# Five Minutes to Midnight

# Five Minutes to Midnight

## Why the Nuclear Threat Is Growing Faster Than Ever

by United States Senator Tom Harkin

with C. E. Thomas

A BIRCH LANE PRESS BOOK
Published by Carol Publishing Group

A Birch Lane Press Book
Published by Carol Publishing Group

Editorial Offices        Sales & Distribution Offices
600 Madison Avenue    120 Enterprise Avenue
New York, NY 10022    Secaucus, NJ 07094

In Canada: Musson Book Company
A division of General Publishing Co. Limited
Don Mills, Ontario

Manufactured in the United States of America
10 9 8 7 6 5 4 3 2 1

Carol Publishing Group books are available at special discounts
for bulk purchases, for sales promotions, fund raising, or
educational purposes. Special editions can also be created to
specifications. For details contact: Special Sales Department,
Carol Publishing Group, 120 Enterprise Ave., Secaucus, NJ 07094

**Library of Congress Cataloging-in-Publication Data**

Harkin, Tom.
    Five minutes to midnight / by Tom Harkin with C.E. Thomas.
      p.  cm.
    "A Birch Lane Press book."
    Includes index.
    ISBN 1-55972-042-5
    1. United States--Military policy. 2. Nuclear warfare. 3. World
politics--1985-1995. I. Thomas, C. E. (Carlton Eugene), 1939-
II. Title. III. Title: 5 minutes to midnight.
UA23.H364  1990
355'.033573--dc20           90-19405
                      CIP

# Contents

# Foreword

by William E. Colby
Former Director of the CIA

The Emperor had a burst of inspiration. He conceived and produced a magnificent new material and commissioned the royal tailor to stitch it into a fabulously beautiful garment, which highly pleased the Emperor. The fact that only the Emperor could feel and see the new material was quite appropriate, because it was obviously beyond the comprehension of mere subjects.

But one day as the Emperor paraded in his finery surrounded by the plaudits of his loyal—and sycophantic—courtiers, a little boy on the edge of the crowd tugged his father's sleeve and said in the uninhibited voice of a child, "The Emperor is naked, Daddy!" The boy's cry caused the crowd to look again, and admit that he was right. The Emperor indeed had nothing on.

The Emperors of the superpowers during the past forty-five years have lived a similar myth, but a more dangerous one, that nuclear weapons were the clothing of national security. The huge arsenals of these superpowers, some 50,000 total warheads in the United States and the Soviet Union, were supposed to protect our populations and our allies from being conquered, and loyal subjects questioned neither the cost nor the concepts involved (which were in any event kept in deep secrecy, denying them to the "enemy" but also to the possibly questioning citizens they ostensibly served).

Mikhail Gorbachev is the little boy of the nuclear clothing. He has stated that nuclear war cannot be fought, and when one considers the question even for a moment, he is right. Any use of these weapons since both sides developed them would entail instant—and devastating—retaliation. There is much gossamer reasoning that avoids this raw fact, and puts their utility in deterrence, the "perception" of power and generating a fear of uncertainty, but the bottom line over the years has been that the weapons cannot be used, i.e., are "useless." In various crises in Berlin, Cuba and the Mediterranean, the two superpowers have tiptoed around this fact, and carefully avoided allowing even minimum combat between their conventional forces for fear of escalation to an unacceptable nuclear level.

Beyond inutility, of course, they are unbelievably dangerous, as any contemplation of a breakdown of central authority in the Soviet Union makes clear when it translates into fear that these weapons could fall into "irresponsible" hands. Gorbachev has carried his cry of nakedness into specific concessions of long-term Soviet objections to arms reductions to equal levels, defensive sufficiency (meaning only that, not an offensive capability), intrusive verification and a host of other steps to reduce the waste and danger of the arms race generally.

Albert Einstein is the author of the summary lament of the whole experience, that the "power of the atom has changed everything save our modes of thinking." Henry Kissinger once cried out in frustration, "What in the name of God is nuclear supremacy?" but the cry was lost in the wilderness of the Cold War. But perhaps Mikhail Gorbachev, as the little boy, has started this process of change in our thinking, belatedly but finally.

But Gorbachev has not acted alone, and cannot. He has been preceded and is today accompanied by an increasing host of thinkers and doers who would educate the public in the follies and futilities of nuclear arsenals. The subject has come out of the closet of secrecy in which it has grown so rankly and the light of an informed citizenry now can come to bear on its arcane rationales and constructs.

Among the leaders of this effort has been Senator Tom Harkin. No hapless dove, this former Navy jet pilot is solidly grounded in Midwestern American values. But he is aware that national security does not stem from piling up more and more dangerous and costly weapons. He, with the good help of C.E. "Sandy" Thomas, has taken a practical look at the real requirements of our country for security—and security from all those other threats to the safety and welfare of our citizens beyond the useless nuclear weapons aimed at us. He has mercifully approached the subject in plain Iowan English instead of the jabberwocky in which the debate has been conducted for so many years.

Senator Harkin's book is important, and offers a roadmap to sane defense policy and planning in the years ahead. His formula for minimum deterrence, for example, recognizes that nuclear weapons cannot be done away with by an easy wave of the hand, but says we *and the Soviet Union*, by hard agreement, should reduce to the numbers

. which will certainly deter each side but not threaten either. He calls for reasonable reductions of our conventional forces in recognition of the fact that the main threat they have been raised to meet has just blown away—the Warsaw Pact. He deals in specifics, but sensibly and not in mind-numbing jargon. He points out especially that the Bush Administration is frantically trying to protect a host of new and more dangerous weapons systems (such as the absurd B-2 bomber at over $800 million *a copy*) while it complains that the nation is broke and cannot meet the challenges of better lives for our people at home and a vigorous leadership role in producing a better new world abroad.

In recent years, the world as a whole each year spent some $1 trillion (yes, million million!) on military forces and weapons. Of this some 30 percent was spent by the United States, some 30 percent by the Soviet Union and some 20 percent by their NATO and Warsaw Pact allies, i.e., some $800 billion annually was devoted to the Cold War between the two superpowers and their allies. That war is over. Surely a major "peace dividend" is available, and Senator Harkin shows us what it is and where it should be spent to overcome the real problems we face after we realize that the threat of nuclear war between the superpowers has evaporated.

Senator Harkin is not naive. He knows that there are still real threats to the safety and welfare of our citizens. He is particularly concerned that the nuclear genie is out of the bottle of the superpowers, and can get into the hands of dangerous demogogues and ethnic and religious zealots. So his formula for the future is a sober one, of allocating our resources sensibly and with high intelligence to meet the actual defense needs of the future, to capture the peace dividend (in monetary terms and in reducing fear) which lies before us and to allocate needed resources against our economic, educational, health and social problems which also pose dangers to the future safety and welfare of our citizens.

There are two ways to defend our country against military threat. The first is to maintain sufficient military forces to defeat or deter attack against us. The second is to convince a possible adversary to lay down his arms. We have largely applied the first, for good reason against an obdurate and openly threatening Soviet Union (although we certainly long ago passed the limit of sufficiency). We now face a Soviet leader who is willing to use the second, and we should be as energetic in accomplishing the goal of minimum mutual safety as we together can achieve. Our experience with the Soviet Union shows that a specific and clear agreement is generally complied with by a government successor to the one which made it, but a "sweetness and light" assertion of general good will ("The Spirit of Camp David") can disappear in short order. If we believe President Gorbachev is firmly in power there, we should move as fast as we can to benefit from his willingness to agree to major arms and forces reductions on both sides. If we believe that his future is in some doubt, we should move even faster. Senator Harkin shows us in clear language the way to go.

# Acknowledgments

We would like to acknowledge the many contributions to the national security debate over the years by members of Congress, the executive branch, the arms control lobby organizations, ordinary citizens and members of academia. We particularly appreciate the contributions of so many members of the armed services and past administrations who speak out eloquently about the folly of the nuclear arms race *after* they leave office and positions of responsibility.

We appreciate those who reviewed parts or all of the early manuscripts of this book including Admiral Eugene Carroll (USN-ret.), Dave Hafemeister, Sam Marullo, Ted Taylor and Anne Thomas. Each made valuable contributions. We especially credit the many direct and indirect contributions of Bob Sherman, who has counseled both of us on the intricacies of the arms race for many years. Bob's tutoring courses on nuclear weapons have become legendary in the House of Representatives. One of his sessions led directly to the banning of depressed trajectory missiles which was subsequently adopted by the Bush administration as a bargaining position in 1989.

Special appreciation goes to members of the staff, including Richard Bender, Kay Casstevens, Don Foley and Ed Long, who contributed many hours evenings and weekends to reviewing material and suggesting changes. And an apology to our families, who endured many hours away from family activities during evenings, weekends and holidays for what was strictly an off-the-job, extracurricular activity, even though related to our legislative responsibilities.

# Five Minutes
## to Midnight

Part One

# THE REAL THREATS
# TO NATIONAL
# SECURITY

# CHAPTER 1

# Toward a Stable Peace: Restructuring Nuclear and Conventional Forces for the 1990s

Few would deny that the chances of a direct superpower war have diminished dramatically since the revolutions of 1989 swept every hard-line Communist government from power in Eastern Europe. The Warsaw Pact is no longer an effective fighting force. The Soviet Union would have to fight its way through Poland, Czechoslovakia and East Germany to reach the West. The Cold War is over.

And yet, by releasing the Eastern European nations to seek their own destiny, free of Soviet domination, Mikhail Gorbachev has inadvertently created greater instability and greater opportunity for violence in Europe than at any time since the two world wars. We all rejoiced as people-power toppled Communist governments from Poland to Romania, but these same forces could erupt in uncontrollable ethnic violence or anarchy in several hot spots within the Soviet Union and its former Warsaw Pact allies. As usual, the price of freedom and democracy is high, and Europeans may have to pay more in the years ahead to maintain or extend their recent gains. But increased U.S. military strength will not prevent internal turmoil within the former Soviet empire. New nuclear weapons will not aid Lithuania or Latvia or Estonia as they fight for their independence, any more than overwhelming American nuclear superiority helped the brave Hungarian freedom fighters in 1956 or the Czechoslovakians in 1968 as Soviet tanks squashed these early attempts toward freedom.

For many Americans, the virtual collapse of the Soviet threat has eliminated our number one preoccupation for 40 years: stopping Soviet Communist expansionism throughout the world. Our national security has been defined almost exclusively by the military force needed to defeat the Soviets. Now that they have been turned into mere economic competitors, the primary threat to our national security has been tamed.

We are concerned, however, that the Soviet menace has masked two major threats to our national security: the threat of nuclear war and the threat of internal societal decline. These threats are growing faster than ever, and will continue to expand unless we change course.

You may be surprised that nuclear war is still on the list. Most Americans conjure up visions of a Soviet-American conflict as the most likely route to nuclear war. They conclude that improved U.S.-Soviet relations means reduced risks of a nuclear holocaust.

Not necessarily. Here is a clear example of the danger of focusing on the wrong enemy. The chances of nuclear war between the two superpowers is negligibly small, and, with the possible exception of the Cuban missile crisis of 1962, probably always has been. But a nuclear war could start if less stable Third World nations acquire and use nuclear weapons, or if client‑states of the two superpowers sucked their supporters into a major conflict. The United States and the Soviet Union could become the best of friends without diminishing the chances of war with Iraq. If Iraq acquired nuclear weapons, they might very well be used. The most likely route to nuclear war has always been through client-state or Third World nation proliferation; improved superpower relations would not necessarily change this equation.

In our judgment, the risks of nuclear war are growing substantially, as both superpowers continue the destabilizing *qualitative* advances in nuclear weaponry. That is, we have become obsessed in arms control negotiations with the *number* of nuclear weapons, when we have long exceeded the quantity of nuclear weapons that would destroy any society. A few hundred are enough, while each side has over 11,000 deliverable nuclear bombs. Yet, in spite of improved relations and despite arms control progress, both sides are continuing to develop new types of nuclear weapons that will make nuclear war more likely in some future international crisis, as we discuss in later chapters.

This qualitative arms race would continue even if we sign the proposed Strategic Arms Reduction Talks (START) agreement to cut the numbers of nuclear weapons by 10 to 40 percent. These quantitative cuts are militarily insignificant. If a few hundred would destroy a civilization, does it really matter if we reduce from 13,000 to "only" 11,000? The START treaty would not stop the development and deployment of new, more destabilizing weapons. The newer weapons would merely replace older systems to stay within the agreed numerical limits.

As long as the qualitative arms race continues, it will be extremely difficult to stop the proliferation of nuclear weapons to other nations, the most likely route to nuclear war. How can the nuclear weapons nations continue to develop and test new nuclear weapons, while they tell smaller nations to desist? How do we explain that developing new nuclear weapons is essential for our national security, but detrimental for others? While the acknowledged nuclear weapons states (U.S., Soviet Union, U.K., France, China and India) have more or less stable governments, we could not rule out the use of nuclear weapons if they were acquired by a future Hitler, Khomeini, Gadhafi, or Saddam Hussein.

Our second concern involves internal enemies. Many internal threats are degrading our national security now. These threats may eat away at our social fabric more slowly and less visibly than an external enemy, but they could be as damaging as any foreign invasion in the long term. We are plagued by environmental deterioration, unmet social needs including hunger, poverty and homelessness in the midst of plenty, the spreading scourge of drug abuse, unrepaired infrastructure, falling commercial competitiveness, grotesque trade deficits and a growing federal debt. Unless we are able to redirect our priorities and our nation's resources away from a fixation on the 1950-era external military threats, and toward the actual 1990 internal threats to our security, we may well find ourselves a declining world power as we enter the 21st century, subject to foreign control through economic, not military take-over.

We have two purposes in writing this book: first, to share our concerns about the continuing threat of nuclear war and the myriad of internal threats to our nation, and, second, to propose solutions to these two threats. In Part 1 (Chapters 2 and 3), we describe the two threats in more detail. In Part 2 (Chapters 4 through 8), we describe an auxiliary fear: that the Bush administration will continue the status quo, conducting national security affairs as we have for four decades, without adapting to the realities of the post-Cold War Gorbachev era. In Part 3 (Chapters 9 through 12), we offer alternatives to the status quo to improve our future national security.

Our fear of business-as-usual within the Bush administration has been borne out in the fiscal year 1991 defense budget request. This was the first budget prepared entirely by the Bush team. Despite the virtual collapse of the Warsaw Pact in late 1989, the administration requested increased funds for every major new nuclear weapon system and most new conventional weapons, even though these weapons were initially justified on the basis of stopping a surprise Soviet attack on Western Europe with only 10 to 14 days' warning. The military budget continues at levels near the peak of the Vietnam War, despite glasnost, perestroika, and the collapse of the Berlin Wall. The official "Defense Planning Guidance" to the military issued on January 24, 1990, stated that it would be "imprudent" to change the Cold War assumption that the Soviets could attack the West with only 14-day warning time, and that "fundamental Soviet objectives in the Third World do not appear to have changed."[1]

The Bush administration urged caution. They worried that a future Soviet hardliner might reoccupy Eastern Europe, even though the Director of the Central Intelligence, William H. Webster, testified before Congress on March 1, 1990, that "the changes are probably already irreversible in several critical respects," offering "little chance that Soviet hegemony could be restored in Eastern Europe." Webster stated that "even if a hardline regime" were to replace Gorbachev, because of internal strife and economic woes, that regime "would have little incentive to engage in major confrontations with the United States" and "would be unlikely to indulge in a major military buildup."[2] Ironically, Secretary of Defense Dick Cheney urged caution and testified to a different committee at almost the same time that we must continue to prepare for possible Soviet military excursions.

Mr. Cheney requested $306.9 billion for the Pentagon in 1991, an

---

[1]Patrick E. Tyler, "New Pentagon 'Guidance' Cites Soviet Threat in Third World," *Washington Post*, February 13, 1990, p. 1.

[2]Patrick E. Tyler, "Webster Sees No Revival of Soviet Threat," *Washington Post*, March 2, 1990, p. 1.

increase of 1.7 percent over the $301.6 billion 1990 defense budget. He was able to claim that this was a 2.6 percent "cut," however, since inflation increased by about 4 percent. That is, with a "cost of living" adjustment to cover inflation, the Pentagon would have received $315 billion in 1991.

Incredibly, the administration requested an average increase of 30 percent in the top 11 strategic weapons systems for 1991, as summarized in Table 1-1. They originally asked for $5.5 billion to build five more B-2 Stealth bombers, part of an $80 billion-plus program to add 132 long-range nuclear bombers to our fleet, only cutting this request back to 75 bombers when it was clear that Congress would never approve full funding. They asked for $2.8 billion more for the MX missile to place 50 of these monsters with 500 hydrogen bombs on railroad cars, so that they could be driven around on the nation's commercial rail lines in time of crisis.

In one of the most graphic indications of lingering Cold War mentality, the Bush administration originally requested a 247 percent increase for the Lance missile program. The U.S. has about 640 older Lance missiles stationed in West Germany, Italy and the Netherlands with 88 Lance missile launchers. Each Lance missile carries a hydrogen bomb with an explosive power up to 100 kilotons, six times the power of the bomb that destroyed Hiroshima. With a range of 80 miles, the Lance missile could destroy several hundred cities and towns in the old East Germany. The administration requested $112 million to begin improving the Lance range up to 240 miles, so that we could drop nuclear weapons on Lech Walesa's Poland or Czechoslovakia. Congress would never have approved these funds, and the newly unified German government would never allow the Lance to be deployed on their soil, so President Bush reluctantly agreed to cancel this program. But the administration continues to push for the rest of the new nuclear weapons programs listed in Table 1-1.

The Bush budget also includes a 181 percent increase in funding for anti-satellite (ASAT) weapons, the first fruits from the Reagan Star Wars research program. Although President Reagan believed that Star Wars could only be used in a defensive role to stop nuclear-armed ballistic missiles, in fact it is much easier to shoot down satellites than missiles or nuclear warheads. The Bush administration is pushing ahead with the development of ASAT weapons that will jeopardize the peaceful uses of space as the Soviets or other future adversaries copy our lead and build their own dedicated ASAT weapons. The administration is taking the first steps to extend the nuclear arms race into outer space.

TABLE 1-1.   MAJOR NUCLEAR AND DEFENSIVE WEAPONS PROGRAMS IN THE FISCAL YEAR 1991 BUSH BUDGET REQUEST

|  | 1990 Actual: | 1991 Request: | Percent Increase: |
|---|---|---|---|
|  | ($ Billions) | | |
| Star Wars | 3.80 | 4.66 | +23 |
| B-2 Stealth Bomber | 4.30 | 5.54 | +29 |
| MX Rail Garrison Missile | 1.72 | 2.84 | +65 |
| Lance Missile Follow-On | 0.032 | 0.112 | +247 |
| SRAM-T Missile | 0.055 | 0.119 | +117 |
| Kinetic ASAT Weapon | 0.074 | 0.208 | +181 |
| Midgetman Missile | 0.100 | 0.202 | +102 |
| Trident-II (D-5) Missile | 1.662 | 1.746 | +5 |
| 18th Trident Submarine | 1.281 | 1.453 | +13 |
| Tomahawk Cruise Missile | 0.628 | 0.863 | +37 |
| Advanced Cruise Missile | 0.368 | 0.541 | +47 |
| Totals: | 14.02 | 18.28 | +30 |
| Department of Energy Nuclear Weapons: | 9.653 | 10.97 | +14 |

We do not need and cannot afford these costly and destabilizing new weapons systems. We clearly have the best opportunity in 40 years to stop and reverse both the nuclear and conventional arms races. Reduced Soviet threat, the fall of Communist governments, the growing public awareness regarding budget deficits and environmental degradation, and the success of U.N. peacekeeping forces in several former hot spots around the world all provide opportunity for establishing a lasting, stable peace.

Even before the fall of the Berlin Wall, Walther Stutzle, the Director of the Stockholm International Peace Research Institute (SIPRI), wrote in 1988 that the chances for peaceful resolution of conflict became "better founded than in any other year since the end of the Second World War."[3] He noted reduced hostilities in Iran-Iraq, Ethiopia-Somalia, Chad-Libya, Angola, Namibia, Afghanistan, Cambodia and Nicaragua. External threats such as terrorists and drug traffickers continue, and others will certainly emerge in the future, but the trends

---

[3]Gison Rapp, "Soviet/US Thaw Cuts Global Conflict," *Jane's Defence Weekly*, May 27, 1989, p. 992.

toward peaceful resolution of the inevitable conflicts between nations is most encouraging.

In our judgment, the U.S. can significantly cut military spending while providing military forces necessary to meet our real security needs in the coming decades. We can create a "peace dividend" that can go a long way toward reducing the federal budget deficit and restoring needed domestic spending that was gutted during the Reagan years. We can cut $30 billion from the military budget in 1991, with cuts reaching $100 billion annually by 1995 and $150 billion or 50 percent by the year 2000.

The Bush administration has claimed that there can be no peace dividend, now that U.S. forces have been used to stop Iraq from attacking Saudi Arabia. However, less than 10 percent of our 2.1 million troops have been dispatched to Saudi Arabia. Total costs of this mission are uncertain, with estimates ranging up to $10 billion per year if our troops remain in the desert, or less than 4 percent of the military budget. Increased oil prices could double this cost.

However, the U.S. should not bear the full burden of protecting Saudi Arabia. Costs should be shared by nations able to pay and those most dependent on Persian Gulf oil. the U.S. consumes about 20 percent of the oil exported from the Persian Gulf, while the European community uses about 35 percent and Japan 43 percent. On this basis, the U.S. fair share of the operation would fall from $10 billion to $2 billion, assuming that the desert operation tempo continues for a full year. And the Kuwait government in exile along with Saudi Arabia should contribute to the costs of their own defense. The interest alone from Kuwait outside assets, estimated at over $100 billion, could pay for the entire operation. In any case, the U.S. portion of costs should be less than $2 billion, which is much less than the $30 billion peace dividend that we have projected based on the reduced Soviet threat.

We can reap a peace dividend, but we must change our way of doing business. It remains to be seen whether the Bush administration can adapt to the 1990s or whether we will be wedded to the Cold War mentality of the 1950s and 1960s until new leaders are elected.

# CHAPTER 2

---

# The Growing Threat of Nuclear War

### SUMMARY

Mention "nuclear war" and most citizens visualize a Soviet-American holocaust involving thousands of nuclear weapons exploding on both nations. In reality, chances of a direct U.S.-Soviet war have never been large, and are becoming extremely low. The real danger lies in other, less stable nations acquiring and using nuclear weapons, or in client-states of the two superpowers starting a war that mushrooms out of control.

Unfortunately, improved dialogue between the U.S. and the Soviet Union is not sufficient to reduce the chances of nuclear weapons being used again. In fact, by continuing the four-decade-old superpower nuclear arms race, the Bush administration is creating conditions that will increase the risks of a nuclear war in the future.

Nuclear war involving unstable Third World nations is not only possible, but becoming *more likely*, despite improved relations between the Soviet Union and the United States, and despite the continuation of superpower arms control dialogue. Indeed, improved relations may indirectly contribute to the growing risk of nuclear war, by lulling the

10

public into a false sense of security. Since the Soviet Union has been billed as our primary enemy, many citizens are relaxing now that the "evil empire" has been transformed overnight into a mere economic competitor.

The real threat of nuclear war does not stem from the Soviet Union, but from other, less stable governments either acquiring their own nuclear weapons—called nuclear proliferation—or from less stable countries dragging a nuclear-capable nation into a war that spirals out of control. Senator John Glenn has called nuclear proliferation "one of the gravest threats facing global security and our Nation's future."[1] While Senator Glenn is also very much concerned with the proliferation of chemical and biological weapons to Third World countries, he stated that "our preoccupation with such weapon systems might distract our attention from the still serious, and I am afraid growing, nuclear threats we face from abroad."

Suppose, for example, that the next time a war breaks out between some future Iran and Iraq, one or both of the belligerents have nuclear weapons. Iran and Iraq had no compunctions about using chemical weapons. Would some future Saddam Hussein resist using nuclear weapons in support of a holy war? Surely we cannot rule out this path to nuclear war, and therefore we must do everything in our power to stop the spread of nuclear weapons to other nations. Iraq has already demonstrated the capability to launch satellites, and therefore has the ability to build ballistic[2] missiles that could deliver nuclear weapons.

Or suppose that the war in Lebanon ignites a full-scale battle between Syria and Israel. What would happen if Syria, backed by a more aggressive Soviet Union, began serious bombing inside Israel? Would Israel, in desperation, use nuclear weapons in a severe crisis, to avoid what appeared to be imminent defeat? Again, this scenario is possible. The U.S. and the Soviet Union should be modifying their nuclear weapon arsenals for maximum stability, discarding weapons that increase the chance of nuclear escalation in some future crisis such as an Israeli-Syrian war.

---

[1]John H. Glenn, Jr., "Supercomputers and Super Bombs," *The Congressional Record*, October 31, 1989, p. S 14382.

[2]A "ballistic" missile is one that is powered early in flight, and then coasts to its target much like a bullet. Ballistic missiles usually have multiple stages, with the first two stages filled with propellant to accelerate the third stage containing the nuclear weapon(s) or "warhead(s)." The warhead(s) travel through outer space on a "ballistic" trajectory before reentering the atmosphere above the intended target.

Unfortunately, the Bush administration is failing in both categories: they are pursuing nuclear weapons policies and practices that encourage—or at least fail to inhibit—other nations from building their own nuclear weapons. As we discuss in more detail in Chapters 4 and 5, the next generation of nuclear weapons planned by the Bush administration are dangerously destabilizing: in a crisis, these new weapons are more likely to be used. Thus a conventional war between Israel and Syria would much more likely escalate to nuclear war if we go ahead with President Bush's plans to develop and deploy the next generation of destabilizing nuclear weapons.

For most citizens, contemplating war in time of peace is difficult. The Soviet threat has diminished dramatically. But there were 19 other wars going on in 1988 with fatalities exceeding 1,000 per year.[3] At least two involved countries with possible nuclear weapons connections: South Africa and Lebanon (through Israel). And the despicable Chinese reaction to Tiananmen Square illustrates that unexpected setbacks and brutal repressions still occur on the world scene. We cannot rule out totally unexpected surprises and the eruption of major wars in the future. But we can work now to reduce the chances of any war escalating out of control. We and the Soviets can minimize, if not eliminate, the chances of other nations acquiring nuclear weapons.

To prevent nuclear weapons from ever being used again, we should analyze how a nuclear war might start. In our judgment, there are six possible paths to nuclear war, listed below in decreasing order of probability:

• Nuclear weapon proliferation to less stable nations.
• Client-state war escalating out of control.
• Accidental nuclear war.
• Unauthorized nuclear war.
• Escalation from a superpower conventional war.
• Bolt-from-the-blue attack.

We believe that the first two routes to nuclear war (nuclear proliferation and client-state war) are not only possible, but the threat is growing faster than ever as the superpowers continue the qualitative nuclear arms race. The next two paths (accidental and unauthorized nuclear war)

---

[3]Ruth Leger Sivard, *World Military and Social Expenditures, 1987-88*, Washington, D.C.: World Priorities, 1987, p.28.

are much less likely, but we could reduce these risks even further by stopping the nuclear arms race. Senator Sam Nunn, the chairman of the Senate Armed Services Committee, stated that, although the risk of superpower war has decreased, "the danger of unauthorized or accidental [launches], in my opinion, has not gone down."[4] Although it would not lead to nuclear war, the risk of an accidental nuclear explosion during the routine handling of nuclear weapons is larger than necessary, and may have even increased in the last decade with the introduction of new weapons such as the U.S. D-5 and Soviet SSN-23 submarine launched ballistic missile. We consider the last two paths (superpower escalation and bolt-from-the-blue attacks) to have negligible probability, even though they have received much attention in the past.

## NUCLEAR PROLIFERATION: THE LIKELY PATH TO NUCLEAR WAR

Six nations have exploded nuclear weapons, and five acknowledge having a stockpile of nuclear weapons as listed in Table 2-1. The four major members of this exclusive club have relatively stable governments, with no strong propensity to attack other nations. The United States, the Soviet Union, France and England are not likely to use nuclear weapons under any conceivable scenario.

TABLE 2-1.  THE NUCLEAR WEAPONS CLUB[5]

|  | Number of Nuclear Explosions | Nuclear Weapons in Stockpile |
|---|---|---|
| United States | 910 | 22,500 |
| Soviet Union | 635 | 33,000 |
| France | 172 | 450 |
| Britain | 41 | 300 |
| China | 34 | 350 |
| India | 1 | ? |

India may feel directly threatened by Pakistan, but India's membership in the nuclear club is based on a single "peaceful" nuclear explosion in 1974. Most intelligence analysts do not believe that India has a significant nuclear arsenal, although they are trying to improve their

---

[4]Melissa Healy, "Nunn Asks U.S.-Soviet 'Fail-safe Review' to Avert an Unwarranted Missile Launch," *Los Angeles Times*, February 11, 1990, p. 8.
[5]Nuclear Notebook, *The Bulletin of the Atomic Scientists*, May, 1989, p. 57.

nuclear weapons capability to stay ahead of Pakistan. Since Pakistan and India are both pursuing nuclear weapon capability, and since they have fought on three previous occasions over Kashmir, this could be the next nuclear battleground. China, the sixth member of the club, may be the least stable, but their primary threat is internal, not due to any external enemy that might lead to the use of nuclear weapons.

In short, the nuclear "have" nations, with the possible exception of India, are not likely to use nuclear weapons unless sucked into a conflagration in the developing world.

The same cannot be said for less developed countries, should they ever acquire nuclear weapons. Countries such as Libya, North Korea, Cambodia, Iran and Iraq might have less stable governments, lower standards of living, and therefore less to lose by going to war with hostile neighbors. Mix in fatalistic religious fanaticism, and the chance of nuclear weapons use increases substantially. Clearly we cannot rule out the use of nuclear weapons should they fall into the hands of some future Amin, Gadhafi, Khomeini, or Pol Pot.

Up to a dozen other nations may have the capability to build nuclear weapons in the next decade. Israel and South Africa may already have tens to hundreds of undeclared atomic bombs; they certainly have the technical knowledge and access to the necessary materials. Argentina, Brazil, Iran, Iraq, Libya, North Korea and Pakistan could probably develop their own nuclear weapons by the end of the decade. Iraq and Pakistan are attempting to develop nuclear weapons manufacturing capability, and Libya reportedly has tried to acquire nuclear weapons.

As more nations join the nuclear weapons club, the chances for accidental war would increase. These nations might not have the sophisticated interlock or safety features that have been developed over the years to prevent the accidental firing of American or Soviet nuclear weapons.

While use of nuclear weapons by Third World nations might not cause the superpowers to fire any weapons from their massive nuclear arsenals, damage could still be extraordinary. Recall that two small atomic bombs destroyed Hiroshima and Nagasaki, killing over 200,000 people, or almost four times the total U.S. fatalities in the Vietnam War. While it is hard to imagine any leader intentionally using nuclear weapons, we must all remind ourselves that our own nation, after a long and costly world war that included massive firebombing of major German and Japanese cities, decided almost without debate to explode nuclear weapons in Japan. Certainly we cannot exclude the strong possibility that other leaders may be pressed to use nuclear weapons in a desperate situation, or that terrorist groups might steal and use or threaten to use nuclear weapons.

As long as the nuclear weapons states continue to build new nuclear weapons, the proliferation of nuclear weapons technology to other, less stable nations will be possible. Nuclear weapons proliferation is increasing the risks of nuclear war.

## CLIENT-STATE WAR

The second most likely route to nuclear war is through a conflict between two nations, each allied with or supported by one of the superpowers or another nuclear-armed nation. The smoldering Israeli-Arab conflict could erupt in warfare at any moment, as it has several times in the last few decades. At this writing, Iraq has stopped its advance after conquering Kuwait, but no one can predict the outcome where religious fanaticism plays a role. Conflicts are much more likely in unstable parts of the world, where countries feel threatened or feel that they have nothing to lose by pursuing armed conflict to achieve their objectives, where populations deprived of basic needs or rights are willing to risk all for a cause.

War is much more likely in areas where the superpowers have no direct, central stakes. One can imagine, for example, a war between Israel and Syria escalating out of control. What would happen if the U.S. aided our ally Israel with conventional force? Growing dependence on Middle East oil could provide additional incentives for further U.S. military intervention. Would the Soviet Union stand by and allow Syria to be destroyed? Would some future Soviet leader, more aggressive than Mikhail Gorbachev, undertake a military excursion to "save" Syria as a means of unifying the USSR and diverting attention from strife at home? It seems quite possible that the two superpowers could get sucked into a Middle East conflict. In the resulting "fog of war," what would happen if Israel set off a few nuclear weapons? Or if the U.S. Navy used tactical nuclear weapons to stave off imminent defeat? Could the Soviets tell if these were U.S. or Israeli nuclear explosions? Would it make any difference?

*This is just the type of crisis that could escalate out of control.* All the rational thinking that would inhibit the use of nuclear weapons during peacetime would be submerged in the "fog of war." A key threshold would be crossed when the leaders of one or both sides came to believe that the opponent might use nuclear weapons soon. If the leadership of either side became convinced that nuclear war was inevitable, then the calculus of such conflict would change. The threat of a few hundred surviving nuclear warheads would no longer be sufficient to deter. The question would become whether there would be any significant advantage (or the perception of such an advantage) in striking first, instead of waiting for the (thought to be inevitable) strike by the opponent.

The client-state war is a likely route to a nuclear Armageddon. Any national security policy should reduce the chances of nuclear escalation in the midst of such an unexpected war in any one of the world's trouble spots. Nuclear weapons arsenals and policies should be designed to survive under the most stressful crisis situations, up to and including a major conventional war by the two superpowers. Unfortunately, the Bush administration is continuing the old way of thinking, piling up new and more sophisticated nuclear weapons as though they were just more powerful conventional weapons, ignoring the fact that these new weapons would be more likely to be used in a crisis.

We discuss more precisely in Chapters 4 and 5 how the next generation of nuclear weapons, if deployed as planned by the Bush administration, would decrease stability and increase the risks of nuclear war in the event of a major client-state conflict. Before discussing the destabilizing nature of these weapons, we address several other possible, but less likely, paths to nuclear war.

## ACCIDENTAL NUCLEAR WAR

We should distinguish between an accidental nuclear explosion during manufacture or handling of a weapon, and a nuclear war started by accident. An accidental nuclear explosion on U.S. soil or at a U.S. base overseas would not start a nuclear war. Yet the consequences of even a single explosion could be so devastating as to make the Chernobyl nuclear reactor accident seem insignificant.

The chances of a single accidental detonation, although small, may be growing. The Department of Energy, which manufactures all of our nuclear weapons, was so concerned about the safety of a nuclear 8-inch artillery shell, that they secretly immobilized these nuclear weapons stored in West Germany, Italy and the Netherlands in 1989 until repairs could be made. Computer simulations indicated that this shell could have been detonated by a stray bullet striking at a critical location, and one military official admitted that "we were also worried that these things might go off if they fell off the back of a truck and landed in a certain way."[6] Similarly, an isolated accidental nuclear explosion might be possible with the short range attack missile (SRAM-A) carried on our nuclear bombers, and even the new W-88 warhead designed for the Trident-II D-5 missile that just entered service in 1990.

A nuclear weapon is actually quite explosion-proof. Unlike conventional chemical explosives, a nuclear weapon would not normally explode if heated in a fire. The atomic bomb trigger of all hydrogen bombs requires a carefully controlled implosion: the enriched uranium or plutonium must be uniformly compressed to reach a critical mass. Chemical explosives are distributed around the outside of the weapon core and detonated in unison to compress the nuclear fuel. In a fire, the bomb materials might melt, and the chemical explosives might detonate, but they would not be coordinated, and the nuclear materials would generally not reach the critical mass necessary to sustain a nuclear chain reaction.

A nearby chemical explosion might conceivably trigger a nuclear weapon, but this circumstance is fairly remote, with one possible exception: the Trident-II D-5 missile, the most recent addition to the U.S. nuclear arsenal. Generally, the more modern weapons are considered less prone to accident. Since the late 1970s, most new weapons have used an "Insensitive High Explosive" or IHE to implode the nuclear core. This IHE chemical trigger is much less vulnerable to accidental detonation than earlier explosives. However, the new W-88 warheads for the D-5 missile use the older, more accident-prone chemical explosive. Designers intentionally chose the older explosive to pack greater nuclear yield in a smaller volume, a clear example of sacrificing safety to achieve better nuclear war-fighting capability. The W-88 warhead has a yield of about 450 kilotons, over four times greater than the W-76 warhead it replaces on the Trident-I missile. Worse yet, the eight W-88 warheads are packed in a circle around the third stage rocket of the D-5 missile, instead of the usual configuration found in other missiles with the warheads mounted on top of the third stage, away from the rocket fuel. If the D-5 third stage rocket were to explode accidentally, then the eight nuclear weapons might also be triggered because of their older accident-prone chemical detonators. Eight 450-kt explosions on a single D-5 missile would decimate any naval port, the

---

[6]R. Jeffrey Smith, "Defective Nuclear Shells Raise Safety Concerns," *Washington Post*, May 23, 1990, p. 1.

equivalent of 240 Hiroshima explosions at one location. By replacing the Trident-I missile with the Trident-II, the risks of an accidental nuclear explosion may increase.

The SRAM-A short-range attack missile carried on U.S. B-1, B-52 and FB-111 bombers are also constructed with the older accident-prone chemical explosive. While the nuclear warheads might not detonate, a bomber fire could still release large quantities of radioactive plutonium. The three directors of the national laboratories responsible for building our nuclear weapons all recommended in 1990 that these missiles be removed from active alert status at our bomber bases, because of the risks of an accident. Siegfried Hecker, director of the Los Alamos National Laboratory that designed the SRAM-A warhead, stated that "from a safety standpoint, I do not feel comfortable" with these weapons being mounted on alert bombers.[7] These SRAM-A missiles have been removed from all bombers on alert.

A single nuclear accident, however destructive, would not start a nuclear war. Some citizens worry that nuclear war could start by accident, citing numerous accidents involving high technology systems such as the Chernobyl nuclear reactor or the explosion of the Space Shuttle Challenger. However, these accidents occurred when the systems were *operating*, whereas nuclear weapons are kept in a quiescent or dormant state. Missiles are never launched with live nuclear warheads, and bombers no longer patrol with nuclear weapons on board. Both superpowers have also placed electro-mechanical controls on their nuclear weapons to prevent them from becoming energized by accident.

An accidental nuclear war would require the combination of two highly unlikely events: an accident leading to one or more nuclear explosions on the opponent's territory, and, given such an occurrence, escalation to an exchange of nuclear weapons between the superpowers.

The probabilities of these two events depend on the international situation. In peace, the chances of an accidental launch are minuscule, and, should one occur anyway, the chances of escalation are small, at least with today's weapons. In a crisis situation, such as a Middle East conventional war, the possibility of an accident and the chances of escalation both increase. Accidental nuclear war would still be less likely than a client-state nuclear war or Third World proliferation

---

[7] R. Jeffrey Smith, "Pentagon Urged to Ground Nuclear Missile for Safety," *Washington Post*, May 24, 1990, p. A1.

leading to the use of nuclear weapons, but we should be doing everything in our power to reduce the chances of nuclear war by any route.

During normal peacetime conditions, the probability of a nuclear accident on the adversary's soil is negligible. A bomber cannot take off by accident, of course, so any accidental nuclear explosion on enemy soil would require the accidental launch of ballistic missiles, either land-based or submarine-based. The historical record is perfect—there have been no accidental detonations—but we cannot extrapolate on the basis of three decades without accident into the indefinite future, particularly if the numbers of nuclear missiles increase and other, less stable nations acquire nuclear weapons that might have less sophisticated controls.

On the U.S. side, there are several mechanisms that prevent accidental launch of land-based ballistic missiles. Signals are required from two launch control officers in their underground center, after they receive the message from the President to fire their missiles, called an "execute order." This execute message includes a "Permissive Action Link" or PALS electronic code to unlock the weapon's firing mechanism. Even if these two launch signals were accidentally generated, by an extraordinary electrical storm, for example, or a computer error, the fire command could be overridden by another of the five launch control centers for each missile squadron.

An accidental missile launch from a submarine would be virtually impossible. The submarine crew must go through several detailed physical steps to prepare a missile for launch. The only non-zero chance of an accidental launch would be if the submarine received a launch order by mistake, similar to the time a training tape was accidentally played into a computer, creating signals that simulated a Soviet attack.

If a missile was accidentally launched, either from land or sea, the warhead would not necessarily detonate without proper arming signals. It has been reported that the United States has six interlocking control devices on some nuclear weapons, each of which would prevent a nuclear detonation if not properly triggered, even if the missile was launched.

Before the United States suspended bomber flights with live nuclear weapons, there were 18 reported accidents. Bombers crashed on takeoff, bombers collided in mid-air, and in several cases, the conventional explosive detonator fired, distributing radioactive debris over wide areas. Four hydrogen bombs were dropped on the coast of Spain after a bomber collided with its refueling tanker in 1966. In no case did the nuclear weapon detonate.

In 1980 a workman dropped a wrench into a missile silo near Damascus, Arkansas, severing a liquid fuel line to one of our old Titan missiles. Several hours later, fumes from the spilled fuel ignited, lifting the missile out of the silo and sending its nine-megaton warhead into a field. The interlock devices prevented the hydrogen bomb from exploding.[8] (We have since removed all of our liquid-fueled Titans, and now rely exclusively on the more reliable solid-fueled rockets.)

If a missile was accidentally launched, and if the nuclear warhead trigger signals were transmitted to the warhead, then a nuclear explosion could not be avoided. Once launched, a ballistic missile would continue its dreadful journey, propelling its hydrogen bomb or bombs through outer space, reentering the atmosphere and exploding over its intended target some 25 minutes later. The United States has no capability to stop a nuclear warhead hurtling through space at speeds of 15,000 miles per hour, except by exploding one of our own nuclear warheads in the path of an incoming Soviet warhead. However, the United States does not have the radar and battle-management capability in place to direct Minuteman or MX missile warheads in this defensive role.

The Soviets have a limited defensive system around Moscow, with up to 100 nuclear-tipped interceptor rockets, as allowed by the 1972 Anti-Ballistic Missile (ABM) Treaty. If an American missile was fired by accident, and if it was also aimed at Moscow, then the Soviets might be able to destroy it above the city by exploding a megaton class nuclear bomb in its path. While there would be some radioactive debris, damage would be insignificant compared to a bomb going off on the ground or in the air over the city. If the accidental U.S. missile was aimed somewhere other than Moscow, then they could do nothing to stop it.

Thus the chances are nearly 100 percent today that any accidental launch of a ballistic missile, accompanied by appropriate arming signals, would result in a nuclear explosion on the opponent's soil. However, the probability of these two events occurring simultaneously are presumably very, very small. If the probability of an accidental launch and the probability of the warhead becoming armed were each one in ten

---

[8]David P. Barash and Judith E. Lipton, *Stop Nuclear War, a Handbook*, Grove Press, 1982, p. 246.

thousand, then the chances of both occurring simultaneously, assuming independent events, would be one in one hundred million.

We could prevent an accidentally launched missile from delivering its nuclear bomb by placing a self-destruct explosive device on each missile. Most U.S. test missiles and most unmanned space-launch missiles are equipped with explosive destruct mechanisms, so that a "range safety officer" can destroy the missile after launch, should it head out of control toward populated areas. Many errant missiles have been intentionally blown up in the past.

Our nuclear-armed ICBMs and SLBMs could be equipped with these self-destruct devices, too, but the military has objected, fearing that the destruct signal might be acquired by our adversary. In a war, the enemy could then disarm our nuclear missiles.

However, in this age of high speed computers and sophisticated codes, we should be able to encode the self-destruct signal with negligible probability of intercept by any adversary. These computer-generated codes could be changed every day, or every hour. It therefore seems reasonable and prudent that both superpowers should equip their ballistic missiles with self-destruct devices in case we ever do have an accidental missile launch. Senator Sam Nunn, Chairman of the Senate Armed Services Committee, has endorsed this action: "In this kind of age of technology, to have no fail-safe destructive mechanisms on missiles does not make sense to me . . . I think we ought to be seriously pursuing that."[9]

Even if one nuclear explosion did occur, as devastating as that would be if it landed near a city, escalation to nuclear war would not be likely with current weapons. Both sides know that they have adequate retaliatory capability. Neither side would fear that all or even a large fraction of their retaliatory forces would be destroyed, particularly if they detected only a single accidental launch. Both sides could afford to wait out a single explosion, to see if it was an accident, or if other missiles were on the way. With the upgraded Hot Line between Washington and Moscow, assurances could be given that this was indeed an accident.

The probability of escalation after one bomb went off would increase, however, if we and the Soviets continue to add first strike capable weapons. If the Bush administration adds thousands of accurate Trident-II (D-5) submarine-launched missiles as planned, then the Soviets

---

[9]Melissa Healy, ibid.

would be much more likely to fire their missiles early: they would fear that the accurate D-5 warheads could in theory destroy the bulk of their retaliatory capability if they waited.

Still, in peacetime, it seems unlikely that either side would retaliate after one nuclear explosion. If nothing else, neither side would have their leadership in a position to make such an apocalyptic decision within half an hour.

The situation could become more unstable if a missile with multiple warheads were accidentally launched. Soviet SS-18 and U.S. MX missiles carry ten nuclear warheads each and all Trident submarine-launched missiles carry eight to ten. One accidental missile launch resulting in ten nuclear explosions on the opponent's soil would certainly increase anxiety and the impulse to respond. This is one of many good reasons to eliminate multiple warhead (MIRV'd) missiles on both sides. (We discuss other reasons in Chapters 4 and 5.)

During an international crisis, the chances for accidental war would increase. At higher levels of alert, for example, some peacetime inhibitions or even physical interlocks to prevent firing of missiles might be removed. Even during peacetime test alerts, some interlocks may be removed; the first stage of an MX missile was totally destroyed in June of 1988 when it accidentally fell seven inches while it was "on alert."[10] If a real crisis lasted for long periods, stress would increase on launch control crews, both underground and underwater. Launch crews and our leaders would be more likely to believe missiles had been launched as part of a planned attack if an international crisis were unfolding, such as a client-state war in the Middle East.

If one or more nuclear bombs did go off by accident, certainly the other side would be primed to respond more quickly in a severe crisis situation than in peacetime. With new weapons like the Trident-II (D-5) missile and its Soviet counterpart, the time pressures would be so acute that leaders might react immediately when they received electronic radar or satellite signals of enemy missiles being fired, launching their missiles when they saw what was actually an accidental launch.

Thus a crisis increases both the chances of an accident (by moving to a higher state of alert with fewer interlocks), and the chances of retaliation (due to the alert status of the opponent). New, accurate "counterforce" weapons like the MX and the D-5 submarine weapons and their Soviet

---

[10]R. Jeffrey Smith, "Falling Missile Jars Loose Shower of Bills," *Washington Post*, February 15, 1989, p. A23.

counterparts further increase the chances of an accidental nuclear detonation or major nuclear exchange.

While we know little about Soviet precautions against accidental launch, we assume that they have the technical capability to add protective equipment. We should be taking advantage of glasnost or openness to work together with the Soviet Union and the four other known nuclear powers to install self-destruct mechanisms on missiles of all nations, and to install other safety interlock features. We should be working to improve communications, including a jointly manned crisis control center. So far, the Bush administration has not taken the initiative to pursue these sane measures.

## UNAUTHORIZED NUCLEAR WAR

In addition to an accidental launch of ballistic missiles, nuclear weapons could be fired without the approval of national leaders. Given the destructive power of nuclear weapons, a few demented individuals could wreak unprecedented havoc.

Consider the firepower available to one submarine commander and his crew. A single Trident submarine carries 24 ballistic missiles. Each Trident-I missile can carry eight 100-kiloton (100,000 tons of TNT equivalent) hydrogen bombs, or a total firepower of over 19 megatons (19,000,000 tons of TNT) in 192 hydrogen bombs. For comparison, the biggest conventional bomb used in World War II was equivalent to a few tons of TNT, and the total explosive power of all the bombs dropped in World War II has been estimated at four megatons. Thus one Trident submarine equipped with Trident-I missiles carries almost five times the explosive power of all the bombs dropped in the Second World War! This is equivalent to over 1,200 Hiroshima bombs in destructive power. Incredibly, the latest generation of Trident submarines entering service equipped with D-5 missiles carry 4.5 times more nuclear firepower, or 5,700 Hiroshimas!

It is believed that the submarine commander and three of his officers have the capability to fire all of their missiles without receiving any external codes or messages. In practice, more crew members would probably have to cooperate to prepare and launch their missiles. Of course, regulations require that the commander wait for the President's signal, but there is nothing to prevent a deranged crew from virtually destroying an entire civilization in an afternoon by exploding 192 nuclear weapons.

In a crisis, the stress on submarine crews could become unbearable. Suppose a conventional war did break out. Suppose further that both sides had developed anti-satellite (ASAT) capability, and the adversary destroyed all communications satellites and shot down or electronically jammed the radios on airplanes carrying messages to the submerged submarines. The submarine commander could only receive very low capacity signals from the very low frequency network, coupling through the ground and water. If this network was destroyed or temporarily out of service, the submarine could be without any communication. What would they do?

Presumably nuclear war-planners have considered the scenario where the Soviets do attack the U.S. with nuclear weapons and knock out most of our communications and most of our leaders. Certainly we would want the Soviets to believe that the submarines would fire their missiles eventually if they received no communications signals for a prolonged period, to deter the Soviets from ever attempting to knock out our communications nodes. How can the submarine commander distinguish between nuclear war and a conventional assault on our communications channels only? Or a massive power blackout on the U.S. mainland, for that matter? How long does he wait to fire his missiles?

Unauthorized launch of land-based ICBMs would be more difficult, because one launch control center can override another's launch signal. But the probability of an unauthorized launch is not zero; after all, someone generates the launch code, and someone carries it around with the President (and presumably other military officers designated to release nuclear weapons if the President is incapacitated). And cooperation between two launch teams or failure to override a launch command cannot be ruled out. If two teams conspired to launch nuclear weapons without authorization, one team could enable their firing circuit and the second team could immediately validate the fire signal, blocking out the override signal from the other three launch centers.

As with an accidental nuclear explosion, a single unauthorized nuclear detonation might not lead to all-out nuclear war, particularly in peacetime. But in a crisis, such as a major conventional war, an unauthorized launch could very well trigger a nuclear exchange. Adding new destabilizing weapons like the MX and the D-5 submarine-launched ballistic missile (SLBM) would increase the risks of escalation, even if the initial launch was unauthorized.

## SUPERPOWER CONVENTIONAL WAR

Most of our post-World War II military planning has been based on stopping the Soviet Union from conquering other nations, particularly in Western Europe. While this was a reasonable assumption for Stalinist Russia immediately after the war, it has grown less and less likely over the years, to the point where conventional war between the superpowers in Europe was very unlikely, even before the revolutions that swept Eastern Europe in 1989. On the other hand, the retreating Soviet army is creating the greatest instability since the end of the war in the nations they are vacating. After four decades of authoritative rule that subjugated centuries-old religious and ethnic animosities, some nations emerging from Communist rule may not be able to constrain internal strife. Armed conflict in response to ethnic turmoil cannot be ruled out within Eastern Europe.

We must distinguish between internal violence within former Warsaw Pact nations, and Soviet external aggression against NATO. Internal ethnic violence within Eastern Europe would be unlikely to involve the use of nuclear weapons under any conceivable circumstances, even if American military force were used to restore order. Soviet external aggression against Western Europe, now highly unlikely, bordering on inconceivable, could have involved the use of nuclear weapons. We therefore have the fortunate situation that the most likely use of force in Europe would not involve nuclear weapons, and the only reasonable avenue to nuclear weapons use, Soviet attack, is extremely remote.

If the Soviets ever did revert to an aggressive leadership and attempted an attack on NATO, escalation to nuclear war would be likely with today's nuclear weapons deployments. Tactical or short-range nuclear weapons are integrated into every branch of the armed services. The Army has thousands of nuclear artillery shells and short-range nuclear-tipped missiles in Europe. (Intermediate and medium-range missiles with ranges between 300 and 3,300 miles were eliminated under the Intermediate Range Nuclear Forces or INF Treaty of 1987.) Most Air Force fighters and bombers are dual-capable: they can carry conventional or nuclear bombs. And the Navy has nuclear depth bombs, nuclear-armed aircraft, and nuclear-armed cruise missiles in addition to their long-range nuclear-tipped ballistic missiles.

It might be difficult to keep short-range tactical nuclear weapons from being used in a sudden conventional war, particularly if local NATO commanders feared that advancing Soviet forces might overrun our ground-based nuclear weapon systems. In desperation, NATO commanders might be pressured into firing their nuclear weapons rather than suffer imminent defeat or allow the enemy to capture our tactical nuclear weapons.

Proponents of continual improvement in nuclear weapons claim that this coupling of nuclear and conventional weapons generates great caution. They conclude that the fear of nuclear war prevents any war. They credit nuclear deterrence with bringing the longest period of peace to central Europe in the last two centuries.

Of course, no one can prove what prevented a non-event. Perhaps there would have been no superpower war since 1945 without nuclear weapons. Perhaps the Soviet Union had its hands full with the countries subsumed under its "sphere of influence" at the end of the war, and had no will to risk even conventional war to achieve further expansion. But certainly the risk of nuclear war would weigh heavily in favor of restraint, should the notion of armed aggression arise again in central Europe. We contend, however, that a few hundred survivable strategic (long-range) nuclear weapons fired from submarines or from carrier-based aircraft would convey the same sense of restraint on the Soviets as our current arsenal of over 13,000 strategic nuclear weapons and several thousand additional tactical nuclear weapons stationed on European soil.

In any case, the chances of direct superpower war in Europe are negligible. The Warsaw Pact has ceased to exist as a fighting force. All Soviet troops may be out of Eastern Europe within a few years, and the Baltic states may be independent nations once again.

Even before the fall of the Berlin Wall, the Soviets had none of the classical excuses to risk war against the West. They had no territorial claims in Europe. They were not in desperate need of any critical resources outside their vast borders. And they had no "debts to settle" or any reason for a war of retribution. In short, the Soviet Union has no motivation to risk the terrible consequences of even a conventional war, assuming that they somehow believed they could avoid a nuclear conflict. The risk of escalation to a nuclear holocaust by even a few nuclear weapons simply reduces an already negligible risk to doubly negligible.

As the Soviet Union lets its former allies choose their own destiny in Eastern Europe, however, the chances for internal violence and chaos are increasing. At some point, civil war or armed conflict between former Warsaw Pact nations is quite possible. But even if armed conflict should break out in Eastern Europe, the chances of U.S. intervention are low. We refused to aid the Hungarians in 1956 and the Czechoslovakians in 1968 when they tried to free themselves from Soviet rule. In the Gorbachev era, it seems more likely that we might even join forces with the Soviets, as we did in World War II, to help stop internal violence in the East European theatre. These peace-keeping type operations would have little chance of escalating to nuclear war, since the troops would not take nuclear weapons into battle. There would be little chance of nuclear weapon systems stored in West Germany (assuming that a new, unified Germany allows any nuclear weapons to remain on its soil) being overrun if we should join a peace-keeping force to restore order in, for example, Czechoslovakia or Romania.

To summarize this chapter, nuclear war would most likely result from the escalation of a conventional war between two lesser-developed countries after one or both acquired nuclear weapons or dragged a nuclear-capable nation into a military conflagration. For this reason, the two superpowers, along with the other major nuclear nations (France, Great Britain and China) have a special obligation to prevent the spread of nuclear weapons to other nations—horizontal proliferation in nukespeak.[11] We can stop horizontal proliferation by agreeing to a global ban on all nuclear weapons testing, and a verifiable ban on the production of fissile or fissionable material—highly enriched uranium and plutonium—the fuel of all nuclear weapons, as we discuss in Chapter 9. But first we have to stop testing and producing fissile material ourselves. Otherwise our ability to persuade other nations to do as we say and not as we do is minimal. The Bush administration is ignoring these prudent measures to reduce the risks of nuclear war.

Is nuclear war possible? Absolutely! And, despite improving superpower relations, the chances of nuclear war will grow substantially in the future, if President Bush continues his policies based on past habits of developing and building new and more destabilizing nuclear weapons with little regard for proliferation.

We describe in Chapters 4 and 5 why these new nuclear weapons now under development would be dangerously destabilizing. But first, we broaden our definition of "national security" in the next chapter to include other internal threats to our society.

---

[11]The term "horizontal proliferation" is used to distinguish the flow of nuclear technology to other nations from "vertical proliferation"—the increase in nuclear technology sophistication within the arsenal of a nuclear-capable nation.

# CHAPTER 3

# Internal Threats to National Security

SUMMARY

Nuclear war is not the only threat looming on the horizon. Our nation has accumulated serious social and economic deficits that, over time, could degrade or destroy our society as surely as any external enemy. President Bush has failed to address the mountain of debt created during the Reagan administration, a debt that could strangle our economy if left unchecked. Federal budget deficits continue in spite of all the balanced budget rhetoric. The military has ordered more weapons than we can possibly afford over the next decade; major weapons systems will have to be cut just to keep the real federal budget deficit at current $250 billion per year levels (excluding the trust fund surpluses).

Other internal threats to our security include drug abuse, environmental pollution, growing dependence (once again) on imported oil, negative international trade imbalances, declining commercial competitiveness in the international marketplace, and inadequate education, particularly in science and math.

We cannot blame all these deficits on high military spending. Even dramatically reduced military budgets could not alone free

28

enough resources to pay for all of our past debts, either financial or social. However, redirecting our scientists and engineers from military research to solving our environmental, energy and other societal needs will help alleviate the greatest threats to our national security in the 21st century, and Congress can cut more dollars out of the military budget than out of the "social budget" without jeopardizing vital national interests—military, social, or economic.

Nuclear war is not the only threat to national security that will increase unless we change our current course. The U.S. economy is in serious trouble. No one can predict how the huge national debt or the takeover of U.S. assets by foreign investors will affect our future, but continuing our present habit of consuming more and saving less, neglecting investments in future production and innovation, may severely curtail economic growth.

Inflation could once again roar out of control. We all remember the discomfort and worry when inflation rates reached into the low teens during the late 1970s. But imagine the economic turmoil if inflation rose over 100 percent per year. Or over 1,000 percent each year, as in some South American nations (Bolivia's inflation rate reached 24,000 percent in 1985). With 1,000 percent inflation, a car costing $10,000 this year would cost $110,000 next year. A monthly paycheck of $2,000 would be worth just $1,092 if you waited one month to spend it.

Sound unbelievable? Probably. But at least one businessman, a member of President Reagan's Grace Commission that was formed to explore ways to cut government spending, suggests that the U.S. economy may be only a decade away from such hyperinflation.[1] The Grace Commission projected that U.S. annual deficit could reach $2 trillion by the year 2000, and $1.6 trillion would be needed each year just to pay interest on the federal debt that they estimate could reach $13 trillion. The U.S. economy, although very robust, now has some of the attributes of Brazil, Argentina, and Bolivia several decades before their economies were racked by triple digit inflation: they all had huge deficits, rapidly expanding money supplies, rising international trade imbalances, and low savings rates. Hyperinflation in the U.S. is

---

[1] Harry Figgie, "Are Hyperinflation, Chaos on Tap for U.S. Economy?" *Engineering Times*, July 1989, p. 5.

unlikely, but significant inflation is a possibility if we continue current habits.

Shifting from economic to environmental horror stories, imagine what might happen if the protective ozone layer in the upper atmosphere were destroyed by the chlorine that modern society has dumped into the air. This ozone in the stratosphere shields us from harmful ultraviolet rays that produce cancer and could reduce crop yields. Too much ground-level ozone, the main ingredient of smog, may already be curtailing farm production. One study predicted that existing urban ozone pollution levels could cut cotton production by up to 35 percent, wheat production by 51 percent, soybeans by 24 percent, and corn production could decline by up to 5 percent.[2] Another model predicted that, by the year 2050, global warming could reduce corn yields by up to 65 percent.[3]

Or imagine the consequences if the average global temperature rose six to 14 degrees Fahrenheit, one extreme prediction of warming over the next 50 years due to the "greenhouse effect"—global warming due to the accumulation of extra carbon dioxide and other greenhouse gases in the atmosphere. This extra heat could melt enough ice and cause the oceans to expand such that the sea level could rise up to 25 feet, in addition to the one foot rise registered in the last century. Since many of our major cities are near sea level, effects would be dramatic.

Other studies of global warming predict much less dramatic effects, with temperature increases of four to nine degrees Fahrenheit and the sea level rising only three to five feet. Some scientists have suggested that cloud cover and ocean currents might reduce global warming, and one model predicts that temperatures could even fall in Antarctica, preventing any rise in sea level due to melting of the West Antarctic ice sheet.[4] While there is still great uncertainty regarding both the degree and the effects of warming, rising temperatures in combination with increased ultraviolet light from a thinning of the earth's protective ozone layer could disrupt or even destroy many important agricultural crops.

These scenarios illustrate just two extreme "opportunity costs" of the arms race: we forgo the opportunity to correct glaring societal problems

---

[2]"Urban Ozone and the Clean Air Act: Problems and Proposals for Change," Washington, D.C.: Office of Technology Assessment, April 1988, p. 41.
[3]Carol Rose, "Global Warming's Effect on Iowa Farming Studied," *Des Moines Register*, November 17, 1989.
[4]William Booth, "Computer Predictions of 'Greenhouse Effect' Have a Northern Accent," *Washington Post*, December 7, 1989, p. A13.

by focusing too much attention and too many resources on unlikely military threats. While we cannot blame every ill in our society on excessive military spending, we believe that there is a strong connection between growing and largely unattended social problems and our continued support and feeding of massive military forces in peacetime.

Sometimes we can see these connections between military spending and missed opportunities better in other nations. For example, the World Commission on Environment and Development estimated that Ethiopia could have controlled desertification by spending up to $50 million to plant trees. Instead, the Ethiopians dumped $275 million per year into weapons from 1975 to 1985, and more than a million Ethiopians died in 1985 as the expanding desert eliminated food-producing land.[5]

The military not only consumes vast resources that could be utilized elsewhere, but the annual debate over the military budget devours thousands of hours of our leaders' time within the executive and legislative branches of government. The White House and the Congress only have so much time to consider national problems. Every hour spent debating the fate of the MX missile or SDI research is an hour lost to finding solutions to global warming or the war on drugs. Furthermore, as we'll elaborate in Chapters 9 through 11, our nation needs a fundamental overhaul in our notion of national security, and this sea change in our way of handling national security will require strong, visionary leadership in the White House, and the rebuilding of a national consensus on security matters in Congress and the American public. We are wasting precious political capital debating individual weapons systems, when we should be discussing the overall strategy and policies to match limited resources to the real national security threats of the 1990s.

Since World War II, discussions of "national security" have focused rather narrowly on potential external threats to our nation, most notably the fear of the huge Soviet military and the possibility of world Communist domination by the Soviets or through its client-states. As long as these external enemies were perceived as the major threat to national security, then a strong military seemed to be the proper remedy or preventive. But the many growing internal deficiencies within our society could also weaken or severely disrupt our civilization. The impacts of global warming could be more damaging to the world in

---

[5]Michael G. Renner, "What's Sacrificed When We Arm," *World Watch*, September/October 1989, p. 9.

the 21st century than any past war, second only to the catastrophe of a nuclear war. A continuation of our relative economic decline could ruin our nation as surely as any external invasion.

In one very real sense we are at war today. Not against an external enemy, but a daily battle within our towns and cities—a war that is killing and ruining the lives of hundreds and thousands of our most vulnerable citizens—the illicit drug war. At first, the military was reluctant to join in the fight against drug abuse, fearing that it would detract from their historic mission of battling external enemies. With Congressional pressure, however, the Defense Department is using some of its resources to help provide surveillance in the border areas, offering assistance to law enforcement officials and to South American nations that are fighting drug cartels. We should ask ourselves if it makes more sense to station U.S. troops in central Europe, where the threat of Soviet surprise attack has vanished, or whether some of those troops would not serve U.S. interests better at the U.S.-Mexican border, providing surveillance of drug traffic for our law enforcement officers.

But the real emphasis to curb the drug war must be on education and rehabilitation, activities that vie for the same tax dollars spent on the military. Over 70 percent of the drug war funds now go to law enforcement and interdiction. We must expand our efforts to curtail the demand for drugs. We must provide hope for our youth in the inner cities, particularly for minorities who are disproportionately the victims of the drug war.

Based on saving lives, any war on "drugs" should also attack alcohol and tobacco abuse. According to the National Council on Alcoholism, alcohol is implicated in 50,000 to 200,000 deaths annually, tobacco allegedly kills 320,000 prematurely each year, while only 4,138 deaths were related to legal and illegal drug abuse, other than alcohol and tobacco, in 1986.[6]

In short, our "enemies" are changing. International terrorists and drug lords are becoming the "clear and present danger" to our society, replacing to a large degree the Communist threat. We should be adapting our military posture and spending priorities to combat these new enemies.

We can no longer afford the simplistic enemy image approach to

---

[6]"The Challenge of the Drug Crisis: To Heal a Wounded Nation," *Washington Newsletter*, Washington, D.C.: Friends Committee on National Legislation, February 1990, p. 2.

national security. We must expand our definition of national security to include a broad range of internal as well as external threats to our national survival and well-being. We must balance the need for military strength with the need for a sound economy, a clean environment and healthy citizens.

Senator Mark Hatfield has long recognized this need for a broadened definition of national security; he frequently refers to President Eisenhower, calling him "the only President in my lifetime who understood national defense. Others have been seduced into believing it is measured only in terms of military hardware and measurements of megatons, whereas President Eisenhower so clearly understood the national defense as involving many components."[7] Senator Hatfield noted that Eisenhower, a career military man and fellow Republican, introduced the national highway system and new educational programs as part of our nation's security. Hatfield liberally quotes Eisenhower's famous statement connecting military spending and unmet domestic needs:

> Every gun that is made, every warship launched, every rocket fired signifies, in the final sense, a theft from those who hunger and are not fed, those who are cold and not clothed. This world in arms is not spending money alone. It is spending the sweat of its laborers, the genius of its scientists, the hopes of its children.[8]

Senator Hatfield concluded that "we are vulnerable in the nation's security picture, but it is not because of lesser moneys that we are spending [on the military]. It is because of the lesser amounts of moneys that we are spending for science, research, education, housing, nutrition, and all of these factors."

In a similar vein, Senator Al Gore ranks environmental degradation as a threat to national security. Speaking to the National Academy of Sciences, he expressed concern about our ability to cope with environmental problems, but went on to say that he does "believe we have the capacity for what is needed—because the challenges can now be accurately described in terms of national security."[9]

In this chapter, we analyze these non-military threats to America's security, including current trends in the U.S. economy, describing how

---

[7]Senator Mark O. Hatfield, *Congressional Record*, July 27, 1989, p. S 8910.
[8]Ibid, August 2, 1989, p. S 9439.
[9]Flora Lewis, "Environment Is Security," *New York Times*, May 24, 1989.

the Bush administration has failed to deal with the tragic economic legacy from the borrow-and-spend Reagan administration. We then describe the other "deficits": areas of our society that have been largely ignored over the last decade. These deficits include:

- Reduced personal and national **savings**
- Falling **competitiveness** in the civilian economy
- Neglect of **education**, particularly in science and math
- Reduced research on alternative **energy** options
- Deterioration of the **environment**
- Reduction in stock of low-cost **housing**
- Inadequate maintenance of **transportation** infrastructure

Correcting these deficits will cost many hundreds of billions of dollars over the next several decades. But investing in these areas will lead to the growth in real national wealth needed to "defeat" the new internal enemies of our national security.

Assuming President Bush does not impose major tax increases, then we must reduce other federal programs to make the necessary investments in our nation's future. As we discuss at the end of this chapter, we can safely reduce more from military spending than from the so-called social programs, but cuts in the military budget alone would not pay for all the debts coming due in the years ahead. Choices will have to be made. We will have to decide which of the many societal and economic deficits most threaten the long-term health of our nation. We will have to apply our limited resources to the most damaging threats, while still preserving a military capability suitable to the real external threats of the 1990s.

Economic Security Threats

Many Americans are now realizing that our national security does not depend on military strength alone. In one public opinion survey, 43 percent said that strengthening our economy should be the federal government's number one priority, 38 percent chose social programs such as education, homelessness and poverty for special attention, while only 15 percent felt that a strong military should be our first priority.[10]

Paul Kennedy, in his landmark analysis of the major nation-states over the last five centuries, "The Rise and Fall of the Great Powers," points

---

[10]*Americans Talk Security*, August 1988, p. 16.

out that great power status depends as much if not more on economic strength as on raw military power.[11] Many young nations start off with economic development as a primary mission while minimizing military prowess. They develop military strength much later to protect their accumulating wealth. Certainly our nation followed this prescription, developing the world's greatest industrial machine while disdaining any significant peacetime military establishment or foreign entanglements prior to the 1940s. As a result, when two major wars came to Europe in this century, the American industrial machine was ready and our industrial capability provided the staying power needed for Allied victory. We had no significant standing peacetime armies, no stock of weapons, and yet our private industrial might provided the margin of victory.

Japan seems to be on this early path, emphasizing economic development after military conquest failed them at the beginning of the century. Japan now devotes most of its resources to economic development, with a military burden six times less than that of the United States on a per capita GNP basis.

Paul Kennedy goes on to state that many nations in the last 500 years have overextended themselves once they reached great-power status, relying too much on military strength while letting their underlying economic base erode. He calls this "imperial overstretch." He suggests that any nation should balance three components of the state budget: military costs, socioeconomic needs of citizens, and investment for economic growth. If "too large a proportion of the state's resources is diverted from wealth creation and allocated instead to military purposes, then that is likely to lead to a weakening of national power over the longer term." Kennedy notes that once this imperial overstretch takes hold and a nation begins to decline in relation to other world powers, "great powers in relative decline instinctively respond by spending more on 'security,' and thereby divert potential resources from 'investment' and compound their long-term dilemma."

Kennedy's conclusions should be required reading for all those concerned about the future of our nation:

The history of the past five hundred years of international rivalry demonstrates that military "security" alone is never enough. It

---

[11]Paul Kennedy, *The Rise and Fall of the Great Powers: Economic Change and Military Conflict from 1500 to 2000*, Random House, 1987.

may, over the short term, deter or defeat rival states (and that, for most political leaders and their publics, is perfectly satisfactory). But if, by such victories, the nation overextends itself geographically and strategically; if, even at a less imperial level, it chooses to devote a large proportion of its total income to "protection," leaving less for "productive investment," it is likely to find its economic output slowing down, with dire implications for its long-term capacity to maintain both its citizens' consumption demands and its international position. Already this is happening in the case of the USSR, the U.S., and Britain.[12]

Does this mean that we are doomed to follow a path of steady economic decline? Not necessarily. Historical trends are never sufficient to predict the future. But certainly the signs are not reassuring. Decline is not inevitable . . . unless we fail to recognize the warning signals and take corrective actions.

We have the world's best and most flexible economic system, vast resources and the world's most democratic and potentially the most responsive political system, a model for nations emerging from four decades of Communist rule. We have an energetic, creative workforce that has produced economic plenty for a majority of Americans. We have the tools to avoid economic decline; whether we choose to heed the warning signals is up to us.

Let's look at some of the trends in economic indicators over the last decade (See Figure 3-1 and Table 3-1). Key trends are mostly negative; trade, savings, and productivity growth have been declining, while interest rates and inflation were reduced by Reaganomics.

*Trade.* The United States trade balance erosion in the 1980s was one of the most dramatic economic reversals since the Great Depression (Figure 3-1). The U.S. had exported more goods and services than we imported during most of the post-Second World War period, with negative balances of at most $28 billion in the late 1970s. Then the bottom fell out beginning in 1983, as Americans continued a gluttonous consumption binge that was sustained by importing goods and services from abroad. Paul Volcker, chairman of the Federal Reserve from 1979 to 1987, wrote that "We have become dependent on—really addicted to—foreign capital to finance our investment and our spending."[13]

---

[12]Ibid., p. 539.
[13]Paul Volcker, "The Costs of Leadership?" *Washington Post*, December 17, 1989, p. B1.

The trade deficit reached a peak of $152 billion in 1987—American businesses exported $152 billion less in goods and services than we imported from abroad. Actually, U.S. exports reached an all-time high in 1988 ($321 billion), but we imported even more ($441 billion) to feed our consumption habit. The trade balance did improve to just over $100 billion in 1989, but many economists expect the trade imbalance to increase again in the 1990s as we import more oil and pay interest on our growing foreign debt. Oil imports alone cost the U.S. economy approximately $64 billion in 1989, and one oil company executive predicts this oil drain could reach $100 billion annually by 2000.[14]

FIGURE 3-1.    UNITED STATES TRADE BALANCE[15]

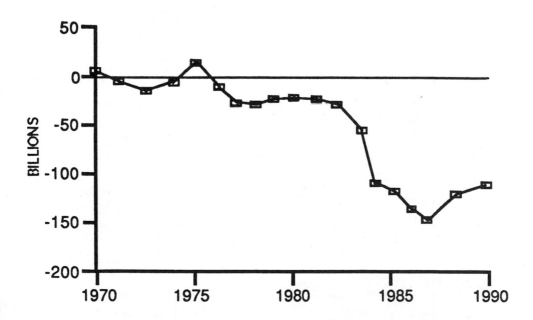

To sustain this trade imbalance and our huge federal budget deficit, foreign investors began acquiring real estate, businesses and other American assets. In 1980, direct foreign investments in U.S. businesses and real estate were estimated at $83 billion by the Department of

[14]Robert L. Hirsch, "U.S. Oil and Gas Consumption: Is Another Crisis Ahead?" *Science*, March 16, 1990, p. 1280.
[15]*United States Trade Performance in 1988*, U.S. Department of Commerce, September 1989, p. 82; and *Economic Indicators*, February 1990, p. 35.

TABLE 3-1.   TRENDS IN SAMPLE ECONOMIC INDICATORS

### Savings (percentage of GNP)[16]

|                              | 1960s  | 1970s | 1980s |
|------------------------------|--------|-------|-------|
| Personal savings:            | 4.6%   | 5.6   | 3.8   |
| Business retained earnings:  | 3.5    | 2.5   | 1.8   |
| State & Local government:    | 0.1    | 0.8   | 1.3   |
| Federal savings:             | −0.3   | −1.7  | −3.9  |
| Net national savings:        | 7.9    | 7.3   | 3.0   |

### Productivity growth (average annual percentage)[17]

|                         | 1948-73  | 1973-79 | 1979-87 |
|-------------------------|----------|---------|---------|
| Business sector         | 2.9%/yr  | 0.6     | 1.4     |
| Goods-producing sector  | 3.2      | 0.5     | 2.4     |
| Service sector          | 2.5      | 0.7     | 0.7     |

|       | Inflation | | Interest |
|-------|-----------------|--------------------------|-----------------------------|
|       | GNP Deflator | Consumer Price Index | 3-month Treasury Bills |
| 1950s | 2.6%  | 2.2  | 2.0  |
| 1960s | 2.4   | 2.5  | 4.0  |
| 1970s | 6.8   | 7.4  | 6.3  |
| 1980  | 9.7   | 12.5 | 11.5 |
| 1981  | 9.7   | 8.9  | 14.0 |
| 1982  | 6.3   | 3.8  | 10.7 |
| 1983  | 3.5   | 3.8  | 8.6  |
| 1984  | 3.0   | 3.9  | 9.6  |
| 1985  | 3.0   | 3.8  | 7.5  |
| 1986  | 2.4   | 1.1  | 6.0  |
| 1987  | 2.8   | 4.4  | 5.8  |
| 1988  | 3.3   | 4.0  | 6.7  |
| 1989  | 4.2   | 4.8  | 8.1  |

---

[16]Gail E. Makinen, "Savings Trends and Productivity," *CRS Review*, June 1989, p. 6.
[17]Edward Knight, "Productivity in the Service Sector," *CRS Review*, June 1989, p. 19.

Commerce. By 1989, these cumulative foreign direct investments had more than tripled to $390 billion, or about 3 percent of total U.S. assets of $12 trillion. In 1980, U.S. companies had invested about 2.7 times more overseas than foreign companies had invested in our economy. By 1989, after nine years of rampant foreign purchases of U.S. assets, foreigners owned $390 billion of U.S. direct assets versus $359 billion that Americans owned abroad.[18]

These direct investments in companies and real estate do not include other financial assets such as stocks and bank accounts. The 10 largest banks in the world are all Japanese; the largest U.S. bank, Citibank, is 24th on the list, with 17 Japanese banks, three French banks, two British banks and one German bank having more assets. Including all investments and financial assets, foreigners own about $2 trillion of U.S. assets while we own about $1.4 trillion overseas. The U.S. has become the world's greatest debtor nation, owing about $630 billion to foreign interests.

While we experienced trade imbalances in most manufacturing areas in the 1980s except chemicals and commercial aircraft, the U.S. economy did maintain a net surplus in services overseas: we collected more interest, rents, dividends and profits from tourism, insurance and other professional services than foreign competitors earned here. But even the service sector trade balance went negative for the first time in the second quarter of 1989, as foreign owners reaped more profits from interest on their growing U.S. holdings.

TABLE 3-2. MAJOR FOREIGN INVESTORS IN U.S. (AS OF 1988)

| | |
|---|---|
| United Kingdom | $88 billion |
| The Netherlands | 51.7 |
| Japan | 48.5 |
| Canada | 24.3 |
| West Germany | 21.3 |
| Switzerland | 15.2 |
| France | 12.2 |

A key issue for the 1990s and beyond is whether we can tolerate a continuation of these trends. Foreign investment so far has been essential to keep interest rates down and to provide domestic employ-

---

[18]"Foreign Investments Top U.S. Holdings Abroad," *Washington Post*, March 14, 1990, p. F1.

ment. However, as more businesses and real estate fall into foreign ownership, major decisions affecting the economy of our nation and, ultimately, our national security, will be made overseas.

Suppose we do have a major world recession. Will the Honda Corporation choose to cut back manufacturing in Japan, or in Marysville, Ohio? If the oil industry suffers economic hard times, will British Petroleum, which has taken over control of the Standard Oil Company of Ohio and now ranks as the number one oil producer in the U.S., decide to cut back U.S. drilling instead of fields closer to London? Ironically, other countries are assuming effective control of vital assets in our nation through economic takeovers, something they could never accomplish militarily. Only time will tell how serious this foreign control will become. Obviously we cannot go on indefinitely selling off our national assets to foreign firms and expect to remain a sovereign nation.

*Savings.* Savings are essential for a dynamic, growing economy. Savings provide the capital for expanding businesses, for conducting private research and development, for developing new products and processes, and for developing and buying more productive equipment. Savings provide the seed money to stay competitive or to leap-frog the competition by starting new enterprises. As shown in Table 3-1, the United States net national savings fell by a factor of more than two from the 1970s to the 1980s. Today our personal savings rate is four to five times less than Japan's, and ten times less than that of South Korea.[19] (See also Figure 3-2.) Instead of investing in new equipment for the future, we are consuming for today.

President Bush's Director of the Office of Management and Budget (OMB), Richard Darman, labeled our behavior "cultural now-ism," defining it as our "collective short-sightedness, our obsession with the here and now, our reluctance adequately to address the future."[20] Clearly we must reverse our poor savings habits of the last decades, if we are to maintain our standard of living and remain a dominant world power.

*Productivity growth.* The rising standard of living that Americans have taken for granted since the Second World War has been due

---

[19]Norman R. Augustine, "U.S. Credibility and Viability in Worldwide Competition," *Key Speeches*, Aerospace Industries Association, Vol. 2, No. 5, June 1989, p. 6.
[20]Jeffrey Bell, "Darman's Hidden Agenda," *Washington Post*, September 17, 1989, p. C1.

FIGURE 3-2.   NET SAVINGS RATES[21]

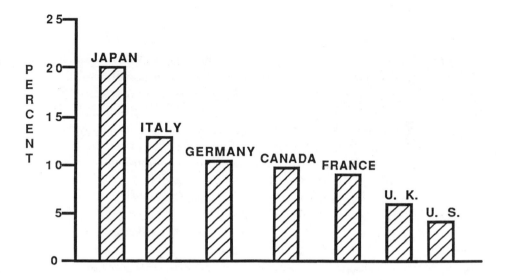

primarily to increased worker productivity. New machines and new processing techniques allow workers to produce more, so that the average American can afford to buy additional consumer goods for each hour of work. As shown in Table 3-1, worker productivity grew at a rate of about three percent per year from the end of World War II until 1973, when it fell to less than one percent per year average growth. While worker productivity grew back into the one to two percent per year range in the 1980s, it is still lower than during the three postwar decades. Furthermore, the service industries now account for about 76 percent of all non-farm jobs and 70 percent of our GNP, and there has been no measurable increase in productivity growth in the service industries. At least part of this failure to maintain productivity growth can be attributed to reduced investment in new plants and equipment, a result of low savings. And much of the new investment has been made by foreign sources as described above.

*Commercial competitiveness.* Many factors contribute to a competi-

---

[21]*Budget of the United States Government*; Fiscal Year 1991 (Washington, D.C.: U.S. Government Printing Office, 1990), p.44.

tive position in the world market: adequate energy, a well-trained, well-educated labor pool, investment in modern and efficient production facilities, adequate transportation, raw materials, and research and development. Our vast military establishment also requires most of these same ingredients. Is it any wonder that Germany and Japan, our two former World War II enemies, are rapidly catching up to us in the economic arena, when they devote less of their resources to their military and more to commercial enterprises? For example, while the United States devotes 75 percent of its federal research and development (R&D) dollars to the military and NASA, Japan spends only four percent and West Germany only eight percent on their military services. We spend 5.5 percent of our GNP on military programs, while Japan devotes about 1 percent and West Germany about 3.1 percent.[22]

Should anyone be surprised that we do not make any VCRs or cameras, or that we have only *one* color TV manufacturer left in the United States (down from 27), when many of our scientists are busy developing and building cruise missiles and stealth bombers and space-age Star Wars weapons? Since 1970, the U.S. share of color television production has dropped from 90 to ten percent, numerically controlled machine tools from 100 to 40 percent, and our share of the semiconductor market from 89 to 64 percent.

Still, we have the world's highest per capita income and the highest worker productivity. But other nations are catching up. An average worker in Japan produced only 18 percent of the output of an American worker in 1950; today the Japanese worker is up to 60 percent of the American productivity and rising. German workers have gone from producing about 35 percent of an American's output in 1950 to 75 percent today.[23] We are still number one, but we are in relative decline compared to other industrialized nations.

*Federal debt and the budget deficit.* The federal government's sea of red ink is astounding. It took the United States government over 200 years to accumulate its first trillion (1,000,000,000,000) dollars of debt, but only four years (1983-1986) to reach the next trillion, and we added the third trillion of debt in 1990. And this obscene mountain of debt occurred on the watch of a President who promised voters in 1980 that

[22]Kosta Tsipis, "New Tasks for Arms Controllers," *Bulletin of the Atomic Scientists*, July/August 1989, p. 8.
[23]Mary Jane Bolle, "Productivity, Income, and Living Standards," *CRS Review*, June 1989, p. 4.

he would balance the budget! As David Stockman, Director of the Office of Management and Budget during the first Reagan term, put it:

> The records will show that within the span of a few short years, the United States flung itself into massive hock with the rest of the world. And it occurred so swiftly that it was hardly even debated or remarked upon until it was too late.[24]

Actually, there is some controversy regarding the detrimental effects of the deficit. Some economists are deeply concerned, suggesting economic disruption or recession and falling standard of living for Americans, while others claim it is not all that bad for the government to go deeply into debt. At the very least, the interest on the national debt is robbing needed funds for Paul Kennedy's three priorities: military, social needs and investment. For 1990, over half of our income taxes went to pay interest on the federal debt ($260 billion out of $489 billion collected), or 24 percent of all government general fund receipts. This is $260 billion that cannot be used for other domestic needs.

The American public was told by the administration that the federal budget deficit would be only $124 billion in 1990. However, this is *not* the true deficit; in 1990, the actual deficit in federal funds was closer to $250 billion. That is, the government took in $250 billion less than it paid out, excluding the various trust funds such as Social Security that ran large surpluses. The federal debt is projected to increase from $2.866 trillion in 1989 to $3.113 trillion in 1990, an increase of about $250 billion.

The government was able to report only $124 billion as "the deficit" by a bookkeeping sleight-of-hand: the Office of Management and Budget (OMB) included the $125.7 billion *surplus* which accumulated in various trust funds during 1990, as part of the "unified" federal budget. That is, taxpayers and employers paid money into 12 trust funds to cover everything from social security payments to highway maintenance (see Table 3-3). Almost all of these trust funds are accumulating surpluses, so that they can make the planned payments to individuals as they retire, are disabled, or become sick. Interest on these funds is necessary to meet future obligations. These surpluses were not intended to be used to reduce the federal budget deficit. And yet the

[24]Quoted from Stockman's memoir by Haynes Johnson, "The Annual Budget Charade," *Washington Post*, February 2, 1990, p. A2.

administration deceives the public by adding these annual surpluses to the even larger federal government operating losses, thereby reducing the proclaimed "deficit."

Senator Moynihan has publicized this deficit-hiding subterfuge, by pointing out that the Social Security trust fund surplus of $62 billion masks part of the deficit. But Social Security is only half of the trust fund surpluses, as shown in Table 3-3.

This deficit-hiding scam will get worse over the next five years, unless Congress acts. The administration predicts that trust fund surpluses will increase from $125 billion in 1990 to $220 billion in 1995, creating an even larger shield to hide the true deficits. In fact, the reported "deficit" will reach zero by 1993 according to rosy administration projections, even though the non-trust funds would still be running an actual deficit above $100 billion (See Figure 3-3).

TABLE 3-3.   OUTLAYS AND RECEIPTS FROM THE TRUST FUNDS FOR 1990[25]

| Trust Fund: | Outlays: | Receipts: |
|---|---|---|
| | (billions of dollars) | |
| Social Security (Federal old age, survivors, and disability insurance): | 249.4 | 311.4 |
| Railroad retirement trust fund: | 9.7 | 10.5 |
| Veterans life insurance trust: | 1.2 | 1.5 |
| Federal employees retirement trust: | 31.8 | 52.6 |
| Military retirement fund: | 21.5 | 33.5 |
| Unemployment trust fund: | 19.5 | 26.2 |
| Health insurance trust funds: | 108.2 | 127.0 |
| Highway trust funds: | 14.9 | 16.3 |
| Airport and airway trust fund: | 3.5 | 5.1 |
| Foreign military sales trust fund: | 9.0 | 8.8 |
| Other trust funds: | 3.1 | 4.8 |
| Totals: | 471.9 | 597.6 |

*SURPLUS IN TRUST FUNDS FOR 1990: $127.5 BILLION*

A similar bookkeeping trick makes the government interest payments look smaller. The usual federal budget summary provided to the public reports "net interest," the interest paid on the debt *minus* the interest paid from the federal government's general fund to the various trust funds. For 1990, the net interest was estimated at $176 billion,

_____

[25]*Budget of the United States Government, Fiscal Year 1991*, p. A-86.

FIGURE 3-3.    FEDERAL DEFICITS WITH AND WITHOUT TRUST FUND SURPLUS[26]

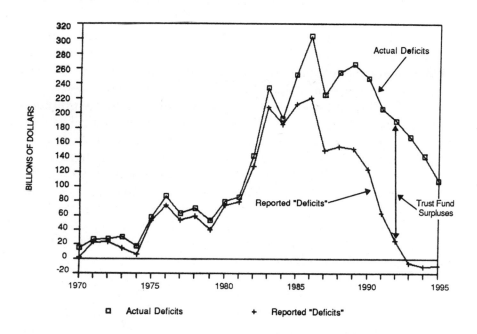

compared to $255 billion in actual interest payments on the total debt. The difference, $79 billion, was paid as interest into the trust funds. Without these interest payments, the federal government could not meet its obligations to workers as they retire in the next century without major increases in taxes, forcing our children and grandchildren to bear the burden of our retirement.

The U.S. Congress has set a goal of reducing the annual federal budget "deficit" to zero by 1993, via the Gramm-Rudman law. However, this would not reduce the national debt to zero. Far from it. We would have a national debt of some $3.7 trillion by 1993 even if we were able to comply with the Gramm-Rudman (G-R) prescription for deficit reduction. And since G-R uses the fictitious budget deficit including the trust fund surpluses, we would still have to pay back those surpluses to keep the trust funds solvent.

The Bush administration has made some minor deficit reduction progress over the last few years, but much of the claimed deficit savings

---

[26]Ibid, p. A-85.

were one-time accounting tricks that did little to reverse long-term deficit trends. They made one-time gains by selling off federal assets. They postponed certain payments from the last day of the fiscal year until the first day of the next year, to make this year's deficit appear smaller. The telephone companies were required to pay the government $102 million in telephone taxes one week early to add revenue for fiscal year 1990, helping the 1990 deficit but adding $102 million to the 1991 deficit. The Bush administration moved the Postal Service "off-budget" in fiscal year 1990, because it finished the year in the red prior to an expected postal rate increase in 1991 that would show a profit.

But President Bush has not made the hard decisions that will be necessary to restore fiscal responsibility. He has merely postponed the day of reckoning, making our choices that much more difficult in the years ahead. Rather than taking charge and immediately installing a long-term economic plan to redirect our priorities, he has taken the easy approach: coast along, following the Reagan borrow and spend habits and hope for a miracle.

## SOCIAL DEFICITS

The annual federal budget deficits and the trade deficits do not tell the full deficit story. There are several other major societal debts coming due in the decades ahead that are not included in the usual predictions of federal obligations. We as a nation should be spending many hundreds of billions of dollars to clean up radioactive waste at nuclear weapons manufacturing plants across the country; to clean up toxic waste dumps; to replenish the deteriorating stock of public housing, roads, bridges and sewers; to improve the air traffic control system; to clean up the air we breathe; and, like it or not, we are going to have to dish out at least another $125 billion and possibly as much as $500 billion to bail out the failing savings and loan industry. Some of these societal bills may be placed "off-budget" or simply excluded from the G-R calculations by edict to make the deficit seem smaller, but this will not change the reality. The total societal deficit is highly speculative, but Table 3-4 lists some estimates for these unpaid bills.

Some social deficits cannot be easily quantified, but they will degrade our society and ultimately our national security if not corrected. We discuss the shortfalls in education, energy, the environment, housing and transportation in the following sections.

Table 3-4.    Estimates of Future Federal Government Costs

(In addition to usual government expenditures,
in billions of dollars over the next 20 years)

|  | Low | High |
|---|---|---|
| Toxic Waste Cleanup (Superfund) | $100 | $500 |
| Nuclear Weapons Plant Cleanup | 50 | 250 |
| Savings and Loan Industry Bail-out | 125 | 500 |
| Air Traffic Control and Airport Improvements | 25 | 50 |
| Infrastructure (Highways, bridges, sewers, etc.) | 100 | 3000 |
| Low income housing rehabilitation | 25 | 80 |
| Clean air | 130 | 200 |
| Total: | 555 | 4,580 |

*Education.* Children are our greatest resource for the future. To remain competitive in high technology international markets, we must have citizens adequately trained in math, science and engineering. Unfortunately, we have not kept pace with the other industrialized countries. American students were once the envy of the world.

Today, our students are falling behind their counterparts in other nations in basic math and science skills. One study compared 13-year-old students from the United States, Korea, Ireland, Spain, the United Kingdom and four provinces in Canada. The American students rated last in overall math proficiency with Korean students at the top; U.S. students were close to the bottom in science, with only students from Ireland and two Canadian provinces scoring worse. While 78 percent of Korean children could solve two-step math problems, only 40 percent of American children succeeded. In science, 70 percent of students from Korea and British Columbia could use scientific procedures and analyze data, compared to only 35 to 40 percent of U.S. students.[27]

Another study showed that American 14-year-olds scored lower on a science achievement test than students from Japan (first), Canada, Sweden, Australia, Italy and the United Kingdom. American 17-year-old students scored last in biology, second from last in chemistry (Canada last) but fourth in physics (Sweden, Italy, and Canada worse).

---

[27]Archie E. Lapointe, Nancy A. Mead, and Gary W. Phillips, "A World of Differences," Educational Testing Service Report No. 19-CAEP-01, January 1989, p. 10.

Students from the UK were first in all three science tests, and Japanese students did better than American students on all three tests.[28]

President Bush has acknowledged the need for better education in America, asking that he be remembered as the "education president." His first actions spoke louder than his words, however, as he proposed *cutting* federal education by $100 million below the previous year's inflation-adjusted level. Predictably, he called this an increase for education, while he trumpets a similar less-than-inflationary boost for the military as a two percent *cut*.

For whatever reason, our schools today are not motivating young people to study technical subjects. A lower percentage of American high school students took advanced placement or second-year physics than foreign students (see Table 3-5). In 1984 and 1985, less than eight percent of all first degrees awarded at American universities were in engineering. Comparable numbers for our allies: 19 percent in Japan, 14 percent in the United Kingdom and West Germany. In the Soviet Union, 39 percent of university degrees went to engineers.[29]

TABLE 3-5.    PERCENTAGE OF 18-YEAR-OLDS TAKING ADVANCED PLACEMENT OR SECOND-YEAR PHYSICS.[30]

| | |
|---|---|
| United States | 1 |
| Hungary | 4 |
| England | 6 |
| Singapore | 7 |
| Poland | 9 |
| Norway | 10 |
| Japan | 11 |
| Australia | 11 |
| Hong Kong | 14 |
| Finland | 14 |
| Sweden | 15 |
| Italy | 19 |
| Canada (English-speaking) | 19 |

[28]Kenneth Redd and Wayne Riddle, "Comparative Education: Statistics on Education in the United States and Selected Foreign Nations," *CRS Report 88-764 EPW*, November 14, 1988, p. 57.
[29]"Shortage of Engineers Needs Solution," *Engineering Times*, July 1989, p. 5.
[30]Michael Neuschatz, "Reaching the Critical Mass in High School Physics," *Physics Today*, August 1989, p. 30.

This is one debt that cannot be repaid overnight. If we do not invest soon in new education techniques to reverse our relative decline in science and math education, then we risk producing a generation of students ill-equipped to compete in the global marketplace of the 21st century.

We must invest in our children's future. Instead of a massive military-industrial complex, we need an educational-industrial complex to reinvigorate businesses across the nation.

Just as John F. Kennedy challenged our scientists and engineers to land a man on the moon before the end of the 1960s, we need a President with vision to challenge our educators to restore our educational system to its former preeminence, the equivalent of an educational moon-shot by the end of the decade. We must give our teachers the resources they need to accomplish this new mission. We need to establish "centers of excellence" at universities, private colleges and community colleges to spur new innovation and growth. We must demystify science, so that all students are expected to take core science courses, not just those on a college track. We cannot afford a scientifically illiterate work force for the 21st century.

*Energy.* By burning fossil fuels, we are creating an annual energy deficit: each year we burn fuel that took millions of years to accumulate. We also have an energy research deficit; we have not adequately funded research to develop low-cost, clean, renewable sources of energy for the next century.

The supply of fossil fuel is limited. Let there be no doubt: there will be other energy crises. The next oil crisis may come next year, or in ten years, but it will come. Our nation, after outstanding conservation efforts in the 1970s succeeded in cutting back our consumption— without the predicted decline in our economy—is once again relying more and more on imported oil. As shown in Figure 3-4, we are now importing more and producing less oil than just before the 1973-74 energy crisis. Our imports of crude oil increased by 77 percent from 1973 to 1989, and our domestic production dropped by 17 percent since 1973. Furthermore, our dependence on the Arab OPEC nations has more than doubled, from 5.3 percent of all U.S. petroleum products in 1973 to 12.3 percent in 1989. Our dependence on all OPEC nations has risen from 17.3 percent to 23 percent.[31]

---

[31]*Monthly Energy Review: December 1989*, Washington, D.C.: Energy Information Administration, U.S. Department of Energy, March 1990.

One oil company official, after analyzing the oil and gas situation, before Iraq invaded Kuwait, and noting the long time required to find new sources of energy, wrote that "these facts, coupled with the nation's generally short-term orientation, suggest a strong likelihood of a new U.S. energy crisis in the early to middle 1990s."[32]

James Schlesinger, well qualified to address the national security implications of energy dependence as a former Secretary of both the Defense and Energy departments, warned in testimony to Congress in March of 1990 that control of the oil market "is once again within the grasp of those major producers in the Gulf that have excess and or expandable capacity." Schlesinger ended his testimony with these somber words:

> Time is beginning to run out. The damage that has already occurred is far greater than is generally recognized. We may as well acknowledge that over the past decade the United States, as a practical matter, abandoned the quest for energy independence—indeed, even the quest for low energy dependency. If we are to limit our future vulnerability, either for national security or international financial reasons, we shall have to reverse course—and take vigorous action.[33]

Our growing dependence on foreign oil creates twin threats to U.S. security: our nation's economic health depends on inexpensive energy, and fear of energy shortages could spark a military confrontation as our military buildup in Saudi Arabia graphically illustrates. Lack of energy could be the trigger that ignites World War III.

Eventually, the human race must find one or more alternatives to fossil fuels. Economic sources of oil will decrease substantially sometime in the 21st century at our current consumption rates. As oil, gas and coal reserves decrease, exploration and production costs will rise. In addition, society must pay for the costs of cleaning up the environment, directly or indirectly. As we seek to reduce carbon dioxide gases (the end product of all fossil fuel burning) to retard the greenhouse effect, as we mandate reduced sulfur dioxide pollution from coal-fired

[32]Robert L. Hirsch, "Impending United States Energy Crisis," *Science*, Vol. 235, March 20, 1987, p. 1467.
[33]James R. Schlesinger, testimony before the Committee on Energy and Natural Resources, United States Senate, March 26, 1990.

electrical generation plants, the real costs of producing energy from fossil fuels will rise even more.

FIGURE 3-4.   OIL CONSUMPTION AND DOMESTIC PRODUCTION

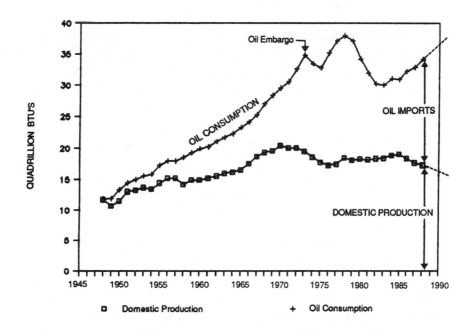

World energy demand will also increase at the same time that fossil fuel costs are rising. Population growth and increased standards of living will both conspire to increase the planet's use of energy in the decades ahead. Eventually the cost of obtaining energy from fossil fuels will be excessive, restraining economic growth and standards of living. Alternative energy sources will be needed in the 21st century if we are to maintain anything like our current high-technology, energy-intensive civilization.

There are only a handful of alternative energy choices: solar energy, wind, geothermal, biofuel, ocean thermal, nuclear energy (fission or fusion), conservation and improvements in energy efficiency.

Solar energy is economic now in remote areas, away from the power grid, and in the southwestern U.S. for reducing utilities' peak electrical air conditioning loads on hot summer afternoons. Both solar thermal systems (where solar energy heats oil or water to drive electrical turbines) and photovoltaic (PV) systems (where solid state solar cells convert sunlight directly into electricity without any moving parts) will become more competitive as fossil fuel costs rise, and as new solar manufacturing techniques are developed. The challenge is to improve the efficiency of these solar systems, along with reduced manufacturing costs and, eventually, improved methods for storing solar energy or electricity at night and on cloudy days. Solar energy may be the ideal source for the environmental age, since it creates no greenhouse gases or air pollutants in operation. Solar energy would also be ideal for our national security, removing any foreign dependence.

Unfortunately, solar energy has two major drawbacks: it is very diffuse and intermittent. Very large solar arrays of photovoltaic cells or large solar thermal mirror collectors are needed to produce energy equivalent to that from one large electrical power plant. A 1,000-megawatt solar plant would need at least 1,600 acres of land, assuming 15 percent solar conversion efficiency, which is optimistic by today's standards. Worse yet, the sun must be shining to produce any energy, so the area must be increased to at least 10,000 acres, depending on the local climate, and excess energy must be stored on sunny days to provide energy at night and during cloudy weather. With current solar and energy-storage technology, it is unlikely that solar energy could provide major contributions to our nation's energy needs anytime soon.

One possible long-range solution might be a solar-hydrogen economy. During sunny periods, hydrogen would be generated by electrolyzing water. The hydrogen gas would be stored for later use in furnaces, or stored in a metal hydride that could become the source of energy in future automobiles. Since hydrogen turns to pure water when it is burned, it would be the ideal environmental fuel: no greenhouse gas, no toxic chemicals, no acid rain, no radioactive waste and no ozone-forming compounds that now produce smog in excess of healthful levels in over 100 cities in the U.S.

Growth of greenhouse gases such as carbon dioxide could also be reduced by burning biofuels, fuels derived from agricultural or forest products. All plants absorb carbon dioxide as they grow. If we could produce liquid fuels from biomass crops, then the carbon dioxide released during burning in car engines would be offset by the gas absorbed in the growing process. About 900 million gallons of ethanol derived from corn are used in the United States annually in the form of "gasohol," a mixture of 10 percent ethanol with gasoline. The Clean Air Amendments of 1990 passed by the Senate require increased use of oxygenated fuels such as ethanol to reduce carbon monoxide in high altitude cities such as Denver in the wintertime, and fuel additives such as ethanol are also mandated in the most smog-choked cities as a partial substitute for aromatic hydrocarbons in gasoline such as benzene (a known carcinogen) and xylene (an ingredient of smog). The Department of Energy is investigating the growth of other woody crops such as fast-growing trees to produce either methanol or ethanol for transportation fuels. These biofuels may provide the best short-term alternative to gasoline to reduce our dependence on foreign oil and to reduce air pollution.

Nuclear energy would also eliminate the generation of most greenhouse gases in plant operation, although fossil fuels would be utilized in other manufacturing steps to build nuclear power plants and to fabricate nuclear fuel rods. Despite safety and licensing problems that have brought new nuclear power plant construction to a standstill, other forms of nuclear energy production might be suitable for the next century.

All existing nuclear power plants rely on the fission reaction: heavy atoms such as uranium and plutonium are split into two smaller atoms, the same process that drives the atomic bomb. These split atoms, the necessary residue from any fission reaction, always have extra neutrons, making them highly radioactive for thousands or hundreds of thousands of years. The U.S. Department of Energy (DOE) is funding the development of new "inherently safe" reactor designs—reactors that would automatically shut down under any failure mechanism—but until we find an acceptable method to store the radioactive waste products for tens of thousands of years, public acceptance of nuclear power will be questionable. If DOE and the nuclear energy industry can produce a single modular reactor design that is safe, the industry hopes that licensing and construction can be streamlined, instead of designing and licensing unique plants for each utility.

Nuclear energy can also be generated, in theory, by the *fusion* reaction: two light atoms of hydrogen are combined—fused—at enormous temperatures and pressures to release extra energy. A fusion power station would consume deuterium and lithium—both obtained from sea water—and would generate no radioactive fuel waste. The end product of the fusion reaction is helium gas, an inert gas itself in short supply; there would be no radioactive waste from spent fuel in a fusion power plant. However, the fusion reactor itself would become radioactive from neutron bombardment, and would have to be permanently protected after the plant was shut down at the end of its useful life.

Unfortunately, scientists have not been able to develop a controlled fusion reaction suitable for generating electricity. The only method to produce a large fusion reaction today is to set off an atomic bomb, hardly a practical approach to utility power generation. Controlled fusion power plants will require at least two or three more decades of well-funded research and development, and many engineering challenges would have to be overcome before fusion power plants could provide electricity by burning sea water. Still, on a time scale of several decades, fusion may offer the best hope of relatively inexpensive, renewable energy for our grandchildren.

For the short term, our best hope to reduce reliance on foreign oil and to reduce the heating of the atmosphere by the greenhouse effect may be to reduce energy consumption. Energy consumption can be reduced by conservation, curtailing some energy-intensive activities, and by improving energy efficiency: performing the same task using less fuel or electricity. After the oil crisis in 1973-74, some people feared that conservation efforts would constrain economic growth. Others envisioned gross hardship (by American standards): giving up air conditioning or restricted car travel, for example.

In practice, Americans proved that we could significantly reduce energy consumption without giving up comforts that we have come to expect. From 1973 to 1986, energy efficiency was improved by 35 percent in automobiles, by 20 percent in homes, by 10 percent in commercial buildings and by 30 percent in manufacturing processes, where companies had a strong incentive to produce their products using less of what had become very expensive energy. These improved efficiencies save the U.S. economy about $100 billion per year in avoided oil import costs; if we were still using energy at the 1973 rate, the U.S. trade imbalance would be doubled to over $200 billion per year.[34] Some energy consumption was reduced by turning off unused lights or by turning up the thermostat on air conditioners (or down on heating units), but, in general, the United States is today enjoying the same comforts using less energy per task.

The fear of slowed economic growth was not justified. We consumed less energy for each dollar of GNP, and still produced more goods and services. Between 1973, before the Arab oil embargo, and 1989, the U.S. GNP increased by about 45 percent, while our energy consump-

---

[34]"Global Warming," *LBL Research Review*, Lawrence Berkeley Laboratory, Summer 1989, p. 2.

tion increased by only 7 percent. Energy consumption per dollar of GNP economic activity fell by about 26 percent.

Not all of this improvement in energy consumption per unit of GNP can be attributed to energy efficiency, however. Perhaps one third of this improvement is due to our economy shifting from energy-intensive industry such as steel mills to more service-related work including shopping malls and offices requiring far less energy per unit of work.[35]

For the future, conservation and improved energy efficiency can still reduce our demand for energy, but the task will be more difficult than in the 1970s. We have skimmed off the easy efficiency gains. We have curtailed the less objectionable energy wastage. From now on, energy conservation and efficiency improvements will be more costly.

Even so, many experts estimate that improved energy efficiency is the cheapest approach to cut our reliance on foreign oil. For electric utilities, the cost of paying their customers to use less electricity is two to ten times less than the cost of building new electrical generation plants. Some utilities are paying builders up to $3,000 per house to incorporate energy efficiency devices and practices.[36] The challenge for our engineers and scientists for the 21st century will be to build automobiles, appliances, buildings, factories and homes that run on a fraction of the energy consumed today.

Consumer education will also be required. The Department of Energy found that given the choice between an energy efficient refrigerator costing $800 and a less efficient unit at $700, consumers would usually choose the cheaper unit, even though the energy savings would pay for the more expensive refrigerator within two years. After that, the $800 refrigerator would save the owner $60 per year in reduced electricity bills. Similarly, energy-efficient fluorescent light bulbs may last ten times longer and consume four times less energy for the same light output, but many homeowners are not willing to pay 20 times more initially to save energy and costs over the long term. Consumers will have to be taught the value of life-cycle costing if we are to fully capitalize on energy efficient products.

Our European friends have set a good example: they generally consume about half the energy for the same economic activity, while enjoying almost the same standards of living. As shown in Table 3-6,

---

[35]Private communication, David Hafemeister, San Luis Obispo, California, February 25, 1990.
[36]Ibid., p. 11.

only Canada consumes more energy than the United States per dollar of GNP. We could cut our energy consumption in half if we could copy the energy habits of our West European and Japanese friends.

TABLE 3-6.   ENERGY CONSUMED PER DOLLAR OF GNP and GNP per capita

| | Energy consumption (megajoules) per $GNP[37] (1985) | GNP per capita[37a] (1984) |
| --- | --- | --- |
| Canada | 36.0 | 13,250 |
| United States | 27.5 | 15,541 |
| Australia | 20.3 | 11,570 |
| Netherlands | 16.2 | 9,392 |
| United Kingdom | 15.8 | 8,616 |
| Italy | 14.9 | 6,901 |
| West Germany | 14.0 | 10,985 |
| Japan | 13.1 | 10,300 |

To prepare for a secure energy future, we should be conducting large, coordinated energy research and development programs. The federal government should be the prime source of alternative energy research funding. No private industry has the resources or the long-term staying power to develop new sources of energy. This is a national problem, requiring massive, dedicated resources. Unfortunately, the Bush administration has inherited an energy research program that was decimated during the Reagan years. Federal energy programs are saddled with two burdens: private industry ideology and competition with nuclear weapons research.

A quirk of history has placed federal energy research into direct competition with nuclear weapons research: the old Atomic Energy Commission was set up as the civilian agency overseeing nuclear weapons and nuclear energy production. The AEC became the nucleus for an integrated national energy program with the formation of the Energy Research and Development Agency (ERDA) which in turn evolved into the current Department of Energy. The DOE brought with it the nuclear weapons baggage.

---

[37] "Energy Conservation in IEA Countries," International Energy Agency, 1987.
[37a] Ruth Leger Sivard, *World Military and Social Expenditures*, 1987-88, 12th Edition, 1987, p. 46.

The Department of Energy's budget (Table 3-7) illustrates the impact of the Reagan military buildup on energy research. The Reagan administration made a clear choice in the 1980s: nuclear weapons took top priority over energy research. The development of new sources of energy was relegated to private industry. The DOE funding for the development of new nuclear weapons warheads received a phenomenal 264 percent increase from 1980 to 1989. During this same period, solar energy research was cut by 83 percent and energy conservation research was reduced by 60 percent, gutting many programs that began in the aftermath of the 1970s energy crisis. Even these figures conceal the real intent of the Reagan and Bush administrations: Congress actually restored much of the renewable energy research funds cut by the executive branch throughout the 1980s, avoiding even larger reductions. And President Bush continued the short-sighted, "let private industry do it" attitude of the Reagan administration with his first budget, requesting cuts in renewable energy research as illustrated by the third column of Table 3-7. The Bush administration asked for a healthy 18 percent hike in nuclear weapons programs for fiscal year 1990, while energy programs were at best held constant or were cut again, including another 70 percent cut requested in just one year for conservation research.

As usual, Congress avoided this short-sighted plan to further erode energy R&D, reinstating and even increasing some funds as shown by the last column. The $357-million increase in nuclear weapons funds granted by Congress was for cleaning up nuclear waste; actual weapons production activities were not increased. Congress not only restored the 70 percent cut in energy conservation requested by the Bush administration, but increased conservation research by 30 percent. In any case, these small increases still leave our primary federal funding of energy research two to three times lower than they were in 1980.

On the positive side, Admiral Watkins, the Secretary of Energy, has stated his support of renewable energy and conservation activities as a vital ingredient of our national energy strategy. He asked for a healthy 24 percent increase in solar and renewable energy research for 1991, reversing nine years of budget cutting requests by the Reagan and Bush administrations. The biggest hike went to biofuels, with a 73 percent increase to research better methods for growing and converting woody plants to methanol or ethanol as motor fuel vehicles. According to Watkins, biofuels research "will go a long way toward laying the groundwork for a transition away from oil over time as our primary transportation fuel."[38]

TABLE 3-7.   SELECTED DEPARTMENT OF ENERGY RESEARCH BUDGETS
(Millions of Current Dollars)

| | 1980 | 1989 | Fiscal Year 1990 Bush Request | 1990 Cong. Budget |
|---|---|---|---|---|
| Nuclear weapon activities: | 2,943 | 7,783 | 9,387 | 9,656 |
| Nuclear Fission Energy | 1,081 | 352 | 350 | 356 |
| Nuclear Magnetic Fusion Energy | 350 | 350 | 349 | 331 |
| Inertial Confinement Fusion | 208 | 163 | 169 | 174 |
| Solar Energy | 559 | 92 | 71 | 95 |
| Conservation | 779 | 315 | 95 | 410 |
| Geothermal Energy | 149 | 19 | 15 | 19 |
| Energy Research Subtotals: | 3,126 | 1,291 | 1,049 | 1,385 |

Both Reagan and Bush (prior to the arrival of Admiral Watkins) reduced energy research in the belief that private industry should fill the gap. But the oil, gas and coal industries are the only major energy enterprises. Oil companies did invest in renewable energy development in the late 1970s, when the high price of oil generated excess profits. Several big oil companies started photovoltaic (PV) development projects. After the precipitous drop in the price of oil in December of 1985, however, every oil company cut back or disbanded its PV operations with the exception of ARCO Solar. Even ARCO Solar was sold in 1989 to the German Siemens company! American renewable energy technology is falling into foreign ownership.

The oil companies not only have dropped most renewable energy projects, but they have stopped prospecting for their bread and butter: drilling for new oil wells has fallen to new all-time lows, lower than at the time of the 1973 oil embargo. In March of 1989, the number of active drilling rigs in the U.S. fell to 753, down from 4,530 rigs drilling for oil in December of 1981.

There are no major solar, conservation, or nuclear energy companies that can afford the type of long-range research needed to put this nation on a firm energy foundation for the 21st century. Regardless of their

---

[38]Mark Crawford, "DOE's Born-Again Solar Energy Plan," *Science*, March 23, 1990, p. 1403.

motivation, the actions of the Reagan-Bush administrations have gutted our nation's energy research programs, leaving us more vulnerable to oil imports than we were before 1973, and ill-equipped to enter the 21st century.

*The Environment.* The earth's environment is being assaulted on all sides by activities of the human species. We have allowed a series of deficits to accumulate in the form of excess pollutants in our water, soil and air. Chlorofluorocarbon (CFC) gases from refrigerators, air conditioners and spray cans are depleting the protective ozone layer in the upper atmosphere that shields us from the sun's deadly ultraviolet rays. Ironically, while the stratosphere is losing ozone, our cities are being choked by too much ozone, the primary ingredient of urban smog. Ozone is produced by a photochemical reaction of hydrocarbon and nitrous oxide emissions from motor vehicles and industrial plants. While ozone in the upper atmosphere protects us from ultraviolet rays, ozone in our cities causes lung damage.

Carbon dioxide from our massive burning of fossil fuels, along with CFCs, methane from farming and other gases may increase the earth's temperature by trapping infrared rays—the greenhouse effect—which could melt the polar ice caps and flood coastal cities. While the greenhouse effect is a global problem, requiring cooperation of major nations around the world, the U.S. is a prime contributor and therefore should be a leader in studying and preventing excessive global warming. With only 5 percent of the world's population, we Americans generate about 23 percent of the world's carbon dioxide. On a per capita basis, we generate about 18 tons of carbon dioxide, compared to only 7.6 tons in Western Europe and a world average of just 3.88 tons.[39] Only East Germany produces more carbon dioxide per capita.

Acid rain, caused primarily by sulfur dioxide emitted from coal-burning electrical power plants, is already killing plants and fish in lakes and forests in the eastern United States and Canada. Industrial plants release hundreds of toxic chemicals into the air each year; of some 300 chemicals known to be harmful to humans, the Environmental Protection Agency has developed regulations for just seven in the last 20 years.

In one direct sense, nuclear weapons are already killing us. For decades the radioactive waste generated by 17 major nuclear weapons production facilities scattered across the country in 13 states has been endangering 80,000 workers and many thousands of residents living

---

[39]*Sierra*, July/August 1989, p. 32.

near these plants. The process of manufacturing enriched uranium and particularly toxic plutonium, the weaponeer's preferred bomb fuel, has generated tons of radioactive waste. No satisfactory method has been developed to dispose of these wastes from the nuclear weapons production facilities, so they have been stored on-site in temporary holding tanks. Many of these tanks are now leaking, contaminating ground water. In other cases, radioactive materials were released into the air.

However, the Department of Energy and its predecessors, the Atomic Energy Commission and the Energy Research and Development Agency, have hidden these gross environmental violations under the mantle of "national security." As the current Secretary of Energy, Admiral Watkins put it, when he took over control of DOE, "The underlying operating philosophy and culture of DOE was that adequate production of defense nuclear materials (bombs) and a healthy, safe environment *were not compatible objectives.*"[40] Admiral Watkins has vowed to reverse this "culture," placing safety as the first priority, above nuclear weapons production goals. However, the Admiral stated that he had been stymied by inadequate data, one-sided staff briefings, "insufficient scientific information," sloppy contracts with civilian plant managers, lack of trained personnel, and "serious flaws" in discipline.[41]

Dealing effectively with these diverse sets of potential environmental disasters will require some of the same types of national commitments previously devoted to the military. In addition to building satellites to monitor Soviet missile launches, we will need satellites to monitor ozone, methane, CFCs, and $CO_2$. Instead of exploding nuclear weapons underground, we will need to devise ways to store radioactive waste safely underground for thousands of years. Instead of devising schemes for better fusion bombs, we will need clever techniques to harness the fusion reaction for civilian power generation.

President Bush has made some progress in dealing with these environmental plights, particularly when compared to his predecessor. Admiral Watkins has brought a fresh candor to DOE, an agency characterized by decades of disregard for the public health and worker safety. President Bush's rhetoric on clean air has been refreshing, again

---

[40]Department of Energy news release of June 27, 1989.
[41]Thomas W. Lippman, "Watkins Finds Energy Department 'Culture' of Mismanagement and Ineptitude," *Washington Post*, June 28, 1989, p. A3.

after total disdain for environmental issues in the Reagan administration.

However, the actual clean air proposals submitted to Congress fall short of what is needed to vigorously attack acid rain, smog and air toxic chemicals. In too many instances, the Bush administration has been tilting toward relief for industries over public health. When the Senate Environment and Public Works committee passed a strong Clean Air Bill in 1990, the Bush White House threatened a veto, forcing Senate leaders to water down key provisions of the bill to assure passage of any clean air legislation. In too many cases, President Bush has been substituting words for actions.

*Housing.* We don't normally think of housing as a high technology item, requiring government research or development. But housing in this country has reached crisis proportions. As many as three million Americans may be homeless, and one Congressional study predicts that homelessness could increase to 19 million over the next 15 years. It is a blight on our national conscience that many go to bed on heating grates in the capital city of the earth's wealthiest nation. Surely our engineers could develop alternate low-cost housing techniques if they were given a national priority. Surely we can afford incentives to maintain and expand affordable housing.

But federal assistance to housing has fallen from $32 billion per year in 1980 to $7.5 billion per year in 1989. Another clear indication of our shifting priorities: in 1981 the federal government was spending about $7 on the military for every dollar spent on housing. Today that ratio has increased over six times to $44 on the military for every dollar to housing. Worse yet, as we learned after the fact, many of those housing dollars went to line the pockets of friends of Reagan appointees to the Department of Housing and Urban Development. The Secretary of HUD, Samuel Pierce, apparently was so uninterested in the homeless that he effectively turned control of the agency over to underlings who steered housing money to consultants and friends of the Reagan establishment.

HUD now estimates that it would cost at least $20 billion to repair deteriorating public housing facilities. Billions more would be required if the nation made a commitment to place a roof over the head of every American man, woman and child who could not afford to pay for their own housing. President Bush's Secretary of HUD, Jack Kemp, will have his hands full restoring credibility of the department, let alone reversing the steady decline in low-income housing.

*Transportation.* If we can spend billions of dollars to transport nuclear weapons 6,000 miles from North Dakota to Moscow in 25 minutes, why can't we solve the problem of transporting our workers 10 or 20 miles from the suburbs to the city workplace each day in less than 60 minutes, without polluting our air, clogging our freeways, ruining our roads and bridges in the process? Instead of "modernizing" our nuclear weapons, maybe we should be directing some of our scientists and engineers to modernize our mass transit, automobiles, and highway systems to simultaneously reduce energy consumption and air pollution, as well as commuter fatigue, frustration and lost time on the job. When major cities such as San Francisco and Washington, D.C., did build modern mass transit systems over the last few decades, there were no American firms in the mass transit business; light rail cars had to be ordered from Italy.

We should be working to improve our national rail system. Sending freight by train requires about three times less energy than delivery by truck, and 40 times less energy than by air freight. We are letting our rail system fall into disrepair, which will reduce our commercial competitiveness.

For the future, magnetically levitated (maglev) trains operating at 250 to 300 miles per hour could relieve much of the congestion at airports. Maglev trains, suspended 4 to 8 inches above the track by magnetic forces, would use about one-fourth the energy and produce about one-fourth the carbon dioxide of airplanes per passenger mile. Since half of all airline flights cover less than 500 miles, maglev trains could actually reduce total travel time for many passengers while freeing congested airports to handle primarily long distance flights. Unfortunately, maglev research ended in the U.S. in 1975. The State of Florida is planning a 15-mile maglev train from Orlando to the tourist attractions, but they will rely on Japanese financing and German maglev technology, a clear signal of changing world conditions.[42]

Even our conventional transportation systems are deteriorating. As of 1988, 41 percent of the 575,000 bridges in the United States failed to meet federal highway standards, with 24 percent being structurally deficient. The cost to repair or replace crumbling bridges: $50 billion annually according to the Federal Highway Administration.[43] Similarly,

---

[42]Larry R. Johnson, "Putting Maglev on Track," *Issues in Science and Technology*, Spring 1990, p. 71.
[43]Edward Abrahams, "Silent Decay," *Washington Post*, October 27, 1989, p. A19.

sewers, roads, airports and buildings are deteriorating faster than they are being repaired. Estimates range upward to $3.5 trillion to fix all of the nation's infrastructure. The Bush administration's solution: let the state and local governments do it.

To summarize this section, our nation has been neglecting several major areas in our society. In education, renewable energy, the environment, housing and transportation, we have accrued "deficits" that will have to be repaid if we are to maintain our current standard of living. Dealing with these social shortfalls will be difficult given our precarious economic situation, and given our continuing excessive expenditures on the military establishment.

## THE MILITARY RESOURCE DRAIN

We should be devoting more of our federal resources and scientific talents toward resolving this myriad of economic and social problems facing our nation. But many of these same resources and talents have been harnessed to the Pentagon's weapons procurement system for many decades. An estimated 30 percent of all American scientists and engineers now work on military projects.

Compared to our gross national product (GNP—the total economic value of all goods and services produced in the country), military spending may seem small, about 5.5 percent of our GNP. But in terms of research and development (R&D), the engine that drives industrial development in our high technology world, the military looms much larger: military R&D grew from 50 percent of all federally funded R&D in the 1970s up to 67 percent in 1989, before declining slightly to 65 percent in 1990. Another 8 percent of federal R&D was consumed by NASA, which has substantial military functions. Only 24 percent of federal R&D was for civilian applications in 1987.[44] As mentioned above, West Germany allocates 92 percent and Japan 96 percent of R&D funds to stimulating their civilian economies.

Numbers do not reveal the complete picture. Military projects often attract the highest paid technical teams, and the work is technologically challenging. Building an advanced cruise missile or developing nuclear-pumped, directed energy weapons is much more exciting for a physicist than working on improved washing machines, cameras or VCR's. As a

---

[44]"National Patterns of Science and Technology Resources: 1987," National Science Foundation, Report No. NSF 88-305, p. 50.

result, many of our best and brightest young scientists and engineers are beginning their careers working exclusively on military projects, often in their universities before they even graduate. Pentagon funding at colleges and universities almost tripled between 1980 and 1988, rising from $455 million to $1.3 billion per year.[45] Both undergraduate and graduate students frequently pay for their education by working on military projects on campus. Often their education and career path are set by the needs of the military.

Once trained in the "gold-plated" techniques of the Pentagon, where performance is everything and cost is secondary at best, it is very difficult for an engineer to switch to the commercial world, where products must be safe, reliable, but also low-cost to stay competitive. A physicist working for the Navy, noting the lack of compatibility between military and civilian research, told a *Los Angeles Times* reporter that "10, 15, 20 years down the road ... the U.S. will have lost an entire generation of real scientists," comparing this loss to that of China when its universities were shut down during the Cultural Revolution.[46]

Military research not only drains scientists and engineers from commercial enterprises, but also distorts their educational choices. Due to military demands, U.S. universities turn out more aeronautical and electrical engineers than civil or mechanical engineers, and more physicists and mathematicians than chemists and biologists. This is a long-term distortion that can only be changed with the next generation of engineers.

Prior to 1980, federal research and development was equally divided between civilian and military projects, about 0.6 percent of GNP each. (See Figure 3-5.) The Reagan administration changed that balance dramatically, with military R&D escalating to 0.9 percent of GNP in 1987, while civilian R&D fell to about 0.4 percent of GNP. This trend must be reversed if we as a nation hope to stay competitive, while still protecting our civilization from environmental degradation and providing sources of renewable energy for the 21st century.

The first Bush budget is not encouraging. As in so many issues, President Bush has chosen to continue dangerous and short-sighted Reagan policies, in this case spending twice as much on military as on civilian research. This ratio of federal military to civilian research is one

---

[45]*Research and Development: FY 1989*, Washington, D.C.: American Association for the Advancement of Science, 1988, p. 11.
[46]"attle of the Labs," editorial in the *Los Angeles Times*, April 16, 1987, p. 4.

key indicator of the Bush administration's failure to begin restoring balance to federal priorities.

Some proponents of reduced military spending imply or claim that military cut-backs could fund many or most of the social and economic deficits listed above. Others claim that military spending is so small (5.5 percent of the GNP) that even major cuts could not begin to address our social needs. The truth undoubtedly lies in the middle: reduced military spending could free substantial federal dollars, but not enough to solve all our problems. But even within the federal budget, there are different claims as to the relative magnitude of military spending.

FIGURE 3-5.   MILITARY AND CIVILIAN RESEARCH FUNDED BY THE FEDERAL GOVERNMENT

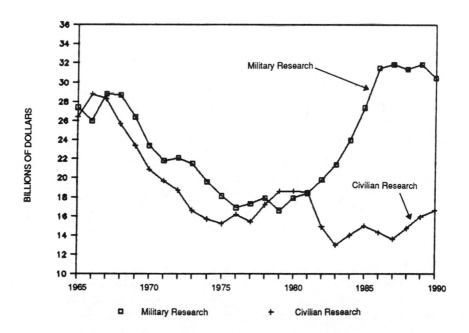

The actual percentage of federal government funds spent on the Pentagon is often claimed to be relatively small: 25 percent for fiscal year 1991 according to OMB summaries. Like the distorted federal budget "deficit," this estimate of military spending is very misleading, and for the same reason: the inclusion of the trust funds. Furthermore, the major component of this unified federal budget (43 percent in 1991)

reported by the administration via OMB is designated as "direct benefit payments for individuals" or simply the social fund. The implication is often drawn that 43 percent of the federal dollar goes for welfare payments. This is false.

First, the trust funds are not "welfare." As shown in Table 3-3, the trust funds are primarily set aside for working people, to help cover the costs of retirement, health and unemployment insurance. Other trust funds are collected to maintain our highways and airports. These funds are established for specific purposes, and should not be withdrawn for other functions such as welfare payments or military projects, without changing the law.

The breakdown of the actual (non-trust fund) federal budget is shown in Table 3-8, along with the picture typically shown by the administration. The Pentagon consumes about 34 percent of the federal general fund, the largest percentage, followed by interest on the debt at 29 percent. The military and the interest on the debt together account for 63 percent of the federal funds. The "means-tested" entitlements or welfare payments to needy individuals are about 13 percent of the federal funds.

Whenever proponents of continued high military spending talk about cutting "social programs," you should refer to Table 3-8. Where would you cut more to reduce the deficit, or to fund the war on drugs? From energy research? From education? From veterans' benefits?

But even this doesn't tell the full story about military spending as a function of government *discretionary* funds. About 58 percent of federal spending is mandatory, set by previous laws. Congress has no direct control over entitlements and interest payments, for example. Even the general fund contains some entitlements such as veterans' health and retirement benefits, housing and education benefits that are paid automatically, unless Congress changes the laws mandating these payments. As a result, for fiscal year 1991, only $512 billion of the $1.23 trillion Bush request for outlays are appropriated by Congress. The other $721 billion in outlays is automatically paid. Thus the *military spending requested by the Bush administration for 1991 is **59.2 percent*** of the discretionary funds available to Congress.

In short, the usual OMB-derived implication that the federal budget is 43 percent "welfare" and 25 percent military is highly misleading. The federal general funds, excluding the trust funds, are 34 percent military and 13 percent for actual human services for the nation's elderly, poor, handicapped and children of these less fortunate citizens. The rest of the federal funds are divided between a myriad of small programs, most of which are fully justified, have been pared back too far during the Reagan years, and often are quite important in their own right for our real national security. And the military budget is 59 percent of the discretionary federal funds actually allocated by Congress in 1991.

TABLE 3-8. COMPARISON OF FEDERAL BUDGET WITH AND WITHOUT THE TRUST FUNDS FOR FY 1991.

Typical Federal Budget Breakdown including Trust Funds:
(As reported by OMB)

| Benefit Payments to Individuals: | 43% |
|---|---|
| National Defense: | 25 |
| Net Interest: | 14 |
| Grants to States and Localities: | 12 |
| Other Federal operations: | 6 |

Federal budget general funds (excluding trust funds):

| National Defense: | 34% |
|---|---|
| Gross Interest on the Debt: | 29 |
| Human Services payments: | 12.5 |
| Education, Training: | 4.6 |
| Veterans benefits: | 3.4 |
| Natural Resources and Environment: | 2.1 |
| International Affairs: | 2.1 |
| Science and Space: | 1.9 |
| Commerce and Housing credit: | 1.9 |
| Agriculture: | 1.7 |
| Administration of Justice: | 1.4 |
| Government Operations: | 1.3 |
| Health: | 1.2 |
| Transportation: | 1.0 |
| Community and Regional Development: | 0.9 |
| Energy: | 0.3 |

Federal Discretionary Funds (excluding mandatory payments)

| Total Federal Outlays: | $1,233 billion |
|---|---|
| − Mandatory payments: | − 712 |
| Discretionary Funds: | $ 512 billion |

Military as percentage of Discretionary Funds: 59.2%

The military budget is a substantial source of funds to begin to reduce our other economic and social deficits, and, as we'll discuss in Chapters 9 and 10, there are very compelling reasons to reduce excessive and destabilizing military expenditures.

To summarize this chapter, the resources devoted to building weapons of war restrict our ability to avoid looming economic, energy, and environmental disasters. These overriding societal problems are too large and too long-term to be handled by private enterprise alone, as prescribed by the Reagan and Bush administrations. We need a national commitment to a balanced national security policy, emphasizing economic strength through investment, the long-term health of our people, as well as adequate military strength. The Bush administration has failed so far to make the visionary changes necessary to prepare the nation for the 21st century, choosing instead to maintain the Reagan emphasis on borrowing to fund excessive military spending while ignoring investment in our nation's future.

Part Two

# DANGERS OF BUSINESS-AS-USUAL

CHAPTER 4

# Our Current Posture: The Nuclear War-Fighting Strategy

SUMMARY

The United States and the Soviet Union need only a few hundred survivable nuclear weapons to deter each other from ever unleashing a nuclear war. Today the United States has over 13,000 strategic nuclear warheads or bombs that could reach the Soviet Union, and the Soviets have over 11,000 that could reach the U.S. Both also have over 10,000 short-range or tactical nuclear weapons for use in local battles. And yet both governments continue to spend tens of billions of dollars and rubles each year to build more nuclear weapons.

Why? Because neither side has been content with simply deterring nuclear war. Both nations have accumulated obscene arsenals of nuclear weapons to support a nuclear war-fighting strategy: despite glasnost and perestroika, we are preparing to fight, survive and "win" a nuclear war, treating nuclear weapons as if they were just more powerful versions of conventional weapons.

71

This is the old way of thinking. Both the quantity and quality of nuclear weapons in the arsenals of the superpowers far exceed that needed to prevent nuclear war.

Most Americans would be shocked to learn that the Bush administration is continuing to build a nuclear war-fighting capability, that we are preparing to fight a protracted nuclear war, should deterrence fail. In 1988, Americans were asked in a national poll if they would support the use of nuclear weapons by the United States if "the Soviets have invaded Western Europe and are winning without using nuclear weapons." Even if NATO was losing the war, only 8 percent would recommend that the United States initiate the use of nuclear weapons to stop Soviet aggression.[1] Apparently, most citizens do not know about (or do not condone) the official NATO policy since 1949 to use nuclear weapons *first* if we are losing a conventional war. President Bush modified this posture rhetorically in mid-1990 by stating that NATO would no longer consider "early first use" of nuclear war, but NATO would still reserve the option of exploding nuclear weapons first.

We have built nuclear war-fighting weapons to back up this stated policy of the "first use" of nuclear weapons to stop a conventional attack. Remarkably, only 37 percent of U.S. citizens would favor the use of nuclear weapons if "American military forces are subjected to a limited nuclear attack while they're in combat," and only 50 percent would retaliate even if "one American city is destroyed in a limited nuclear attack."[2] In other words, there was a gaping discrepancy between American/NATO policy and public acceptance, long before the fall of the Berlin Wall. A bare majority accepted pure deterrence, and only 8 percent condoned official NATO policy to use nuclear weapons first.

We do keep nuclear weapons to deter nuclear war, but both nations long ago exceeded the number of weapons that would dissuade the opponent from ever attacking. Yet we (and the Soviets) have continued building additional weapons to be able to fight, limit, survive and "win" a nuclear war. The Bush administration is continuing all of the programs started by its predecessors to develop new weapons that would make nuclear war more likely in some future crisis.

This does not imply that our leaders are madmen bent on unleashing

---

[1]*Americans Talk Security*, National Survey No. 6, Boston: Martilla and Kiley, June 1988, p. 41.
[2]Ibid., p. 72.

a nuclear holocaust. No one wants to fight a nuclear war. Certainly not President George Bush, nor Secretary of Defense Dick Cheney, nor National Security Advisor Brent Scowcroft. But there are many rationalizations conjured up to build more weapons, as we explore in more detail in Chapter 7. Some nuclear warriors yearn to regain the nuclear superiority that the United States enjoyed for the first two decades of the nuclear age. Most are trapped by the following mental gymnastics: in order for nuclear deterrence to be credible, they say, nuclear weapons must be *usable*. If the President is afraid to use nuclear weapons, and the Soviets know (or believe) that he is so paralyzed, then they might not be deterred. In a crisis, they might be tempted to use nuclear weapons, believing that the U.S. President would not retaliate.

Thus, according to this reasoning, we must *lower* the threshold for nuclear war—make nuclear war *more likely*—so that the Soviets will believe that our President would push the button. We must be prepared to fight and win a "protracted" nuclear war to convince the opponent that we are serious—a game of nuclear chicken! In short, **to make nuclear war less likely, we must make nuclear war more likely.**

Despite our best intentions, these efforts to make the nuclear deterrent more credible have bought us a nuclear war-fighting capability far in excess of what we need to deter Soviet aggression. These war-fighting weapons have increased the risks of nuclear war by lowering the nuclear threshold, while draining our national treasury. We discuss in Chapter 5 why war-fighting weapons make nuclear war more likely, and how the next generation of nuclear weapons, if we continue our current course, would further degrade our national security. But first, we describe why our current weapons are really designed for nuclear war-fighting and not for simple deterrence of nuclear war. While we concentrate primarily on excessive U.S. weapons, our comments apply also to the Soviet arsenal. They too have built a nuclear war-fighting capability far in excess of their legitimate defensive needs.

QUANTITY OF NUCLEAR WEAPONS: HOW MUCH IS ENOUGH?

Our nuclear war-fighting posture can be illustrated by the physical characteristics of the nuclear arsenal, and, to a lesser degree, by the statements of our national leaders regarding our nuclear intentions. Two physical attributes of our nuclear arsenal distinguish a war-fighting capability from a pure deterrence posture: the *quantity* of nuclear weapons and their *qualitative* characteristics.

Consider first the number of nuclear weapons in our arsenals, compared to the number needed for effective deterrence. Since the beginning of the nuclear age, many analysts have concluded that a few hundred survivable nuclear warheads would suffice for deterrence. During the Kennedy administration, Secretary of Defense Robert McNamara predicted through computer simulation that 200 to 400 megatons of nuclear firepower would destroy approximately 75 percent of all Soviet industry and would immediately kill about 25 percent of the Soviet population. McNamara concluded that a few hundred was enough for deterrence. These calculations were based on "prompt" fatalities—those killed by the immediate effects of nuclear weapons blast and radiation.

More recent studies have concluded that firestorms generated by multiple nuclear detonations could kill even more people. These new models predict that 40 equivalent megatons of nuclear explosives would kill 25 percent of the Soviet population, compared to 200 megatons estimated by McNamara in 1968.[3] Just 300 nuclear warheads on submarines would meet this criterion for deterrence. Another computer simulation predicted that just 239 Soviet nuclear warheads aimed at U.S. energy production and storage sites would eventually kill 140 million Americans due to starvation.[4] Today we have over 5,000 nuclear weapons on submarines alone.

The United States has accumulated over 3,100 equivalent megatons of explosive power, or between 15 to 75 times more than we would need to meet the McNamara criterion for deterring the Soviets, and the Soviets now have over 6,200 equivalent megatons, or 30 to 150 times more than they need to deter the U.S. from attacking.[5]

[3]Harold A. Feiveson and Frank von Hippel, "Stability of Nuclear Balance After Deep Reductions," to be published in *Verifying Nuclear Warhead Reductions*, a joint book of the Federation of American Scientists and the Committee of Soviet Scientists, and Frank von Hippel, Barbara G. Levi, Theodore A. Postol and William H. Daugherty, "Civilian Casualties from Counterforce Attacks," *Scientific American*, September 1988, pp. 36-42.
[4]M. Anjali Sastry, Joseph J. Romm, and Kosta Tsipis, *Nuclear Crash: The U.S. Economy After Small Nuclear Attacks* MIT Report #17, June 1987.
[5]"U.S. Strategic Nuclear Forces, End of 1988," *The Bulletin of the Atomic Scientists*, January/February 1989, p. 68, and "Soviet Strategic Nuclear Forces, End of 1989," *The Bulletin of the Atomic Scientists*. March 1990.

But you don't need to be a think-tank analyst with a supercomputer to predict how many nuclear weapons would deter nuclear war. Recall that one small atomic bomb, with an explosive power equivalent to about 13 thousand tons of TNT (13 kilotons) killed over 100,000 Japanese citizens at Hiroshima on August 6, 1945. A second atomic bomb dropped on Nagasaki three days later led to Japan's immediate, unconditional surrender.

Today's hydrogen or fusion bombs are generally three to one hundred times more powerful. Given that the Soviet Union has fewer than 250 cities with a population above 100,000, would not the mere possibility of one bomb going off over every major city deter any rational Soviet leader from ever using nuclear weapons?[6]

McGeorge Bundy, the National Security Adviser to President Kennedy, put it this way:

> Think-tank analysts can set levels of acceptable damage well up in the hundreds of millions of lives. They can assume that the loss of dozens of great cities is somehow a real choice for sane men. They are in an unreal world. In the real world of real political leaders— whether here or in the Soviet Union—a decision that would bring even one hydrogen bomb on one city of one's own country would be recognized in advance as a catastrophic blunder; ten bombs on ten cities would be a disaster beyond history; and a hundred bombs on one hundred cities are unthinkable.[7]

Ten hydrogen bombs would be a "disaster beyond history," and yet we and the Soviets are each prepared to unleash over 10,000 hydrogen bombs. By this standard, we have over 1,000 times more than we need, and yet we are told that we must continue to build "better" nuclear weapons. Think-tank analysts and many of our leaders continue to think the unthinkable.

Additional nuclear weapons might be justified if our weapons became vulnerable to attack. To be an effective deterrent, a few hundred nuclear weapons must be able to *survive* a surprise strike by the opponent. Any

---

[6]As we discuss in Chapter 7, those who manage our nuclear arsenals have indeed conjured up many reasons to build more nuclear weapons; they have convinced themselves that a few hundred nuclear weapons is not enough to deter. We find these reasons hard to swallow, and believe most Americans, given the facts, would agree that a few hundred is indeed enough.

[7]*Foreign Affairs*, October 1969.

weapons that were vulnerable to attack might invite the Soviets to strike first in a crisis, to eliminate as many of our nuclear weapons as possible. This survivability-vulnerability concept is illustrated in Figure 4-1.

FIGURE 4-1.   ILLUSTRATION OF SURVIVABILITY VERSUS VULNERABILITY.

## SURVIVABLE MISSILE <u>DETERS</u> ATTACK

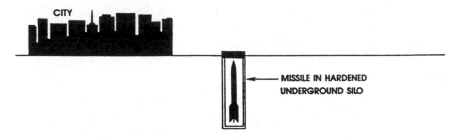

## VULNERABLE MISSILE <u>INVITES</u> ATTACK

The top sketch shows an ICBM that has been "hardened" against nuclear attack by placing it in an underground concrete silo. This ICBM can survive all but a direct nuclear hit. This survivable missile *deters* attack, since the opponent knows it could rise out of the ashes to retaliate if the city were ever destroyed.

In the bottom sketch, the ICBM has been placed above ground, making it vulnerable to a nearby nuclear explosion. This vulnerable missile *invites* attack, since the opponent can eliminate it by striking first, thereby reducing the damage to his homeland. Thus survivable weapons deter war, while vulnerable weapons could encourage war, or at least the escalation from conventional war to nuclear war.

Both superpowers have built three different vehicles to deliver nuclear weapons: bombers, land-based intercontinental ballistic missiles (ICBMs), and submarine launched ballistic missiles (SLBMs). These three redundant delivery systems are called the "strategic triad."

Fortunately, the bulk of our nuclear arsenal can survive a nuclear attack, stored safely on submarines at sea and bombers on alert. Our nuclear-powered submarines, carrying over 5,000 hydrogen bombs, are considered virtually invulnerable while under the world's oceans; seawater is opaque to the radar waves and infrared waves that make airplanes and surface ships subject to constant, worldwide surveillance. Secretary of Defense Frank Carlucci attested to the value of nuclear submarines in 1989:

> When at sea, our SSBNs [nuclear ballistic missile submarines] are considered to be 100 percent survivable by all recent assessments and are projected to remain so against foreseeable threats.[8]

Submarines equipped with nuclear-armed ballistic missiles are therefore excellent retaliatory weapons. Since the enemy cannot find them, there is no chance of a preemptive attack suddenly disarming the United States. Approximately 60 percent of our submarine force is at sea every day, so that even a surprise, bolt-from-the-blue Soviet attack would face retaliation by 3,000 submarine-launched hydrogen bombs, or ten times more than we need for effective deterrence. Thus our nuclear bomb-equipped submarine missiles alone could deter the Soviets, even if we had no other nuclear weapons.

In addition, many of our 324 long-range bombers[9] are on alert, able to take off within the 25-minute warning of attack provided by our satellite-based sensors that hover over the Soviet Union and monitor all Soviet missile launches. While bombers would take 10 to 12 hours to reach the Soviet Union, those on alert could take off and escape destruction before the first Soviet bombs went off on U.S. soil. These surviving bombers could deliver up to 2,000 more nuclear weapons to the Soviet homeland, even if the Soviets struck first without any warning.

Land-based ICBMs, the subject of much heated debate over the last two decades, are now buried in underground concrete silos, protecting

---

[8]Frank C. Carlucci, *Annual Report to Congress*, Washington, D.C.: Department of Defense, January 17, 1989.
[9]The Department of Defense lists only 263 nuclear long-range bombers. They do not count 48 FB-111 nuclear capable bombers with 1,550-mile range that can reach the Soviet Union from Great Britain, or 61 B-52G long-range bombers that have been assigned conventional missions. These B-52Gs are still nuclear capable, so the United States would have up to 372 bombers available for delivering nuclear weapons in an allout war.

them from all but a very close hit by nuclear weapons. Alleged improvements in Soviet missile accuracy, however, have raised the possibility that the Soviets could destroy many of our missiles in their silos by a surprise first-strike attack with pinpoint accuracy. This threat to our land-based missile fleet was dubbed the "window of vulnerability" in the 1980 Presidential campaign. Candidate Ronald Reagan used this potential vulnerability as a scare-tactic to convince voters that President Jimmy Carter had let our nuclear forces become vulnerable to Soviet attack.

In reality, the "window of vulnerability" applies only to our land-based ICBMs. This threat may or may not be valid, given the uncertainties of the Soviets ever launching thousands of warheads over the North Pole, a route never flown before, but in any case this threat has little strategic significance. The United States has wisely chosen to place less than 19 percent of its nuclear warheads on potentially vulnerable land-based ICBMs. Even if the Soviets did succeed in destroying *all* of our land-based missiles, *all* of our submarines in port, and *all* of our bombers not on alert, we could still retaliate with over 4,000 hydrogen bombs from submarines at sea and bombers that took off on warning of attack.

Ironically, President Reagan's own Commission on Strategic Forces admitted in 1983 that the "window of vulnerability" was not important. This commission, headed by Brent Scowcroft, President Bush's National Security Adviser, effectively said that we do not need ICBMs for deterrence: our nuclear weapons on submarines and bombers on alert are more than adequate to deter, even if the Soviets were able to destroy all our ICBMs. They even recommended that the multiple warhead MX missile be placed in old Minuteman missile silos, the same vulnerable silos that President Reagan used as the basis of the "window of vulnerability" scare. This is a clear example of exaggerating a military threat for political purposes during an election campaign. In the future, we must base strategic decisions on realistic threat assessments, not inflated threats concocted for political convenience.

Our nuclear overkill capability is best illustrated by estimating the number of nuclear weapons that would survive a surprise, bolt-from-the-blue attack, the worst case. As shown in Table 4-1, both sides would have over 2,500 nuclear weapons left after the other side struck without any warning, far more than the few hundred needed for deterrence.

But a bolt-from-the-blue attack is not plausible. Any conceivable use of nuclear weapons would surely involve a long deterioration in superpower relations, including conventional hostilities or at least mobilization of conventional forces. These actions would give many months if not years of warning. Under these conditions, even more nuclear weapons could be placed on alert. As shown in the last column of Table 4-1, both sides would have over 7,000 survivable nuclear weapons with warning of attack.

*If the consequences of 100 hydrogen bomb explosions are "unthinkable," deterring any rational leader, how could anyone conclude that 7,000 survivable warheads is not enough?* And yet the Bush administration is telling us that we absolutely must add MX missiles on commercial railcars, Midgetman missiles, Trident-II submarine-launched missiles, new B-2 bombers and new air-launched and sea-launched cruise missiles. Despite improved relations and mounting budget deficits, the Bush administration has endorsed every new nuclear weapons system. The 1991 budget request includes an amazing 30 percent increase for the 11 top strategic nuclear weapons systems. And our scientists are fast at work developing a new generation of nuclear weapons, as we discuss in Chapter 5. While the Soviets are cutting back conventional forces, they too are adding more modern nuclear weapons at great cost to their weaker economy.

QUALITY OF NUCLEAR WEAPONS: WAR-FIGHTING CHARACTERISTICS

Any attempt to "fight and win" a nuclear war would depend not only on the *quantity* of weapons, but also on their *quality*. In particular, war-planners would like to have better accuracy, so that they could hit specific "hardened" or well-protected targets; prompt delivery; and good communications and control over those nuclear weapons. Only one leg of our strategic triad combines all three war-fighting attributes: land-based ICBMs.

Bombers have good accuracy and reasonable communications, but they are very slow, taking up to 12 hours to reach their targets. The threat of retaliation in 12 hours is perfectly adequate to deter the Soviets from ever attacking, but nuclear war-fighting strategists would like to attack Soviet forces much more quickly using ballistic missiles.

Submarine-launched missiles can be delivered promptly, with even shorter delivery times (10 to 15 minutes) than ICBMs from waters close to the Soviet Union, but SLBMs have had poor accuracy in the past, and communicating with underwater submarines is very difficult, for the same reasons that protect submarines from detection. The accuracy of

TABLE 4-1.   SURVIVABLE STRATEGIC NUCLEAR WEAPONS

| | Total Deployed Warheads:[11] | Worst-case Estimate of Survivable Warheads[10] | |
| --- | --- | --- | --- |
| United States | | Peacetime: | With Warning: |
| ICBM | 2,450 | | |
| SLBM | 5,312 | 3,180 | 5,000 |
| BOMBER | 5,238 | 1,500 | 4,700 |
| TOTALS: | 13,000 | 4,780 | 10,200 |
| Soviet Union | | | |
| ICBM | 6,450 | 2,050 | 3,500 |
| SLBM | 3,642 | 540 | 2,500 |
| BOMBER | 1,228 | 0 | 1,100 |
| TOTALS: | 11,320 | 2,590 | 7,100 |

NUMBER OF SURVIVABLE WARHEADS NEEDED FOR DETER-
RENCE: 200 TO 400

U.S. SLBMs was improved dramatically with the introduction of the Trident-II (also known as the D-5) missile in 1990, but less than optimum communications will continue to limit the utility of our submarine missiles in the eyes of the nuclear war planner. Submarines now receive low data rate communications from command headquarters continuously, but they cannot routinely respond. Submarines could therefore receive the signal to fire their missiles according to a prearranged SIOP (Single Integrated Operational Plan) target list. However, the National Command Authority could not send detailed new targeting instructions promptly, and they might not immediately receive confirmation from distant submarines that missiles had been launched.

---

[10]The assumptions used to calculate survivable warheads include: 60 percent of U.S. and 15 percent of Soviet submarines are on patrol during peacetime, which represents typical operating conditions; 30 percent of U.S. bombers and no Soviet bombers are able to take off after enemy missile launches are detected; U.S. could destroy 68 percent of Soviet ICBMs with a surprise attack, using 900 Minuteman-III and 500 MX warheads, with two warheads aimed at each of 700 Soviet silos, about half their total fixed ICBMs. (The surviving 2,050 Soviet warheads on fixed missiles will become vulnerable to American D-5 submarine-launched warheads if we go ahead with D-5 deployment, but Soviet SS-24 and SS-25 mobile missiles will counteract D-5 accuracy to some degree.

[11]"U.S. Strategic Nuclear Forces, End of 1988," *Bulletin of the Atomic Scientists*, January/February 1989, p. 68, and "Soviet Strategic Nuclear Forces, End of 1989," *Bulletin of the Atomic Scientists*, March 1990.

This leaves the land-based ICBM as the war-fighter's weapon of choice. The U.S. MX missiles now have accuracies better than 100 meters; they can usually come within 100 meters of the intended target (the length of a football field), after traveling 6,000-7,000 miles via outer space. The best Soviet ICBMs (SS-18, mod 5) have estimated accuracies of about 100 meters.[12] Coupled with powerful nuclear bombs, these ICBMs could in theory destroy even buried, underground missiles, provided that they are fired first, and provided that the opponent does not "launch on warning."

That is, faced with accurate missiles on the other side, one missile commander might opt to launch his missiles immediately when warning signals indicate the other side has fired. Thus, even if we or the Soviets attempted to destroy the opponent's land-based missiles by striking first, we could never be sure that the opponent's missiles would still be in their underground silos when our bombs went off 25 minutes later.

ICBMs meet the war-fighter's other criteria, too: they can be fired promptly, reaching the opponent's targets within 25 minutes, and communications between the National Command Authority and the underground missile launch control centers are excellent—at least before the first bomb goes off!

Note that none of the three war-fighter's criteria—accuracy, speed, and good command control—are necessary for a pure retaliatory or deterrence role. We don't need high accuracy to destroy conventional military installations, ports, airfields, fuel depots, industrial centers or cities.[13] We don't need prompt retaliation to deter the Soviets; they would be deterred just as much by the fear of societal collapse in 12 hours as by a 25-minute holocaust. And the Soviets would be deterred by the fear of massive retaliation from submarine-launched nuclear warheads, even if the retaliatory attack were not precisely timed or coordinated by a central command authority. The fear that many if not all submarine commanders would eventually get the message to retaliate would be sufficient to deter.

---

[12]The 180 meter accuracy of the new SS-18 mod 5 missile is estimated based on the statement that each SS-18 mod 5 has the same silo kill capability as two SS-18 mod 4 warheads.

[13]The nuclear war-fighters would like us to believe that existing weapons can only be used to attack cities, and therefore we must have newer, more accurate weapons like the MX missile and the D5 submarine-launched missile to attack military targets. As discussed in detail in Chapter 5, existing weapons are adequate to attack virtually all military targets *except* underground missile silos and buried command and control bunkers.

In summary, both the increased numbers of deliverable nuclear warheads and the qualitative improvements—accuracy, speed, and command and control—in the nuclear delivery systems made over the last three decades are only needed to be able to fight and attempt to "win" a nuclear war. They are not needed, in our judgment, to prevent a nuclear war. This is the primary indication of the nuclear war-fighting aspects of the nuclear arsenals of the two superpowers. President Bush and Secretary of Defense Cheney have endorsed all of the nuclear war-fighting weapons ordered by earlier administrations.

For any of our readers who are concerned about our apparent disdain for weapons needed to "win" a nuclear war, do not despair; we are not advocating that the United States should intentionally *lose* a nuclear war. We are advocating the *prevention* of nuclear war. We subscribe to the thesis that there can be no winners. As the Physicians for Social Responsibility say, prevention is the only cure. President Reagan and Secretary General Gorbachev jointly agreed that a nuclear war cannot be won and must never be fought. We agree, but our deeds must match our words.

The nuclear dilemma is not a football game. No one would win a nuclear war. We are not advocating unilateral disarmament so that the Soviets might "win." We are in the nuclear game together, and, like it or not, we share a common fate. We must work with the Soviets and the other nuclear powers to reduce the risks of any nuclear detonations to as close to zero as is humanly possible. Both superpowers are responsible for 40 years of unbridled nuclear competition that has brought us our vast overkill capability. Both superpowers will have to work to reduce the danger to manageable levels in the years ahead.

If the thousands of additional weapons needed in the futile attempt to "win" a nuclear war had no effect on the chances of a nuclear war starting, then we wouldn't be writing this book. Building 13,000 nuclear weapons when a few hundred was adequate would be just a tragic waste of taxpayer money. However, these new weapons are also *destabilizing*, as we discuss in more detail in the next chapter: these war-fighting weapons increase the chances of nuclear war. We do have much better options; we prescribe a safer and less costly deterrent posture in Chapter 9.

## WAR-FIGHTING RHETORIC AND REALITY

During the 40 years of the nuclear age, the actual war-fighting plans of the United States have been clouded by secrecy, by the differences between declared policy and actual policy, and by the double-talk of "nukespeak" that often distorts or hides the real meaning of announced decisions and confuses ordinary citizens. Leaders have rarely talked about fighting and winning nuclear wars. When the Reagan administration mentioned firing nuclear warning shots and being able to fight and limit a nuclear war, many people were scared into joining grass-roots movements such as the Nuclear Weapons Freeze Campaign. The administration cooled the rhetoric, but not the development and procurement of nuclear war-fighting weapons.

Looking back over the last four decades, the United States has always had some form of nuclear war-fighting capability and intent. The type of war-fighting plans have shifted over the years, but we have clearly exceeded a deterrence-only posture since at least the mid-1950s.

While shrouded in secrecy at the time, we now know that during the 1950s, the United States had basically one nuclear war plan: the "spasm" attack, an all-out obliteration of not only the Soviet Union but Eastern Europe and China as well. Virtually all of our bomber force, the only delivery vehicles available at the time, would have been sent to pre-assigned targets, with little flexibility for a limited attack and apparently no provision to hold some nuclear weapons in reserve. The stated goal of the Air Force in this pre-ballistic missile era was to achieve a "credible first-strike capability."[14] That is, they hoped to be able to destroy most or all of the Soviet nuclear-equipped bombers before they could take off.

General Curtis LeMay, commander of the Strategic Air Command in the 1950s, was responsible for our entire nuclear force on strategic bombers. General LeMay even considered a preemptive nuclear strike against the Soviet Union as a viable option. He stated that "if the U.S. is pushed in the corner far enough we would not hesitate to strike first."[15] General LeMay had no qualms about attacking cities. He once objected to targeting Soviet atomic bomb facilities because there were no cities nearby, and therefore little "bonus damage" from attacking these isolated facilities.[16]

Herman Kahn, a physicist with RAND Corporation, the Air Force think tank set up after the war, believed that fighting a nuclear war would not be that much different than a conventional war. His writings

---

[14]Alain C. Enthoven and K. Wayne Smith, *How Much Is Enough? Shaping the Defense Program, 1961-1969*, Harper & Row, 1971, p. 170.
[15]Peter Pringle and William Arkin, *S.I.O.P.: The Secret U.S. Plan for Nuclear War*, W.W. Norton and Co., 1983, p. 45.
[16]Ibid., p. 63.

may have given military men such as General LeMay some comfort as they planned their nuclear strikes:

> If proper preparations have been made, it would be possible for us or the Soviets to cope with all of the effects of a thermonuclear war in the sense of saving most of the people and restoring something close to the previous standard of living in a relatively short time.[17]

In 1962, Secretary of Defense Robert McNamara quoted this paragraph from an Air Force document:

> The Air Force has rather supported the development of forces which provide the United States a first-strike capability credible to the Soviet Union, as well as to our Allies, by virtue of our ability to limit damage to the United States and our Allies to levels acceptable in the light of the circumstances and the alternatives available.[18]

The all-out LeMay spasm attack plan was changed dramatically during the Kennedy administration, at least on paper. McNamara, after briefings by the RAND Corporation, was convinced that the all-out attack against cities was not credible or moral. No American President would unleash such a massive attack in response to limited Soviet aggression, and possibly not even in response to their use of tactical nuclear weapons in Europe. He called for a "no cities" policy of "flexible response," giving the President flexibility to order limited strikes against purely military targets, sparing Soviet cities initially, hoping to keep the nuclear war limited. If the Soviets launched a limited attack against our missile fields, for example, or if they accidentally fired one or two missiles, then the President could reciprocate with a limited response. Hopefully, if we avoided a direct attack on any Soviet city, then the USSR would show similar restraint.

Secretary McNamara announced his new "no cities" or "flexible response" strategy in June of 1962 at the University of Michigan. His message implied, however, that nuclear weapons were not that much different from conventional weapons, possibly influenced by Herman Kahn:

---

[17]Herman Kahn, *On Thermonuclear War*, New York: Free Press, 1969.
[18]Robert S. McNamara, *Blundering into Disaster; Surviving the First Century of the Nuclear Age*, New York: Pantheon Books, 1986, p. 51.

The United States has come to the conclusion that, to the extent feasible basic military strategy in a possible general war should be approached in much the same way that more conventional military operations have been regarded in the past. That is to say, principal military objectives, in the event of nuclear war stemming from major attack on the alliance, should be the destruction of the enemy's military forces not his civilian population. The very strength and nature of the alliance forces make it possible for us to retain reserve striking power to destroy an enemy society if driven to it. In other words we are giving a possible opponent the strongest imaginable incentive to refrain from striking our cities.[19]

McNamara quickly became disenchanted with the open-ended implications of this nuclear war-fighting strategy, however, fearing (correctly) that the target lists and the "required" weapons would grow without limit. Within months, he switched his *declared* policy, stating that we would follow a policy of "assured destruction," later changed by others to "mutual assured destruction" or MAD for short: we would henceforth keep only enough nuclear weapons to retaliate, to assure that we could destroy the Soviet Union in event of attack.

Despite the declared policy of MAD, the President still maintained the "flexible response" options for fighting a nuclear war. He could choose limited options such as attacking only Soviet nuclear forces, Soviet air defenses away from cities, air defenses near cities, communication centers or a "spasm" attack including cities.

In reality, MAD has never been our policy since 1961, in the sense that all we could attack was cities. By providing the President with many options, the weaponeers have justified the vast buildup in nuclear war-fighting weapons. Some proponents of President Reagan's "Star Wars" defensive shield claimed that all we have is a MAD policy, asking whether it isn't better to defend our country with a defensive shield, rather than to rely on the immoral MAD policy by attacking cities. As we discuss in more detail later, the President has had options other than directly attacking cities since the early 1960s.

Secretary McNamara was seriously troubled by the implications of building more weapons than we needed for deterrence in the early 1960s. A decade later, James Schlesinger, Secretary of Defense under President Ford, had no such qualms. He actively pushed for the

---

[19]Arthur Macy Cox, *The Dynamics of Detente*, W.W. Norton & Company, 1976, p. 23.

acquisition of accurate, first-strike capable weapons to be able to destroy Soviet missile silos and command and control bunkers, further accelerating the acquisition of war-fighting weapons that continues today.

President Carter, who came into office openly discussing nuclear disarmament, was subsumed into the nuclear establishment. Before leaving office, he and Zbigniew Brzezinski, his National Security Adviser, added several new dimensions to the nuclear war-fighting goals, including decapitation (destroying Soviet leadership as a specific target), ethnic targeting (to create internal political disruption within the Soviet Union), and the concept of a protracted nuclear war (making plans and procuring weapons to fight with nuclear weapons over many months or years).[20]

There was little public discussion of the implications of these new goals or new weapons to meet those goals. A series of arguments spewed out of the think tanks and the Pentagon to justify what were clearly war-fighting options. The most enduring theme has been "flexible response": we can't tie the President's hands, but must offer him multiple options to respond to all possible contingencies. We must have accurate "counterforce" weapons to attack Soviet missile silos, to limit damage to our homeland by attacking their nuclear missiles first.

Building new weapons to provide "flexible response," or counterforce capability, or to limit damage all sound more credible and hence easier to sell to the American public and Congress than stating that we are seeking a nuclear warfighting capability. But the hardware is the same. Only the name has been changed to protect the military budget.

At times, some of our leaders have lowered their guard and admitted that we have a nuclear war-fighting policy:

"Our policy is "counterforce" or "war-fighting" . . . the two are synonymous."—General Bernard Davis, Strategic Air Command (1982)

"I think we need to have a counterforce capability. Over and above that, I think that we need to have a war-fighting capability."— Frank Carlucci, then deputy to Secretary of Defense Caspar Weinberger.

---

[20]Philip K. Lawrence, *Preparing for Armageddon*, Sussex, U.K.: Wheatsheaf Books, 1988, p. 100.

'You have to have a war-winning capability if you are to succeed.'—
Secretary of the Navy John Lehman.[21]

More frequently, accurate new weapons are justified on the basis of
improving deterrence. General John Chain, Commander of the Strategic Air Command, testified that "the primary purpose of these forces is
to deter a nuclear war ... yet allow effective warfighting should
deterrence fail and nuclear war ensue."[22] The nuclear establishment in
the U.S. (and presumably the Soviet Union) clings to deterrence as the
primary policy, but usually adds a caveat, possibly the world's six most
dangerous words:

**IF DETERRENCE FAILS, WE MUST PREVAIL.**

How does one "prevail"? Then Secretary of Defense Caspar Weinberger, while claiming that we are not arming to fight or to "prevail" in a
protracted nuclear war, nonetheless stated that:

> our policy requires that, if necessary, we prevail in denying victory
> to the Soviets and in protecting the sovereignty and continued
> viability of the United States and of the Western democracies as
> free societies.[23]

We will not "win," but we will "prevail in denying victory to the
Soviets"!

A White House memorandum in 1972 talked of "strategic sufficiency,"
implying that we were not seeking superiority or the capability to win a
nuclear war. But this memo went on to define "strategic sufficiency" as
the nuclear weapons necessary "to ensure that the U.S. would emerge
from a nuclear war in discernibly better shape than the Soviet Union."[24]
Did anyone ever stop to think what would happen as the Soviets also
sought such "sufficiency"? How could both countries emerge from a
nuclear war in "discernibly better shape"?

Colin Gray and Keith Payne of the conservative Hudson Institute
think tank were more blunt in their 1980 article "Victory Is Possible",

---

[21]Peter Pringle, *S.I.O.P.: The Secret U.S. Plan for Nuclear War*, W.W. Norton & Co.,
1983, p. 243.
[22]John T. Chain, Jr., testimony before the Senate Appropriations Defense Subcommittee, May 3, 1990.
[23]Caspar W. Weinberger, letter of May 20, 1983 to Theodore Draper, *The New York
Review of Books*, August 18, 1983.
[24]Gregg Herken, *Counsels of War*, Knopf, 1985, p. 266.

when they called for a nuclear strategy that "would have to envisage the
demise of the Soviet state." They went on to state that:

> Washington should identify war aims that in the last resort would
> contemplate the destruction of the Soviet political authority and
> the emergence of a postwar world order compatible with Western
> values.[25]

And President Bush, then running against Ronald Reagan for the 1980
presidential nomination, when asked how you could win a nuclear
exchange, replied:

> You have a survivability of command and control, survivability of
> industrial potential, protection of a percentage of your citizens,
> and you have a capability that inflicts more damage on the
> opposition than it can inflict upon you. That's the way you can have
> a winner ... [26]

According to one account, President Bush had modified the SIOP,
the Single Integrated Operational Plan for targeting nuclear weapons, to
attack Soviet leadership very early in a war, hoping to win a decisive
"victory." Incredibly, this SIOP plan now reportedly includes over
15,000 separate target sites inside the Soviet Union. This SIOP-7 may
partially explain why the administration continues to push for more
accurate, first-strike capable weapons like the MX and the Trident-II
(D-5) missiles. But as Desmond Ball, an expert on nuclear targeting and
Director of Defense Studies at Australian National University, has
stated, "The new SIOP will increase the risk that the Soviets will go first
in a crisis."[27] This super secret SIOP must be reduced to eliminate one
major driver of the arms race.

This desire to deny victory to the Soviets, to inflict more damage on
the Soviets than they can inflict on us, and to destroy the Soviet Union
can all justify new, more accurate, more destabilizing nuclear weapons—the weapons to fight, limit, survive and "win" a nuclear war.

---

[25]Colin S. Gray and Keith Payne, "Victory Is Possible," *Foreign Policy*, Summer 1980,
p. 14.
[26]Robert Scheer, *With Enough Shovels: Reagan, Bush & Nuclear War*, Random
House, 1982.
[27]Robert C. Toth, "U.S. Shifts Nuclear Response Strategy," *Los Angeles Times*, July
23, 1989.

In short, the rhetoric often sounds reasonable: who could be opposed to limiting damage to the U.S., should deterrence fail and a nuclear war began? From a moral perspective, shouldn't we target Soviet nuclear weapons instead of cities? These plans sound rational and moral, unless they increase the chances for nuclear war. As we will discuss in the next chapter, however, the acquisition of these nuclear war-fighting capabilities has increased the probability of nuclear war in some future crisis, and the next generation of weapons now under development would further degrade our national security.

# CHAPTER 5

# Dangers of the Qualitative Nuclear Arms Race

SUMMARY

The Bush administration is squandering the best opportunity in 40 years to end the dangerous and costly nuclear arms race. Instead of working vigorously with the Soviets to jointly construct a new, more stable relationship at much lower levels of nuclear weapons, President Bush's national security team has endorsed and is actively developing all the new nuclear war-fighting weapons begun by previous administrations. These new weapons will make nuclear war more likely in a crisis (crisis instability), and they will spur the other side to add more weapons in a classical action-reaction cycle (arms race instability).

In the last decade of the 20th century, the two superpowers face a fundamental choice: we can follow the business-as-usual approach—adding each new nuclear weapon innovation under the guise of "modernization," while signing cosmetic arms control treaties that at best retire older, less dangerous weapons. Or we and the Soviets can stop both the *quantitative* and *qualitative* arms races by agreeing to ban all nuclear explosions (the comprehensive test ban), all missile flight

90

tests, all anti-satellite (ASAT) weapons tests, and by banning all weapons in outer space.

There are three potentially grave dangers to our national security if we continue our old habits of building new nuclear war-fighting weapons as fast as they are invented:

1. **Crisis Instability:** The probability of nuclear war would increase in some future crisis if we and the Soviets develop and build the next generation of destabilizing nuclear weapons that are now under development.

2. **Arms Race Instability**: Both superpowers would be forced to add more nuclear weapons at ever increasing costs to counter the additions of the adversary and to preserve their ability to retaliate, blocking any effective arms control, let alone arms reduction agreements.

3. **Societal Degradation:** The continued escalation of the technological arms race would divert tens of thousands of our best and brightest scientists and engineers from addressing other pressing societal needs as discussed in Chapter 3, further degrading both nations' economic security and well-being.

If superpower relations continued to improve and no conflicts erupted within the Soviet sphere, then these dangers would recede over time. But we cannot plan on perpetual peace and endless photo opportunities at superpower summits. U.S.-Soviet relations could sour overnight if internal turmoil turns to bloodshed within the Soviet Union or former Warsaw Pact nations. If confrontation returns, the nuclear arms race could accelerate with a vengeance.

In this chapter, we consider how previous technology advances have contributed to the first two dangers—crisis instability and arms race instability—and how future nuclear weapons developments would further degrade our security.

## CRISIS STABILITY

Crisis stability refers to that condition when neither superpower could gain a significant advantage by using nuclear weapons first, even in a crisis situation, such as a major war or confrontation.

Stability can be illustrated by a simple physics problem. Consider two balls: one placed on the top of a hill, and the other in a valley

(Figure 5-1). Both balls are in equilibrium, and would remain stationary unless perturbed by an outside force. The ball in the valley is in a stable equilibrium position; even if moved by an outside force, it will return to its initial rest position. The ball on the hill, however, is in a position of *unstable* equilibrium; if someone gives this ball a slight push, it will roll down the hill.

FIGURE 5-1. ILLUSTRATION OF STABILITY

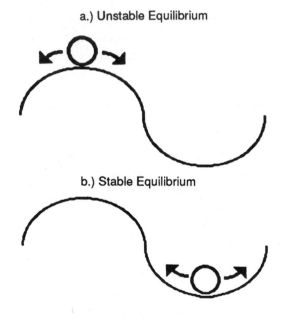

a.) Unstable Equilibrium

b.) Stable Equilibrium

In a similar fashion, nuclear weapons in the arsenals of the super-powers can be represented by one of two states of equilibrium: stable or unstable. In this analogy, severe international tension caused by events like the Berlin blockade or the Cuban missile crisis is the force that pushes the nuclear ball. The ball on the hill moves from equilibrium (peace) and rolls down hill (nuclear war) if pushed—crisis *instability*; while the ball in the valley returns to its equilibrium position (nuclear war is avoided) after the crisis recedes—crisis stability.

In peacetime, it doesn't matter whether the nuclear ball is on the hill or in the valley. In either case no force is applied so it remains stationary. Nuclear weapons are not used. Therefore one cannot say that we have crisis stability by noting the absence of nuclear war during peacetime. Just because no nuclear weapon has been used in anger since 1945 does not indicate that our nuclear weapons are stable. The real test is whether nuclear weapons would be used in a crisis, buffeted by the stresses of war or fears of war. Hence the emphasis on "crisis stability" to define combinations of weapons that would not be used, even in a crisis.

We could design our weapons to be stable in the most severe crises, up to and including a conventional war between the superpowers, or even an accidental launch and detonation of several nuclear weapons. Unfortunately, the U.S. and USSR have followed and are continuing to follow a different path: we are creating and building destabilizing weapons, analogous to placing balls on the tops of hills. The Bush administration is moving full steam ahead with a whole new generation of destabilizing nuclear weapons, requesting a 30 percent funding increase for the major nuclear weapons systems in 1991.

During normal, peacetime conditions, we do have a stable balance of terror today: no rational leader would dare attack the other for fear of nuclear retaliation by even a few hydrogen bombs. You might say we have peacetime stability, or first-strike stability. Even a nuclear ball on the hilltop will remain stationary without an external perturbing force.

During a crisis, the nuclear equation changes. If a conventional war breaks out, for example, and one or both of the superpowers becomes convinced that nuclear war is inevitable—that the adversary will use nuclear weapons in the next hour or day or week—then the leaders may begin to consider the relative consequences of using nuclear weapons first, versus the consequences of waiting for the expected nuclear attack. If either side perceives a significant *advantage* in striking first, such as a reduction in the expected damage level, then the incentive to push the button increases, and our security decreases.

The decision to use nuclear weapons first would not require any illusion of a successful first strike, in the sense of destroying all or even most of the opponent's nuclear weapons. If they really believed that nuclear war was inevitable, then leaders immersed in the chaos of war, particularly if they were losing, might be persuaded to use nuclear weapons first in an attempt to limit damage to the homeland, or to emerge in a better relative position after the war.

The choice would not be between zero or a few hundred nuclear explosions on U.S. soil, the normal peacetime calculus, but between 5,000 Soviet bombs on the U.S. if we wait, versus "only" 500 if we strike first—the lesser of two unimaginable disasters. While many citizens might protest that 500 hydrogen bombs exploding on the U.S. is so devastating as to be indistinguishable from 5,000, military leaders or Presidents coached by think-tank analysts might perceive an advantage, particularly if those leaders have been telling each other for years that we must "prevail" in a nuclear war or must come out in a "better relative position" than our adversary.

On paper, 500 nuclear explosions might look better than 5,000. For example, computer simulations might predict that 500 explosions aimed primarily at nuclear weapons sites would kill "only" 5–20 million Americans, at least in the first day of war, and leave some infrastructure and a few industries untouched, so that civilization could start over, while 5,000 nuclear detonations might kill 20–160 million with far less chance of recovery to anything resembling society as we know it.[1] With this computer simulation calculus, the President (or General Secretary) could conclude that he or she would save 15–140 million lives by striking first.

To maintain crisis stability, then, we should avoid any combination of weapons that gives either side an advantage *or the perception of an advantage* by using nuclear weapons first during a crisis. Or the perception of a disadvantage by waiting until the other side goes first.

In particular, no nuclear weapons should be vulnerable to an attack. This is a much more stringent requirement than first-strike or peace-time stability. In peacetime, no President would ever contemplate pushing the nuclear button *even if he or she could be assured of destroying 95 percent of all Soviet nuclear weapons.* The remaining 5 percent, over 500 Soviet hydrogen bombs, would destroy our nation as a viable civilization. We would be deterred. The fact that 95 percent of the Soviet arsenal was vulnerable to a preemptive strike would not matter in peacetime calculations.

In a crisis, however, when nuclear escalation seemed inevitable, a leader might think about pushing the button to gain such an advantage, if *any* nuclear weapons were vulnerable on the other side. Complete crisis stability would therefore require totally invulnerable weapons on both sides. Our challenge is to minimize any weapons vulnerability or perceived advantage to the side going first.

Consider next how previous nuclear weapons advances have created

---

[1]*The Effects of Nuclear War*, Washington, D.C.: Office of Technology Assessment, United States Congress, May 1979.

rewards for using nuclear weapons first. Two major destabilizing technological innovations of the last two decades are improved missile accuracy and MIRV—"multiple independently targetable reentry vehicles." MIRV is the innovation of mounting more than one warhead or nuclear bomb on each missile, like loading ten bombs on one airplane, or six bullets in one gun. Each U.S. MX missile and each Soviet SS-18 missile carry ten nuclear warheads; each missile could attack 10 targets of the opponent, a seemingly prudent and efficient technique for delivering the most damage per missile from a military viewpoint.

But because of its high offensive value, a MIRV'd missile also becomes a very lucrative target, offering the opponent the opportunity to knock out 10 threatening warheads with one shot. In addition, each MIRV'd missile, once launched, could eliminate five to ten of the opponent's missiles, giving the owner of that MIRV'd missile very strong motivation to fire it early in a crisis, before it could be destroyed on the ground and before the opponent's silos were emptied.

But missiles must have good accuracy to destroy the opponent's ICBMs. Both superpowers have buried their nuclear-tipped missiles in underground concrete silos to protect them from nearby nuclear detonations. With sufficient accuracy, a nuclear warhead could be exploded within a few hundred feet of a silo, crushing the silo or burying it in debris from the bomb crater, preventing the ICBM from being launched, assuming that the side with accurate warheads strikes first *and* that the opponent does not launch his missiles during the 25-minute ICBM flight time of the attacking missile. With modern satellite reconnaissance satellites, both sides know exactly where the opponent's missile silos are located to within a few tens of feet. These missile silos are sitting duck targets if the opponent's missiles have sufficient accuracy.

Nuclear-war planners calculate the probability that any nuclear warhead can destroy an opponent's missile silo, called the "silo kill capability." This capability depends primarily on the hardness of the opponent's silos, and the accuracy, reliability and yield of the warhead/ missile combination. The progressive improvements in missile accuracies are shown in Table 5-1, along with the estimated silo kill probability assuming two shots at each target. Each liquid-fueled missile is assumed to have 70 percent reliability and each solid-fueled missile is assumed to successfully deliver its warhead to the target 80 percent of the time.

Soviet missile silos are alleged to have greater hardness (more difficult to destroy) than American silos, so the calculations for Table 5-1 assume Soviet silos are hardened to 4,000 pounds per square inch (psi), while U.S. silo hardness is taken as 2,000 psi. There is great uncertainty in most of these assumptions regarding accuracy, reliability and silo hardness, so these results only indicate trends. The general conclusion is that U.S. accuracy is generally better, and therefore the U.S. MX and Minuteman-III equipped with the more powerful Mark 12A warhead has higher silo kill probability (94 and 71 percent) against 4,000 psi Soviet silos than the much vaunted Soviet SS-18 Mod 4 has against softer 2,000 psi silos (67 percent). The new Soviet SS-18 Mod 5 does have higher kill probability (88 percent) than the U.S. Mark 12A.

Higher yield or explosive power can make up for poor accuracy to some degree. Thus the old Soviet SS-18 Mod 3 had a single 20 megaton warhead with worse accuracy than the Mod 4 or Mod 5 MIRV'd SS-18s, but higher two-shot silo kill capability at 90 percent. The lethality of a weapon increases very slowly with increased yield (mathematically to the 2/3 power), while lethality grows with the square of the CEP accuracy, where CEP is the "Circular Error Probability"... representing a circle surrounding the intended target into which half of all warheads would fall. Thus if the accuracy is doubled from .1 to .05 nautical miles (smaller CEP is more accurate), then the weapon becomes four times as lethal. If the explosive yield is doubled, the lethality is increased only 59 percent. Therefore both superpowers have been moving toward smaller yield weapons with better accuracy.

Accurate MIRV'd missiles are particularly destabilizing, as illustrated by two cases in Table 5-2. In the first case, assume that both sides have 10 MIRV'd missiles, each with 10 warheads. Assume further that two warheads must be aimed at each missile silo of the opponent to assure reasonable probability of destruction, say 90 percent versus 70 percent if only one warhead is fired at each silo. If the attacker attempts to destroy all 10 missiles of the opponent, then it must fire 20 nuclear warheads.

With MIRV'd missiles (Case 1), the attacker can destroy 90 percent of all enemy missiles by firing just two MIRV'd ICBMs with 20 warheads. After this first strike, the attacker has an eight to one advantage. The attacker clearly "wins" by striking first in this hypothetical situation.

With single-warhead missiles (Case 2), the attacker would have to fire just one warhead at each of the opponent's silos. Even if the attacker fired all 10 missiles, he could at best destroy 70 percent of the victim's missiles. In this case, the attacker is disarmed and the victim emerges

TABLE 5-1. TRENDS IN ICBM ACCURACY AND SILO KILL CAPABILITY.[2]

| U.S. ICBMs: | MIRVs | Yield (MT) | CEP* (N.M.) | Two-Shot Kill Probability Against 4,000 psi Silos: |
|---|---|---|---|---|
| Titan | 1 | 9 | .8 | 15.4 percent |
| Minuteman-II | 1 | 1.2 | .34 | 24.2 |
| Minuteman-III | | | | |
| Mark 12 | 3 | 0.17 | .10 | 56.4 |
| Mark 12A | 3 | 0.335 | .10 | 71.4 |
| MX | 10 | 0.30 | .05 | 94.6 |

| Soviet ICBMs: | | | | Two-Shot Kill Probability Against 2,000 psi Silos: |
|---|---|---|---|---|
| SS-18 Mod 1 | 1 | 24 | .23 | 90.5 percent |
| SS-18 Mod 2 | 8 | 0.9 | .23 | 47.8 |
| SS-18 Mod 3 | 1 | 20 | .19 | 90.9 |
| SS-18 Mod 4 | 10 | 0.5 | .14 | 66.5 |
| SS-18 Mod 5 | 10 | 0.75 | .09 | 88.6 |

*CEP = Circular Error Probability or accuracy of missile/warhead combination in nautical miles (6,080 feet).

with three missiles and warheads. Thus single warhead missiles are considered stabilizing since they offer no advantage, but rather a major disadvantage in striking first.

The most destabilizing combination would be a fleet of accurate MIRV'd warheads facing an opponent with many warheads on a few MIRV'd missiles stationed in fixed silos. Unfortunately for us and for the rest of the world, this destabilizing combination is becoming a reality: the Soviet Union has about 5,700 warheads (50 percent of all Soviet warheads) on 1,128 land-based missiles in fixed underground silos. In 1980, 72 percent of all Soviet warheads were in fixed silos, but the Soviets have been adding submarine-launched missiles and mobile land-based missiles, reducing some of their vulnerability. The Soviets now have over 200 mobile missiles on trucks or railcars. In principle the U.S. might destroy these mobile missiles if we knew where they were parked and we struck without warning, but presumably the Soviets would move these mobile missiles around during any crisis that might conceivably lead to a U.S. attack.

---

[2]For formulas on silo kill probability, see Chapter 6 by David Hafemeister: Kosta Tsipis, David W. Hafemeister and Penny Janeway, *Arms Control Verification: The Technologies That Make It Possible*, Washington: Pergamon-Brassey's, 1986, p. 44.

TABLE 5-2.  COMPARISON OF STABILITY: MIRV'd vs. SINGLE-WARHEAD
MISSILES

CASE 1.   10-WARHEAD MIRV'd MISSILES:

(Attacker uses two missiles with 20 warheads to destroy 10 enemy
missiles.)

|  | Attacker: | | Victim: | |
|---|---|---|---|---|
|  | Missiles: | Warheads: | Missiles: | Warheads: |
| Initial: | 10 | 100 | 10 | 100 |
| 1st Strike: | − 2 | − 20 | − 9 | − 90 |
| After: | 8 | 80 | 1 | 10 |

(Attacker kills 90 warheads with two missiles, emerging from battle with an
eight to one advantage. FIRST STRIKE PAYS!)

CASE 2.   SINGLE-WARHEAD MISSILES:

(Attacker fires all 10 missiles, destroying only 70 percent of opponent's
weapons.)

|  | Attacker: | | Victim: | |
|---|---|---|---|---|
|  | Missiles: | Warheads: | Missiles: | Warheads: |
| Initial: | 10 | 10 | 10 | 10 |
| 1st Strike: | − 10 | − 10 | − 7 | − 7 |
| After: | 0 | 0 | 3 | 3 |

(Attacker is disarmed, and victim emerges with advantage. FIRST
STRIKE LOSES, so single warhead missiles are stabilizing.)


The Soviets may move even more of their land-based missiles to
mobile trucks or trains in the coming years, which would reduce the
threat from accurate U.S. missiles. At this time, however, over half their
11,300 strategic nuclear warheads are at 1,128 fixed, known sites that have
been carefully surveyed by our spy satellites. The United States could
therefore kill up to 5,700 nuclear birds with only 1,128 stones, if we
struck first with accurate warheads. Conservative military-war planners
assume that we would have to aim two warheads at each Soviet silo to
make sure we could destroy it, so they would claim that we would need
about 2,300 accurate warheads to destroy 1,128 Soviet ICBMs in their
silos. This would still be a bargain; we could eliminate up to 5,700 Soviet
hydrogen bombs by striking first with 2,300 bombs ... in nukespeak, a
good "cost exchange ratio" of 2.5 to 1.

Wait, you say: we are the good guys—we would never strike first! That is true, but it is irrelevant. Perceptions are paramount for deterrence. The Soviets do not believe that we wouldn't strike first in a crisis; after all, official NATO policy for 40 years has been to use nuclear weapons first to stop a conventional Warsaw Pact attack in Europe, even if the Soviets have not used nuclear weapons. And of course, the United States did use nuclear weapons first in World War II.

The Soviets might perceive only one option to prevent the loss of most of their ICBMs in a deteriorating international crisis if the United States ever deployed 2,300 or more accurate ballistic missile warheads: they would have to launch their ICBMs first, or at least "launch on warning" or "launch under attack." Therefore U.S. acquisition of accurate nuclear delivery systems gives the Soviets strong incentive to use nuclear weapons first in a crisis—to "use them or lose them."

The United States has acquired enough accurate nuclear warheads, part of our nuclear-war-fighting capability, to threaten the 1,128 Soviet ICBM silos with one warhead each. We have retrofitted 900 of the moderately accurate and higher yield Mark 12A warheads (600 feet accuracy) into 300 older Minuteman-III missiles, and we have added 500 very accurate warheads (300 feet accuracy) on 50 MX missiles, replacing 150 less accurate Minuteman warheads. While these 1,400 accurate warheads are not enough to hit each Soviet silo with two explosions, it certainly threatens much of their retaliatory forces. In a crisis, the Soviets would perceive an advantage in firing their missiles before half of them could be destroyed.

Furthermore, since all 1,400 accurate U.S. warheads are mounted on 350 ICBMs in fixed silos, the Soviets could in theory destroy most of the threatening U.S. land-based missiles only by striking first themselves, hoping to blast our missiles in their underground silos or on railroad cars garrisoned near silos (if we deploy the MX Rail Garrison system) before they could be fired. In short, Soviet leaders today would have a double incentive to push the button in a crisis, a twin advantage created by our addition of 1,400 accurate warheads. Similarly, U.S. leaders have strong incentive to launch our land-based missiles due to the addition of 308 accurate Soviet SS-18 missiles. **Both superpowers *have degraded their own security by adding accurate MIRV'd nuclear weapons such as the SS-18 and the MX missile.***

The Soviets have 4,880 warheads on 608 SS-18 and SS-19 missiles, or enough to target up to four warheads against each U.S. missile silo, far more than they need to wipe out most of our ICBMs with a high-probability two warheads per silo attack. They have 4,880 accurate warheads and we have only 1,400, so their actions are more destabilizing, right?

Not exactly. Stability depends not only on the weapons, but also on the vulnerability of the opponent's retaliatory force. The weapons of the two superpowers have to be considered together; they can't be analyzed in isolation. If all U.S. warheads were on invulnerable submarines, for example, then it wouldn't matter how many accurate warheads the Soviets had. All of our warheads would survive on submarines hidden under the world's oceans.

In fact, we are close to that ideal case. The U.S. has wisely placed only 19 percent of its warheads on vulnerable land-based missiles. No matter how many or how accurate Soviet ICBMs become, they cannot threaten the majority of our nuclear weapons on submarines or weapons in bombers on alert. Perfect pinpoint accuracy is useless if submarines can't be found.

Unfortunately, Soviet deployment strategy has created a destabilizing imbalance with their overreliance on land-based missiles in fixed silos. From a purely bean-counting approach, the Soviets could theoretically destroy some 2,450 U.S. warheads on ICBMs or 19 percent of our retaliatory force, while we could theoretically destroy 5,700 Soviet warheads, 50 percent of their arsenal. Because of this built-in asymmetry due to vulnerable Soviet basing decisions, **the Soviet Union is more vulnerable to accurate warheads than is the U.S.**

This dangerous, destabilizing nature of accurate, MIRV'd missiles was acknowledged by the key national security leaders in the early 1970s. For example, when Senator James Buckley (R.- N.Y.) introduced an amendment to the 1971 defense authorization bill to improve the accuracy and yield of the Minuteman-III missile warheads so that they could be used to destroy Soviet ICBMs, it was soundly defeated.

Even the Department of Defense objected to the quest for accurate missiles at the time, writing:

It is the position of the U.S. to not develop a weapon system whose deployment could reasonably be construed by the Soviets as having first strike capability. Such a deployment might provide an incentive for the Soviets to strike first.[3]

---

[3]Arthur Macy Cox, *The Dynamics of Detente: How to End the Arms Race*, W.W. Norton & Co., 1976, p. 86.

Senator John Stennis, the conservative southern Democrat from Mississippi and pro-defense chairman of the Armed Services Committee, also spoke out against Buckley's amendment giving the Minuteman-III "counterforce" capability, the accuracy and yield to destroy Soviet ICBMs in their underground silos. His statement appears to have represented the consensus view in 1971:

> The explanation of this amendment includes the word "counterforce." Those familiar with these terms know that essentially means a first-strike capability. We have stayed within the terms of deterrence, deterrence, deterrence. That is what we are talking about at the SALT talks. We do not need this type of improvement in the payload and guidance now. Our accuracy is already sufficiently good to enable us to attack any kind of target we want and to avoid collateral damage to cities. The only reason to undertake the type of program the amendment suggests is to be able to destroy enemy missiles in their silos before they are launched. *This means a U.S. first strike*, unless the adversary should be so stupid as to partially attack us, and leave many of his ICBMs in their silos for us to attack in a second strike.[4]

By 1974, however, the Pentagon and Congress had succumbed to the nuclear-war-fighting fever, and approved the Minuteman-III counterforce improvement program. Senator Stennis and others became enthusiastic supporters of later, far more dangerous counterforce weapons like the MX missile. The MX has twice the accuracy with 10 instead of just three Minuteman-III warheads that Senator Stennis called a first-strike weapon a decade earlier. Each MX warhead has nearly twice the probability of destroying a Soviet missile silo as the Minuteman-III missiles that Congress rejected just a few years earlier.

Today, very few voices are raised in the halls of Congress when new counterforce weapons are proposed, even though the early arguments of Senator Stennis and many others are just as valid today as they were in 1971. Some leaders, such as the current Chairman of the Senate Armed Services Committee, Senator Sam Nunn, would prefer that we had only single-warhead missiles. In June of 1989 Senator Nunn stated that:

> ... if we both had single warhead mobiles on land, neither side would be nearly as tempted to strike first in a crisis. Neither side

---

[4]Ibid.

would feel as vulnerable in a crisis and therefore both sides, in my view, would take that finger a little bit further off of the nuclear trigger.[5]

The newest addition to our nuclear war-fighting capability is the Trident-II or D-5 submarine-launched ballistic missile (SLBM). Historically, SLBMs have been rather inaccurate, since they are fired from a moving, underwater platform, instead of a carefully pre-surveyed spot on the earth's surface. But the D-5 has almost the same accuracy as the MX, and a high probability of destroying Soviet ICBMs, *if we strike first*. The Pentagon originally requested 4,800 D-5 warheads, enough to fully saturate the existing Soviet missile fields containing some 1,128 ICBMs, with plenty left over for command and control bunkers and other hardened military targets. The Bush administration is moving ahead with plans to outfit up to 21 or more Trident submarines with over 4,000 destabilizing D-5 warheads.

The D-5 has one large advantage over the MX missile: the MX is both threatening to Soviet retaliatory forces *and* vulnerable to attack. The MX is doubly destabilizing, giving the Soviets two major incentives to attack and destroy the MX before it can be launched. The D-5, carried by submarine, is not vulnerable to a Soviet first strike, which explains why the D-5 has received far less condemnation than the MX in Congress. However, the accuracy of the D-5 would still pressure the Soviets to fire their ICBMs early rather than late. The D-5 and similar Soviet SLBM's are still very destabilizing.

In one sense, the D-5 is more destabilizing than the MX: since SLBMs can be fired from waters closer to the Soviet missile fields, warning time can be as short as 10 to 15 minutes, compared to the 25-minute warning time for ICBMs fired from the continental United States. This time difference is crucial. Military planners now count on 20 minutes to receive Presidential approval to launch under attack, to fire our missiles as the first Soviet warheads start arriving on U.S. soil. If anything, the Soviets have had an even more centralized control of nuclear weapons. The D-5 reduces Soviet response time, and may force them to decentralize control, at least in a crisis. Knowing that they would have only 15 minutes to decide, they might delegate launch authority to a military officer or even to a computer, increasing the hair-trigger nature of modern nuclear weapons.

---

[5]Sam Nunn, Speech to the Institute for Foreign Policy Analysis, Washington, D.C., June 13, 1989.

Before we began deploying our accurate ICBM warheads in the late 1970s, there was never any pressure on either side to fire its missiles early, even in a stressful war situation; they knew that their ICBMs would survive under any circumstance. They could carefully analyze any signals from their early-warning infrared satellites or ground-based radars that constantly search for U.S. missile launches. If these electronic listening devices indicated a U.S. attack, they could afford to wait, to see if these were false signals or a real attack. They could even wait for the sure confirmation of a nuclear detonation on Soviet soil before committing nuclear suicide, assured that all of their nuclear arsenal would survive. There was simply nothing to be gained by launching their missiles on the basis of warning signals, and everything to lose if the early-warning signals proved false. We had crisis stability.

Our accurate, war-fighting nuclear weapons have reduced this stability. Today, if a crisis developed, leaders would be under strong pressure to fire their missiles early, knowing that delay could mean that most of their retaliatory force might be destroyed. They would carefully analyze all signals from their early-warning systems. But they would at least have 25 minutes to verify the validity of any missile launch signals from their early-warning satellites or ground-based radars.

Accurate submarine-launched missiles like the D-5 would reduce this reaction time. With the prospects of only 10 or 15 minutes of warning from accurate submarine-launched missiles off their shores, Soviet leaders might have to rely on automatic computer processing to analyze early-warning signals. During a crisis situation, they might go to "launch on warning," effectively turning control for starting World War III over to electronic sensors and computers. *Are we really more secure by adding weapons that make our security depend on the reliability of Soviet computers?*

Accurate SLBM warheads like those on the D-5 missile and Soviet counterparts have also complicated the task of Soviet early-warning systems. Submarine-launched missiles, with shorter range and less powerful rockets than ICBMs, emit weaker infrared signals. In addition, SLBMs have no fixed point of origin. Several years ago, the military planners knew that all accurate warheads that could threaten their land-based missiles would originate only from land-based ICBMs, the only accurate missiles. Each side knows from spy satellites the exact location of every ICBM silo of its adversary.

As part of their early-warning system, then, they could exclude any infrared signals emanating from other than the known missile fields,

eliminating many potential false alarms based on geography. An oil well
fire in Texas might look just like a missile launch to Soviet spy satellites,
but a quick computer check would reveal that there are no U.S. ICBMs
in Texas, so the Soviets could rule out this infrared signal as a false
alarm.

With the addition of the accurate D-5 missile, however, the Soviets
must assume that a bright infrared signal originating from any of the
world's oceans could be from an accurate, silo-busting missile. They
have no geographical reference to separate real missile launches from
other extraneous sources of infrared energy such as gas fires, glint from
cloud edges, or short-range missile launches from ships at sea. Since
they must look for weaker infrared signals to detect SLBMs compared to
ICBMs, the chances of false alarms and an accidental nuclear war
increased significantly when we added the accurate D-5 submarine
launched missiles. The Bush administration continues to push for
deployment of these destabilizing D-5 missiles; they are planning to
replace the older Trident-I (C4) missiles with the nuclear war-fighting
D-5 missiles, even though the existing C4s have many years of service
life remaining. When the Soviets follow our lead and add accurate
SLBMs like the D-5, then U.S. response time will be cut, and our
President will be under greater pressure to "use them or lose them" in a
future crisis.

The destabilizing nature of the current superpower arsenals can be
illustrated by estimating the advantage gained by striking first with
nuclear weapons. Two measures of potential advantage are the ratio of
warheads launched to warheads of the opponent destroyed, and the ratio
of remaining warheads after the battle. John Steinbruner of the
Brookings Institution has calculated that if the Soviets struck first, they
could destroy about 7,000 U.S. warheads by firing 4,000 of theirs, or a
1.8 to 1 ratio. The Soviets would have a 2.1 to 1 advantage in surviving
warheads after they struck first.

Similarly, if the U.S. struck first with today's arsenal, then we could
theoretically destroy 8,300 Soviet warheads with 4,400 of ours, a 1.9 to 1
cost exchange ratio. We would have a 3.3 to 1 advantage in remaining
warheads after we struck first. Thus both sides would could gain an
advantage in striking first in a crisis; the current arsenals are unstable
primarily because of multiple warhead land-based missiles.[6]

---

[6]John D. Steinbruner, *Restructuring American Foreign Policy*, Washington, D.C.:
The Brookings Institution, 1989, p. 105.

If both sides moved to single warhead missiles, this crisis instability would be diminished. Two missiles would have to be fired to give reasonable assurance that one warhead would be destroyed on the other side. The cost exchange ratio would be less than unity. The side striking first would essentially disarm itself, coming out in a worse relative position, as illustrated in Table 5-2. Clearly both sides should be eliminating MIRV'd missiles, as proposed by Senator Sam Nunn and apparently accepted by the Bush administration for future arms control discussions.

Before leaving the issue of past technological developments, we should mention that not all improvements are destabilizing. For example, SLBMs were one of the most stabilizing developments of the nuclear age, providing an invulnerable haven for retaliatory weapons that has prevented either side from achieving a first-strike capability. More recently, the development of mobile missiles, particularly on the Soviet side, has improved stability by reducing their reliance on increasingly vulnerable ICBMs in fixed silos. And spy satellites deployed in the late 1950s dramatically improved arms race stability, by giving both sides confidence that the other did not have secret ICBM silos or other major military installations hidden in some remote valley.

What of the future? Can things get worse? Are there other technological developments that would further reduce crisis stability?

## NEW WEAPONS DEVELOPMENTS

Unfortunately, the next generation of nuclear weapons promoted by the Bush administration would degrade stability even further. Unknown to most Americans, we, and presumably the Soviets, are developing revolutionary new war-fighting weapons. If we and the Soviets continue to develop and eventually deploy these new weapons, they could add further incentives to strike first or to use nuclear weapons first in a crisis.

These are the weapons that are now under various stages of development within the weapons laboratories:

*Earth-penetrating warheads.* As the name implies, these weapons would burrow into the earth before exploding, increasing their ability to destroy underground missile silos and command and control bunkers, by coupling more of their explosive energy directly into the earth. Like missile accuracy, this capability may appeal to the nuclear war-fighting strategist, but it too contributes to crisis instability.

We cannot improve our security by putting Soviet command structure at risk. In a crisis, they would be more inclined to fire their missiles early, fearing a loss of control if their communications and command centers were destroyed. Note that targeting command bunkers might even increase pressure on Soviet leaders to fire their mobile missiles. The mobile missiles themselves might survive, but they would be useless for retaliation if they did not receive the launch message. By threatening the existence of Soviet commanders, we increase the pressure on them to strike early.

Weapons designed to destroy Soviet command and control bunkers also conflict with one oft-declared U.S. nuclear weapons policy: to limit any nuclear war or to terminate a conflict before it could escalate out of control. Why should we strive to build weapons to destroy the Soviet leadership, while one of our declared policies is to negotiate with those leaders to terminate the war early? Unless one believes that Soviet military officers in the field would stop all hostilities once their leaders were eliminated, these weapons would seem to contradict our declared policy of early war termination.

The Pentagon approved the earth-penetrating warhead for engineering development in late 1988, the stage prior to production and deployment.

*Precision guided reentry vehicles.* All warheads on today's ballistic missiles follow free-fall trajectories once they are lifted into outer space. For MIRV'd missiles, each warhead is aimed in space by small maneuvering rockets on the post-boost vehicle (PBV), or "bus" that carries the multiple warheads. This PBV begins releasing reentry vehicles (RVs—the capsule containing the nuclear weapon) soon after the missile engines turn off high above the launch pad. No correction in each warhead's flight can be made once it is released by the bus in outer space. The warhead coasts thousands of miles through space to its fiery reentry into the earth's atmosphere before exploding over its intended target. Any deviation in the warhead's path due to heavy winds in the atmosphere or due to errors in the initial aiming cannot be corrected.

The United States has tested maneuvering reentry vehicles (MaRV), warheads with moveable weights or fins that can maneuver the warhead once they reenter the atmosphere above the target. This technology was originally developed so that the warheads could dodge interceptor rockets fired by Soviet terminal defenses, such as those around the city of Moscow. (The Soviets could use MaRVs to defeat proposed Star Wars terminal defenses.) In principle, warheads could be slowed down and even fly long distances in the atmosphere. Once free of the blinding, hot plasma that surrounds the warhead on reentry, these MaRVs could use smart sensors to detect the exact position of the target, again increasing the capability to attack hardened targets like missile silos and command bunkers. Eventually, smart MaRVs could in principle attack mobile missiles. MaRVs equipped with conventional warheads might even attack ships or airplanes. This is just one more step in the evolution of accurate and destabilizing war-fighting weapons.

*Strategic relocatable target (SRT) weapons.* The Pentagon is now funding research on sensor technology to be able to find relocatable targets like mobile missiles, mobile radars and mobile communication vans. This is a very challenging task. There are two primary mechanisms to detect military targets: passive sensors like our eyes that look for light reflected from or infrared energy radiated by targets, or active sensors like radars that paint the scene with electromagnetic radiation and look for reflections from missiles or trucks. Neither approach is well suited to finding mobile missiles or communication vans in the vast expanse of the Soviet Union. Passive sensors can be fooled by camouflage, and radar detectors can be fooled by simple "corner cube" reflectors[7] that return huge echoes, saturating the radar receivers with false targets. Mobile missiles could be shuttled between multiple garages, similar to the racetrack shell game basing scheme once proposed by the Carter administration for our MX missile.

Even without camouflage, decoys or multiple protective shelters, distinguishing military vehicles and trains from ordinary trucks or trains could be a major challenge, particularly during cloudy weather. The most likely solutions would probably use space-based radar satellites with very large antennae. Several satellites might be ganged together to form a large "phased array" radar antenna in space. Even with massive space-based radars, hiding existing mobile missiles and communication vans in the Soviet Union should be relatively easy.

The Air Force is studying methods to destroy Soviet mobile missiles under the MSTART (Missile System to Attack Relocatable Targets) program. Defense contractors are analyzing means to equip ICBM

---

[7]A "corner cube" reflector could be formed by covering the inside of two adjacent sides and the bottom of a cardboard box with aluminum foil to reflect radar waves. These three reflecting planes, the inside of a partial cube, would then return radar waves back on themselves; rays coming from a radar in any direction would be directed back to the transmitter, saturating the radar receiver or generating such strong signals that adjacent (real) targets would be obscured.

warheads to search out and eliminate mobile targets, and to compare such smart ICBM warheads with manned bombers for achieving the same objective.[8]

While detection of mobile targets is unlikely in the foreseeable future, note that the SRT project, if successful, would undermine deterrence. Mobile missiles are considered stabilizing, since they can't be located, yet we are pursuing technology to find mobile missiles. Tomorrow's technology development erases yesterday's stabilizing advances.

*B-2 Stealth Bomber.* The Stealth bomber is designed to penetrate future Soviet anti-aircraft defenses, so that Air Force pilots can fly over the Soviet Union 10 or 12 hours after a nuclear war to bomb any surviving targets. Given our vast arsenal of more than 7,000 warheads on ballistic missiles, it seems ludicrous in the extreme to imagine why we would need to fly over the Soviet Union to drop another 5,000 hydrogen bombs, particularly since we already have 97 brand-new B-1 bombers and 234 B-52 bombers that could be equipped to fire air-launched cruise missiles from outside Soviet air space. (The B-1 was sold on the basis of being able to penetrate Soviet defenses, but the Air Force admits that it cannot accomplish this mission against future Soviet air defenses due to electronic countermeasure deficiencies.)

Furthermore, these existing bombers could easily blast corridors into the Soviet Union, firing their nuclear-armed SRAM missiles more than 100 miles in front of their path, obliterating any anti-aircraft installations left standing after the barrage by several thousand SLBM and ICBM nuclear explosions hours earlier. But, in the usual conservative military fashion, war planners assume that each bomber would have to fend for itself, facing the full complement of Soviet anti-aircraft fire all the way.

Most members of Congress supported the B-2 Stealth research program during the late 1970s, preferring this new technology over the planned B-1 bomber which used older technology. The stealth technology could make our future bombers less susceptible to enemy radars for both conventional and nuclear missions. President Carter agreed, cancelling the B-1 bomber in favor of building cruise missiles and continuing research on the B-2.

Unfortunately, President Reagan resurrected the less effective B-1 system during the defense boom days of the early 1980s, without

---

[8]J. R. Wilson, "US Study Targets Mobile ICBMs," *Jane's Defense Weekly*, May 27, 1989, p. 996.

stopping other hardware programs. As a result, the United States has started procurement of more new military weapons systems than we can possibly afford. Now we are faced with a choice of fiscal responsibility (cancelling the B-2) while keeping the inferior weapons system (the B-1).

The Pentagon initially stated that the primary mission for the B-2 would be to hunt down and destroy mobile missiles, or, in nukespeak, "strategic relocatable targets (SRT)." Assuming that mobile missiles could be targeted, attacking them with the B-2 would simply add more pressure on any surviving Soviet crews to launch their mobile weapons too. At best, there seems little rationale to build the expensive B-2 at over $800 million per plane. At worst, it would further undermine crisis stability or at least contribute to additional nuclear weapons exploding on American soil by pressuring the Soviets to fire their mobile missiles, missiles that are now considered survivable and thus stabilizing.

General John Chain, Commander of the Strategic Air Command and Director of Strategic Target Planning, indirectly admitted to this destabilizing nature of the B-2 during testimony before the Congress on May 3, 1990. At one point, to justify the MX-Rail Garrison missile, General Chain expounded on the virtues of mobile missiles, stating that "making ICBMs mobile will add increased stability in a crisis," since mobile missiles are more survivable. We agree. But to justify the B-2 bomber, he also testified that "a penetrating bomber is the only weapon system that has the ability and the capability to be enhanced to hold mobile targets at risk."[9] He discounts the B-2's ability to destroy mobile missiles because the manned bomber is not a prompt weapon. Thus the B-2 might not contribute to immediate crisis instability at the beginning of a war, since the missiles would undoubtedly have arrived several hours earlier. However, the B-2 could very well pressure Soviet commanders to fire their surviving mobile missiles, thereby increasing damage to the U.S. *Do we really want to add weapons that maximize damage to the U.S.?*

The B-2 might also decrease stability by reducing warning time to the Soviets. If the B-2 did succeed in foiling Soviet radars and infrared detection systems, then the Soviets would have less time to react. In a crisis, they might be prompted to fire early, fearing that (possibly false) radar signals were last-minute detections of stealth bombers that had

---

[9]John T. Chain, Jr., testimony before the Senate Appropriations Defense Subcommittee, May 3, 1990.

succeeded in penetrating outer defenses. In this sense the mere presence of B-2s in the U.S. arsenal could create itchy fingers on Soviet nuclear triggers, even if they never entered Soviet airspace. In reality, long-wavelength radars will detect the B-2, but with less accuracy, making it more difficult to pinpoint the exact position of the B-2 so that interceptor rockets or planes could attack. The B-2 will not be invisible, it will just be harder to track.

The Pentagon must believe that there is at least a small possibility of the B-2 being able to penetrate Soviet airspace, because they are even designing a stealth bomb! That's right, a bomb with minimal cross section so that Soviet radars could not detect the bomb itself when it was dropped from the bomber.

*Sea-launched cruise missiles (SLCM).* Both the United States and the Soviet Union are developing and deploying sea-launched cruise missiles—pilotless jet aircraft. These SLCMs can be fired from virtually any type of ship. Today, we know that Soviet long-range sea-based nuclear weapons are confined to submarines. But if SLCMs are allowed to proliferate, any Soviet ship could be carrying nuclear weapons. The Soviets have tried to ban SLCMs in the START negotiations, or at least to limit the number of nuclear armed SLCMs (they can also carry conventional warheads), but in the past the United States has refused to limit these weapons.

If both sides were allowed unlimited nuclear SLCMs, the U.S. would be at a relative disadvantage due to our exposed coasts. A 1989 bipartisan study conducted by several executive and legislative branch national security leaders, co-chaired by Harold Brown, former Secretary of Defense, and Brent Scowcroft, before he became President Bush's National Security Advisor, concluded:

> With regard to nuclear-armed SLCMs, there is a basis for concluding that parallel U.S. and Soviet deployments would yield the Soviets a net advantage. Unlike the situation of the Soviet Union, many of the most lucrative targets in the United States are near the coasts—locations that are vulnerable because of the short flight time from Soviet ships and submarines.[10]

---

[10]Harold Brown, Representative Les Aspin, Senator William Cohen, Amos A. Jordan, Robert C. McFarlane, Senator Sam Nunn, Senator John Warner, and R. James Woolsey, "Deterring Through the Turn of the Century," The Foreign Policy Institute and The Center for Strategic and International Studies, January 1989, p. 16.

On another occasion, General Scowcroft stated that "the U.S. technological edge in SLCMs will prove temporary while the geographical asymmetries between the superpowers are permanent—and permanently favorable to the Soviet Union."[11] This candid analysis of the effects of the Soviets copying our weapons plans is refreshing. Unfortunately, President Bush has apparently failed to heed this warning, since he is refusing to limit nuclear-armed SLCMs in the START negotiations, agreeing instead to a "gentleman's agreement" of no more than 880 SLCM's.

While the Soviets could more easily attack the U.S. with SLCMs, at least we would have an hour or two of warning, since current cruise missiles are slow and relatively easy to detect. However, the next step in cruise missile development could remove most or all warning time:

*Stealth cruise missiles.* The stealth technology, used to make the B-2 bomber and new fighter planes less visible to radars and passive infrared sensors, is also being applied to pilotless cruise missiles. The Advanced Cruise Missile (ACM) was supposed to replace or augment the Air-Launched Cruise Missiles (ALCM) carried on B-52 bombers by 1990, but development problems have delayed their introduction into the arsenal. The ACM not only would be less detectable than the ALCM, but is supposed to fly at supersonic speeds, making it much more difficult to shoot down. This design goal may be elusive, however, since a high-speed cruise missile becomes hot due to air friction, making it more easily detectable by heat-sensitive infrared sensors.

If cruise missiles ever became truly invisible to radar and other detection devices, which now seems unlikely, then they would become first-strike capable weapons. Cruise missiles already have very high accuracy, using terrain following radar or correlation techniques to home in on their assigned targets. But the current ALCM takes several hours to reach its target, giving the enemy plenty of notice of an impending attack. And air-to-air missiles fired from fighter aircraft might destroy some of today's slow, non-stealthy cruise missiles.

The ACM might still take an hour or more to reach its target, but if an adversary could not detect it, then ACMs could in principle be used to strike first, knocking out hardened targets like ICBM silos without warning. In fact, perfectly stealthy cruise missiles would be more destabilizing than accurate ICBMs, because ICBMs can always be

---

[11]James P. Rubin, "Limiting SLCMs—A Better Way to START," *Arms Control Today*, April 1989, p. 10.

detected during their fiery launch, giving the opponent 25 minutes warning. It is unlikely that either side could ever hide the tremendous heated gas plume from the launch of a heavy ballistic missile from infrared satellites in space. A very stealthy cruise missile, on the other hand, might give no warning.

Imagine the fear that would sweep over the U.S. if a belligerent Soviet leader came to power after the USSR had armed its submarines with thousands of long-range, supersonic, stealthy cruise missiles with nuclear warheads. A few submarines could sneak up within a few hundred miles of our east and west coasts, and fire their silent weapons at military targets across the country. In principle, they could coordinate an attack so that cruise missiles aimed at inland targets would be fired first, and those intended for coastal targets last, so they would all detonate at about the same time, giving our leaders little time to react. This scenario would make the ICBM "window of vulnerability" scenario look like a Sunday school picnic.

Some readers may feel that such an SLCM attack would be absurd. Surely no Soviet leader would dare try such a risky venture. But as Theodore Postol, an MIT professor and arms control expert points out:

> My experience with similar military planning concerns leads me to predict that our military will take the threat of such a sneak attack seriously. They will adapt U.S. operations to attempt to compensate for it, they will spend money to defeat it, and they will adjust assessments of U.S. nuclear-force capabilities to take it into account. Their concerns will also grow as Soviet SLCMs improve in stealth and range.[12]

In other words, the military will take such a threat seriously when the Soviets begin deploying stealthy SLCMs, and this will force another costly and dangerous acceleration of the arms race.

The development of stealth cruise missiles could be dangerously destabilizing. There has been almost no public discussion of these dangers, however. We pursue technology as though only the United States of America is capable of building these weapons, often failing to consider the consequences when the Soviets (or other future adversaries) copy our lead.

---

[12]Theodore A. Postol, "In Soviet Arms Talks, U.S. Takes Troubling Stance on 'Stealth' Missiles," *Los Angeles Times*, September 10, 1989, p. IV-3.

*Depressed trajectory missiles.* Currently, ballistic missiles are fired on parabolic "minimum energy" trajectories, carrying their deadly nuclear cargo high into space before falling back into the atmosphere over their targets. Missiles can be fired at other angles, either higher or lower, but it takes more energy, reducing the range of the missile. If the firing angle is reduced or "depressed," the warhead could stay mostly within the atmosphere, reducing flight time and possibly avoiding or delaying detection by radar systems. For example, the usual minimum energy submarine launched ballistic missile (SLBM) would take about 15 minutes to travel 1,500 miles from an off-shore submarine. A depressed trajectory SLBM might take only six minutes to reach the Pentagon or the White House, again tightening the nuclear hair trigger.

A depressed trajectory missile fired from a submarine off our coast could in principle be used to attack our bombers on the ground, catching them before pilots could scramble and take off. It could also be used to circumvent any Star Wars space-based defensive system, or to wipe out our national command authority (NCA)—-the President and designated button-pushers in waiting.

Today our nuclear arsenal has triple redundancy. We can retaliate with submarine launched missiles, land-based missiles, and bombers on alert. The Soviets could in principle fire their ICBMs to hit our bombers on the ground as well as our ICBMs, but the timing is wrong: bombers on alert can be airborne in eight to 10 minutes, and our early-warning infrared satellites would give us 25 minutes warning, the flight time of an ICBM. The Soviets could fire SLBMs from off-shore submarines to catch most of the bombers before they could take off, but then nuclear detonations on our airbases would provide ample justification to launch our ICBMs before Soviet ICBMs arrived 25 minutes later. Since Soviet SLBMs do not yet have the accuracy to destroy ICBMs, our land-based missiles could survive this SLBM first strike.

If the Soviets developed a submarine-launched depressed trajectory missile, then they might be able to simultaneously attack our National Command Authority in Washington, bombers on alert and our early-warning radars near the coasts. With the NCA, early-warning radars and quite probably most communication links destroyed, surviving U.S. military officials would face a daunting decision: early-warning infrared (IR) sensors would probably detect the subsequent Soviet ICBM launches, but there would be no radar confirmation and no message from the President to authorize the release of their nuclear weapons. It is possible that the officers who constantly watch for any signs of attack would lose all communications and receive no other indication of attack.

What would they do? Should they be instructed to fire their ICBMs whenever communications go dead? What if there were a massive electrical power grid failure? An earthquake near Washington that cut all communications?

Remember that a decision would have to be made in less than 25 minutes. The ICBMs would be on their way as soon as the first depressed trajectory SLBMs were landing. Power black-outs have lasted for many hours.

The development of depressed trajectory missiles could contribute to a first-strike capability, enhancing nuclear war-fighting capability, and further pressuring authorities to fire nuclear weapons early. Fortunately, President Bush has recognized the danger in this development, after the House of Representatives attached an amendment to the 1989 defense bill that banned the testing of depressed trajectory missiles as long as the Soviets did not test such flight profiles. President Bush subsequently asked the Soviets to ban depressed trajectory missiles in the START arms control negotiations. This is the only new weapons development that this administration is seeking to curtail through negotiations, and it is the only arms control initiative that would actually improve crisis stability by preventing a destabilizing addition to our arsenals.

*Anti-submarine warfare* (ASW). Both superpowers are working on offensive and defensive techniques to fight a war under the sea: offensive ASW involves primarily sensor developments to attempt to locate submerged submarines. Defensive techniques attempt to foil the enemy's sensors or make submarines more invisible. As with most high technology projects, the United States is thought to have much better ASW capability. U.S. submarines are historically quieter and more difficult to detect. Future innovations could improve our ability to hide under the sea, such as adaptive skins on submarines that would pick up the enemy sonar signals and either cancel out the signals or return false echoes creating imaginary targets at distant locations. These defensive measures are stabilizing, maintaining an invulnerable haven for retaliatory nuclear weapons.

Effective ASW sensor developments would be extremely destabilizing. With accurate warheads to attack silo-based ICBMs and command and control bunkers, depressed trajectory SLBMs to take out the

National Command Authority and bombers on alert, and ASW technology to locate submarines before the attack, one side would be able in principle to eliminate most of the opponent's forces in a preemptive first strike. The side with effective ASW sensor capability would certainly anticipate a significant advantage in striking first during a crisis, the essence of crisis instability.

Fortunately, for those who believe as we do that crisis stability is essential for U.S. and Soviet security for the indefinite future, detecting submarines is extraordinarily difficult, bordering on the impossible. Furthermore, the difficulty derives from fundamental laws of physics, that, barring any breakthrough, should protect submarines under water for many, many decades.

Submarines are safe primarily because water is opaque to electromagnetic radiation. All common sensors used to detect airplanes or satellites use electromagnetic radiation: either light waves or infrared waves for passive sensors such as eyes or cameras, or microwaves for radar systems. But microwaves penetrate only a few millimeters in water. In very clear water away from coastal areas, blue-green light may penetrate tens of meters into the ocean, but most sea-water obscures any submerged submarine from visual or optical detectors. This leaves only sound waves and other secondary effects such as magnetic field changes, garbage or effluent from the submarine, or changes in the ocean's surface waves to detect submarines.

Sound detection or sonar is the most common ASW sensor. A passive sonar system listens for the noise from the submarine (along with all the other noises such as waves, fish, other ships, etc.). An active sonar sends out sound waves, much like a radar system, and listens for echoes from the submarine.

In either case, sound waves are far less well behaved than light waves or microwaves that normally travel in straight lines. Sound waves travel much slower than light waves, and are bent and distorted by ocean density variations. Sound waves also yield very poor resolution, requiring huge sensor arrays with dimensions that are on the order of miles instead of feet for their optical or radar counterparts. For all the recent improvements in acoustical data processing and the expenditures of billions of dollars per year for decades on anti-submarine-warfare research, there is little likelihood of any ASW system being able to routinely detect and locate distant submarines.

Furthermore, even if such a breakthrough occurred, the adversary could instigate countermeasures. These might include generating extraneous noise sources, spoofing the ASW system, deploying sound generating decoys to lure the ASW system away from the submarine, or simply destroying the adversaries, vast array of acoustical sensors that, in the case of the United States, now extend for hundreds of miles along the sea floor at "choke points" all across the globe. The measure-countermeasure options are as limitless as the ocean.

Periodically (usually at budget time), there are rumors or press leaks about a Soviet ASW breakthrough in non-acoustic techniques that will render our submarines vulnerable (and therefore we must build some new ICBM or nuclear bomber to preserve our nuclear deterrent). One possible non-acoustic detection scheme would use a blue-green laser, based either on an airplane or a satellite, to probe the ocean, looking for laser light reflected from a submerged submarine. This type of laser radar could cover only a very small patch of ocean, however; its beam would have to be focused to a relatively small spot to produce enough laser energy to penetrate into the water more than a few feet. With such a small beam, this blue-green laser could at best pinpoint the position of a submarine whose general location was determined by other means. Even this operation would be extraordinarily difficult, however, since the reflectivity of submarines in the blue-green region is very low, and could be reduced more with black paint!

Another popular ASW approach that pops up in the press from time to time is space-based synthetic aperture radar. Less well informed articles occasionally imply that such radars can "see" submarines directly. In fact, no microwave radar can penetrate sea water more than a few millimeters. Space-based radars would have to detect the sub-marine "wake," any change in the ocean's surface characteristics made by the submarine moving below the surface. There have been exagge-rated claims that submarine wakes persist for hours or even days, but the U.S. has never been able to utilize such wakes for routine submarine detection.

Admiral C. A. H. Trost, Chief of Naval Operations, felt obligated to respond to one 1989 article which charged that the Navy was inten-tionally blocking ASW research, that the oceans were becoming "transparent," and our submarines could in fact be detected by the Soviets using non-acoustic ASW systems. Admiral Trost wrote "the fact is that the oceans are simply not becoming more transparent. Instead, they are becoming more opaque." He went on to say that "nearly all non-acoustic detection technologies can detect a submarine, but only under contrived scenarios—-not under realistic operating conditions."[13]

*Nuclear-pumped directed energy weapons (NDEW)*. Previously, we have been describing nuclear weapon delivery system technology improvements: advances in ICBMs, SLBMs, SLCMs, etc. But the physicists and engineers at the nuclear weapons laboratories at Los Alamos, New Mexico, and Livermore, California—and probably their colleagues in the Soviet Union—are busy, too. They are working on the "third generation" of nuclear weapons.

The first generation was the atomic or fission bomb: energy was released by splitting large atoms such as uranium or plutonium. The bombs that destroyed Hiroshima and Nagasaki were atomic bombs.

The second-generation weapons were the more powerful thermonuclear or fusion or hydrogen bombs: hydrogen isotopes[14] are fused together at extremely high temperatures and pressures to release fusion energy, the engine driving the sun. To date, the only way scientists can achieve fusion temperatures and pressures for the hydrogen bomb is by exploding an atomic bomb. (An atomic bomb is required to trigger every hydrogen bomb.)

From a military viewpoint, these nuclear weapons are not very efficient. Their energy spews out in all directions in a rapidly expanding fireball. Despite the enormous release of energy, damage is limited to a radius of "only" a few miles. If even a small fraction of that bomb energy could be focused into a narrow pencil-beam of energy, it could destroy objects thousands of miles away. This is the objective of the third generation of nuclear weapons: action at a distance.

The basic concept of third-generation nuclear weapons is quite simple: take some of the plentiful energy from the bomb explosion, and focus it in one direction, much like the mirror of a searchlight collects

---

[13]C. A. H. Trost, "The Navy v. (Enemy) Subs," *Washington Times*, September 5, 1989, p. C2.

[14]Isotopes are atoms with a different number of neutrons. Thus ordinary hydrogen gas, the lightest and most plentiful atom in the universe, has but one proton and one electron ... and no neutron in its nucleus. The first "isotope" of hydrogen, called deuterium, has one neutron. About 0.7 percent of water contains the heavier deuterium atoms instead of hydrogen; this "heavy water" is used in some types of nuclear reactors. The second isotope of hydrogen is tritium which has two neutrons. Tritium is used in modern nuclear weapons to increase the yield or explosive power of the atomic bomb trigger. Being radioactive with a relatively short half-life of 12.3 years, this tritium in modern bombs must be replenished every four or five years.

the light from a carbon arc and focuses it into a beam of light. Nuclear explosions contain a rich mix of energy, including high energy neutrons, gamma rays, X-rays, ultraviolet, visible light, infrared and even microwaves. Schemes have been devised to accentuate the production and focusing of most of these radiations.

The most famous third-generation weapon is the X-ray laser, promoted by Edward Teller as a potential candidate for Ronald Reagan's Star Wars ballistic missile defensive system. The X-ray laser concept proposes using thin metal fibers driven by a hydrogen bomb explosion. Energy from the explosion would ionize the fibers, forming a pencil-beam of X-rays for a brief instant before the laser was destroyed. In the Star Wars scenario, Dr. Teller proposed that many individual bundles of thin metal fibers would be mechanically pointed toward each Soviet ballistic missile. When they were all lined up with their targets, the bomb would be detonated. If pointed correctly, the resulting powerful beams of X-rays would destroy the missiles.

The X-ray laser has one major drawback: the X-ray beam would be stopped by air! Even the very thin air some 60 miles above the earth's surface would be enough to dissipate the beam. Thus the X-ray laser would only work in outer space, and it could only shoot down objects that were at least 60 miles above the earth.

If the X-ray laser technology ever proved feasible, it would make a very potent anti-satellite (ASAT) weapon. Since any Star Wars missile defense system would depend on satellites, a Soviet X-ray laser could be used to defeat Star Wars. In fact, the first Livermore X-ray program, dubbed Excalibur, was proposed as an offensive weapon to shoot down any future Soviet Star Wars battle stations. The higher brightness, second-generation Super Excalibur would have been used as a ballistic missile defensive weapon, according to Livermore plans.

The X-ray laser is but one of several nuclear bomb-pumped directed energy weapons now under development. Another third-generation nuclear weapon could penetrate the atmosphere and attack targets on the ground: a microwave laser. Certain microwave frequencies do travel through the atmosphere with very little attenuation. A nuclear bomb-pumped microwave weapon in space could damage targets on the ground, including communication gear, radars and mobile missiles. Because of its extraordinary power, a bomb-pumped microwave laser could illuminate a large area on the ground. It would not need to determine the exact location of mobile missiles, but could flood a relatively large area with a high-energy pulse of radiation, destroying the electronic systems of any missiles in the area. Once again, this new development would render mobile missiles vulnerable, decreasing crisis stability by pressuring the adversary to fire mobile missiles early, before the microwave weapon could destroy them.

Alternately, ground-based, nuclear bomb-pumped microwave weapons could destroy or disrupt the electronics on satellites in space, another possible Soviet countermeasure to defeat a U.S. Star Wars system. But these ground-based weapons might also be used to blind an opponent's communication and early-warning satellites, creating grave instabilities in a crisis.

Finally, nuclear bombs can be used to propel pellets, a nuclear shotgun. While physical pellets cannot be focused into a narrow cone like a beam of light, a nuclear shotgun could still destroy targets over many hundreds or even thousands of miles in outer space. The SDI organization has proposed using a nuclear shotgun called "Prometheus" to blast away Soviet decoys that would likely surround reentry vehicles during a nuclear war.

So what are the dangers of these third-generation weapons? Proponents claim that these weapons would be more humane: since the energy is concentrated into narrow beams, the user can be more discriminating, aiming at only military targets and sparing cities. Lowell Wood, who heads the X-ray laser work at Livermore, stated that "the obvious direction of weapons design is to increase the utility of weapons and at the same time decrease the disadvantages intrinsic to their use."[15]

That's the problem. These nuclear weapons would be more usable. Without any fear of "collateral damage" (people killed), these weapons could become just another war-fighting weapon in the 21st century. Leaders who wouldn't dream of using hydrogen bombs to take out an offending missile launch facility for fear of nuclear retaliation, might use an orbiting, bomb-pumped microwave laser for a surgical strike. But how could we be sure that the adversary would not retaliate with less discriminating nuclear weapons? *Do we really want to make nuclear weapons more usable?*

The speed and long range of nuclear-pumped directed energy weapons (NDEW) compared to bullets or missiles would be very destabilizing in a crisis, particularly in outer space. Our military forces now rely on satellites for global communications, for navigation, and for

---

[15]Michael D. Lemonick, "A Third Generation of Nukes," *Time*, May 25, 1987, p. 36.

early warning of missile attack. In the next war, even if it lasts only a few minutes, satellites would be crucial to monitoring Soviet missile launches, and for communicating between the National Command Authority and the launch control centers.

The Soviets also rely on satellites. Suppose that both sides have NDEWs in some future crisis. These weapons kill at the speed of light over thousands of miles. The side striking first could blind the enemy. Two friendly NDEW battle stations in orbit on opposite sides of the earth could in principle destroy all opposing satellites in seconds. Without any communications or confirmation of missile attack, the blinded side would be totally vulnerable. It would be unlikely to get off many missiles in the 25-minute time interval from loss of communication to the arrival of enemy warheads over its missile fields and command bunkers.

To summarize, the development of NDEWs would give major advantages to the side striking first. Warning time for ballistic missile attack would be reduced from 25 minutes now, or 15 minutes since the U.S. is deploying accurate SLBMs like the D-5, to a few seconds, the time for an NDEW beam to reach a distant early warning or communication satellite. *Do we really want hair-trigger weapons systems with a few seconds' warning time?*

*Anti-satellite (ASAT) weapons.* We have already mentioned the dangers of a shoot-out in outer space, should both sides develop advanced directed energy weapons such as laser or neutral particle beams to destroy opposing satellites. But we do not have to wait for exotic laser beam or particle beam weapons to enter dangerous territory in outer space. Conventional ground-based, "hit-to-kill" rockets equipped with heat-seeking sensors or homing radars could be built today to attack each other's satellites. These "kinetic kill" weapons destroy their prey by direct collision.

If we proceed as planned by the Bush administration and build a dedicated ASAT weapon system, then the Soviets and other future adversaries will follow our lead. Enemy ASAT weapons will eventually threaten our critical satellites, with the potential of turning outer space into a battleground.

## ARMS RACE STABILITY

Arms race stability refers to a condition when no nation feels compelled to build more weapons. Unfortunately, most of the advanced weapons described above would pressure the opponent to add more. New war-fighting weapons on one side create vulnerabilities or the perception of vulnerabilities on the other side, so new weapons are added to breach the gap. This action-reaction cycle will continue until both sides recognize that nuclear superiority is a mirage. There is no American security without Soviet security ... there is only common security.

*Accuracy.* Accurate Soviet weapons such as their SS-18 and SS-19 ICBMs created the "window of vulnerability," the potential that they could destroy most of our ICBMs in a surprise first strike.

Unfortunately, leaders in the United States used the "window of vulnerability" as an excuse to build another war-fighting weapon: the 10-warhead MX land-based missile. After discarding 35 different schemes to provide some survivability for the MX, President Reagan chose to put the first 50 back into vulnerable Minuteman silos. Thus, in this case, the accuracy of Soviet missiles was used as a whipping boy to push through a very dangerous and destabilizing weapon system, escalating the arms race. In the end, the Reagan administration failed to correct the original threat: vulnerable land-based ICBMs.

In the case of the Soviet Union, the increasing accuracy of U.S. ICBMs (and now the increased accuracy of the D-5 submarine-launched missiles) may have driven the USSR to building the mobile SS-25 single-warhead truck-based missile, and the 10-warhead SS-24 that can be carried on trains. They may be forced to build more command and control bunkers. They could have avoided these costly projects if the U.S. had resisted the temptation to add so many accurate warheads.

*MIRVing.* Multiple warheads, when combined with improved accuracy, also places pressure on the other side to add more nuclear weapons. Single-warhead missiles would be far less threatening. Possible reactions to MIRVing in peacetime would be to add more land-based missiles (increase the number of targets for the opponent's MIRV'd missiles), add mobile missiles (the Soviet choice), or add more SLBMs or more bombers.

*Anti-submarine warfare* (ASW). Certainly, if either side developed (or was thought to be developing) an effective ASW sensor capability, the other would be deeply concerned. Since we rely on submarines much more than the Soviets, the United States would probably react with new weapons developments. Recall the wailing and gnashing of teeth when the "window of vulnerability" was brought forth in the late 1970s. The window of vulnerability was applicable to just 19 percent of our nuclear force—our land-based ICBMs—although ICBMs are the darlings of the nuclear war-fighting adherents. Imagine the reaction in the U.S. if the Soviets could potentially destroy 60 percent of our nuclear warheads on submarines and ICBMs instead of only 19 percent on ICBMs.

Probable responses to effective ASW developments would include adding ASW countermeasures such as acoustical decoys, sound jammers to saturate Soviet sonar receivers, and possibly disruption or destruction of their sonar arrays. There would surely be strong pressure to add many more U.S. submarines, just in case the old ones did become vulnerable. Indeed, the Scowcroft Commission that advocated placing MX missiles in vulnerable silos combined with building the small ICBM (Midgetman), also recommended developing a small submarine as a hedge against future Soviet ASW breakthroughs.

*Earth-penetrating warheads and precision-guided MaRVs.* Both weapons would increase the risk to ICBM silos and other hardened targets such as command and control bunkers. Likely reactions include building more mobile missiles, mobile communications vans and airborne command posts.

*Strategic relocatable target (SRT) weapons and B-2 bombers.* These weapons, to the degree that they would be successful in locating and destroying mobile missiles and mobile vans would increase pressure to build more offensive weapons, to add countermeasures to better hide weapons, decoys, and possibly better defenses to destroy our weapons. Other options include building more bombers and submarine-launched ballistic missiles.

*Nuclear-pumped directed energy weapons (NDEW).* The primary battleground for NDEWs would be in outer space. If either side begins deploying these weapons, the other side would feel compelled to add more communication, navigation and early-warning satellites. These satellites would be hardened, as much as possible, to improve their chances of surviving an attack by NDEWs. Possible survivability techniques include extra fuel for maneuvering, mechanical shielding and decoys.[16] All of these changes would add to the cost and weight of future satellites, further burdening our limited space launch capability.

---

[16]Decoys would have to be permanently deployed around the parent satellite, since there would be no warning time with speed-of-light NDEW weapons; thus the other side could study the decoys for months or years before attack, making it very likely that the decoys would be identified as such before the attack, thereby losing their effectiveness.

The ultimate response, as usual, is for the opponent to make its own NDEW, to be able to shoot back (or shoot first). Thus the pursuit of NDEW capability could lead to the space-age "shoot-out" at high noon ... severe crisis instability with the prize going to the side that shoots first.

To summarize, the administration (and most likely the Soviet Union) is developing a whole new generation of destabilizing nuclear weapons systems. If deployed, these weapons would threaten the retaliatory capability of the Soviet Union, increasing the risks of escalation to nuclear war in some future crisis, and increasing the pressure in peacetime to add ever more costly weapons to maintain an invulnerable deterrent. The nuclear arms race is alive and well, despite all the hype about imminent arms control treaties.

# CHAPTER 6

# Arms Control Treaties: Limit or License?

SUMMARY

Previous arms control treaties, with the exception of the Anti-Ballistic Missile (ABM) Treaty and the Intermediate Range Nuclear Forces (INF) Treaty, merely sanctified the largest number of nuclear weapons then in existence or planned by either superpower. Loopholes were left so that all new weapons developments and deployments could continue full speed ahead. While the INF Treaty and the Strategic Arms Reduction Treaty (START) actually reduce the *numbers* of deployed nuclear weapons for the first time, they do not stop the *qualitative* or technological improvements that fuel the arms race. The INF Treaty is also unique since it eliminates an entire class of nuclear weapons (those with ranges between 300 and 3,400 miles), but these represent less than 4 percent of the nuclear arsenals.

Hardliners have opposed effective arms control treaties because they fear the Soviets could gain an advantage by cheating. They claim that we do not have the technology or intelligence resources to detect all Soviet violations, when in fact we do have the ability

124

to detect any militarily significant violations in time to take corrective action.

## PAST ARMS CONTROL TREATIES

The two superpowers have signed 15 treaties related to nuclear weapons since the dawn of the nuclear age (See Appendix B). Several treaties have banned nuclear weapons from certain areas including the Antarctic, outer space, Latin America and on the sea bed (but not from submarines in the sea, our primary vehicle for hiding nuclear missiles). Several other treaties seek to prevent a surprise nuclear war by improving communications between the U.S. and the Soviet Union through "hot lines"; to notify each other in advance of missile launches; and to promptly report any accidents and to consult with each other in the event of conventional war. While these treaties may help reduce the risks of nuclear war in some circumstances, they did nothing to stop the development and deployment of ever more destabilizing nuclear weapons by both sides.

Substantial efforts were made over four decades to end the testing of nuclear weapons, to control the addition of new offensive nuclear weapons, and to stop an arms race in defensive weapons. By any objective measure, the first two efforts failed, and the success of the Anti-Ballistic Missile (ABM) Treaty which bans all but one missile defense system is now being eroded as the U.S. and the Soviet Union are exploring technologies to shoot down ballistic missiles in flight, and the U.S. has announced its intent to make a decision by 1993 whether to deploy a Star Wars defensive system which would violate the ABM Treaty.

With the arrival of Mikhail Gorbachev on the international scene, we have the best opportunity since nuclear weapons were invented to constrain future destabilizing weapons developments and to slow if not stop the proliferation of nuclear weapons to other countries. Unfortunately, the Bush administration is not pursuing these opportunities with vigor. Indeed, it is impeding progress by refusing even to discuss any restrictions on nuclear weapon testing and by refusing to negotiate with the Soviets to prevent the development of anti-satellite (ASAT) weapons or to prevent an arms race in outer space, the last weapons-free environment.

## The Comprehensive Test Ban

Ending all nuclear testing was the goal of every President from Eisenhower to Carter. A comprehensive test ban (CTB) would. not remove any weapons. But a CTB would prevent the superpowers from developing the next generation of nuclear weapons, which, as we discussed in Chapter 5, would increase the risks of nuclear war in some future conflict. In addition, a CTB would help to prevent other, less stable nations from acquiring nuclear weapons. Nations might build nuclear weapons and threaten to use them without any testing, but they would not have much confidence in weapons that had never been fired. Since the threat of nuclear war is growing primarily through nuclear proliferation, a CTB could be the most important step in reducing the risks of a nuclear Armageddon.

The Soviets first proposed ending all nuclear tests at a UN meeting in May of 1955, as part of a general package to reduce conventional forces and to eliminate all nuclear weapons. Progress on a CTB was constrained by linkage to other arms reductions and the Soviet insistence that no on-site inspections would be required to verify a test ban. In June of 1957 the Soviets offered to place control posts manned by international inspectors on their territory. In March 1958 the Soviet Union declared a unilateral moratorium on nuclear testing, and invited the other nuclear powers to cease their tests. The U.S. and Great Britain refused to stop initially, but all three nations ended testing for three years until the Soviets started testing again in August of 1961. The U.S. resumed two weeks later.

Finally, on June 10, 1963, President Kennedy announced a unilateral U.S. moratorium on further testing of nuclear weapons in the atmosphere, after the U.S. had exploded a record 96 nuclear weapons the year before. On July 2, 1963, Premier Khrushchev agreed to end all atmospheric tests, and a Limited Test Ban Treaty (LTBT) was signed on August 5, 1963, ratified by the Senate 80 to 19 on September 24, and signed by President Kennedy on October 7, just one month before he was assassinated.

The LTBT prohibits nuclear explosions in the atmosphere, under water or in outer space. It did not, however, prevent the continuation of underground nuclear testing. Both superpowers continue to this day to explode nuclear weapons in tunnels or deep wells. Since 1963, the U.S. has exploded about 625 nuclear weapons underground, while the Soviets have set off about 465 underground explosions. Furthermore, neither France nor China have signed the LTBT, although no nation has exploded a nuclear weapon in the atmosphere since the last Chinese atmospheric test on October 16, 1980.[1] In effect, the LTBT was an environmental treaty: it eliminated the radioactive fallout from atmospheric testing that was contaminating milk with radioactive Strontium-90. The LTBT did not stop the arms race.

The superpowers and Great Britain agreed in the preamble to the LTBT to work for a comprehensive test ban (CTB) "to achieve the discontinuance of all test explosions of nuclear weapons for all time," stating that they were "determined to continue negotiations to this end."[2]

President Reagan was the first President in almost 30 years to refuse to negotiate limits to nuclear testing. By the time Mikhail Gorbachev came to power, the Reagan administration had launched one of the largest peacetime military buildups in history. This buildup included developing a new generation of nuclear war-fighting weapons along with the third generation of nuclear weapons as a key element of the Star Wars defensive dream. Underground nuclear explosions were essential to test these new war-fighting weapons.

The Reagan administration could not admit to the American public that it favored developing new nuclear war-fighting weapons, so several excuses were fabricated to explain their refusal even to negotiate with the Soviets on nuclear testing. First they said that a CTB could not be verified. When scientific evidence proved otherwise, the administration said that testing was needed to prove the reliability of existing weapons, even though very few stockpile reliability tests have been conducted in the past. When public pressure forced them to continue some negotiations, they threw up a smoke screen over the ability to monitor compliance with a decade-old pair of unratified treaties that set a limit of 150 kilotons on underground explosions. These diversions effectively stalled all progress on a CTB.

## TEST BAN VERIFICATION

Most scientists agree that a CTB can be effectively verified by a combination of seismic detectors, the same instruments used to record earthquakes around the world, and other intelligence sources. Any

---

[1]*Bulletin of the Atomic Scientists*, October 1989, p. 48.
[2]*Arms Control and Disarmament Agreements*, Washington, D.C.: The United States Arms Control and Disarmament Agency, 1980, p. 41.

nuclear explosion sends shock waves through and along the surface of the earth. These acoustical waves can be detected by seismic stations, and the location of the event can be pinpointed by triangulation from several seismic receivers. There will always be some uncertainty about very low-yield nuclear explosions. Very weak explosions, say less than one kiloton, can be confused with an earthquake or even a very large chemical explosion, such as those used in construction or mining. In a cooperative regime, however, large chemical explosions could be announced in advance, and their seismic signals ignored.

Earthquakes can be distinguished from nuclear explosions to some degree. Their characteristics are different. Nuclear explosions tend to produce proportionately more high frequency signals than earthquakes. Nuclear explosions produce more waves that travel through the earth, while earthquakes create more surface waves. Research is continuing to improve our ability to distinguish nuclear seismic patterns from earthquake signals.

Remote seismic detection capabilities are excellent for most nuclear explosions. An array of seismic detectors in Norway was able to clearly monitor a 0.5 kt Soviet explosion at a distant of 3,800 kilometers in 1987. This particular explosion, which was 25 times weaker than the Hiroshima bomb, occurred about 70 seconds after an earthquake in the Soviet Aleutians. This earthquake completely masked the nuclear explosion in the 1.2 to 3.2 hertz frequency channel, but was clearly detected in the higher frequency 3.2 to 5.2 hertz band.[3]

A nation could partially muffle the shock waves from a nuclear explosion by digging a large cavity, or by exploding a nuclear weapon in a large underground cavern. This "decoupling" could in theory make a 100 kiloton explosion produce external seismic signals equivalent to those from a 1-10 kiloton explosion. If the seismic detection network could detect only explosions above half a kiloton, then explosions under 50-KT in a very large cavern might not be reliably detected.

In any case, detection capability can be improved by placing arrays of seismic detector stations inside the Soviet Union. Several years ago, this possibility seemed remote, given the secretive nature of Soviet society. But a private U.S. environmental organization interested in implementing a CTB, the Natural Resources Defense Council, was allowed to place experimental seismic monitoring devices within 100 miles of the

---

[3]Harold A. Feiveson, Christopher E. Paine and Frank von Hippel, "A Low-Threshold Test Ban Is Feasible," *Science*, October 23, 1987, p. 456.

main Soviet nuclear testing range at Semipalatinsk in 1986. Large chemical explosives were set off to measure the geological characteristics of the region. Five new U.S. seismic stations were placed in the Soviet Union in 1989, and the Soviets will share data from five seismic station in the U.S., and they will set up their own stations at Albuquerque, New Mexico and Blacksburg, Virginia. Many more could be added if the Bush administration would resume CTB negotiations in good faith.

The advantages of in-country seismic monitors was demonstrated on September 3, 1987, when the NRDC recorded a 10-ton chemical explosion of TNT, set off to calibrate their seismic instruments. This explosion was 1,300 times weaker than the Hiroshima atomic bomb. By coincidence, a large magnitude 7.2 earthquake occurred in the Macquarrie Islands in the Western Pacific about 80 seconds before the chemical explosion. The signal from the nearby simulated nuclear explosion of 10 tons was twice as large as the signal from the real earthquake. [4]

The consensus in the scientific community is that explosions above 3 to 10 kilotons can be routinely monitored with 15 seismic stations inside the Soviet Union, even if the Soviets were to excavate huge cavities to decouple the explosion from the earth, or down to one kiloton without decoupling. [5] Since decoupling requires the excavation of large quantities of material, satellites could probably detect these activities. Future research could probably lower the detection threshold to fractions of a kiloton without decoupling, or to about a kiloton with decoupling. Since the atomic bomb trigger of most hydrogen bombs is in the 5-KT to 15-KT range, no nation could secretly test the components of a hydrogen bomb. [6]

Seismic detector arrays alone might not catch a rogue nation that set off a few very small nuclear explosions underground. But other intelligence sources might pick up such an infraction. Nuclear weapon development and production require unique materials, skilled people, special diagnostic instruments and earth drilling equipment. Over time, chances are good that these activities would be detected. In any case, a few clandestine explosions below one kiloton would not have

---

[4]"Nuclear Glasnost," *The Amicus Journal*, Fall 1987, p. 14.
[5]W. J. Hannon, "Seismic Verification of a Comprehensive Test Ban," *Science*, January 18, 1985, p. 256.
[6]*Seismic Verification of Nuclear Testing Treaties*, Congress of the United States, Office of Technology Assessment, May 1988.

much military significance, as long as we maintained a minimum deterrent capability.

As these realities of seismic detection capability became known, the Reagan administration shifted tactics. They implied that seismic detection was not as accurate as another U.S. technique called CORRTEX. Richard Perle, Assistant Secretary of Defense, testified in 1985 that there was "substantial evidence that the Soviets are violating" the 150-kiloton limit specified by the 1974 Threshold Test Ban Treaty.[7] (The U.S. Senate has never ratified this treaty or a companion 1976 Peaceful Nuclear Explosions Treaty that also sets a 150-KT ceiling.) They claimed that seismic monitoring was not accurate enough to determine conclusively that the Soviets had cheated. Therefore we had to make the Soviets accept our CORRTEX approach.

CORRTEX is an intrusive on-site calibration device. A special cable in inserted into a shaft bored parallel to the hole containing the nuclear explosive. As the weapon explodes, the shock wave traveling through the earth crushes the nearby CORRTEX cable. By measuring rate of collapse of this cable with short electrical pulses, scientists can infer the magnitude of the explosion. The Reagan administration implied that CORRTEX was better than seismic detection, and, until the Soviets accepted this superior technique, we could not ratify the 1974 and 1976 treaties, and we could not proceed with the more important task of ending all nuclear explosions.

Like many of the Reagan administration's arms control postures, the CORRTEX proposition was a farce. CORRTEX is a good calibration technique, but it has no remote monitoring capability and cannot replace seismic detection. A few CORRTEX measurements are helpful to calibrate seismic measurements. But it does not work at all for low-yield explosions, requiring at least a 50-KT explosion and preferably 75-KT for high accuracy. And CORRTEX has no capability to detect clandestine explosions. It has to be pre-positioned within 20 or 30 feet of the nuclear explosive to work. If the Soviets ever accepted our CORRTEX as the sole verification approach, we would have no capability to detect Soviet cheating. We have to rely on remote seismic detectors. Of course, the Reagan administration had no intention of negotiating limits on testing, so this stalling technique carried no risk.

The Reagan administration was so successful overselling the virtues

---

[7]John Horgan, "Underground Nuclear Weapons Testing," *IEEE Spectrum*, April 1986, p. 42.

of CORRTEX that *Time* ran a story which claimed that CORRTEX "would allow the U.S. to measure nuclear blasts that are too small to be clearly identified from seismic data alone,"[8] when in fact it cannot be used to measure small yields at all.

One of the Reagan conservatives in the Pentagon, Frank Gaffney, in a more candid moment, openly admitted that CORRTEX was a stalling technique to delay any possibility of a CTB. He wrote:

> The inherent limitations of CORRTEX are regarded as virtues by those in the U.S. government who hope to slow the rush toward additional constraints on—or the complete banning of—nuclear testing. The thinking goes like this: The more time is wasted on discussions and experimentation of monitoring techniques irrelevant to the verification of an environment in which there are no legal tests, the easier it will be to stave off demands for the more constraining comprehensive test ban.[9]

In effect, our tax dollars were used to conduct joint tests with the Soviet Union to waste time on discussions, to delay any chance of a CTB, while the President piously stated that we absolutely needed these CORRTEX tests to verify old treaties.

With regard to Soviet compliance with the 150-KT limit on underground testing, the Congressional Office of Technology Assessment pointed out that there is some uncertainty in all scientific measurements, but

> all of the estimates of Soviet tests are within the 90 percent confidence level that one would expect if the yields were 150-KT or less. Extensive statistical studies have examined the distribution of estimated yields of explosions at Soviet test sites. These studies have concluded that the Soviets are observing a yield limit. The best estimate of that yield limit is that it is consistent with compliance with the 150-KT limit of the Threshold Test Ban Treaty.[10]

---

[8]"When in Doubt, Check It Out," *Time*, January 11, 1988, p. 64.
[9]Frank Gaffney, Jr., "Test Ban Would Be a Real Tremor to U.S. Security," *Defense News*, September 5, 1989, p. 35.
[10]Ibid, OTA, p. 126.

In other words, as best they can tell, the Soviets have not violated the Treaty as the Reagan administration charged.

Ironically, the U.S. inadvertently violated the 150-KT limit on August 18, 1988 with Soviet inspectors at the Nevada test site for the first time. The U.S. set off what was supposed to have been a 145-KT explosion to demonstrate the CORRTEX technique to the Soviets. Two CORRTEX sensors registered 163 and 155 kilotons, slightly above the treaty limit. Nonetheless, the U.S. ambassador on nuclear testing, Paul Robinson, dismissed this embarrassing incident with the statement that "the test yield was clearly below the [treaty] threshold, and neither we nor the Soviets have a problem with that."[11]

## Nuclear Weapons Reliability

When previous arguments against a CTB lost credibility, the Reagan tune changed to reliability. Deterrence requires reliable weapons, and therefore we must continue exploding nuclear weapons underground at the Nevada test site, they said, as long as we rely on nuclear deterrence for our national security. This has a reasonable ring, as did most of the PR-conscious Reagan pronouncements. But the reliability argument has several flaws.

First, historically, the United States has not tested weapons frequently once they have been placed in the stockpile. It has been estimated that fewer than one shot out of 15 to 20 per year was to check the reliability of our existing nuclear weapons. (Most nuclear explosions are for developing new weapons or for testing the effects of explosions on other electronic devices.) Since the U.S. has about 25 different types of nuclear weapons in the active inventory, presumably each weapon type could only be tested once every 30 years. Firing one or two nuclear warheads of a given type is not adequate for determining reliability. Even if a given weapon was unreliable, it might not be detected with just one or two test explosions.

Second, most defects in weapons can be determined without an actual nuclear explosion. If metal parts or electronic components of the triggering circuits are rusting or deteriorating due to radiation or heat, for example, then this can be monitored by removing weapons from the stockpile and disassembling them. The triggering circuits can be

---

[11]R. Jeffrey Smith, "Data from Atom Blast Adds to Treaty Verification Questions," *Washington Post*, September 8, 1988, p. 3.

checked, and the conventional high explosive can even be detonated with the nuclear material, plutonium or uranium, removed or substituted by dummy components.

Test ban opponents often cite 14 nuclear explosions since 1958 where, they say, testing revealed defects in weapons that could not have been discovered by other means, proving the need for more testing. James McNally, a scientist from the Los Alamos National Laboratory, wrote that "The only really strong case we have" was testing to validate changes made to the Sergeant missile warhead. According to McNally, "we are on thin ground on some of the examples we cite."[12] Ray Kidder, a longtime nuclear weapons scientist from the Lawrence Livermore National Laboratory, concluded:

> A detailed review of the problems encountered with the 14 weapon designs since 1958 that have been frequently and prominently cited as evidence that an LTTB (Low Threshold Test Ban) or a CTB would preclude the possibility of maintaining a reliable stockpile, shows that this experience has little if any relevance to the question of maintaining the reliability of the stockpile of nuclear weapons that exists in 1987.[13]

Dr. Kidder concludes that "the nuclear test record of the past decade, together with properties intrinsic to nuclear weapons themselves, leaves no doubt" that current nuclear weapons are reliable. He goes on to say that existing nuclear weapons designs could be manufactured in the future without the need for nuclear test explosions above one kiloton, "that the nuclear weapons in the present U.S. stockpile are sufficiently robust to allow reliable replication."

Some government officials also claim that maintaining the nuclear weapons needed for deterrence requires an active test program to keep scientists at the two government nuclear weapons laboratories ... white-collar welfare! If we had a CTB, the scientists would become bored and leave. Within a decade, we could not remanufacture nuclear weapons using the old designs without the guidance of the weapons designers. (Some add that the Soviet Union could force their scientists to stay on, thereby creating a weapons designer gap in favor of the Soviet Union.)

---

[12]David C. Morrison, "Test on Testing," *National Journal*, March 4, 1989, p. 557.
[13]R. E. Kidder, *Maintaining the U.S. Stockpile of Nuclear Weapons During a Low-threshold or Comprehensive Test Ban*, Lawrence Livermore National Laboratory, Report No. UCRL-53820, October 1987, p. 11.

Dr. Kidder concludes that if we began with a low threshold test ban at one kiloton, for example, that "there would be time to make necessary changes to reduce the present reliance of the production complex upon the advice and counsel of weapons lab personnel."[14] According to Kidder we could then safely move to a total ban on nuclear testing: "It should also eventually be possible to maintain the reliability of the stockpile within the limits of a CTB."

But suppose Dr. Kidder is wrong. Suppose we agreed with the Soviets to a CTB and the lack of testing did result in some loss of reliability. Presumably the Soviets would lose confidence in their nuclear arsenal too. Nuclear weaponeers may argue that ours are more complex and therefore more susceptible to degradation, but then we should be considering more robust designs. (Indeed the Congress did direct the Department of Energy to conduct a study of weapons reliability and to prepare for a CTB or at least limits on testing.)

Eventually, if both sides began to lose confidence in their nuclear arsenals, this would be a disadvantage to the side contemplating a first strike. That is, the nuclear aggressor would need high confidence that most of his weapons would work. The side that renounced first strike intentions, however, and relied only on retaliation, would not have to seek such perfection. If only half our weapons worked in retaliation, this would still be devastating to the opponent, and would still deter him.

This may seem counterintuitive: how could unreliable weapons improve stability? Basically, attempting a first strike is a much more difficult task than retaliating, requiring many more weapons and excellent control and timing. To minimize damage to the homeland, the first strike aggressor should fire hundreds of missiles with thousands of warheads in a coordinated attack, so that the warheads arrive on their targets more or less simultaneously. Timing does not matter for the retaliator. The fear that a few dozen nuclear weapons would eventually reach the aggressor nation would be enough to deter.

As an analogy, suppose you were competing in a sporting event where you were required to walk across the street, but your opponent had to walk ten miles. Under these circumstances, it would be to your advantage if both competitors had to place a dozen tacks in their shoes. You could easily manage to cross the street with tack-filled shoes, but your opponent would be at a large disadvantage walking ten miles under these conditions. In this sense, a loss of reliability would be to the

---

[14]Ibid, p. 1.

relative disadvantage of the attacker attempting a nuclear first strike, since this is a more difficult task.

Furthermore, the aggressor would not *know* if the opponent's nuclear weapons would work or not. The aggressor would have to assume that most of the opponent's weapons would work in retaliation as advertised. He could not gamble his nation's survival on the assumption that the adversary's retaliatory weapons might have become unreliable.

Any nation contemplating a first strike, however, would know much more about its own weapons. If non-nuclear inspections had shown degradation, for example, then an aggressor would have less confidence in carrying out a first strike. Thus **a loss of reliability improves stability** by creating uncertainty in the mind of any potential nuclear aggressor.

Ironically, one of the last remaining rationales for a leaky Star Wars defense is that it "would create uncertainty in the minds of the Soviet attack planners." This uncertainty is touted as a major advantage of a partial defense, acknowledging that a nation bent on a first strike must have reliable weapons. Well, a CTB could create uncertainty in the minds of Soviet attack planners without any technological break-throughs, without spending hundreds of billions of dollars, and without risking grave crisis instability inherent in SDI. And this uncertainty would improve with age like a good wine, if we accept the administration's argument that a CTB would lead to unreliable weapons.

In short, a first strike requires higher reliability than retaliation. If deterrence is our only goal, we shouldn't fear a CTB. We should enthusiastically embrace it. But President Reagan and now President Bush have stalled negotiations on a CTB.

Ironically, just as President Reagan was the first to renounce negotiations for a CTB, President Gorbachev was the first Soviet leader in several decades to enthusiastically endorse the CTB in word and deed. On August 6, 1985, he unilaterally stopped all nuclear testing, inviting Reagan to join the moratorium. Gorbachev extended his test moratorium for 18 months, despite continued U.S. testing.

In another post-Cold War turnaround, the Soviet Union announced in early 1990 that they had cancelled 11 of 18 planned nuclear test explosions and would end all testing at their main facility at Semi-palatinsk by 1993, in response to citizen environmental protests. Additional nuclear tests would be conducted at their remote Novaya Zemlya island within the Arctic Circle. Meanwhile, U.S. citizens protesting at the Nevada test site are virtually ignored by our government.

Unfortunately, the Bush administration has shown even less enthusiasm for a nuclear test ban than the Reagan team. President Reagan promised to begin negotiations with the Soviets regarding further testing limits after the Threshold Test Ban Treaty was ratified. President Bush backed off from this pledge to Congress in the spring of 1990. Spurgeon Keeny, the President of the Arms Control Association, blasted this decision:

> At this time of great promise for arms control, it is indeed unfortunate that the Bush administration has reneged on President Reagan's commitment to pursue negotiations for further limits on nuclear testing immediately after ratification of the Threshold Test Ban Treaty (TTBT). This gratuitous backsliding seriously undercuts U.S. nuclear nonproliferation policy and diminishes U.S. credibility as a negotiating partner.[15]

President Bush made great fanfare over the signing of a verification protocol to the TTBT at the 1990 superpower summit. Both superpowers have observed the 150-KT limit of this treaty for 16 years, so signing a verification protocol and getting final Senate ratification has little practical significance. The real litmus test is whether President Bush will reverse his decision not to negotiate further limits to nuclear testing.

### NUCLEAR WEAPONS ARMS CONTROL

Early attempts to curb nuclear weapons involved major sweeping disarmament proposals such as the U.S. Baruch plan in 1946 to turn control of nuclear weapons over to an international agency. Beginning in 1964, however, the U.S. began a more pragmatic approach, proposing that the two superpowers should "explore a verified *freeze* of the number and characteristics of their strategic nuclear offensive and defensive vehicles."[16] Sixteen years later, when citizen activists proposed such a freeze on all weapons, they were derided as naive and the Freeze was characterized as "unilateral disarmament" by the Reagan administration. The Soviets refused to discuss a freeze on delivery vehicles in

---

[15]Spurgeon M. Keeny, Jr., "Nuclear Backsliding," *Arms Control Today*, February 1990, p. 2.
[16]Ibid., ACDA, p. 132.

1964, and both sides went ahead adding offensive nuclear weapons while preparing to deploy ground-based missile defenses.

Negotiations on nuclear weapons were planned in 1968, but the Soviet invasion of Czechoslovakia intervened. President Nixon initiated the Strategic Arms Limitation Talks (SALT I) on November 17, 1969. Over two years later, the SALT I treaty was signed. The treaty included the ABM Treaty, a permanent ban on all except two (later changed to one) ground-based rocket interceptor fleet, and an interim agreement on offensive weapons. Negotiators had great difficulty crafting an arms control agreement on offensive forces, so the interim restrictions on offensive weapons were binding for only five years, with the assumption that a more comprehensive SALT II treaty would follow.

The SALT I interim agreement was basically a freeze on missile launchers either in the field or under construction at the time. While it did not remove any nuclear weapons, it did put a cap on one aspect of the arms race. SALT I did not cover warheads or bombers. The United States was not prevented from adding more warheads to existing missiles (MIRVing), nor from adding bombs or air-launched cruise missiles (ALCMs) to bombers. Thus the number of deployed nuclear warheads increased dramatically for the U.S. and later for the Soviet Union as both sides added MIRV'd warheads during the 1970s. SALT I did not stop the arms race. It merely set an upper limit on the number of ballistic missile launchers.

We missed a major opportunity to stop the deployment of more nuclear warheads in 1972 by not banning MIRV'd missiles. At the time, we had a technological lead over the Soviets, and did not want to bargain this lead away. We disdained the arms control approach, and several years later the Soviets added MIRV'd warheads which now threaten our missiles. By December, 1974, Henry Kissinger expressed some regret over not including MIRVs in the SALT treaty: "I would say in retrospect that I wish I had thought through the implications of a MIRV'd world more thoughtfully in 1969 and 1970 than I did."[17]

Even the meager SALT I limitations expired in 1977 before the SALT II negotiations could be completed. SALT II was signed on June 18, 1979, but the Soviet invasion of Afghanistan in December of 1979 eliminated any chance of the Senate ratifying this controversial treaty. In reality, SALT II was quite modest. Like SALT I, it did not directly limit nuclear warheads. A ceiling of 2,400 (later reduced to 2,250)

---

[17]Ibid., Kull, p. 242.

launchers (ICBMs, SLBMs, bombers and air-to-surface ballistic missiles) was established, but with "sub-ceilings" on various missiles carrying MIRV'd warheads. Both sides agreed to a limit of 1,320 MIRV'd missiles and bombers carrying air-launched cruise missiles (ALCMs). Thus SALT II attempted to indirectly limit the total number of warheads. The ceilings were so high, however, that only the Soviets would have had to remove a few hundred nuclear warheads to stay in compliance.

The Reagan administration did negotiate one landmark treaty, the Intermediate range Nuclear Forces (INF) treaty of 1988. This treaty banned an entire class of weapons with ranges between 300 and 3,400 miles, removing Soviet SS-20 and American Pershing-II and ground-launched cruise missiles (GLCM) from the European theatre. Unfortunately, this range interval included less than 4 percent of all nuclear weapons. Both sides could easily cover the intended targets for these missiles by retargeting other weapons. The U.S., for example, asked Great Britain to permit nuclear-capable B-52s and F-15E aircraft to be based on their airfields to help attack targets in central Europe formerly covered by INF weapons.

## VERIFICATION

The failure of past arms control efforts was due in part to controversies over Soviet treaty compliance. Hard-liners claim that the Soviets have violated every treaty they ever signed. They fear that the Soviets will cheat on future treaties unless we have excellent, bordering on perfect, verification capability. In effect, they say we must be able to detect any degree of Soviet violation, even if inadvertent or technical in nature.

In our judgment, this is too severe. With a far-flung nuclear weapons establishment, involving tens of thousands of people and tens of thousands of weapons, accounting errors or misinterpretations of technical details are possible without any intent on the part of national leadership to violate the main provisions of a treaty. Some provisions of these treaties are intentionally crafted with vague language so that one or both sides will be able exploit loopholes to develop new weapons. In fact, most alleged "violations" have been relatively minor, and in no case has the Soviet Union violated the main numerical provisions imposed by past treaties.

For example, the Soviets were accused of violating the Limited Test

Ban Treaty by venting radioactive material beyond its national borders, which violates one of the LTBT provisions. Both superpowers have accidentally vented radioactive gases from some of their underground nuclear tests. Technically, some radioactive particles probably were carried outside their borders, but neither nation has exploded nuclear weapons in the atmosphere, the primary objective of the LTBT. As President Bush admitted in his 1990 message to Congress on arms control compliance, Soviet venting of radioactive material "does not pose calculable health, safety or environmental risks, and the infractions have no apparent military significance."[18] Nonetheless, this accidental venting is listed as a treaty "violation."

The Soviets were accused of exceeding the 150 kiloton limit of the (unratified) Threshold Test Ban and Peaceful Nuclear Explosion (PNE) treaties. As noted earlier, the Office of Technology Assessment stated that, within measurement error, it appears that the Soviets have not exceeded the 150-KT limit. Furthermore, the TTBT specifically allows for a few accidental excursions beyond the 150-KT limit, knowing that nuclear bomb yields are sometimes higher than anticipated. So, technically, even if the Soviets did exceed 150-KT once or twice, it would not have been a violation.

The Soviets were accused of violating a provision of the SALT II treaty that places some limits on the radio signals or "telemetry" used during missile flight tests. The treaty vaguely limits the degree of "encryption" or encoding of radio signals used to report back missile flight characteristics, so that the other side can monitor the flight tests. Actually, the SALT II treaty *permits* encryption:

> Each Party *is free* to use various methods of transmitting tele-metric information during testing, *including its encryption*, except that . . . neither Party shall engage in deliberate denial of telemetric information, such as through the use of telemetry encryption, whenever such denial impedes verification of compliance with the provisions of the Treaty.[19]

Who determines if encryption is "deliberate," or whether that encryption "impedes verification"? Clearly this provision leaves much

---

[18]George Bush, *Report to Congress on Soviet Noncompliance with Arms Control Agreements*, February 23, 1990.
[19]*Arms Control and Disarmament Agreements*, Washington, D.C., The United States Arms Control and Disarmament Agency, August 1980, p. 227.

room for creative interpretation. Hardliners consistently accused the Soviets of using too much encryption. However, the Soviets did not exceed the numerical limits of the SALT II treaty, even though the U.S. Senate never did ratify the treaty.

In fact, it was the United States that violated the numerical limits on SALT II in December of 1986. Both sides had agreed to abide by the numerical limits, including the provision that no more than 1,320 multiple warhead systems including bombers equipped with ALCMs would be deployed. President Reagan intentionally violated this provision by permitting the 131st B-52 bomber equipped with cruise missiles to enter service without retiring other MIRV'd missiles or bombers. President Reagan took this action against the advice of Congress (57 Senators wrote to him on December 15, 1986, asking that he stay in compliance with SALT II as long as the Soviets remained in compliance), many ex-Secretaries of Defense, Brent Scowcroft, the current National Security Advisor, and even the Commander of the Strategic Air Command, General Bennie Davis, who testified on March 6, 1985 that "I have made that assessment privately today that we should continue to abide by the SALT II limitations."[20] They believed that the Soviets were in a much better position to expand nuclear weapons, and that the SALT II limits at least provided an upper cap on the arms race.

The Soviets did clearly violate one provision of the ABM Treaty, which forbids large phased array radars at sites away from a nation's borders. The intent of this provision was to prevent either side from building large radars as part of a nationwide ballistic missile defense system. The Soviets did begin to build such a radar near Krasnoyarsk, far from their border, claiming that it was to be used for tracking satellites and not for ballistic missile defense. Although Gorbachev stopped construction and has begun to dismantle the radar buildings, this is a technical violation. Even in this case, however, the Krasnoyarsk radar is not really suitable for an effective ballistic missile battle management radar, and would not have led to a nationwide ballistic missile defense system. The proper U.S. response was to protest this infraction and demand its destruction to preserve the ABM Treaty. We should not use this violation as an excuse to block future arms control limitations that are in our best interests. Furthermore, the U.S. has come close to violating this same provision of the ABM Treaty by

---

[20]General Bennie Davis before the Strategic and Theater Nuclear Forces Subcommittee of the Senate Armed Services Committee, March 6, 1985.

building new phased array radars at Thule, Greenland and near Fylingdales Moors in England. We claim that these new radars are modifications of two existing radars, as permitted by the ABM Treaty, but the new Fylingdales radar is eight miles from the old system, stretching the credibility of the U.S. claim.

Rather than insisting on perfect verification to monitor all activities in the Soviet Union, a more appropriate measure would be to insist on adequate verification. That is, we should have the capability to detect any Soviet violations that are militarily significant. And we should be able to detect those violations in time to take corrective action before our national security would be threatened. In this sense, the Krasnoyarsk radar episode demonstrated that we do have adequate monitoring capability: we discovered the radar several years before construction would have been completed, and many years before the Soviets could have constructed anything approaching a nationwide ballistic missile defense system.

Today, we have adequate verification capability, and it is getting better. The United States has the capability to monitor activities inside the Soviet Union using spy satellites, or "national technical means" (NTM) of verification in nukespeak. Satellites in geosynchronous orbit high over the Soviet Union monitor all Soviet missile launches with infrared eyes.

We have visible and infrared cameras in low earth orbit to photograph any part of the Soviet Union. These spies in the sky have resolutions down to four to six inches. That is, any object bigger than four to six inches can be photographed from space. Since missiles are typically many feet in diameter, a spy satellite could spot any new missile silo, assuming we knew the general area to search and assuming clear weather during some part of the construction phase. We can detect and count tanks, ships, planes, fuel depots and even individual troops on maneuver.

Infrared imaging systems are particularly useful at night, since they measure the heat radiated from buildings and vehicles. Since all military activity including training exercises involves the generation of heat, infrared sensors can often spot activities better than visible cameras. For example, infrared sensors can determine whether a factory building is heated, permitting verification that missile plants or nuclear reactors have been shut down. Infrared mappers can even reveal events that happened hours before the satellite passes overhead. For example, airplanes parked on a sunny runway create a cold area on the pavement.

Hours after they take off, infrared detectors can sense and count how many planes were parked there earlier.

Other detection systems include electronic intelligence (ELINT) satellites that listen in on Soviet communications and radar transmissions, and other ELINT equipment on ships, planes and ground listening posts that surround the Soviet Union. During a Soviet test missile firing, U.S. infrared satellites first detect the launch and alert other radar sensors around the world. Ground-based radars in Turkey and in China monitor the missile flight, typically from west to east, ending in the Kamchatka area near Japan, or in the Pacific Ocean. Shipboard radars such as the Cobra Judy track the missile (dummy) warhead as it nears splash down in the Pacific, and ground-based radars in Alaska such as the Cobra Dane at Shemya Air Force Base also track and record the characteristics of Soviet missile warheads. They can detect when and how many MIRV'd warheads are released. They can estimate missile accuracy and determine if the Soviets develop decoys to fool any attempt by the U.S. to deploy Star Wars defensive systems.

The original spy satellites required clear, daylight weather to take actual photographs which were later sent back into the atmosphere for pick-up by aircraft in the Pacific. (The capsule containing the photographs released a parachute, and airplanes with long hooks grabbed the parachute strings and reeled in the film capsule.) Later versions use electronic sensors, much like a video camera, so that the electronic images can be sent back to ground stations quickly. The U.S. White Cloud ocean surveillance system has one central satellite plus three subsatellites to triangulate ship positions. The latest White Cloud constellation reportedly uses infrared detection.

The most recent U.S. Lacrosse spy satellites carry synthetic aperture radars. Radar waves emitted by the satellite are reflected off objects in the Soviet Union during all weather conditions, day or night. The reflected radar waves are recorded as the satellite flies overhead, building up a synthetic image over long distances, producing much better resolution than an ordinary radar. While actual results are classified, it is believed that these Lacrosse radar satellites can detect objects as small as a foot or two in diameter, which would include most weapons of military value.

Finally, the U.S. undoubtedly relies on covert intelligence sources both in the Soviet Union or from defecting Soviet citizens. Any major weapons development includes complex operations including design, testing, building and deploying weapons in the field. The chances for spies, informants or nowadays even tourists reporting some of these activities are good.

Despite all of this technical and intelligence capability, there is no denying that a future Soviet government could probably hide some nuclear weapons indefinitely without detection. However, hidden weapons serve no useful purpose for deterrence if the enemy doesn't know about them, and hidden weapons cannot function reliably for an aggressor if they cannot be fired. Useful, reliable weapons such as missiles must be tested occasionally, if nothing else to train new launch control officers. The U.S. can detect any missile launch. This is the choke point. The Soviet Union (or any other nation) cannot periodically test hidden missiles, nor can they develop and test new missiles without our eyes in the sky seeing and measuring the characteristics of those launches.

### CURRENT ARMS CONTROL TREATY NEGOTIATIONS

The United States and the Soviet Union have concluded the basic ingredients of three new treaties: a treaty to ban all chemical weapons, the Conventional Armed Forces in Europe (CFE) treaty and the Strategic Arms Reduction Talks (START) treaty. These treaties may help to slow both conventional and nuclear arms races, but they fall short of what could have been accomplished to improve stability.

*Conventional Armed Forces in Europe (CFE).* The CFE proposal between the 23 NATO and Warsaw Pact nations now calls for reducing both Soviet and American troops to 195,000 in central Europe, with the U.S. allowed to maintain another 30,000 in other parts of Europe since we have been invited there by the host countries. About 80,000 U.S. troops will be withdrawn, while the Soviets will remove 405,000. Meanwhile Eastern European nations including Hungary and Czechoslovakia have asked all Soviet troops to leave, and any remaining Soviet forces in the former East Germany will soon become an anachronism. In a bizarre turn of events, the new German government has offered to pay the Soviet Union for some of the expenses of keeping Soviet troops in the old East Germany. There is some possibility that the 195,000 CFE ceiling may give a future Soviet leader a certain legitimacy for keeping troops in Europe that would otherwise be lacking.

Nonetheless, CFE is a landmark treaty, since it requires large asymmetric Soviet reductions in almost all categories of conventional weapons. For example, the Soviets will have to destroy 15 times more tanks (30,000 vs. 2,000 for NATO), 42 times more troop carriers (42,000 vs. 1,000), and 22 times more artillery pieces (27,000 vs. 1,200). The two sides are far apart on their definition of combat aircraft: by Warsaw Pact definitions, NATO would have to give up 1,600 aircraft to 400 for the Warsaw Pact, while NATO definitions of combat aircraft would include many more Soviet trainers, medium bombers and fighter interceptors, so that the Warsaw Pact would have to eliminate 8,000 aircraft to only 900 for NATO.[21]

The U.S. Air Force would probably give up 900 older aircraft such as the A-10, which would not strain their combat capability. In fact, retired Air Force General John W. Vogt, who commanded NATO air forces, said that "getting rid of it [the A-10] would be a plus," since the controversial A-10s are susceptible to anti-aircraft fire.[22] In other words, current U.S. conventional force reductions would not require much commitment to major cuts on the part of President Bush, but it has a major stabilizing influence by removing Soviet numerical superiority.

CFE will also set up very intrusive on-site inspections to verify that troops and weapons are indeed removed. These inspection procedures will permit NATO personnel to monitor Soviet troop and equipment movements, virtually eliminating any chance of a clandestine Soviet buildup as a precursor to a surprise attack. The U.S. will also monitor the destruction of thousands of Soviet weapons under CFE, a major advantage over the Soviets merely shipping these weapons back to the Soviet Union.

*Strategic Arms Reduction Talks (START)*. In some ways the START treaty is a disappointment, given what could have been accomplished with visionary leadership. Originally advertised as a 50 percent cut in nuclear weapons, U.S. nuclear weapons may be cut by as little as 10 percent. The 50 percent reduction affects only the Soviet ballistic missile warheads. The treaty limits nuclear warheads to 4,900 on all land-based or sea-based ballistic missiles. Since the U.S. has 7,762 warheads on missiles, we would have to cut about 37 percent in this category. The Soviets, with just over 10,000 warheads on ballistic missiles, would have to cut just over 50 percent. Worse yet, the START treaty does not stop the development and deployment of destabilizing new nuclear weapons.

[21]Jonathan Dean, "Conventional Talks: A Good First Round," *The Bulletin of the Atomic Scientists*, October, 1989, p. 26.
[22]R. Jeffrey Smith and George C. Wilson, "Hill wary of proposal to scrap military planes," *The Washington Post*, June 1, 1989, p. 33.

The START treaty sets a limit of 6,000 on all nuclear weapons mounted on missiles, bombers or cruise missiles. If one side chose to place the full 4,900 warheads on missiles as permitted by the treaty, then only 1,100 nuclear bombs would be allowed on other delivery vehicles. But the treaty undercounts all nuclear weapons on "slow-flyers": bombs carried on aircraft and cruise missiles. Since bombers are slow and can be recalled, they are considered more stabilizing. Under START, all bombers are counted as carrying one bomb, even though each of our B-1s may be loaded with up to 24 nuclear weapons. Similarly, B-52s with 20 air-launched cruise missiles (ALCM) may be counted as carrying only 10 missiles. There are no limits on the number of ALCMs produced or stockpiled, so that each side could build thousands of nuclear-armed cruise missiles and store them on bomber bases, ready to be loaded before a war. In this sense, the START treaty really sets ALCM limits only during peacetime. Cruise missiles with ranges less than 360 miles are not counted, and the U.S. has "grand-fathered" the long-range Tacit Rainbow cruise missile. The U.S. will be permitted to build 5,000 of these non-nuclear cruise missiles which can fly into the Soviet Union and search out and destroy radar stations by homing in on their radar signals. Distinguishing between these Tacit Rainbow and other cruise missiles could be an arms control verification nightmare.

Sea-launched cruise missiles (SLCM) are not counted at all under the main treaty, although the two sides agree in a side "gentleman's agreement" to deploy no more than 880 SLCMs. START does not include any verification provision to monitor these 880 missiles. Presumably the legislatures of the two nations will be responsible to make sure these limits are enforced through fiscal restraints.

The START treaty also excludes three submarines in port from the final tally, under the assumption that three subs may be undergoing overhaul. This alone eliminates 576 nuclear warheads from the U.S. official warhead count under START rules. Finally, the treaty does not attempt to count nuclear weapon "reserves." By some estimates, the U.S. has a small arsenal of one to two thousand uncounted nuclear weapons that are set aside to reload bombers and submarines after they return from firing their first round of nuclear weapons, and the Soviets may have an even larger stock of missile reloads.

The START treaty is therefore blind to several thousand U.S. warheads or bombs. The Soviets have fewer long-range bombers and therefore will benefit less from the liberal START counting rules, but they too will reduce less than 50 percent in total nuclear weapons. One possible post-START regime would require a nine percent U.S. reduction and a 37 percent Soviet reduction in nuclear warheads.[23] The START treaty is therefore a net gain for the United States, but does not live up to its billing as a 50 percent cut. In fact, *both the U.S. and the Soviet Union will have more strategic nuclear warheads after the START reductions than either had in 1980*, as illustrated in Figure 6-1.

That is, if the U.S. and the USSR had agreed to a nuclear weapons freeze in 1980 as advocated by 70 to 80 percent of the American public, then both sides would have fewer nuclear warheads today than after the START reductions are completed in several years. Worse yet, the additional warheads, particularly on the U.S. side, are destabilizing weapons like the MX and the D-5, far more likely to lead to nuclear war than our 1980 mix of nuclear weapons.

FIGURE 6-1. STRATEGIC NUCLEAR WEAPONS: START vs. NUCLEAR WEAPONS FREEZE

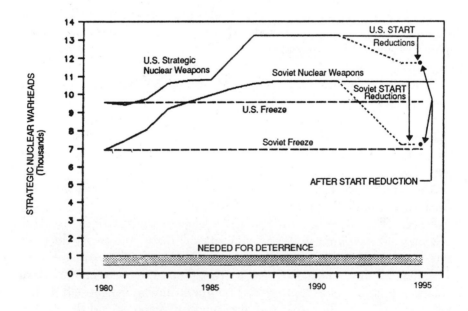

---

[23]R. Jeffrey Smith, "Soviets Press U.S. for Deeper Reductions in Strategic Weapons," *Washington Post*, February 25, 1990, p. A14.

In this sense START is no different than previous SALT treaties. The U.S. does not have to give up any planned additions to our nuclear arsenal. Paul Wolfowitz, Under Secretary of Defense for Policy, testified that:

It is important to be aware that, unlike the INF Treaty, START will not force us to destroy new systems that we are deploying under our modernization program. START allows for replacement of aging systems. None of the new systems requested in the President's budget would be scrapped.[24]

Even Richard Perle, the hardliner known for his opposition to previous arms control treaties, admitted that START is the product of the Cold War mentality, and that we should be making much deeper cuts in nuclear weapons: "Literally, if you did nothing else than divided by two, you'd be better off."[25] Paul Nitze, one of our most senior arms control advisers, added that "we haven't gone far enough" with the START treaty: "Today, one really ought to aspire to do much better."[26]

START also ignores two important issues that could unravel the treaty: sea-launched cruise missiles (SLCM) and Star Wars. The Soviets wanted to ban all SLCMs, but offered to ban only nuclear armed SLCMs when the U.S. military insisted that they maintain conventionally armed SLCMs. However, verifying the difference between conventional and nuclear SLCMs would require either intrusive ship board inspections, clever tagging of SLCMs at the factory, or a large degree of trust. Both sides decided to leave the SLCM issue for START II, including only a side statement that both sides would agree to deploy no more than 880 SLCMs.

These 880 SLCMs would alone constitute a full retaliatory nuclear weapons force. Each nuclear warhead for the U.S. SLCM, the Tomahawk Land Attack Missile-Nuclear (TLAM-N), has a yield of 170 kilotons, 10 times more powerful than the Hiroshima bomb. A force of 880 TLAM-Ns would have an equivalent firepower of 270 megatons, far more than the 50 megatons considered by some as adequate for

[24]Paul Wolfowitz, testimony before the U.S. Senate Defense Appropriations Subcommittee, May 3, 1990.

[25]Frank Starr, "Rethink Arms Control from the Ground Up, Former Reagan Official Advises," *Baltimore Sun*, March 13, 1990, p. 8.

[26]R. Jeffrey Smith, "Treaty Would Cut Few Warheads," *Washington Post*, April 3, 1990, p. 1.

deterrence, and equivalent to over 4,000 Hiroshima bombs. The START treaty has no legally binding restrictions on this massive force, and no provisions to verify compliance with the "gentleman's agreement" not to deploy more than 880 SLCMs.

By ignoring Star Wars, however, START may fall apart in a few years if the Bush administration decides to test a space-based missile defense system. The Soviets originally stated very clearly that they would not sign a START agreement unless the U.S. reaffirmed its commitment to the ABM treaty and vowed not to deploy Star Wars. The Soviets later backed off, agreeing to sign a treaty without assurances about ballistic missile defense, but indicated that they would abrogate any START treaty if we began to test a Star Wars weapons system. The chief Soviet arms control negotiator, Yuri Nazarkin, said that they would probably consider any space-based test of Star Wars as a violation of the ABM Treaty, and "if the ABM Treaty is violated, we will probably use our right of withdrawal" from START.[27]

We would do the same if the Soviets ever began testing a partial space-based defense. By ignoring the Star Wars threat, START is a temporary treaty, designed primarily to boost the political fortunes of Presidents Bush and Gorbachev. Because it would be temporary, Senator Sam Nunn doubts that the Senate would ratify any treaty if the Star Wars issue has not been resolved:

> If a START agreement is presented to us and we do not know what the Soviets will consider a breach of the ABM Treaty . . . it would be very hard to get it ratified.[28]

In one sense, we have no long-range plan to accompany START. What does it accomplish? Would we have a more stable balance after START? As Brent Scowcroft put it, before he became National Security Advisor to President Bush, "Where are we going?" (with INF and START). "They don't seem to lead anywhere that I find comfortable . . . What are we trying to do?"[29] Since START does not remove destabiliz-

---

[27]Randall Palmer, "Soviets Say SDI Test Could Endanger Pact," *Washington Times*, March 1, 1990, p. 10.
[28]Sara Fritz, "Key Lawmakers Discount Soviet Shift on Arms," *Los Angeles Times*, September 26, 1989, p. 1.
[29]Brent Scowcroft, statement to the American Association for the Advancement of Science colloquium, October 13, 1988.

ing weapons such as the Soviet SS-18 or the U.S. MX, it does not improve crisis stability.

There is another inherent danger in the START agreement: people may conclude that we have solved the nuclear problem ... we will have "done" arms control for the 1990s. The public could go back to sleep, allowing the qualitative advances in nuclear weapons to march on silently, without oversight, until it is too late.

Despite our reservations about START, we do not advocate scrapping the Treaty. It is a useful step in the right direction. It may help to keep Gorbachev in power. But it is not enough. It stops some elements of the quantitative arms race, but not the more dangerous qualitative arms race. Arms control should not stop with START. Unfortunately, at this writing, Presidents Bush and Gorbachev seem more interested in signing a watered-down START agreement at any cost, jettisoning any difficult issues that might restrict President Bush's ability to put Star Wars weapons in outer space or build up a new generation of SLCMs.

*Defense and Space Talks.* The two superpowers are also going through the motions of "negotiating" a treaty at the Defense and Space Talks. However, the United States has no intention of restricting weapons in space, and is actively pursuing dedicated anti-satellite (ASAT) capability as well as the capability for deploying space-based Star Wars weapons, no matter how ineffective. Therefore the Defense and Space Talks are just that: talks limited to confidence building measures to inform each other on weapons developments.

*Chemical Weapons Ban.* The U.S. is actively working to ban all chemical weapons. President Bush has taken a personal interest, having presented the U.S. draft position on a chemical weapons ban as Vice President in 1984. President Bush originally backtracked on his commitment to a chemical weapons ban by stating that the U.S. would continue to produce chemical weapons until all nations agreed to a ban. Fortunately, he has now reversed his position, taking the lead by agreeing to stop all U.S. production and to cut stockpiles of chemical weapons by 80 percent. We applaud President Bush for this action, recalling that in 1969 President Nixon unilaterally banned not only the production but all U.S. stockpiles of biological materials, which eventually led to the Biological Weapons Agreement of 1972. We trust that President Bush's agreement to stop all chemical weapons production will lead to a similar worldwide chemical weapons ban in the next few years.

Ideally, if relations between the superpowers continue to improve, then arms control treaties will not be needed. The arms race would wither over time from lack of interest and funds. It is conceivable that both superpowers and the other four nuclear weapons nations would recognize that their own best interests dictate that they divert resources from building destabilizing nuclear weapons to cleaning up the environment, increasing domestic investment and relieving stressed economic systems.

But we cannot base our future security on the hope that Mr. Gorbachev, and particularly his successors, will continue to accept the tenet that a nuclear war cannot be won and must not be fought. We cannot count on future Soviet leaders to be as accommodating at the arms control negotiating table, agreeing to grossly asymmetrical reductions. We should be taking this unique opportunity in history, while we have a rational and accommodating Soviet leader, to reduce both of our nuclear arsenals, guided by verifiable arms control treaties, establish a stable nuclear regime at much lower levels, and stop the qualitative arms race.

We should be moving swiftly to curb weapons proliferation to other nations. We should join together to stop the proliferation of chemical, biological and nuclear weapons and their means of delivery to less stable countries. There are great opportunities for the advancement of arms control and disarmament around the world, but we need strong institutions to capitalize on these opportunities, including a revitalized Arms Control and Disarmament Agency (ACDA).

## The Arms Control and Disarmament Agency (ACDA)

The U.S. Congress created ACDA in 1961, the first nation to establish an agency specifically concerned with controlling and reducing weapons. The intent was to provide an arms control advocate within the executive branch to counterbalance the Pentagon, presumably lobbying for more diplomatic, non-military options for our foreign policy with strong emphasis on negotiated reductions in weapons as part of our national security framework. ACDA was supposed to have been the champion of arms control.

But ACDA has been repeatedly riddled with leaders opposed to arms control during its short life. For example, Kenneth Adelman, President Reagan's choice to head ACDA, was a strong proponent of new nuclear weapons, including the MX, new strategic bombers and new strategic submarines. He once told a reporter for the New York *Daily News*, before he was nominated to head ACDA:

> I can't think of any negotiations on security or weaponry that have done any good. In a democracy, these negotiations tend to discourage money for defense programs. The public says, "Why increase the military when we're negotiating with the Russians?"

Adelman added that he would still continue negotiating with the Soviets, but only for political reasons, to placate the American public. "If anyone brings up the subject, you can say 'we have a guy over there.'"[30] Adelman renounced these words when he was nominated as head of ACDA, but this clearly indicates a lack of enthusiasm for meaningful arms control, particularly for the man charged with carrying the arms control banner (and disarmament, according to the agency's title) into the executive branch inter-agency review process.

Henry Cooper, another ACDA official during the Reagan administration, was in charge of negotiating limits on anti-satellite (ASAT) weapons for ACDA. Before joining ACDA, Cooper was responsible for designing ASAT weapons for the Defense Advanced Research Projects Agency (DARPA). Talk about the fox guarding the chicken coop.

President Bush's first choice for ACDA director was James G. Roche, who worked for Senator "Scoop" Jackson, a leading critic of arms control policy throughout the SALT negotiations. While Mr. Roche declined the offer to become ACDA director, this indicates that the Bush administration is not about to place arms control advocates in charge of the agency. The current ACDA director is Ronald Lehman, also a conservative protégé of Senator Jackson and former Assistant Secretary of Defense for International Security Policy, a key Pentagon position. As one indication of his lack of enthusiasm for arms control negotiations, Lehman joined with another civilian official, Steven Hadly, Assistant Secretary of Defense, in opposing any discussions regarding sea-based tactical nuclear weapons, even though the Chief of Naval Operations, Admiral A.H. Trost, stated his willingness to at least negotiate:

> If we could, with proper confidence in their willingness to abide by an agreement, be assured there were no nuclear weapons that

---

[30]R. Jeffrey Smith, "Some Haunting Words on Arms Control," *Science*, February 1983, p. 1049.

threatened either side's ships at sea . . . it could be in our interest to
enter negotiations.[31]

The former Chairman of the Joint Chiefs of Staff, Admiral Crowe, and
Paul Nitze have both called for negotiations, since nuclear weapons give
the Soviets an advantage at sea. Why does the director of ACDA, the
agency set up to be the advocate of arms control within the executive
branch, refuse even to negotiate when military leaders are willing to sit
down and talk?

Even when ACDA has succeeded in getting an arms control treaty
ratified, its leaders have been rewarded with dismissal to placate
hardliners in Congress. After the SALT I agreements (including the
ABM Treaty) were signed in 1972, all of the senior officers of ACDA
were forced to resign, according to the former Public Affairs Adviser to
ACDA.[32]

In many cases during the 1980s, ACDA has reversed its designated
role, taking the anti–arms control position while the Pentagon and State
Department call for more restraint. For example, ACDA has supported
a more robust Star Wars anti-ballistic missile defense program which
would violate the ABM Treaty, while both the State Department and the
Joint Chiefs of Staff have urged that we maintain the ABM Treaty.
Richard Burt, the chief negotiator on Space and Defense Talks, testified
that any arms control treaties should "fully protect our options for
deploying" a defense against ballistic missiles,[33] even though such a
deployment would end any offensive arms control agreement.

With all the activity in arms control negotiations and treaties, ACDA
should be investigating new techniques to verify compliance with
treaties. The Bush administration, however, requested only $200,000 for
ACDA research in 1990, down from $900,000 the year before. The
Pentagon's research budget for new weapons is 200,000 times greater,
and the Department of Defense exerts great influence over ACDA.
Senator Paul Simon reports that a university's proposal to ACDA for
verification research was held up while ACDA officials checked with the
Pentagon. According to a State Department inspector general's report,

---

[31]Patrick E. Tyler, "Top Admiral Sees Talks on Sea Arms Possible," *Washington Post*,
May 12, 1990, p. A12.
[32]Ralph Smith, Letter to the editor, *Arms Control Today*, January/February 1989, p.
23.
[33]R. Jeffrey Smith, "Burt Says U.S. to Protect SDI Options in Talks," *Washington
Post*, May 6, 1989, p. A13.

ACDA has failed to investigate techniques to monitor a chemical weapons ban in part because of Pentagon objections.[34]

We must reverse these historic trends, and assure that ACDA becomes a source of true arms control advocates. We need not fear that arms controllers will dominate the federal government, given the vast inertia of nuclear war-fighting strategists within the Pentagon and other offices within the State Department. A reinvigorated ACDA could be a prime source of rational long-range planning initiatives and sensible arms control policy.

To summarize, past arms control treaties have set some limits on nuclear weapons, usually at the upper ranges of what either side was planning, and they have helped to stabilize the arms race by providing some predictability and some transparency. Nuclear testing treaties have simply driven the arms race underground. The ABM Treaty represents one excellent example of arms control: a national debate was held before the major weapons were deployed. We looked into the future and predicted that deploying ballistic missile defenses would force the opponent to add more offensive weapons, thereby stimulating the arms race instead of slowing it. We and the Soviets therefore agreed to ban these weapons.

The CFE and START agreements were quite ambitious when first proposed, but have been overtaken by the events of 1989. They are valuable, but should be followed swiftly by new treaties to make deeper cuts now, removing destabilizing weapons on both sides and stopping the qualitative arms race before the Gorbachev window of opportunity closes.

---

[34]R. Jeffrey Smith, "ACDA Research Lags, Report Says," *Washington Post*, May 5, 1989, p. A25.

# CHAPTER 7

# If They're So Dangerous, Why Build Them?

SUMMARY

Despite the dangers and costs, supporters of the status quo, if not quite comfortable, have at least accepted the continuation of the nuclear arms race as a price for peace. The arms race continues in part due to inertia, profits and career advancement. But many rationalizations have also evolved over the years to justify procuring new nuclear weapons, including: the geopolitical advantage perceived by keeping ahead of the Soviets; the perceived need for extending nuclear deterrence to cover our allies and to prevent conventional war as well as nuclear war; the need to "modernize" weapons; the use of weapons as "bargaining chips" in arms control negotiations; the "spinoffs" that accrue to the civilian economy from military research; and, for some, the futile quest for weapons to "win" a nuclear war, should deterrence fail. Taken together, these motivations provide a powerful force within the societies of both superpowers, driving the nuclear arms race while over-whelming and obscuring the long-term risks and costs to society.

In previous chapters, we described how new weapons, once de-ployed, would increase the risks of nuclear war, siphon funds from

154

conventional forces to supply our addictive fix of new nuclear weapons, and divert resources from other pressing societal needs. We suggested earlier that a few hundred survivable nuclear weapons would suffice for deterrence, whereas we have over 13,000 warheads poised to obliterate the Soviet Union and they could explode over 11,000 nuclear weapons on U.S. soil. Why then do the military and civilian bureaucracies of the two nations want to build more?

Surely the people in government, industry and the military who run the vast weapons procurement machine would recognize the dangers listed in the previous chapters (assuming that they took the time to analyze our predicament). No special security clearance or deep insight is required to predict the possible calamities facing both nations if we continue our past habits. Yet our leaders march on, plowing tens of billions of dollars and rubles into the nuclear arsenals each year.

Apparently other, more powerful forces perpetuate the arms race. Apparently, at least in the minds of those running the nuclear establishment, these forces or advantages of building new weapons overwhelm or submerge the dangers that we have described. By analyzing the forces driving the arms race, we may be better able to reverse our historic proclivity to build weapons of mass destruction.

Just what are these forces that cause rational leaders to ignore the dangers that lie ahead? There is no simple answer, but we can list several factors that drive the arms race:

• Inertia and the "Iron Triangle"
• The Quest for Superiority (or parity)
• Extended Deterrence
• Modernization
• The Cities-Only Scenario
• Bargaining Chip
• Spin-offs
• Hard-Target Kill Capability
• War-fighting Preparations

We discuss each of these driving forces behind the arms race below, primarily from the U.S. perspective. Similar forces undoubtedly operate within the Soviet Union, although the details may differ with their more centralized society. Our emphasis on American involvement in perpetuating the arms race does not exonerate the Soviet Union. They share responsibility for our bloated nuclear arsenals, and must work with the United States to end the qualitative arms race and improve stability at reduced levels of nuclear weapons.

*The Iron Triangle.* The "iron triangle" refers to three very influential actors on the nuclear weapons stage: defense industries, the military and Congress. Each has a stake in the arms race. Over 8 million people depend directly on the Pentagon for their next paycheck, including 4.4 million civilian workers (3.3 million in defense industries and 1.1 million civilians who are on the direct Pentagon payroll)[1] and 3.7 million men and women in uniform (2.1 active duty and 1.6 million Reserve and National Guard forces). More workers are paid by the military than grow food (3.1 million) or teach our children (4 million elementary and secondary teachers) in the United States. Similar conditions prevail in the Soviet Union, but we consider the U.S. side in the following discussion, since we are more familiar with conditions in this country.

With no war to occupy our 3.7 million men and women in uniform, their major activities include building, testing and training to use new, ever more complex weapons. Without a war to fight, thousands of military officers at the Pentagon and at military installations around the world depend on new weapons procurements for their career advancement. And many of our elected representatives, even those skeptical of the need for new weapons, continue to vote for military projects to appear "strong on defense" or to guarantee jobs back home.

Many critics of the arms race tend to blame the profit motives of the defense contractors, or the drive of the military to acquire complex new weapons systems. But Congress also perpetuates the arms race. We tend to remember how Congress put the brakes on the worst excesses of the Reagan military buildup in the early 1980s. However, Congress has historically been a prime mover in pushing higher military spending. For the decade from 1957 through 1967, for example, Congress consistently appropriated more money for the military than the Pentagon requested.[2]

Many weapons programs have originated or have been pushed by members of Congress even without military support. The early seeds of Star Wars laser weapons research were planted by Congress in the late 1970s. Senator Malcolm Wallop fought for many years to force DARPA (the Defense Advanced Research Projects Agency) to test a chemical

---

[1]Ronald Fraser, "The Job Measure of Defense," *The Cleveland Plain Dealer*, April 20, 1989, p. 11B.
[2]Alain C. Enthoven and K. Wayne Smith, *How Much Is Enough? Shaping the Defense Program, 1961-1969*, Harper & Row, 1971.

laser for ballistic missile defense in outer space. There was no lobbying by the military. There were no defense contractors pushing proposals in the Pentagon or on the Hill. Scientists at DARPA had little hope of building such laser weapons in the laboratory, let alone in outer space. Senator Wallop's proposal to add $160 million for a space-based laser to shoot down missiles and aircraft was defeated in 1980. He proposed $250 million for space-based lasers in 1981, won a $50-million add-on in the Senate, but had to settle for $5 million after conference with the House of Representatives, which preferred no add-on. The Senate-House conference rejected another attempt by Senator Wallop to mandate space-based deployment of a laser weapon in 1982, and even such stalwarts of the Star Wars missile defense research program as (then Senator) Dan Quayle, John Warner and Senator Pete Wilson voted with the majority (65–27) in 1983 to defeat another Wallop amendment to transfer $125 million to space-based lasers. Their skepticism regarding space-based chemical lasers was validated by the five defense contractors hired by SDI to design a Star Wars system architecture: none of these defense contractors chose the space-based chemical laser favored by Senator Wallop as the weapon of choice for a practical missile defense system. The experts chose kinetic energy rockets and other types of exotic weapons such as neutral particle beam weapons and free electron lasers over the chemical laser.

Yet funds were allocated for chemical laser weapons development, and willing defense contractors came up with proposals to spend the money. Prototype chemical lasers were built, and one project, Zenith Star, still calls for an orbiting test of the chemical laser in the mid-1990s, although it is not a main component of SDI deployment plans. The laser weapons research program originated in Congress. Congress has earned its position over the years as the third leg of the iron triangle.

Some would add two more players to the list of three dominant arms race actors (defense contractors, the military and Congress), forming an iron pentagon: universities and the government weapons laboratories. Some may still envision universities as bastions of independent thinking, where research can flourish without outside influence. But many universities now rely on the Pentagon for research dollars. Between 1980 and 1988, Department of Defense research funded at universities increased by 188 percent, rising from $455 million to $1,312 million. Even after adjusting for inflation, this represents a 96 percent increase.

By 1988, Pentagon money going to universities exceeded total funds provided by the National Science Foundation. Only the National

Institute of Health supplied more research dollars to universities ($3.9 billion for NIH vs. $1.3 billion for defense research). Pentagon money spent at our nation's campuses exceeds that from NASA by a factor of 3.8, and is 2.7 times more than funds from the Department of Energy and 4.3 times more than from the Department of Agriculture.[3]

Worse yet, most of these Pentagon funds are not for basic research, but for applied research and development directed at specific military problems, tying not only university research but also the careers of fledgling scientists and engineers to specific military needs. For fiscal year 1989, only 2 percent of the Defense Department research funds were for basic research, with 6 percent for applied research, and the rest, 92 percent, for specific military projects.

The federal government through the Department of Energy (DOE) also runs nine major national laboratories employing 22,000 scientists and 50,000 technicians with a budget of $3.7 billion per year.[4] The two main nuclear weapons laboratories at Los Alamos, New Mexico, and Livermore, California, are both administered for DOE by the University of California, a bizarre distortion of academic freedom and the independent pursuit of knowledge for the benefit of the human race. What other civilization has turned to its academic institutions to design and test weapons of war, particularly weapons of mass destruction?

While the activities at the Lawrence Livermore and Los Alamos National Labs have expanded over the years to include more than the design and development of our nation's nuclear bombs, this remains their number one priority. During the 1970s, the weapons labs expanded into energy research, but much of this work was diverted back to the Star Wars program in the 1980s.

The scientists from the weapons labs form a powerful lobby on Capitol Hill when others attempt to ban more nuclear weapons tests. During 1986-87, the Lawrence Livermore National Lab hired an outside contractor to help make plans for lobbying Congress in support of continued nuclear weapons testing, the lifeblood of these laboratories. The General Accounting Office concluded that no laws were violated,

---

[3]Intersociety Working Group, *AAAS Report XIII: Research and Development FY 1989*, Washington, D.C.: American Association for the Advancement of Science, 1988, p. 11.

[4]In addition to Los Alamos and Livermore, the national laboratories include Argonne in Illinois, Brookhaven in New York, Oak Ridge in Tennessee, Pacific Northwest in Richland, Washington, Lawrence Berkeley in California, the Idaho National Engineering Laboratory and Sandia in New Mexico.

because the Department of Energy (DOE) had approved the lobbying effort in advance. Nonetheless, DOE used $550,000 of taxpayer money to pay a contractor, RDA Logicon, to help convince key members of Congress to vote against a comprehensive test ban.[5] In addition, weapons scientists paid by DOE lobbied Congress to continue underground nuclear weapons testing. These scientists, along with other DOE officials, conducted 118 briefings for members of Congress in 1987, 96 for House members and 22 for Senators. In addition to lobbying against nuclear testing limitations, these DOE teams were asked after each briefing to rate each member's stand on nuclear testing on a numerical scale from strongly in favor to strongly against testing.

In March 1986, 48 physics professors from the University of California sent a letter to the university president, protesting the actions of their colleagues at the weapons laboratories. According to Glenn T. Seaborg, former chairman of the Atomic Energy Commission, this letter "suggested that questionable arguments were being used by the scientists at Livermore and Los Alamos to oppose a verifiable comprehensive test ban treaty."[6] They asked the university president to direct the laboratories to prepare for an end to nuclear weapons testing. So far, there is no end in sight.

The momentum of the iron triangle (or pentagon) is nearly unstoppable once it gets rolling. And the military-industrial complex is large indeed and on the move. The Pentagon spends more than $1 billion dollars every working day. The assets assigned to the Pentagon exceed those of the top 30 U.S. corporations combined.

It is very difficult to stop a major weapons system like the B-1 bomber or the MX missile once it picks up steam, spreading billions of dollars of contracts in as many states as possible. Companies become accustomed to the large projects and profits, military careers depend on the continued procurement of the weapons (whether they work or not) and the jobs of tens of thousands of blue-collar workers depend on weapons production, with massive layoffs at the end of production. The threat of losing jobs (their constituents and then theirs!) motivates many members of Congress to continue programs that bring even a few dozen jobs to their districts.

---

[5]GAO Report RCED-88-25BR, *Nuclear Test Lobbying: DOE Regulations for Contractors Need Reevaluation*, U.S. General Accounting Office, October 1987.
[6]Glenn T. Seaborg, "Weapons Labs Need New Thinking," *The Bulletin of the Atomic Scientists*, July/August 1989, p. 11.

Each of the millions of workers, military officers and researchers have a stake in continuing the weapons procurement program. Although a minority of the population, these stake-holders are much more active politically, and therefore much more powerful than the average citizen. Given the choice, the majority of citizens might choose to have their tax dollars spent on repairing roads or for energy research rather than the B-2 bomber, but most citizens are not aware of these issues and in any case have little opportunity to make a choice. With no financial stake, they do not take the time to write their elected officials or to vote against those representatives who supported the B-2 bomber. Those whose next paycheck depends on the weapon, however, do work to defeat any elected official who dared to vote against continuation of their weapon program.

Elected officials also fear being labeled "weak on defense" or "soft on Communism" as the inevitable reelection campaign approaches. Our nation certainly is not weak, by any stretch of the imagination, in either conventional weapons or nuclear weapons. Yet perceptions are paramount. The public can be influenced by marginal changes in our defense posture. Attention is focused on new weapons, such as the D-5 submarine-launched missile or the MX missile. Most voters do not have the time or the resources to study the total defense posture, to ask the types of questions we are raising in this book. They may not realize that we already have 13,000 strategic warheads, that adding more D-5 or MX warheads would have little incremental value, and in fact would most likely degrade our security.

But we cannot convey this danger in 30-second sound bites or slick campaign posters, the communication media of elections. Rather, many voters judge elected officials on the basis of their perceived "toughness" in recent weapons votes in Congress (or so the political pundits tell the candidates). Congress does not vote each year for the vast majority of our weapons that are already manufactured and deployed in the field. Decade-old votes for existing weapons are long forgotten. As a result, many in Congress feel compelled to vote for all new weapons systems, however marginal or dangerous their impact.

More moderate members of Congress may oppose some military projects, but then feel pressured to support other new weapons to avoid the "weak on defense" charge. Thus many voted against the MX, but voted for the D-5 missile to balance their voting record, even though the D-5's accuracy and reduced flight time make it a destabilizing weapon. Until the electorate is better informed about the dangers of new weapons, or until more elected officials are willing to stand up and fight the "weak on defense" charges, the arms race will continue to be supported in Congress.

For several years, most members of Congress have been saying that the Pentagon must cancel some weapons systems to reduce our federal deficits. The nation cannot afford to buy all the new weapons ordered during the Reagan administration's spending spree, when most weapons were bought on credit. Instead of canceling weapons outright, the military has been stretching out procurements, ordering fewer weapons per year, which raises unit costs. By stretching out procurements, money is saved in the current year at the expense of increased costs in later years.

When Secretary of Defense Richard Cheney entered office, he continued past practices by endorsing all of the new nuclear weapons systems, including both the rail garrison MX missile and the single-warhead Midgetman missile. But Cheney did attempt to cancel one conventional weapon program completely, the Osprey V-22 tilt-rotor helicopter-aircraft, and called for ending production of F-14 fighters. Instead of welcoming this first cancelation of a major weapon system, Congress, prodded by members with contracts in their districts, reinstated funds to keep both the V-22 and the F-14 programs alive. Military weapons programs are resilient indeed. If one part of the iron triangle tries to kill a program, then another rescues it.

Before leaving the subject of the inertia of the arms race and the "iron triangle," we should also note that civilians in the administration can be a powerful force perpetuating the nuclear arms race. Whether at the White House or in the State Department, senior officials frequently take a more hard-line position than members of Congress or their uniformed counterparts in the Pentagon. Consider, for example, one roadblock to concluding an effective START treaty with the Soviet Union: Star Wars. Although Gorbachev agreed to sign the START treaty without resolving the Star Wars issue, the Soviets made it known that they would pull out of the treaty if the U.S. ever begins space-based tests of Star Wars.

President Reagan, with his dream of a perfect defensive shield, insisted on clinging to his Star Wars security blanket in the START negotiations. When Reagan left Washington, Admiral Crowe and the Joint Chiefs of Staff, our most senior military advisers, advocated that the U.S. drop its insistence at the START negotiations that we would test and deploy a partial defense. This sound advice was overruled by civilians in the Defense Department, the White House and the State Department in the spring of 1989.[7] The civilians took a more militaristic approach than the military, postponing the day when we can sign lasting agreements permanently reducing nuclear weapons.

More recently, the Air Force offered to give up the rail mobile MX missile program as part of their contribution to declining defense budgets. Secretary Cheney, the civilian leader, refused this offer, ordering the Air Force to request more money for the MX program.[8]

*Quest for Superiority—or Even Parity.* Old ideas die hard. Prior to World War II, there was some expectation that a nation with superior military forces would prevail in battle. While clever tactics sometimes permitted inferior forces to win, more tanks, more guns and more troops at the border would generally increase the chances of repelling any invader and protecting the homeland in the pre-nuclear era. Peace through military strength did make some sense prior to World War II, although strength alone is never sufficient.

Two inventions have shattered any remaining validity in the "peace through strength" slogan: the intercontinental ballistic missile (ICBM) and nuclear weapons. Once an ICBM leaves its underground silo, accelerating its deadly cargo into outer space, reaching speeds of 15,000 miles per hour, there is little an opponent can do to prevent that warhead from exploding over any target some 25 minutes later. Even if we never invented nuclear weapons, the ICBM would have drastically changed warfare. The ICBM has eliminated the battlefront. No nation, no city, no military target on the face of the earth is safe from attack within half an hour. The world's largest army cannot repel ballistic missiles arriving from outer space. Equipped with nuclear bombs, ICBMs have the capacity for virtual societal destruction.

We can no longer protect our people or our cities from annihilation. We are the most powerful military nation in the history of the world . . . and the most helpless, pathetically vulnerable. We cannot be invaded, even by the Soviet Union, since they lack the ability both to control the oceans and to transport occupation troops to our shores. We cannot be invaded, but our society can be destroyed in an afternoon. We can retaliate, destroying the opposing society half an hour later, fulfilling

[7]Michael R. Gordon, "Joint Chiefs Urge U.S. Restraint on 'Star Wars' in Strategic Talks," *New York Times*, June 1, 1989, p. 12.
[8]Rowan Scarborough and Bill Gertz, "Revive Railed MX, Cheney Tells AF Budget Officials," *Washington Times*, April 26, 1990, p. 3.

our mutual suicide pact, but the fact remains: we are defenseless, despite spending trillions of dollars on "defense" since World War II.

In the nuclear age, spending more money on the military does not necessarily improve our national security. We can buy more weapons of mass destruction, more ICBMs, more bombers, more SLBMs and more cruise missiles to add to our overkill capability, but the days of protecting our people and cities from attack by military force at the border are gone forever.

Some citizens hope that Star Wars might restore control over our own destiny by providing an effective defense against ballistic missiles. As we discuss in Appendix A, however, even the leaders of the Star Wars program agree that we will never be able to stop all ballistic missiles, and Star Wars has no capability to destroy bombers or cruise missiles. Knowing that we could not possibly protect our people and cities, the Pentagon has set a meager goal for Star Wars of stopping just 15 percent of all Soviet ballistic missile warheads. At best, Star Wars could protect some of our missiles, but not people.

Despite this reality, some still cling to the old ways of thinking. They yearn for the days when military superiority meant better security. The 1980 Republican platform, for example, called for "sustained defense expenditure sufficient to close the gap with the Soviets, and ultimately reach the position of military superiority that the American people demand."[9]

Robert McNamara, our longest serving Secretary of Defense, recognized our quest for nuclear superiority:

> From the dawn of the nuclear age to the present, the United States has sought to maintain "superior" strategic and tactical nuclear forces—or at least forces that could give us an advantage if we, rather than the Soviets, struck the first blow. So long as we maintain this goal, it will be difficult to achieve arms control agreements aimed at stable, low level of weapons on each side.[10]

Others recognize that, in the nuclear age, superiority may have little military significance, but they still hold that superior forces have certain political value. By building more weapons, we give the *appearance* of strength. We show our resolve to meet any challenge.

---

[9]Joseph B. Gorman, *The 1980 Presidential Election*, CRS Report No. 80-180 GOV, October 8, 1980.
[10]Robert S. McNamara, *Blundering into Disaster*, New York: Pantheon, 1986, p. 132.

Conversely, if we let the Russians get ahead of us in some category of nuclear weapons, then others may see us as weak. The Soviets might then try to exploit this perceived weakness in Third World conflicts, according to conventional wisdom. In 1974 Henry Kissinger, who became both National Security Advisor and Secretary of State for President Nixon, expressed his lack of confidence in the military value of nuclear weapons this way:

> While a decisive advantage is hard to calculate, the *appearance of inferiority*—whatever its actual significance—can have serious political consequences.[11]

Therefore we must build more or better nuclear weapons to prove our strength. Nuclear weapons have become a status symbol, a mark of an advanced, modern nation-state.

Steven Kull, a psychologist who interviewed 84 nuclear policymakers from the Pentagon, the administration and the Congress, recorded this candid statement from a staff member of the Senate Foreign Relations committee regarding our need to build nuclear weapons to catch up to the Soviets:

> We need 'em 'cause they got 'em. That's the only reason for having 'em. One should match them point for point for every weapon they have. They aren't useful for military purposes. They're only useful for psychological and political purposes.[12]

Kull notes that many members of the nuclear establishment concede that these new nuclear weapons have little or no military utility, but they are still needed for political purposes.

The importance of nuclear superiority was refuted during the Cuban missile crisis of 1962, according to then Secretary of Defense Robert McNamara. He described that crisis as follows:

> At the time of the Cuban missile crisis, we had on the order of 5,000 strategic offensive nuclear warheads. The Soviets had on the order of 300. We had a ratio, an advantage of 17-to-1.
>
> Suppose we'd launched 5,000 against 300, and say even 10 percent of them survived. And I think, frankly, many more than 10

---

[11]Steven Kull, *Minds at War*, New York: Basic Books, 1988, p. 124.
[12]Ibid., p. 116.

percent would have. Ten percent of 300, 30. Thirty nuclear warheads could have destroyed tens of millions of Americans. We were deterred.[13]

Even with 17 to 1 superiority, we could not use nuclear weapons to our advantage. Nuclear superiority is meaningless. Even Henry Kissinger once questioned the efficacy of nuclear superiority. In a moment of frustration at a press conference in Moscow, when asked repeatedly about Pentagon efforts to block a SALT agreement, Kissinger blurted out:

> What, in the name of God, is strategic superiority? What is the significance of it, politically, militarily, operationally, at these levels of numbers? What do you do with it?[14]

While he later regretted the comment, it may reveal what many of our nuclear deterrent architects feel inwardly, but repress in group or public discussions. In our view, these subconscious doubts about the utility of nuclear superiority are more valid than the usual public statements.

As the quest for nuclear superiority has been renounced by many analysts, some have toned down their goals, donning a mantle of moderation by claiming that they only seek parity. But even parity in all levels of nuclear weapons makes little sense. As we've stated many times before, a few hundred deliverable nuclear weapons is sufficient for deterrence. Seeking to match the Soviets in all categories where they are ahead is a waste of taxpayer dollars, and, in many cases, another justification for adding destabilizing weapons. Thus the Soviets have more accurate counterforce nuclear warheads on their SS-18s and SS-19s. Proponents of the MX missile can therefore claim that they only seek parity with the Soviets by promoting the MX.

Furthermore, parity is an elusive goal. Because of worst-case planning and worst-case threat projections, each side perceives the opponent as being stronger than they really are. The arms race has been driven in part by our misperceptions of Soviet military accomplishments. We projected great capability to Soviet tanks and fighter aircraft

---

[13]Robert McNamara on WETA-TV, PBS network show, *To What End?*, October 18, 1988.
[14]John Newhouse, *War and Peace in the Nuclear Age*, New York: Alfred A. Knopf, 1989, p. 245.

and built our own weapons to counter the perceived threat, only to find years later from captured Soviet equipment that their weapons were not as capable as we had estimated. Star Wars is driven in part by our estimates of Soviet ballistic missile defense research. For several years, the Pentagon referred to a specific laser complex at Sary Shagan as evidence that the Soviets already had the capability to damage our satellites with high power lasers. As part of glasnost, a Congressional team including laser scientists visited this site in the Soviet Union, only to find antiquated laser equipment that was far too weak to damage even an unprotected satellite.

Parity may sound like a more reasonable goal than superiority, but it too can be used to justify superfluous conventional and nuclear war-fighting weapons.

*Extended Deterrence.* Most military analysts agree that a few hundred survivable nuclear weapons would suffice to deter the Soviets, or any other adversary, from ever attacking us with nuclear weapons. However, they go on to speculate, logically, that nuclear war would most likely evolve from a conventional war. The best way to prevent nuclear war, then, is to prevent *any* war between the superpowers or between the NATO and Warsaw Pact nations. Hence the notion of "extended deterrence." We want to extend the nuclear umbrella to cover our NATO allies and to deter a conventional war.

Now the thought process gets more convoluted, but stick with us. This is one of the most commonly used arguments by the nuclear establishment to justify more nuclear weapons, at least before the collapse of the Warsaw Pact. They argued that, to deter a conventional war, say a Soviet invasion of West Germany, large ICBM warheads fired from the United States would *not* be a credible deterrent. That is, the U.S. would be reluctant to use ICBMs, fearing that the Soviets might misinterpret any ICBMs fired from the American homeland as the beginning of a massive U.S. attack. Because the Soviets might then attack our cities, we would be self-deterred, unwilling to risk our cities to stop a Soviet attack in Europe. We would not be willing to sacrifice New York to "save" Bonn.

Therefore, according to this reasoning, we need shorter range tactical nuclear weapons stationed in Europe. The Soviets would recognize that tactical weapons were intended only for the local theatre, so the reasoning goes, and could not be used against the interior of the Soviet Union. Responding to this logic, NATO had deployed about 7,000 short-range nuclear weapons in Europe beginning in the mid-1950s. These tactical nuclear weapons included short-range missiles, nuclear artillery shells, nuclear bombs on short-range aircraft, and even man-transportable nuclear land mines.

The use of tactical nuclear weapons to "save" Europe from Soviet attack has always been suspect. Robert McNamara reports that a 1955 exercise called Carte Blanche simulated the use of just 335 tactical nuclear weapons, a small fraction of the weapons available. In the first two days of this simulated battle, 1.5 to 1.7 million people would die and 3.5 million would be wounded, about five times the total German casualties in World War II. Helmut Schmidt declared that tactical nuclear weapons "will not defend Europe, but destroy it."[15]

Since 1979, NATO unilaterally reduced the total number of nuclear weapons by 2,400, without any fanfare and nothing like the propaganda bonanza reaped by Gorbachev when he announced a unilateral reduction of 500 tactical nuclear weapons in May of 1989. The U.S. removed 429 more nuclear warheads as part of the INF agreement. But we still have several thousand nuclear artillery shells and short-range nuclear missiles and over 1,600 aircraft stationed in Europe that could be used to deliver nuclear bombs to stop a Soviet conventional attack.

If this were not enough, the U.S. could also fire nuclear weapons from submarines offshore and carrier-based Navy fighter-bombers could also attack Warsaw Pact countries with nuclear weapons. Our British and French friends also have close to one thousand nuclear warheads that could be used against the Soviets in central Europe. We do not need more nuclear weapons to assure extended deterrence.

The war-fighting strategists say that we need the flexibility to hit different types of targets under a range of scenarios, and we need the flexibility to deter further fighting on each "rung" of a ladder of escalation. In general, they opt for small nuclear weapons, so that our leaders will have less inhibition about using them. They lobbied for the low yield (1-KT) neutron or "enhanced radiation" bomb which has the same prompt lethal radius (690 meters) for neutron radiation as a 10-KT fission bomb, but roughly half the blast damage radius (550 vs. 1220 meters).[16] The neutron bomb would therefore disable tank operators within a 690-meter radius, while reducing the area of blast damage by a

---

[15]Robert S. McNamara, *Blundering into Disaster: Surviving the First Century of the Nuclear Age*, New York: Pantheon, 1986, p. 33.

[16]Thomas B. Cochran, William M. Arkin and Milton M. Hoenig, *Nuclear Weapons Databook, Volume I: U.S. Nuclear Forces and Capabilities*, Cambridge: Ballinger, 1984, p. 28.

factor of four compared to a 10-KT device, thereby reducing civilian casualties under some circumstances. With the potential for reduced civilian loses, commanders might be more likely to use the neutron bomb. However, popular demonstrations in Europe prevented NATO nations from accepting American neutron bombs.

Some war-fighting enthusiasts lobbied against the INF Treaty, since it removed one class of tactical nuclear weapons (those with ranges from 300 to 3,300 miles) from the European theatre, thereby reducing our flexibility, or so they claimed.

Just prior to the 40th anniversary of NATO in 1989, the Bush administration struggled over the issue of negotiating with the Soviets on reducing or removing the remaining short-range nuclear missiles with ranges less than 300 miles. These short-range nuclear missiles such as the American Lance missile were not covered by the INF Treaty. The West German public understandably favors removing all such missiles, since they would explode only on German soil in event of war.

The initial Bush administration response was to refuse to negotiate. They wanted to "modernize" the Lance nuclear missile by increasing its range from 70 miles up close to the 300-mile INF Treaty limit. The Bush administration had to delay the modernization decision for several years in the face of overwhelming German opposition (only 14 percent of the German people supported Lance modernization),[17] but the administration still refused to negotiate reductions in short-range missiles.

The U.S. and NATO had much to gain from such negotiations. The Soviets have about 3,000 nuclear short-range missiles that can be fired from approximately 1,400 launchers, while the U.S. has only 700 of the old Lance missiles and only 88 launchers to fire those missiles in West Germany. The Soviets will be forced by their former Warsaw Pact allies to remove all of these short-range missiles within a few years, but citizens of our NATO allies may reject American ground-based nuclear weapons, too. We may be wise to negotiate with the Soviets to destroy these weapons before the Soviets withdrawal. Otherwise, the Soviets would move these weapons back into the Soviet Union, and the U.S. would not even have on-site inspection privileges to monitor their location let alone their destruction.

Paul Nitze, a veteran nuclear statesman and senior adviser to President Reagan, advocated in May of 1989 that we negotiate with the

---

[17]Simon Head, "The Battle Inside NATO," *The New York Review of Books*, May 18, 1989.

Soviets on short-range missiles, with a goal of destroying all except 200–300 missiles each.[18] The Soviets would have to destroy about 2,800 missiles while we would give up only 500, or a net five-to-one gain for the NATO position.

Richard Perle, another veteran of the arms control wars and no dove on defense issues, went even further, suggesting we eliminate all short-range nuclear missiles. Perle notes that the short-range Soviet missiles could destroy NATO airfields at the start of a war, removing one of NATO's main weapons and main strategies: the use of nuclear-equipped aircraft to attack deep behind Warsaw Pact lines.

These recommendations by former Reagan officials did not sway the Bush administration, even after the fall of the Berlin Wall. They requested $119 million in the 1991 budget to develop a new Lance missile for deployment in West Germany and a new nuclear artillery shell. This new Lance missile could deliver nuclear weapons to the former East Germany and to half of Poland and Czechoslovakia.

The main stated reason for their refusal to negotiate on short-range nuclear missiles: they feared that the Soviets would force them into accepting the zero option. They feared the elimination of all short-range missiles, even though this outcome would destroy about five times as many Soviet as American missiles; even though we would still have thousands of aircraft-delivered nuclear bombs that we could use in any war; and even though our British and French allies could fire nearly one thousand nuclear weapons into former Warsaw Pact countries, should that ever become necessary. Such is the power of "extended deterrence" thinking within Washington corridors of power.

The basic notion of extended deterrence is to make nuclear weapons usable. If they are usable, or more precisely, if the Soviets believe we would use them, then they will be more credible as a deterrent. Of course, those of us who advocate stability over usability worry that the war-fighting strategists just might achieve their objective: by lowering the nuclear threshold, nuclear weapons may indeed be used in some future conflict. The question is how far we can go in making nuclear weapons more usable, without ever using them.

In a sense, we are walking a nuclear tightrope. We want to be surefooted, so we don't fall, but we want to wiggle and squirm, scaring the Soviet audience below into believing we might fall.

---

[18]Michael R. Gordon, "Reagan Arms Adviser Says Bush Is Wrong on Short-range Missiles," *New York Times*, May 3, 1989, p. 1.

John Steinbruner of the Brookings Institution classifies the "extended deterrence" notion as "metaphysics," and is optimistic that this argument for building more nuclear weapons may be losing credibility:

> I want to suggest to you that this standard metaphysics is breaking down because background political attitudes are shifting. The standard arguments [for extended deterrence] are very vulnerable to a shift in political attitudes because they have no real anchoring in military circumstances. Therefore, they are almost entirely dependent upon people's willingness to believe and that willingness is rapidly declining.[19]

Presumably the revolutions in Eastern Europe in late 1989 accelerated the demise of the extended deterrence rational for more nuclear weapons. Admiral Crowe, after retiring as Chairman of the Joint Chiefs of staff, believes that reducing strategic nuclear weapons would not make conventional war more likely:

> I do not believe the theory that [a strategic arms accord] is just going to make it safe for conventional war—that theory has now become hollow.[20]

We can only hope that this willingness to believe in nuclear metaphysics will decline fast enough to permit a reordering of our nation's priorities before it is too late.

*Modernization.* Another frequent claim in support of new nuclear weapons is that we must "modernize." The implication is often made that, without modernization, our old weapons would no longer deter the Soviets. Dick Cheney cited Soviet nuclear "modernization" as the primary rationale for requesting an average increase of 30 percent in strategic nuclear weapons for 1991. The Soviets are modernizing, so we must too.

Listening to the rhetoric, one would think that our weapons were rusting away. Advocates of higher military spending spoke of our B-52 bombers as being older than the pilots who fly them. Our bomber force

---

[19]John Steinbruner, quoted in "European Arms Control After the NATO Summit," *Arms Control Today*, June/July 1989, p. 5.
[20]R. Jeffrey Smith, "Crowe Suggests New Approach on Naval Nuclear Arms Cuts," *Washington Post*, January 8, 1990, p. A4.

had to be modernized. And so we built 100 new B-1 bombers to replace them. No sooner were the B-1s operational, however, than the Air Force announced that, well, the decrepit B-52s could struggle on a few more years after all, and they converted some B-52s for use in conventional bombing missions.

But the bomber modernization didn't stop there. The Air Force has been working on the B-2 Stealth bomber since the late 1970s. The first Stealth bomber prototype was rolled off the production line in 1989, less than a year after the B-1 bomber force became operational. The B-2 is not needed to replace the B-1, but rather to supplement it. The B-1 is perfectly adequate for deterrence, particularly since it can attack targets deep inside Soviet territory by firing long-range cruise missiles from outside Soviet airspace.

However, the B-2 Stealth bomber is designed to more easily avoid some types of Soviet radar detection, giving it better capability to fly into Soviet airspace. Given that we could explode some 7,000 hydrogen bombs on Soviet soil from submarine and land-based missiles, one wonders how many Soviet radars or fighter aircraft would remain to stop any bomber, or why we should need to fly over all this death and destruction to drop another 5,000 hydrogen bombs on the dead and dying.

The modernization of the ICBM force also brought new capability: a major improvement in our nuclear war-fighting capability with the accurate, 10-warhead MX replacing the less accurate three-warhead Minuteman-III. Again, the modern, solid-fueled Minuteman-III was perfectly adequate for deterrence, but was not optimum for fighting and winning a nuclear war. If the Minuteman-III was becoming unreliable as parts wore out, it could have been replaced with a more modern or more reliable three-warhead missile. Obsolete or faulty parts could have been replaced. For maximum stability, we should have substituted a modern single-warhead missile for the Minuteman-III. Instead, we decreased crisis stability by adding the 10-warhead MX missile in vulnerable silos.

The United States did have 52 older Titan liquid-fueled missiles that were less reliable. The liquid fuel in these missiles had to be drained and replaced periodically. One Titan blew up near Damascus, Arkansas, in 1980 when a worker dropped a wrench that severed a fuel line in the silo. The volatile fuel mixture exploded later, killing one worker and sending a nine-megaton hydrogen bomb into a nearby field. Fortunately, the many interlock safety features prevented the bomb from exploding.

The U.S. has removed all of these old Titan missiles. The Soviets, however, rely primarily on liquid-fueled missiles. They began replacing their older missiles with the new solid-fueled SS-24 and SS-25 mobile missiles several years ago. At least this "modernization" improved crisis stability, since their mobile missiles are more survivable: they do not make a tempting target for U.S. missiles in time of crisis. However, the SS-24 mobile missile has 10 warheads, so the stability created by mobility is offset by the destabilizing nature of multiple warheads.

Our submarine-launched ballistic missile (SLBM) force "modernization" was also oversold: the United States began adding the new 24-missile Trident submarines in 1982, many years before the older Poseidon submarines were to be retired, beginning in 1993. At least two Poseidon subs have since been converted to carrying U.S. "Special Operation Forces," our secret Army and Navy for fighting covert actions around the world.

Finally, the Navy is planning to replace the Trident-I (C-4) missile with the more accurate Trident-I (D-5) missile, again bolstering our nuclear war-fighting capability. There is nothing wrong with the 384 Trident 1 missiles in service. They are perfectly suited for deterrence, and have several decades of service life left. But they are being replaced by the more powerful and more accurate D-5 missiles under the banner of force modernization.

In short, modernization is sometimes required to replace old weapons or less reliable weapons, but, more often than not, "modernization" has been used to camouflage our efforts to build a nuclear war-fighting capability.

*The Cities-Only Scenario.* A popular yarn used in the late 1970s by advocates of nuclear war-fighting capability to justify new, accurate nuclear weapons goes like this: suppose the Soviets used a limited number of nuclear weapons to attack only our nuclear weapons facilities: primarily our ICBM silos and any bombers based away from large cities. They postulate that very few people would die, at least not initially.

What would the U.S. do? The hardliners claim that our old weapons are inaccurate, so that we could only attack Soviet cities, the "cities-only" scenario. We would therefore have only two choices: surrender or unleash a massive attack against Soviet cities. The latter would result in Soviet retaliation against our cities, with over 100 million likely fatalities. No President would start such a deadly exchange. Hence, they say, we would be forced to surrender!

To save us from this dilemma, we must build accurate new weapons, they say, weapons to give us the capability of striking military targets, not cities. With these new weapons, we would have many choices, or flexible response. We could escape the "cities-only" scenario. We could move from killing innocent civilians to attacking only military targets.

This scenario has two major flaws: it assumes few people killed if the Soviets attacked our strategic military forces, and it assumes that we would be forced to attack only cities with existing nuclear weapons. In fact, computer simulations predict that a Soviet attack on our ICBM fields and our strategic bomber bases would kill from 12 to 27 million Americans.[21] The United States has lost just over one million people in all the past wars in our history. It is difficult to imagine a U.S. President not reacting to an attack that killed 10 to 20 million citizens in a single day.

Second, the President would have many options other than attacking Soviet cities. We have had multiple options to attack a broad range of targets for almost three decades. Ever since Robert McNamara and John F. Kennedy discovered that the Eisenhower administration had only one nuclear war-fighting plan—an all-out spasm attack against the Soviet Union, China and the Eastern European countries—this country has had the capability and the plans for many attack options against purely military targets or facilities needed to sustain military operations such as key rail junctions, mines, missile test sites and other key facilities located away from population centers. Yes, civilians living near military installations would be killed, but we would not have to target heavily populated areas to respond to any Soviet attack.

The ability of existing nuclear weapons to destroy most military targets can be demonstrated by comparing the accuracy of these weapons with their lethal radius. Consider the attack illustrated by Figure 7-1; a nuclear warhead is aimed at the intersection of two runways at a military airfield. Because of various errors in the flight path traveling from the U.S., the warhead would usually miss the intended aimpoint.

---

[21]Frank N. von Hippel, Barbara G. Levi, Theodore A. Postol and William H. Daugherty, "Civilian Casualties from Counterforce Attacks," *Scientific American*, September 1989, p. 36.

One measure of this deviation is CEP, which is commonly listed as "circular error probability" but, as Robert Sherman points out, would be better represented by the term "Circle of Equal Probability." The CEP is the radius of a circle into which 50 percent of all warheads would fall, statistically, if we fired many warheads at that same aimpoint. It is equivalent to throwing 10 darts at a dart board and measuring the circle that encloses the five darts closest to the bull's-eye. Suppose, for example, that the actual warhead fell on the outer edge of the CEP circle in Figure 7-1. In this case, the runway, hangars, support equipment and aircraft would still be destroyed, as long as the lethal radius exceeds the CEP.

Figure 7-1. RELATIONSHIP BETWEEN LETHAL RADIUS AND ACCURACY OR CEP OF A NUCLEAR WEAPON.

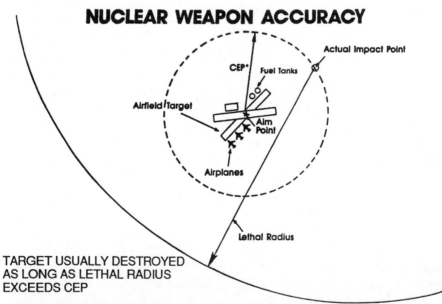

*CEP = Circular Error Probability . . . circle within which 50% of all weapons of particular type will fall

As shown in Table 7-1, the lethal radius necessary to destroy "soft" military targets—targets that are not buried underground to resist nuclear blast—exceeds the CEP for every nuclear weapon in the U.S. arsenal, assuming 12 pounds per inch blast pressure. This would be equivalent to over 400 tons pressure on a two story house; 5 pounds per square inch would destroy most houses. Even the old submarine-launched warheads on Poseidon missiles could be used to attack "soft" military targets. The Trident-I (C-4) missiles have six times greater accuracy than needed for 12 pounds per square inch blast pressure; these C-4 missiles could destroy much harder targets by landing closer, bringing more blast pressure on each target.

This means that we do not need a new generation of more accurate nuclear weapons to avoid the "cities-only" paper tiger. We could use the older C-4 missiles to attack a wide range of military targets including military airfields, radar stations, ammunition dumps, fuel depots, barracks, truck and tank farms, shipping ports, space-launch facilities, research laboratories, power plants, etc. In fact, we could attack virtually all military and economic targets except underground command and control bunkers and buried ICBM silos.

TABLE 7-1.    LETHAL RADIUS AND ACCURACY FOR TYPICAL U.S. STRATEGIC NUCLEAR WEAPONS.

|  | Accuracy CEP (feet) | Lethal Radius-12 psi[22] (feet) | Ratio of Lethal Radius to Accuracy: |
|---|---|---|---|
| ICBMs |  |  |  |
| Minuteman-II | 2,000 | 13,000 | 6.5 |
| Minuteman-III | 600 | 7,000–8,000 | 12.5 |
| MX | 300 | 8,500 | 28.3 |
| SLBMs |  |  |  |
| Poseidon | 1,500 | 4,000 | 1.7 |
| Trident-I (C-4) | 900 | 5,900 | 6.6 |
| Trident-II (D-5) | 480 | 10,000 | 20.8 |

Further, we could fire just one warhead, 10 warheads, or any number we chose. We have total flexibility to select various levels of escalation against military targets of our choice in response to a Soviet limited strike. We are not limited to attacking only cities, and have not been so limited since 1962.

Former Secretary of Defense Harold Brown commented as follows regarding the cities-only scenario:

Even after a total loss of Minuteman missiles, we would *not* face the dilemma of surrender by inaction or mutual suicide by an all-

---

[22]Lethal radius scaled from 1 megaton airburst data from *The Effects of Nuclear War*, Washington, D.C.: Office of Technology Assessment, May 1979, p. 36.

out attack on Soviet cities and industry, provoking an equal attack on ours. We would instead have surviving bomber and submarine forces fully capable of selectively attacking military, economic and control targets, thus negating any gain the Soviet might imagine they could attain by an attack on our ICBM force.[23]

*The "Cities-Only Scenario" was a hoax to justify the quest for a nuclear war-fighting capability.*

*Bargaining Chip.* Another oft-used rationale for new nuclear weapons is the bargaining chip: we build the weapons to cash in at the negotiating table, to force the Soviets to bargain away their weapons. We must negotiate from a position of strength, so they say, or else the Soviets will have no incentive to reduce their weapons, or even to talk about arms control. This rationale may have had some credibility with previous Soviet leaders, but Mikhail Gorbachev seems independently motivated to negotiate limits and reductions in nuclear weapons, including agreements grossly unfavorable to the Soviet Union by previous standards, citing a dual benefit to the Soviet Union of reduced economic burden and reduced risks of nuclear war.

The bargaining chip argument seems to surface whenever other justifications for new weapons are particularly weak, or when the weapons system is under attack for other deficiencies. The controversial MX missile and the Star Wars program have been termed bargaining chips to help offset the destabilizing nature of these two systems. In both cases, it was clear to most observers that the administration had no intention of ever giving up these weapons in exchange for Soviet concessions. Even with the mythical 50 percent reductions of the START treaty, the U.S. will keep all accurate 10-warhead MX missiles, eliminating older but less destabilizing single warhead or, at best, the less accurate triple warhead Minuteman III missiles.

President Reagan made it perfectly clear that he would not exchange his Star Wars dream at the bargaining table even if the Soviets agreed to total elimination of all ballistic missiles, and President Bush has ignored the recommendation of the Joint Chiefs of Staff that we cash in the Star Wars bargaining chip in exchange for substantial reductions in offensive nuclear weapons through the START negotiations. As a result, the START treaty is a temporary agreement, sure to be abandoned if either

---

[23]F. Kaplan, *Dubious Specter*, Washington, D.C.: Institute for Policy Studies, 1980, p. 46.

superpower begins to test and deploy a partial defense. The START treaty may give Presidents Bush and Gorbachev much needed political capital in the short term, but it has no lasting value until the Star Wars issue is resolved.

In some cases, weapons assume a bargaining chip mantle at adolescence, when they have not demonstrated their full military worth, but are growing rapidly and need much care and feeding at the Pentagon trough. Later, as the weapons mature, the military suddenly realize that they cannot live without their fully capable adult weapons, and they withdraw them from the negotiating arena. This pattern was followed with MIRVs and cruise missiles in the SALT I negotiations. Both were advertised early in their life as bargaining chips, but both were later protected as the military decided that early deployment of these weapons by the U.S. was more important than curtailing Soviet advances in these areas. MIRVs have already come home to roost, threatening our land-based missiles and creating the excuse for the "window of vulnerability" hoax. We also expect Soviet or Libyan cruise missiles fired from submarines near our long shores may one day undermine our security, unless we restrict cruise missile developments by mutual agreement and establish global monitoring capability to stop any clandestine efforts to build these weapons.

Nuclear weapons policies as well as actual weapons systems have been dubbed "bargaining chips." Robert "Bud" McFarlane, one of President Reagan's many national security advisers, originally concocted the "broad interpretation" of the ABM Treaty as a bargaining chip with the Soviets. This reinterpretation of the ABM Treaty would allow more Star Wars tests. McFarlane reasoned that this would bring pressure on the Soviets to negotiate, fearing advances in U.S. Star Wars technology.

In this case, the bargaining chip argument backfired, as the hardliners in the Reagan administration, Richard Perle and secretary of Defense Caspar Weinberger, accepted the "broad interpretation" as the official, non-negotiable U.S. position.[24] Like nuclear weapons that began as bargaining chips, this policy bargaining chip was never cashed in, but became part of the administration's position, postponing sensible arms control. Only the insistence of Congress and Senator Sam Nunn in particular kept the original interpretation of the ABM Treaty intact.

---

[24]Strobe Talbott, *The Master of the Game: Paul Nitze and the Nuclear Peace*, New York: Alfred A. Knopf, 1988.

The term bargaining chip has taken on a new meaning with the B-2 and START. The Air Force is effectively blackmailing Congress, stating that they will not support the START Treaty unless the B-2 bomber is approved. The liberal START counting rules favor bombers, with each counting as carrying only one bomb, even though it might actually contain 12 to 24 nuclear weapons. Until May of 1990, the Air Force claimed that it must have 132 B-2s to hit all the targets on the current SIOP target list. When it became obvious that Congress would not appropriate $80 billion or more for 132 new bombers, Dick Cheney did reduce the request to 75 bombers, and overnight 75 was acceptable.

*Spin-offs.* If all else fails, a military program is hailed for its beneficial influence on the civilian economy. In the past, spin-offs from military research and development have helped our commercial markets. The development of military aircraft helped establish the United States as the number one supplier of commercial aircraft, which, with agriculture and the chemical industry, remain as our only major export industries. And much of the electronics and computer industries can trace their roots to military projects beginning with radar in World War II.

But even the spin-off argument is losing ground today. For example, the commercial electronics industry is actually ahead of the military in producing the latest computer chips, in a field that was once driven by military requirements. Because of the long lead-time and general sluggishness of the military procurement establishment, they often end up using antiquated electronic components that were frozen into the weapons design many years earlier.

A recent book by the Brookings Institution concludes that:

> military research and development no longer have the spinoff effect on the civilian sector of the economy that they did in the period when computers and microelectronics were developing . . . the demands of security investment have diverged from those of commercial application.[25]

Many military projects yield little or no commercial benefit. Exotic laser-beam or particle-beam weapons have no apparent civilian use,

---

[25]Kenneth F. Flamm and Thomas L. McNaugher, "Rationalizing Technology Investments," a chapter in *Restructuring American Foreign Policy*, Washington, D.C.: Brookings Institution, 1989, quoted in *Carnegie Quarterly*, Winter 1989, p. 4.

although Lt. Gen. Abrahamson, the original director of the Star Wars program, claimed credit for medical applications of the free electron laser. Actually, this medical research began without SDI funds and does not require SDI power levels. Indeed, an SDI caliber-free electron laser would blow a patient away!

Whereas early military transport or bomber aircraft had civilian application, the B-2 Stealth bomber has very little. The "stealth" technology, developed to reduce the ability of radars to detect military planes and cruise missiles, would actually be counterproductive in the airline business: we want civilian airliners to be seen by radars, and require them to carry "transponders" that automatically report aircraft type and altitude to make them more visible, not less. Military aircraft require high thrust and maneuverability. Commercial aircraft need high fuel efficiency and smooth and quiet flight. The computerized design and manufacturing process used on the B-2 may have some application in future civilian production. Because of the very tight manufacturing tolerances for the B-2, most plans and drawings were made on computers, a procedure which could help U.S. industrial competitiveness on future large scale production projects.

Even when military and industry both utilize new technology such as robotics, their needs may not overlap. One study concluded that "many of the DOD- and NASA-funded efforts in robotics deal with mobility and navigation, the areas deemed least important in a recent Robot Industries Association survey of American Manufacturers."[26]

Joseph Morone, a professor at Rensselaer Polytechnic Institute School of Management, described a fundamentally different culture in military industry versus the civilian economy:

> The defense culture emphasizes design of one-of-a-kind, high-performance and reliability systems that require customized manufacturing. The commercial culture places much greater emphasis on cost, on design for manufacturability, and on flexible, automated manufacturing. These differences become especially significant in light of the tilt in the U.S. R&D system toward military spending. A large fraction of the science and engineering community is being socialized in the one culture rather than the other. As

---

[26]Leo E. Hanifin, "The Paradox of American Manufacturing," *The Challenge to Manufacturing: A Proposal for a National Forum*, Washington, D.C.: National Academy of Engineering, 1988, p. 12.

a result, when scientists and engineers move from the defense to the commercial sector, instead of creating a beneficial transfer of technology, they may actually be contaminating the commercial sector with values and practices that are fundamentally inappropriate to competitive, market-oriented environments.[27]

A recent study on the defense technology base by the Congressional Office of Technology Assessment (OTA) concluded that some military technology may depend on civilian innovations that "spin-on" to the military, a total reversal of the "spin-off" rationale for more military spending.[28] According to OTA, much of this declining military spin-off potential is due to legal, institutional and administrative barriers. Fiber optics companies, for example, have had to set up special divisions with separate accounting, auditing and personnel practices to meet military procurement standards and regulations. Too often, the military prematurely freezes in a particular technology through complex procurement specifications, thereby eliminating future commercial advances in fast-moving fields from entering a military weapon system.

In any case, if our goal is to improve our commercial competitiveness or to ameliorate global warming or acid rain, military spending is not the most efficient approach. Funds applied directly to solving society's real problems would go much farther than waiting for serendipitous fallout from weapons programs.

*Hard-Target Kill Capability.* The nuclear establishment repeats over and over that the United States must acquire nuclear weapons that have "prompt, hard-target kill capability," also known as a "counterforce," or, strictly speaking, "countersilo" capability. They say that we "absolutely must" have the capability to quickly destroy those targets that the Soviets value most: their underground missile silos and the command and control bunkers that would house the Soviet leadership during an international crisis. Therefore we must add nuclear weapons with high accuracy and high explosive power or yield to destroy underground silos.

In a pre-nuclear era, the capability to destroy enemy weapons was wise and prudent. Once a war started, any military establishment would want weapons that could knock out the opponent's offensive potential.

---

[27]Joseph G. Morone, "Federal R&D Structure: The Need for Change," *The Bridge*, Washington, D.C.: The National Academy of Engineering, Fall 1989, p.8.
[28]Peter Grier, "Pentagon Arms Suffer from High-tech Gap," *Christian Science Monitor*, June 8, 1989, p. 7.

But this is not the pre-nuclear age. By acquiring the capability to destroy Soviet ICBMs in their underground silos, we give them strong incentive to fire those missiles early in a crisis, provoking the very nuclear holocaust that we all want to avoid.

Brent Scowcroft, the National Security Advisor to President Bush, R. James Woolsey, our arms control negotiator at the conventional force talks, and Thomas Etzold wrote recently that Soviet prompt, hard-target kill-capable ICBMs "constitute one of the most dangerous elements in current strategic relationships, because they encourage fears of preemptive attack and threaten our ability to do what is prudent in a crisis and necessary in war."[29]

They went on to say that "we would prefer to see both sides verifiably eliminate prompt, hard-target kill-capable ICBMs," but then argued that, in the meantime, the United States should offset this Soviet capability by building our own. In other words, it is dangerous for the Soviets to have hard-target kill capability, even though only 19 percent of our nuclear weapons are on vulnerable ICBMs, while it is acceptable for us to build accurate, hard-target kill weapons to attack 50 percent of Soviet warheads on fixed-silo ICBMs.

Admiral Crowe, while Chairman of the Joint Chiefs of Staff, testified that computer simulations showed that Soviet ICBMs "give the Kremlin a relative advantage in 'damage expectancy.' This means little, however, in the overall nuclear calculus."[30]

It means little, and yet Admiral Crowe also supported the full range of new U.S. nuclear weapons, including prompt, hard-target kill-capable weapons like the MX and the Trident II missiles.

As he interviewed members of the nuclear establishment, Steve Kull discovered two contradictory reasons to justify prompt, hard-target kill capability. One purpose was to *assure escalation* to a full-scale nuclear war, so that the Soviets would be less inclined to attack, and to assure Europeans that we would use nuclear weapons. Supposedly U.S. leaders would be less inhibited about using these accurate weapons compared to older weapons that might produce more collateral damage. The other contradictory purpose was to use precise, hard-target kill-capable weapons to *prevent escalation*, to help keep nuclear war limited

[29]Brent Scowcroft, R. James Woolsey, and Thomas H. Etzold, *Defending Peace and Freedom: Toward Strategic Stability in the Year 2000*, University Press of America, 1988, p. 17.
[30]Admiral William J. Crowe, Jr., Testimony before the Defense Appropriations Subcommittee, March 17, 1989.

once it began (this reasoning parallels the "cities-only" scenario: we need better accuracy to give us more options). Thus before the war, these chameleon weapons deter by fear of rapid escalation, while after the war begins, they are supposed to prevent escalation.

Kull describes one interview with a Pentagon official regarding this destabilizing nature of hard-target kill-capable nuclear weapons. The official admitted that these weapons "would force them [the Soviets] to attack full scale." When Kull questioned him further about supporting such destabilizing weapons, he became flustered and stated that he could not publicly argue against hard-target kill weapons, that his responsibility was to explain administration policy.[31]

Kull interviewed another official who was involved with nuclear war planning at NATO for many years. This NATO official, pressed by Kull, admitted that hard-target kill and countersilo targeting would be inappropriate, and that we should not target command bunkers because "you want to maintain an ability for effective command and control on both sides." But he reverted later to the usual rationalizations for wanting hard-target kill capability. He realized, apparently for the first time, the inconsistencies in his position. Kull came to an astounding conclusion: in years of participation in nuclear war-planning at NATO headquarters, this official had never faced the contradictions in striving for hard-target kill capability despite the dangers:

> ... by the end of the interview he seemed to implicitly confirm that he had not seen the incompatibility of his positions. I asked him if, in all his years at NATO headquarters, anybody had ever pointed out this problem to him, or if he had ever heard anybody else discussing it. He answered negatively.[32]

*War-fighting Preparations.* Finally, we return to our theme from Chapter 4: the nuclear war-fighting strategy. While many of us cringe and are repulsed by the thought of rational men and women planning deliberately for a "protracted nuclear war," in fact thousands of military analysts in and out of uniform do just that in both nations. They justify building and preparing to use new nuclear weapons on the basis of preparing to fight and win a nuclear war. By this preparation, they would argue, the threat of nuclear retaliation becomes more credible. If

---

[31]Op. cit. Kull. p. 112.
[32]Op. cit. Kull. p. 202.

the Soviets believe we are preparing to fight a nuclear war, and preferably if they believe that our leaders are a bit reckless, then they would be less inclined to attack. On the other hand, if the Soviets ever believed that we did not have the equipment or the resolve to fight a nuclear war, then we could be coerced or manipulated, according to this school of thought.

The advocates of a nuclear war-fighting posture do not stop with talk about retaliation or nuclear war-fighting. We must also build war-fighting weapons, to show we are serious. For many individuals in the military, in government and in various academic and think-tank circles, three or four decades of this kind of talk has seemingly dulled their senses, leading many to implicitly accept the notion that we must have a nuclear war-fighting capability.

President Reagan sensed that many members of the nuclear establishment have accepted a certain inevitability about nuclear war, when he ran into substantial resistance to his signing of the INF Treaty. In 1987, he stated:

> I think that some of the people who are objecting the most [to the INF treaty] and just refusing even to accede to the idea of ever getting any understanding, whether they realize it or not, those people basically down in their deepest thoughts have accepted that war is inevitable and that there must come to be a war between the superpowers.[33]

If Ronald Reagan, Mr. Conservative, can bring himself to talk to the Evil Empire and to discuss and sign arms control treaties, then maybe there is hope for changing course. Nuclear war is not inevitable, but we can and must do more to minimize future risks.

This concludes our discussion of the causes or justifications for the arms race. We suspect that few advocates of new nuclear weapons would subscribe to all the rationales we have described above. Most are probably driven by some combination of motives, with varying weights given to each rationale. Few probably have the time or intellectual honesty to stop and analyze their true motivations. We believe that most are driven by some combination of habit (inertia), career advancement, and a gut level feeling that we should stay ahead of our nominal

---

[33]David Hoffman, "Reagan Lashes Conservative Foes of Treaty, Foresees '88 Summit," *Washington Post*, December 4, 1987.

adversary, the Soviet Union, no matter what the cost. In other words, we are driven by the old way of thinking, in Einstein's terminology.

We have discussed reasons for continuing the arms race from the U.S. perspective. Similar reasons probably drive the arms race on the Soviet side. The details may be different. They may not have a free enterprise industrial complex and profit motives per se, but career advancement within the Soviet defense manufacturing establishment and various weapons bureaus is probably similar to motivations that drive the arms race on the U.S. side. The Soviet Union certainly saw nuclear weapons as a power symbol in the first several decades of the nuclear age, confirming superpower status and recognition even if their economic system could not match the West.

There is one big difference in the Soviet Union today: Mr. Gorbachev seems to have recognized the necessity of Einstein's new way of thinking about nuclear weapons. And given the centralized power in the Soviet system, Gorbachev has one big advantage over the United States: he does not have to convince the established bureaucracy in the government, academia or the military to adopt the new way of thinking. He can offer large, asymmetric cuts that favor the U.S. by the old military standards without reaching a consensus, without convening endless inter-agency review panels. Concentrating power in one person does have certain advantages in the short term.

In the long run, the checks and balances of our democratic system protect us from the excesses of a despotic ruler. In the case of nuclear weapons procurement and policy, however, the democratic process has often been circumvented, as we discuss in the next chapter.

# CHAPTER 8

---

# Failure of the Democratic Process

## SUMMARY

The democratic process depends on a well-informed electorate making appropriate choices through their elected representatives. In the nuclear weapons arena, this process has been impeded by a combination of unnecessary secrecy, nukespeak language that often hides the meaning of weapons and policies, unabashed salesmanship that ignores the down-side of weapons and policies, and the lack of long-term planning in military matters. As a result, our nuclear weapons policies and procurement plans have circumvented the democratic process. Decisions are made by a small group of bureaucrats, while Congress plays on the margins, making minor changes to a few military programs, but offering no coherent alternative. The Bush administration seems all too comfortable with the status quo, maintaining most of the secretive, short-sighted, undemocratic features of nuclear weapons policies inherited from previous administrations.

If they were fully informed about the economic, social and military costs and risks of the next generation of nuclear weapons, most

185

Americans would demand an end to the qualitative arms race. But the democratic process has been thwarted by several roadblocks. Secrecy is often used as an excuse to exclude citizen participation in the nuclear debate. The military has even prevented effective civilian oversight of our war-fighting plans, excluding top elected officials from seeing sensitive documents and plans. Nukespeak jargon shields many citizens from the real implications of our nuclear weapons policies and procurement plans.

New weapons programs and nuclear weapons requirements are sold to the public like used cars: any minor virtues are extolled while hiding the defects. And even for those in and out of government who have penetrated the veil of secrecy, jargon and deception surrounding our nuclear war-fighting plans, few have the resources or patience to look ahead 10 to 20 years to predict the implications of adding new weapons technologies today, and fewer still have the power or the will to change our nation's course.

As a result, the democratic process has been subverted in our national security policies and military procurement plans. Instead of developing broad national security objectives based on debate among well-informed citizens and their elected representatives, our national security process is driven by short-term weapons procurements drawn up by the individual military services in conjunction with their industrial benefactors. Weapons procurements define our policy, instead of the other way around.

## SECRECY

Since the beginning of the nuclear age, the real nature of our nuclear weapons and our nuclear war-fighting plans have been hidden from public view to some degree. Some of this concealment was justified in the early years of the nuclear age. Secrecy was clearly justified to keep Hitler from learning about the Manhattan Project that developed the first atomic bomb. During the war, Churchill refused to share the nuclear secret with the Soviets, our nominal allies against the Nazis. He saw the atomic bomb as an "equalizer" to control the Soviets as early as 1943, and refused to consider international control of atomic weapons, since that would have required sharing information with all nations, including the Soviets.[1]

---

[1] Joseph I. Lieberman, *The Scorpion and the Tarantula*, Boston: Houghton Mifflin, 1970, p. 32.

The decision to bomb Hiroshima was effectively made in secret by Gen. Leslie Groves, the military leader of the Manhattan Project whose previous military experience included overseeing the construction of the Pentagon. General Groves selected four potential Japanese cities to bomb a year before the August 6, 1945 attack on Hiroshima. He placed Kyoto on his early target lists, but Secretary of War Henry Stimson had visited Kyoto before the war, and, knowing first-hand of its beauty and heritage as ancient capital, insisted several times that it be stricken from the list. General Groves did not inform the Joint Chiefs of Staff about the plans to drop the atomic bomb on Japan, since one of the chiefs, Admiral Leahy, was known to be opposed. Joseph Lieberman (now a Senator from Connecticut) wrote:

> This was a very brazen decision for a lesser officer to make regarding the authority of the American military establishment and demonstrated the enormous power General Groves had gained for himself in a short period of time. He was altogether correct in his perception of Admiral Leahy, however. Like other members of the Joint Chiefs of Staff, Leahy believed that the Japanese were already defeated by the Naval blockade and success-ful fire bombing of their islands. Equally important to Leahy was his conclusion that the atomic bomb was a "barbarous" weapon. "I was not taught to make war in that fashion," Leahy said, "and wars cannot be won by destroying women and children."[2]

Thus the first decision to use nuclear weapons was made without the tacit approval of our highest military leaders. Harry Truman was not informed about the A-bomb project while he was Vice President. His diary notation on July 18, 1945, less than three weeks before the Hiroshima bombing, indicated his view that Japan was ready to surrender, and Truman wrote that the atomic bomb should *not* be used against civilians.[3]

However, planning for the atomic bombing mission was in full swing when Truman took over the presidency after Roosevelt died on April 12, 1945. By August, the momentum of the atomic bomb project was virtually unstoppable. It would have taken an exceptionally strong leader to reverse the momentum. General Groves' bombing plans went

---

[2]Ibid., p. 95.
[3]Norman Cousins, *The Pathology of Power*, New York: W.W. Norton, 1987.

ahead without much debate by our elected leaders, let alone the development of a democratic consensus. Given the wartime conditions, this lack of democratic process may have been justified. Unfortunately, ending the war did not restore enlightened decision making to nuclear matters.

Once the Soviets built and exploded their own atomic bomb in 1949, many years before General Groves expected them to succeed, classification of all but the technical details became unnecessary. In any case, the mechanical details of nuclear weapons are not needed to make intelligent choices about nuclear deterrence policy. We may not know exactly how the bomb works, but once we learn that one bomb can destroy one city, it does not take a nuclear physicist to decide that 13,000 nuclear bombs are more than enough to destroy a nation.

However, the military has used secrecy to keep nuclear war-fighting plans from our civilian leaders. This secrecy extended all the way to the White House in the 1950s. President Eisenhower did not find out the true nature of our nation's nuclear war-fighting plans until his last months in office. General Curtis LeMay, commander of the Strategic Air Command, was responsible for fighting a nuclear war in those days, despite the Constitutional designation of the President as Commander-in-Chief. There was a general distrust of civilians interfering with the military strategy of how to fight a war, even when that President happened to be a five-star general. In this view, the President might be the commander, but General LeMay and his successors were responsible for the actual planning and execution of a nuclear war.

From 1951 to 1955, the Joint Chiefs of Staff did not even receive a copy of General LeMay's war plans, let alone approve them.[4] In November of 1960, President Eisenhower sent three emissaries to SAC headquarters in Omaha, Nebraska, to determine just how SAC planned to use nuclear weapons in the event of a war. General LeMay's replacement, General Thomas Power, reluctantly revealed that SAC had but one plan: an all-out "spasm" attack, using all his bombers against targets in China and Eastern Europe as well as the Soviet Union. According to LeMay's plans, we would have obliterated China, Poland, Czechoslovakia, East Germany, Hungary and most of Eastern Europe in response to an attack by the Soviet Union. There were no other options, and no weapons were held in reserve.[5]

---

[4]Peter Pringle and William Arkin, S.I.O.P.: The Secret U.S. Plan for Nuclear War, New York: W.W. Norton, 1983, p. 52.
[5]Ibid., p. 54.

When John F. Kennedy won the presidency in 1960, his Secretary of Defense, Robert McNamara, restored civilian control over our nuclear war-fighting plans. The McNamara Defense Department created several options for fighting a nuclear war, starting with limited attacks on Soviet nuclear forces, then attacks on air defenses away from cities, air defenses near cities, command and communication facilities, and finally, the all-out cities attack. In June of 1962, McNamara announced that nuclear weapons were just another way to fight a war, implying that we had a war-fighting strategy. Seeing that this would lead to an open-ended justification for more and more nuclear weapons, he publicly announced a shift in December of 1963 to "assured destruction," later called "mutual assured destruction" or MAD by some . . . implying that we keep only enough weapons to retaliate should the Soviets attack us.

However, despite the declared policy of MAD, the nuclear war-fighting options remained. Our declared policy was not the same as our actual policy. Since 1962, the United States has had the flexibility to attack a range of military targets as well as industrial and urban centers in various combinations. We have never really had a "cities-only" policy. Even the Curtis LeMay "spasm" attack targeted a mixture of military targets such as airfields and industrial targets that were usually in or near cities.

In the 1980s, the Reagan administration extended excessive secrecy from war plans to include the actual nuclear weapons systems. The so-called black budget grew by a factor of eight from 1980 to 1988. The black budget contains weapons projects whose very existence is supposedly a secret, in addition to operating funds for the National Reconnaissance Office (spy satellites), the National Security Agency (communication and electronic intelligence), and the CIA. Including covert operations and the military's "Special Operations Forces," the total black and intelligence budget grew from $4 billion in 1980 to about $38 billion dollars in 1990, or about 13 percent of the total military budget where the black funds are hidden.

The size of the secret "black budget" can be estimated by subtracting the sum of the listed (unclassified) elements of the budget from the total DOD budget. The 1990 budget includes about 100 black programs with mysterious titles like "TRACTOR CRASH," "LINK CYPRESS," "HAVE NAP," "RETRACT MAPLE" and "CHALK POINSETTIA." About 60 of these unidentifiable black programs have no listed funding levels, while funds are listed for the other 40. Approximately 39 other black programs are identified, including the B-2 bomber, the Advanced Tactical Fighter (ATF) and the Advanced Cruise Missile, but no funds are shown. (The B-2 came out of the black in 1990.) In other cases billions of dollars are simply grouped into line items labeled "classified programs" or "classified project." Two conspicuous line items within the Air Force budget are labeled "SELECTED ACTIVITIES" for $4.9 billion (possibly the CIA budget) and "SPECIAL PROGRAMS" for $3.14 billion (possibly the National Reconnaissance Office).

These black budget funds are monitored by a handful of elected officials, including the chairmen and ranking minority members of the House and Senate Intelligence Committees, the armed services committees, and the defense appropriation subcommittees. This represents 12 members of Congress out of 525. Traditionally, these senior members of the military committees have been the most conservative members of Congress. While this is changing gradually, the black programs hardly receive a thorough and fair scrutiny from our elected officials.

Other members can learn about these programs if they ask for classified briefings, assuming that they even know that a particular black program exists (even the names of many projects are highly classified), but in practice few have the time or patience to penetrate the black curtain. Security rules preclude the personal staff of elected officials from attending hearings or learning about black projects. Therefore the members must personally attend these highly classified briefings, and cannot discuss the classified details with staff afterwards. The end result: black programs receive very little scrutiny, possibly one reason for their popularity in some circles.

While the technical details of most weapons systems are highly classified, the existence and general operating parameters of those weapons are known. The general characteristics of the MX missile in terms of its range, the number and yield of its 10 warheads, and even the location of the missile fields are public information. Precise details of operation and the targeting plans are highly classified, which is appropriate.

The Reagan administration, however, tried to keep secret even the existence of weapons like the Stealth fighter, the Stealth cruise missile, and the Stealth bomber. The real impact of the black budget is to keep the funds allocated to these projects a secret from most members of Congress and the American public. This subverts the constitutional responsibility of the Congress to provide funds for the military and to provide for the general welfare and common defense of the country.

In the past, small, tightly controlled and highly classified projects have been successful in avoiding the sluggishness of large military bureaucracies. The U-2 spy plane was produced under very tight secrecy at the Lockheed "skunkworks" in California. But today's mega-skunkworks include tens of thousands of workers, making super secrecy difficult, and creating additional bureaucracy that often avoids the checks and safeguards developed for more conventional military procurement projects. The end result is loss of effective fiscal and technical control over the massive Stealth projects.

Even if cost-effective production is achieved, secret weapons cannot fulfill the stated mission of nuclear deterrence. To deter, the enemy must know that we have certain weapons. We want the Soviets to know that we have bombers on alert, that we have Minuteman missiles and particularly Poseidon and Trident submarine-launched missiles at sea, ready to retaliate should the Soviets ever attack. Secret weapons cannot deter. Secret weapons can only be used to fight a nuclear war, not to prevent one. Thus these black budget weapons must be made public once they are built. They can only be secret in their formative years, when development costs, technical failures and schedule overruns are likely to create problems if they were known to Congress and the American people.

But, again, do not be discouraged or diverted by any claims that secret weapons or strategies would alter the policy debate. Secrecy has no bearing on the main issues. We may not know how many billions of dollars that the Pentagon has spent on the Stealth bomber, but we can still debate the merits and risks of developing the B-2 bomber or the Stealth cruise missile. As Jerome Wiesner, scientific adviser to Presidents Eisenhower and Kennedy, put it:

> It is often argued that secret information exists that would argue against a nuclear freeze or a test ban or some other logical arms-limitation measure. But there are no secrets on the vital issues that determine the course of the arms race.[6]

Overclassification is rampant. In 1970, the Pentagon's Defense Science Board stated that 90 percent of classified scientific and technical data should not be classified, that excess classification stifles inventiveness and useful research.[7] In 1978, Howard Morland, a free-lance

---

[6]Jerome B. Wiesner, "A Militarized Society," *Bulletin of the Atomic Scientists*, August 1985, p. 105.
[7]Arthur Macy Cox, *The Dynamics of Detente: How to End the Arms Race*, New York: W.W. Norton, 1976.

reporter, asked Congressman Ronald Dellums to submit a list of questions to the Department of Energy regarding the need for more plutonium for nuclear weapons. The DOE responded by classifying Morland's questions![8] When Morland tried to publish an article in *Progressive* describing how a hydrogen bomb worked, the government blocked publication, even though all material came from unclassified sources. In the subsequent trial, the government classified an article by physicist Hans Bethe from an eighth-grade encyclopedia, and Morland's college physics book was retroactively classified because Morland underlined certain sections.[9]

Secrecy is often used to suppress embarrassing information. Prior to the Limited Test Ban Treaty of 1963, the U.S. exploded 109 nuclear weapons in the atmosphere at the Nevada test site. The Atomic Energy Commission and its successors, ERDA and DOE, soon realized that citizens and animals living downwind from the test site were being exposed to dangerous levels of radiation. This information was classified, and the AEC instead issued reassuring statements and suppressed a report from the Public Health Service that established a link between leukemia and radioactive fallout.

It wasn't until 1986 that Federal District Judge A. Sherman Christensen accused the federal government of making "intentionally false or deceptive statements," and of "improper but successful attempts to pressure witnesses not to testify as to their real opinions." Another District Judge, Bruce Jensen, after awarding $2.6 million in damages to 10 plaintiffs, stated that "the dereliction of democracy in this case was the ultimate fallout,"[10] and Senator John Glenn commented that "we are poisoning our people in the name of national security."

Senator Glenn wrote that "DOE's radiation health effects research has been operating under unjustified forms of secrecy and has been isolated from the mainstream of public health science." He stated that the massive buildup and leaks of radioactive wastes at the nation's 250 nuclear weapons production facilities were due to "secrecy, isolation,

[8]Stephen Hilgartner, Richard C. Bell and Rory O'Connor, *Nukespeak: Nuclear Language, Visions, and Mindset*, San Francisco: Sierra Club Books, 1982, p. 64.
[9]Ibid., p. 68.
[10]Book review by Nick Kotz, *The Washington Post Book World*, March 19, 1989, reviewing Philip L. Fradkin, *Nuclear Roulette in Nevada: Fallout, an American Tragedy*, University of Arizona Press, 1989.

decentralized management and self-regulation—artifacts of the 1950s Cold War era."[11]

In many cases, the United States classifies information that is readily available to the Soviets. For a number of years, the U.S. Department of Energy classified the so-called hohlraum targets used in laser fusion energy research, even though Soviet scientists talked openly about these targets, and in 1984 the Japanese published a cover-story article on hohlraums in *Laser Focus*, a trade journal.

More recently, the United States and the Soviet Union conducted joint measurements of underground nuclear explosions, using both seismic instruments and the CORRTEX hydrodynamic technique proposed by the U.S. to measure the yield (explosive power) of the explosions. The data from these joint experiments were shared between U.S. and Soviet teams. The Soviets agreed to make these data public, but the U.S. government refused.[12]

It appears that the seismic technique of remotely measuring underground nuclear blasts was just as accurate as the on-site CORRTEX method pushed by the U.S. administration. These results confirm the widely accepted belief that remote seismic measurements are adequate to monitor a ban on all but militarily insignificant nuclear explosions, something the Reagan and Bush administrations oppose. This is a blatant example of using classification or simply withholding information from the public when that information contradicts stated administrative positions.

In a related episode, the Pentagon even classified ordinary rocks from the Soviet Union! These rocks were retrieved by American scientists from bore holes at the Soviet nuclear test sites, part of a U.S.-Soviet exchange visit. The Soviets approved this activity, but when the rocks were returned to the United States, they were promptly classified "Secret," logged in, and stored in a safe.

Worse yet, a $750,000 contract was signed with five universities to analyze these rocks. Since the authentic Soviet rocks have been classified, the university researchers were forced to analyze simulated Soviet rocks from Maine!

Here again, secrecy is obviously not required to keep the Soviets

---

[11]John H. Glenn, "National Security: More Than Just Weapons Production," *Issues in Science and Technology*, Summer 1989, p. 27.
[12]Michael R. Gordon, "U.S. Opposes Release of Soviet Nuclear Test Data," *New York Times*, March 23, 1989, p. 7.

from learning about geological conditions at their own test site; rather, the Bush administration is afraid that knowledge about Soviet underground geology will improve our capability to monitor a ban on underground testing of nuclear weapons, which they strongly oppose.

The government has not only abused secrecy provisions to prevent democratic discussion of policies it opposes, but it has used secrecy to hide embarrassing foreign policy escapades, as in the Vietnam War "Pentagon Papers" released by Daniel Ellsberg. Erwin Griswold, the solicitor general of the United States at the time, was given the responsibility of reviewing all 47 volumes of the Pentagon Papers prior to Supreme Court trial in 1971. All 47 volumes were classified "Top Secret." Griswold read through about 40 items that were deemed particularly sensitive by a team from the Departments of Defense and State and the National Security Agency, selecting 11 items he considered a possible threat to our national security. The Supreme Court struck down this case, declaring that there was no threat to national security by releasing any part of this document, including the 11 most sensitive items. Griswold concluded that "I have never seen it even suggested that there was such an actual threat." He went on to say:

It quickly becomes apparent to any person who has considerable experience with classified material that there is massive over-classification and that the principal concern of the classifiers is not with national security, but *rather with government embarrassment of one sort or another*. There may be some basis for short-term classification while plans are being made, or negotiations are going on, but apart from details of weapons systems, there is very rarely any real risk to current national security from the publication of facts relating to transactions in the past, even the fairly recent past.[13]

Unnecessary secrecy continues to this day to impede civilian control of military planning at the highest levels of government. The Joint Chiefs of Staff, our most senior military officers, generate nuclear war plans through their "Military Operational Procedures—MOPS." But the MOPS are so highly classified that the only civilians allowed to read them are the Secretary of Defense and Deputy Secretary of Defense.

---

[13]Erwin N. Griswold, "Secrets Not Worth Keeping," *Washington Post*, February 15, 1989, p. A25.

Without staff support, these civilian leaders cannot possibly analyze and critique the military war-fighting plans in any meaningful way.

Benjamin Schemmer, editor of the *Armed Forces Journal International*, began his first editorial to the new Bush administration in January of 1989 with this sentence: "The new Secretary of Defense needs to reassert civilian control over the military." He called on Congress to "hold hearings on why civilians should not be involved in the war plans."[14] No dove on defense, Mr. Schemmer obviously believes that secrecy continues to impede proper civilian oversight in the Bush Department of Defense.

## NUKESPEAK CAMOUFLAGE

Excessive and unwarranted classification is not the only barrier that excludes citizens from the nuclear debate. Whether intentional or not, a nukespeak vocabulary has evolved to confuse and distort the real meaning of our nuclear enterprise. We have already discussed some of the nukespeak language earlier. In Chapter 7, we listed the quest for "modernization" as one of the driving factors in the arms race. In fact, much of the modernization is not needed for deterrence, but contributes instead to a war-fighting capability. The uninitiated are taken in by the claims that we must "modernize" our forces, avoiding a debate on the merits and substantial risks of building accurate new weapons. Citizens are led to believe that they are making needed improvements to maintain an adequate deterrence, when in fact the major motivation is to enhance our nuclear war-fighting capability.

Other debate-suppressing code words include "flexible response," "damage limitation," "counterforce" capability and, most recently, "discriminate deterrence." These terms are all variations on the same theme that older, inaccurate warheads can only be used to attack cities in support of that evil MAD doctrine, whereas we want to be able to hit military targets to avoid escalation to an all-out war. In reality, we have had the capability and targeting plans to hit all military targets since the early 1960s. All targets, that is, *except* hardened, underground missile silos and command bunkers.

"Damage limitation" refers to the use of accurate nuclear weapons to destroy Soviet missiles before they can be launched, thereby reducing

---

[14]Benjamin F. Schemmer, "Must We Go Nuke? Let's Mop Up First," *Armed Forces Journal International*, January 1989, p. 5.

or limiting the damage to our homeland. As usual, the motivation is exemplary, but the end result is not. The accurate, high power nuclear weapons needed to limit damage are the same destabilizing nuclear weapons that could be used for a first strike.

The term "counterforce" originally meant the ability to attack the military force of the opponent. Targeting airfields or tank farms or fuel depots was not considered destabilizing. Since the 1970s, "counterforce" has taken on a new meaning: the ability to destroy missile silos. For clarity, the name should have been changed to "countersilo." Countersilo weapons like the Soviet SS-18 and the American MX and D-5 missiles are very destabilizing as discussed earlier. As you may have gathered, all of these terms hide the acquisition of accurate, destabilizing, nuclear war-fighting weapons.

Another popular term in the nuclear analyst's lexicon is "prompt, hard-target kill capability." This phrase is less deceptive than the others, and somewhat remarkable in that the word "kill" survived the Pentagon wordsmith's knife. [15] But implications of this phrase might still escape the nuclear novice. What it really means is that the military wants the ability to quickly destroy Soviet ICBM silos and command and control bunkers, targets that are "hardened" to withstand all but a near direct hit. The "prompt" refers to fast ballistic missiles with 15-25 minute flight time rather than bombers that take 12-14 hours to reach their targets.

This "prompt, hard-target kill capability" could only be utilized if we struck before Soviet ICBMs were fired. We would either have to strike first ourselves, or the Soviets would have to launch part of their ICBM force and not fire their residual ICBMs when we launched our accurate weapons. In either case these weapons would increase the incentives for both sides to launch sooner rather than later in a crisis. These are destabilizing weapons.

In all cases, justifications for new nuclear weapons should be judged not by their intent, but by their actual effect. The intentions of modernization, damage limitation, counterforce or flexible response may be acceptable, but the weapons to achieve those goals are in fact destabilizing.

---

[15] The only other recently used Pentagon term containing the word "kill" was the "Kinetic Kill Vehicle" or KKV of the Star Wars program. The name of this proposed weapon system was sanitized to a more innocent-sounding "Space Based Interceptor" in 1988 and then to "Brilliant Pebbles" in 1989.

## USED-CAR SALESMANSHIP

You don't sell used cars by emphasizing the dents and defects of a car. Salesmen accentuate the positive, even turning faults into virtues (high mileage becomes well broken in, older models are collector's items, etc.). It seems at times that the administration and other weapons advocates are selling used cars. Reports to Congress and the American public turn into unabashed sales pitches for the latest weapon system or policy. Rarely are the risks, trade-offs or alternatives discussed. Half-truths are used to buttress faulty conclusions. ·

The used-car sales approach was quite effective in the late 1970s in scuttling the SALT II Treaty. The late Senator Henry "Scoop" Jackson and various anti-SALT groups presented one-sided descriptions portraying Soviet strengths and American weakness.[16] Soviet superiority was accentuated by quoting the number of ICBMs, missile throw-weight (the weight that could be lifted into space), and the number of submarines. No mention was made of the total number of strategic warheads, the number of bombers, or submarine-launched warheads where the U.S. had significant advantage. It was claimed that the United States stood still in the '70s, while the Soviets added massively to their nuclear arsenals. Never mind that the U.S. strategic nuclear arsenal doubled from about 5,000 nuclear warheads in 1970 to over 10,000 by 1980 and that the bombers, missiles and submarines carrying those weapons were all substantially improved.

In the early 1980s Brent Scowcroft, now the National Security Advisor, chaired President Reagan's Commission on Strategic Forces. This well-respected panel produced a better-than-average report, admitting that deterrence was alive and well because we have over 5,000 nuclear warheads safely at sea on submarines. The potential vulnerability of our land-based missiles was not the critical flaw as claimed by candidate Reagan in the 1980 presidential campaign.

But the Scowcroft Commission report lacked critical assessments of new counterforce weapons. For example, they acknowledged that stability should be our primary objective. Yet they went on to recommend deploying the MX missile, the most destabilizing weapon in our arsenal. There is no discussion of the crisis instability created by the MX. They did mention that 50 MX missiles with 500 warheads would

---

[16]Arthur Macy Cox, *The Dynamics of Detente: How to End the Arms Race*, New York: W.W. Norton, 1976, p. 35.

not be enough to destroy all 1398 Soviet silos, an implicit admission that enough warheads to do so would be destabilizing. But they also endorsed the D-5 submarine-launched missile, even though the Pentagon originally asked for 4,800 D-5 warheads, clearly enough for a first strike against Soviet ICBMs. This first-strike potential of the D-5 missiles was never mentioned in the Scowcroft report.

More recently, Senator Sam Nunn chastised Secretary of Defense Dick Cheney for neglecting to mention certain negative details regarding Soviet strategic nuclear weapons. Mr. Cheney, in his zeal to sell U.S. strategic "modernization" programs, carefully listed those strategic systems that the Soviets were continuing to "modernize." But he neglected to mention that the Soviets had reduced the number of strategic launchers as older models were retired faster than new ones were added; that they had cut back production of the Blackjack strategic bombers that "goes beyond what is required by START" according to CIA Director Webster; halted some SS-18 silo improvements and that they had stopped submarine and bomber patrols near U.S. territory.[17]

We would recommend that DOD begin to mimic the style of Congressional reports including those of the Office of Technology Assessment or the Congressional Research Service. Reports from these two organizations always include the advantages and the disadvantages of a particular weapon system or arms control treaty, highlighting the pros and cons so that the reader can arrive at his or her own decision based on the best available arguments.

Another example of one-sided salesmanship comes from the 1986 Defense Authorization bill. This bill stated flatly that we "absolutely must have" prompt, hard-target kill capability. There was no discussion of why we needed this capability, and no mention of any deleterious effects. If the United States Senate, the "world's greatest deliberative body," cannot produce an honest and candid discussion of the pros and cons of acquiring hard-target kill capability, how can we expect the American public to join the debate?

The annual Pentagon requests for funds for Star Wars and anti-satellite (ASAT) weapons exclude any negative consequences from these programs. After weighing the pros and cons, informed individuals may disagree on whether the United States should proceed to deploy ASAT or Star Wars weapons. But no one could deny that there are some

---

[17]Sam Nunn, "The Changed Threat Environment of the 1990's," *Congressional Record*, March 29, 1990, p. S3448.

disadvantages to at least partially counterbalance the perceived military advantages. Any attempt to deploy a dedicated U.S. ASAT system would surely increase pressures on the Soviets to build their own effective ASAT, which in turn would put our satellites at risk. Pentagon budget justifications never mention let alone discuss the ramifications of these negative factors. They merely state that they must have an ASAT system to destroy Soviet reconnaissance satellites.

Salesmanship sometimes extends to the National Laboratories, where one would think that scientific objectivity would prevail. President Reagan decided to accelerate the ballistic missile defense research program based in part on Edward Teller's efforts to sell the X-ray laser program. Teller stated in a December 1983 letter to the Reagan White House that the technology was ready for engineering, when in fact the work was in the very early research phases. Dr. Teller even went so far as to claim one X-ray laser "the size of an executive desk" could wipe out the entire Soviet ICBM fleet.

Several scientists discounted Teller's claims. Roy Woodruff, the scientist who directed the X-ray laser research as Associate Director at the Lawrence Livermore National Lab, called the statements of Teller and Lowell Wood about the X-ray laser "overly optimistic and technically incorrect." Livermore director Roger Batzel refused Woodruff's request to counter Teller's claim that the X-ray laser was ready for engineering development, and Woodruff was not permitted to send corrected technical data to Washington.[18] Dr. Woodruff was effectively demoted for his efforts to preserve scientific integrity.

Another Livermore scientist, W. Lowell Morgan, quit the X-ray laser program, calling it an "obscene investment of money" and that he "felt that the interpretation and presentation of the few scientific results that we had was fraudulent."[19] Even the promise of early research results from underground nuclear explosions to test the X-ray laser concept at the Nevada test site was later suspect, because of questionable data from improperly calibrated test equipment. The Livermore Lab later acknowledged that they were having great difficulty developing adequate instrumentation to measure properties of the X-ray laser output.[20]

---

[18]Dan Morain and Richard E. Meyer, "Teller Gave Flawed Data on X-ray Laser, Scientist Says," *Los Angeles Times*, October 21, 1987, p. 1.
[19]Theresa M. Foley, "SDIO Studies Basing Small X-ray Laser Weapons on Submarines," *Aviation Week and Space Technology*, August 1, 1988, p. 57.
[20]"Livermore Acknowledges X-ray Laser Problem," *Science*, November 29, 1985, p. 1023.

## LACK OF LONG-TERM PLANNING

There does seem to be one area of consensus in military circles: virtually everyone agrees that the United States government lacks a long-term integrated plan for our weapons policies, procurements and our arms control policies. Thousands of analysts in the Pentagon, the White House, the State Department, and the Congress study our weapons systems and churn out reports, but the vast majority only have time to prepare, defend or critique the budget for the next year. Virtually no one is in charge of implementing any long-term plan. We drift from year to year, making adjustments on the margin, reacting to the momentum of the arms race, like a giant boulder roaring down a hill. We can't stop it. The best we can do is to chip off a few flakes as it flies by, or, with great effort, divert it slightly to the right or left.

John Lehman, the Secretary of the Navy in the Reagan administration, wrote after leaving office:

> There is no integrated defense policy. Thanks to three decades of reforms, the vast Pentagon bureaucracy is occupied almost solely with programming and budgeting, and is currently based on sheer repetitive momentum. Nearly every office in the Pentagon— whether charged with dependents' schools, nuclear research or guerrilla warfare—spends 95 percent of its time on the endless meetings concerned with the annual budget preparation and presentation to Congress.
>
> In today's Pentagon, there is no real integration of policy. The huge staff of the Joint Chiefs of Staff (JCS) churns out its papers, the vast Office of the Secretary of Defense (OSD) staff theirs, and the military departments still others. Nowhere are they brought together except in a procedural sense of staffing paperwork.[21]

Congress came to similar conclusions in the Fiscal Year 1989 Defense authorization bill:

> There is no established process involving the Office of the Secretary of Defense and the Joint Staff in which strategy, policy, operational concepts, and resource constraints are fully debated,

---

[21]John Lehman, "Pentagon RX: Cut the Fat, Build Services' Muscle," *Washington Post*, January 22, 1989, p. D2.

coordinated, and translated into weapon acquisition programs. The dominant role of setting requirements for new weapon systems remains with the headquarters staffs of the military departments, and the requirements developed by those departments often do not appear to have been rigorously evaluated in terms of their overall contribution to national military strategy.[22]

In other words, each branch of the military defines its own weapons requirements, more or less independently of the civilian leaders and the needs of our country in terms of overall national security. The Army defines requirements for tanks, the Air Force for planes, and the Navy for ships. (Actually, four services, the Air Force, Army, Navy and Marines, each purchase their own aircraft, giving the U.S. four robust and virtually independent air forces.)

The federal government is virtually paralyzed by the budget process, determining how much money to throw at which weapons systems. The Pentagon must testify before six major committees of Congress each year: the House and Senate Budget committees, the two Armed Services Committees, and the two Defense Appropriation Subcommittees. Each committee and many other related subcommittees hold hearings on various components of the military budget, including research and weapons procurement programs for each of the services, health care, military dependent issues, as well as force structure, training, readiness and maintenance. In all, the Pentagon must deal with 30 different committees, 77 subcommittees and 4 panels, according to Dick Cheney, the Secretary of Defense. In addition to these formal hearings, many informal presentations are required for professional staff members. Mr. Cheney estimates that senior defense officials give an average of 14 hours of testimony for each day Congress is in session.[23] With this focus on next year's budget, long-term strategy and planning receive little emphasis.

Benjamin Schemmer, in the editorial quoted earlier, wrote that "America's military strategy is bankrupt." He recommended the creation of an Undersecretary of Defense for Program Integration, "someone who's cleared to read the war plans and advise the SecDef how defense 'policy' correlates with his 'acquisition' programs, his 'force manage-

---

[22]*National Defense Authorization Act for Fiscal Year 1989,* Conference report 100-989, September 28, 1988, p. 90.
[23]Dick Cheney, "Defense Management: Report to the President," July 1989.

ment' plans, and arms control."[24] In other words, we need an effective long-term planning capability.

Ideally the Congress should also develop a long-range planning capability. The logical arrangement would be for the House and Senate Armed Services Committees to consider long-range issues, leaving the yearly budget decisions to the Defense Appropriation Subcommittees. In practice, both committees in each house have blurred the distinction between authorizing programs and appropriating money, creating much duplication of effort. As stated by one of the many reports prepared for the new Bush administration, co-chaired by former Secretaries of Defense Harold Brown and James Schlesinger: "The Armed Services Committees should broaden their focus to basic policies and the fundamental contours of military strategy and defense programs and the appropriations subcommittees should narrow their focus to spending issues."[25]

It is unclear whether Congress could in practice separate these functions. Those serving on the Armed Services Committees are keenly interested in allocating funds for preferred weapons systems. And those on the Defense Appropriation Subcommittee want to place their stamp on key arms control and military policy questions. Furthermore, Senators and Representatives, like their counterparts in the military services and the executive branch, have little time or resources for long-range planning.

If anything, the personal staffs of members of Congress have less time to analyze national security issues, since they must consider not only defense issues, but all aspects of our national life. It is a rare Congressman who has the luxury to stop and consider the long-term implications of new weapons systems, when he or she must decide how to vote on next year's budget and weapons mix, plus education, social security, taxes, the environment, transportation, agriculture, veterans issues, health, foreign policy, and so on.

This leaves the staffs of the Armed Services Committees and Defense Appropriation Subcommittees. But many of these aides are also products of the arms race. Their careers have been linked to various weapons

---

[24]Schemner, op. cit.
[25]Harold Brown and James Schlesinger, cochairmen, *Making Defense Reform Work*, Washington, D.C.: The Foreign Policy Institute and The Center for Strategic and International Studies, November 1988, p. 3.

systems. And they generally have little exposure to economic and environmental issues, and therefore are ill-suited to bringing cohesion to our total national security strategy.

Finally, the administration and the Congress would have to reach a consensus on national security policy. After the contentious debate and division during the early Reagan years, the White House and the Congress did agree on the overall funding levels for defense and the civilian budget for fiscal years 1989 and 1990. With the dollar figure set by this so-called budget summit, the Congress was able to avoid lengthy debate and stalemate over the total dollars flowing to the Pentagon. But no consensus was reached on many other issues within the military budget such as SDI, the MX-Midgetman choice, the B-1 vs. B-2 bomber question, and how to reduce and restructure forces after the Cold War. Without agreement between the executive and legislative branches, it is unlikely that major changes could be implemented.

New weapons take anywhere from 5 to 15 years from conception to deployment. The Pentagon puts out a five-year budget plan, but in the Reagan years it assumed such optimistic funding in future years that it was almost useless, or even counterproductive since it perpetuated the myth that military budgets would continue to grow to pay for future weapons procurements. The military services could derive some sense of validity to their grandiose weapons building plans, because the five-year plan promised endless increases in military budgets.

Our elected officials have limited time horizons compared to weapons systems. Presidents have at best four years, Senators six years and Representatives only two years. The time required for reelection campaigning reduces their effective attention spans even more. Is it any wonder that no one formulates or is guided by long-range plans?

This leads us to one conclusion: the American public, academics and activists outside of government must supply the long-term continuity, the long-term vision to guide our nuclear weapons policies, procurements and arms control policies until such time as the administration regains control of and restores sanity to the military planning process. Informed citizens are the only enduring force. A progressive President might be able to bring about nuclear perestroika, but he or she probably couldn't be elected without citizen approval of new weapons policies. We must restore the democratic process to the nuclear weapons arena. We must build and maintain a national consensus. Active citizen participation is essential to avoid the dangers we listed in Chapter 5.

## SUCCESSFUL DEMOCRATIC DEBATE

There were three periods of very productive national debate regarding nuclear weapons policy. In the early 1960s citizens debated and protested the radioactive fallout from atmospheric nuclear explosions by both superpowers. The fears of radioactive strontium-90 in milk helped to push our leaders into signing the Limited Test Ban Treaty of 1963 that ended atmospheric testing. But a minority of Senators still opposed the treaty, and 34 Senators can block any treaty since the Constitution requires a two thirds majority for ratification. To secure the votes of a group of Senators led by Henry "Scoop" Jackson, President Kennedy had to promise that testing would actually increase underground so that new nuclear weapons could be developed. The arms race merely moved underground. But at least radioactive fallout was reduced.

The second national debate was over the issue of ballistic missile defenses in the late 1960s. Scientists played a substantial role in this debate, culminating in the consensus that defenses would be destabilizing. That is, if one side tried to put up a defensive shield, the opponent would add more offensive missiles to guarantee its ability to retaliate. With worst-case analysis, the opponent would always assume that the defense would work better than in actual operation, leading them to add more offensive missiles than necessary. Attempting to build defenses is a sure method of increasing the nuclear arsenals of both sides. Of course, the Star Wars debate has reopened this chapter in the nuclear arms race with a vengeance.

The third national debate in the early 1980s was spurred by President Reagan's bellicose threats against the Evil Empire. Millions of citizens joined groups such as the Nuclear Weapons Freeze Campaign to meet and discuss the nuclear arms race. Although they failed to stop the arms race, public pressure did slow and cap programs such as the MX missile, and the legacy of the Freeze movement is a latent group of citizens who are more knowledgeable about nuclear issues, and ready to respond to visionary leaders.

In summary, the nuclear arms race was born in secrecy, and continues to this day to circumvent the normal democratic process. We do not have a well-informed electorate or anything approaching an informed national debate about the arms race. The annual procurement of new nuclear weapons continues without any meaningful long-range planning. No one considers the long-term implications of building new, more destabilizing weapons. We have not changed our way of thinking, as Einstein said, and hence we drift toward unparalleled catastrophe.

This concludes our discussion of the dangers facing our nation if we continue the qualitative arms race, developing and building "better" nuclear weapons without regard to their long-term effects on our national security. We turn now to our prescription for improving our total security: economic, environmental, social and military.

# Part Three

# ALTERNATIVE NATIONAL SECURITY STRATEGIES

# CHAPTER 9

# A Sane Nuclear Alternative: Deterrence-Only

## SUMMARY

The United States and the Soviet Union could reduce nuclear proliferation, minimize the risk of nuclear war and cut military spending by adopting a deterrence-only policy: we would keep nuclear weapons only to deter war, and renounce all other secondary objectives for weapons of mass destruction. Both superpowers would renounce the quest for nuclear superiority, abandon the outrageous concept of winning or "prevailing" in a nuclear war, and stop building nuclear weapons to destroy underground missile silos and command and control bunkers. Each superpower would keep only a few hundred nuclear weapons on survivable mobile platforms such as submarines and agree to jointly stop all nuclear weapons testing.

The deterrence-only strategy would best be implemented through reciprocal initiatives. We would stop weapon developments for a specific time period, inviting the Soviets to stop, too. We would negotiate treaties to solidify a long-term stable environment without the pressure of continuing technological developments. Weapons reductions could be made in small steps, with each new step contingent on Soviet reciprocal moves. While it might be possible to create a deterrence-only policy by congressional action alone, a bold, visionary President will probably be required.

As a long-term goal, we would seek to remove all nuclear weapons, whenever international relations permit. In the meantime, technology would be developed to monitor a global ban on the production of fissionable material, the essential fuel of all nuclear weapons. While striving for eventual nuclear disarmament, the world would be far more secure with the deterrence-only posture, a stable position that could withstand future international disturbances with far more resilience than our current destabilizing policies and nuclear arsenals.

## THE DETERRENCE-ONLY POLICY

We recommend that the nation adopt a deterrence-only policy: we would officially acknowledge that nuclear weapons serve but one purpose: to deter their own use. Henceforth, we would keep only enough weapons to deter war. This policy has also been called "minimum deterrence" or "finite deterrence."

This concept is not new. Bernard Brody, a political scientist from the University of Chicago, with experience at Yale, the RAND corporation and UCLA, recognized this reality of nuclear weapons at the dawn of the nuclear age in 1945 when he wrote:

Thus far the chief purpose of our military establishment has been to win wars. From now on its chief purpose must be to avert them. It can have almost no other useful purpose.[1]

George Kennan formulated a "minimum deterrence" policy in the State Department in 1949, stating that atomic weapons should only serve "purposes of deterrence and retaliation."[2] This was a clear example of Einstein's call for a new way of thinking about nuclear weapons. Regrettably, the deterrence-only policy was not accepted by our leaders. Over the years, most officials have effectively succumbed to the

---

[1]Jonathan Schell, *The Fate of the Earth*, New York: Alfred A. Knopf, 1982, p. 197.
[2]Steven Kull, *Minds at War: Nuclear Reality and the Inner Conflicts of Defense Policy Makers*, New York: Basic Books, 1988, p. 5.

traditional military view that more weapons equals better security, that nuclear weapons are just another very powerful way of executing a war. They would be hard-pressed to justify the growth in our nuclear arsenal looking back at 40 years of the arms race. Each step along the way may have seemed rational at the time, or at least tolerable, but the end result of 13,000 deliverable strategic nuclear warheads and perhaps another 10,000 tactical nuclear weapons defies all reason.

At least one group of 150 nuclear weapons experts from government, military and academia did agree in 1989 that "nuclear weapons strategy is likely to move toward a 'deterrence-only' policy."[3] A majority of these experts, meeting at a conference held at the Los Alamos Laboratory's Center for National Security Studies, agreed that our current forces are based on nuclear war-fighting capability, but that nuclear forces would probably shrink and contract to the deterrence-only posture. There is no evidence, however, that these experts nudged the nuclear establishment in that direction after they left the conference.

Some of you may be wondering how this policy of deterrence-only would differ from our current posture. Don't we keep nuclear weapons for deterrence now?

Yes, that is *one* of our objectives today, but there are several other secondary objectives that get us into trouble:

*Superiority/Parity.* We must add nuclear weapons to try to catch up to the Soviets in those categories where they are ahead such as total number of ICBMs, "throw weight" (the lifting power of their missiles) and number of submarines.

*Counterforce weapons.* We must add weapons to attack hardened Soviet missile silos and command and control bunkers, the things the Soviets value most.

*Damage limitation.* We must add accurate weapons to limit damage to the U.S. by attacking Soviet ICBM silos, should nuclear war occur.

*War-winning.* We must add weapons to "win" or to "prevail" should deterrence fail, by coming out of a nuclear war in better relative position than the Soviet Union.

All of these secondary goals justify the procurement of "prompt, hard-target kill capability" or weapons to destroy hardened Soviet missile silos and command and control bunkers and, for the future, weapons designed to destroy mobile missiles or even nuclear sub-

---

[3]Peter Grier, "U.S. Conferees See Diminishing Role for Nuclear Weapons," *Christian Science Monitor*, June 28, 1989, p. 7.

marines. Trying to simultaneously pursue these secondary goals along with the primary deterrence goal leads to the dangerous inconsistencies in our current policy. Deterrence of nuclear war requires crisis stability. To maximize crisis stability, our policy should avoid any targeting goals that would give the Soviet Union any incentive to strike first during a crisis situation. But each of the secondary goals requires accurate, silo-busting nuclear weapons.

These secondary goals are dangerous, costly and inconsistent with deterrence. Under a deterrence-only policy, we would officially de-nounce all of these secondary objectives and all the excess baggage that goes with them. Superiority would be replaced by sufficiency, enough to deter. War-winning would be replaced by war-avoidance. Damage limitation by retaliating with many accurate nuclear weapons would be replaced with damage limitation by jointly reducing our nuclear weapons drastically. Deterrence would be not just the primary objec-tive, but the *only* objective for nuclear weapons. We would abandon any attempt to use nuclear weapons for geopolitical persuasion, either overtly or covertly.

It may be difficult for some military planners to relinquish their attempts to limit the consequences of a nuclear war. All Americans share their concern, and would obviously support any damage limitation plans that had no impact on the probability of war beginning in the first place. Unfortunately, reducing damage by building weapons that threaten Soviet retaliatory forces increases the risk of escalation. We must choose between reducing the risks of war and reducing the consequences of such a war. In our judgment, we must choose war avoidance over damage limitation, particularly when our attempts to limit damage by countersilo targeting would in all likelihood *increase* actual damage to the U.S. as the Soviets launched on warning. We must always distinguish between the *intent* of a weapon system and the actual *consequences* of deploying that weapon. The intent of an accurate D-5 to limit damage should war occur may be laudatory, but potential con-sequences of pressuring the Soviets to launch on warning overwhelms any advantage of deploying the D-5 over existing C-4 missiles.

## DETERRENCE-ONLY WEAPONS

To implement the deterrence-only policy, we would need only a few hundred survivable nuclear warheads in place of the 13,000 in our strategic arsenal today. All warheads should be on mobile missiles, either at sea or on land, or on bombers on alert. All fixed-silo ICBMs would be eliminated on both sides as destabilizing, beginning with multiple warhead missiles, since they invite preemptive attack in a crisis, and since their accuracy and prompt retaliatory response time would not be needed for deterrence. No new nuclear weapons systems would be needed, once we renounced any desire to destroy Soviet underground missile silos or command and control bunkers. Weapons could be replaced as they reached the end of their useful service life, but replacements would be functionally equivalent.

Deterrence-only weapons must satisfy one criterion: the few hundred (say 400) nuclear warheads must be able to survive a Soviet first strike, as absurdly unlikely as that may seem in these times of Soviet withdrawal from Eastern Europe. Robert McNamara reports that the U.S. Navy considered a force of about 464 survivable nuclear warheads adequate for deterrence in 1958 and 1959, calling this "an objective of generous adequacy for deterrence alone, not by the false goal of adequacy for 'winning'"[4] We believe that 400–500 survivable warheads on each side is sufficient for deterrence today.

Under the deterrence-only policy, there is no justification for nuclear superiority or war-winning weapons. The paramount requirement is crisis stability, and fixed-silo ICBMs, particularly those with many accurate warheads like the MX, invite attack. Given Gorbachev's flexibility in the arms control arena, he would probably agree to eliminating most if not all of their fixed-silo ICBMs if we agreed to remove ours. But we must ask. We should take the initiative to create a more stable regime.

The 400–500 warheads for the deterrence-only policy must be on survivable platforms. Fortunately, most of our warheads are currently on survivable mobile missiles: submarine-launched missiles moving under the sea.[5] These missiles are safe from attack, as acknowledged by most military experts. We could place all 400 warheads on submarines. Each new Trident submarine carries 192 warheads (eight on each of 24 missiles), but we should not place all of our retaliatory force on just two or three boats.

---

[4]Op. cit., McNamara, p. 123.
[5]The term "mobile missiles" as commonly used should really read "land-mobile missiles," referring to ICBMs on trucks or railroad cars. But submarine-launched ballistic missiles (SLBMs) are by definition highly mobile, and far more survivable than any land-based mobile missile.

Rather, we should place fewer warheads distributed on 10 to 15 submarines. (We currently have 35 ballistic missile submarines, including nine of the new 24-missile Tridents.) Fifteen Trident submarines could carry 360 warheads if each missile had but one warhead. Poseidon missiles each carry an average of 10 warheads and the Trident missiles have eight warheads each. Thus the existing submarines have far more capability than needed for deterrence.

If we still rely on nuclear deterrence when the new Trident submarines are ready for retirement in 20 to 30 years, we should consider building much smaller submarines carrying far fewer missiles. The 17 Trident submarines now ordered are more than adequate for deterrence, and we do not need the first-strike capable D-5 missile. The SLBM's should have long range to increase the volume of ocean each submarine can hide in. We should sacrifice accuracy and payload to achieve longer range, thereby improving stability and our common security. In addition, the yearly operating costs for 35 submarines could be cut at least in half.

Some of the 400 warheads might be placed on mobile missiles on land. The Soviets apparently prefer this option, and have already developed the SS-24 10-warhead, rail-mobile missile and the SS-25 single-warhead, truck-mobile missile. However, detecting mobile missiles on land, while extraordinarily difficult, is easier than finding and tracking submarines at sea. As noted in Chapter 5, the United States has initiated several programs with a goal of finding and destroying Soviet mobile missiles on land. Thus arms control limits on what we now call strategic relocatable target (SRT) weapon systems would be required to maintain crisis stability in a deterrence-only regime, if the Soviets chose to rely on land-mobile missiles for much of their deterrent.

We would not need more MX missiles as currently proposed by the Bush administration, and the proposed fleet of 500 Midgetman mobile missiles could be eliminated or cut down to 50. The annual operating costs for our 1,000 fixed silo missiles could be reduced to operate 50 mobile missiles or be eliminated. We could agree to eliminate all land-based missiles in exchange for the Soviets reducing to 400 warheads on survivable platforms.

Finally, some of the 400 warheads could be placed on bombers that were on alert, so that they could take off on receipt of warning of Soviet missile launch. Future technologies like depressed trajectory missiles and very stealthy cruise missiles would have to be banned to maintain this mode of survivable basing. We would not need to improve the avionics on the B-1 bomber, and we would not need to add any B-2 Stealth bombers.

The potential savings in nuclear weapons budget authority are estimated in Table 9-1. Cost estimates are approximate, particularly after 1991, since the Department of Defense has not submitted its annual five-year plan as required by law. Operating cost savings assume that the United States retires all land-based missiles, reduces the number of submarines from 35 to 17, and cuts bomber operations dramatically. The 1990 operating costs for current strategic weapons systems were estimated at $1.8 billion for all ICBMs, $2.4 billion for SLBMs and $11.8 billion for bombers, for a total annual cost of $16.1 billion to operate and maintain our current strategic nuclear arsenal.[6] We have assumed in Table 9-1 that these operating costs are cut in half by 1995.

Based on these assumptions, the deterrence-only posture could save $17 to $24 billion per year in research and weapon procurements, and $2 to $10 billion per year in reduced operating expenses. By 1995, savings could approach $35 billion per year, or roughly 12 percent of current military spending.

## DETERRENCE-ONLY ARMS CONTROL POLICIES

Arms control treaties would be an integral, coherent component of the deterrence-only policy. There would be none of the inconsistencies of the Reagan arms control circus, such as their official policy to ban mobile missiles in negotiations with the Soviets while the weaponeers deemed them stabilizing and desirable, or their major emphasis on developing strategic defenses in violation of the ABM Treaty, the cornerstone of arms control achievements.

The arms control objectives of the deterrence-only policy would include multi-national, verifiable bans on all nuclear explosions, all missile flight testing, all anti-satellite weapons testing, all weapons in space, all sea-launched cruise missiles and all anti-mobile missile weapon systems. Prohibiting these activities though verifiable treaties would cement the stability of the small, deterrence-only arsenals on each side. Verification technology would be improved as needed to give

---

[6]Stephen Alexis Cain, *Strategic Forces Funding in the 1990s: A Renewed Buildup?*, Washington, D.C.: Defense Budget Project, April 1989, p. 15.

TABLE 9-1.   ROUGH ESTIMATE OF POTENTIAL SAVINGS DUE TO THE "DETER-
RENCE-ONLY" POLICY.

| | ($Billions) | | | | |
|---|---|---|---|---|---|
| | 1991 | 1992 | 1993 | 1994 | 1995 |
| **RESEARCH AND PROCUREMENT:** | | | | | |
| B-2 Stealth Bomber | 5.54 | 5.7 | 5.8 | 5.9 | 6.0 |
| Advanced Cruise Missile | 1.0 | 1.0 | 1.0 | 1.0 | 1.0 |
| MX-Rail Garrison | 2.7 | 2.1 | 1.5 | 0.7 | 0.6 |
| Midgetman SICBM | 0.2 | 0.2 | 0.3 | 0.3 | 0.3 |
| Trident submarines | 1.39 | 1.4 | 1.4 | 1.4 | 1.4 |
| D-5 Missiles | 1.54 | 1.5 | 1.4 | 1.7 | 1.7 |
| Lance Tactical Missile | 0.11 | 0.2 | 0.2 | 0.2 | 0.2 |
| Kinetic ASAT Weapons | 0.21 | .4 | 0.5 | 0.6 | 0.8 |
| Tomahawk SLCM | 0.86 | 1.0 | 0.7 | 0.6 | 0.6 |
| Star Wars Research | 3.1 | 4.0 | 6.6 | 8.0 | 8.7 |
| DOE Nuclear Weapons | 1.0 | 1.5 | 2.0 | 2.5 | 3.0 |
| Subtotals: | 17.65 | 19.0 | 21.4 | 22.9 | 24.3 |
| **OPERATING COSTS:** | | | | | |
| Submarines (17 vs. 35) | 1.1 | 1.1 | 1.1 | 1.1 | 1.1 |
| Remove ICBMs | 0.5 | 1.0 | 1.5 | 1.5 | 1.5 |
| Reduce Bomber flights | 0.5 | 1.5 | 2.0 | 3.0 | 3.0 |
| Subtotals: | 2.5 | 3.6 | 5.6 | 8.6 | 10.6 |
| Total Savings: | 20.15 | 22.6 | 27.0 | 31.5 | 34.9 |

each superpower adequate warning should any future adversary attempt to build destabilizing weapons in violation of any treaty. Verification will never be perfect, but it need not be perfect to assure common security. Verification need only provide enough warning of militarily significant violations to permit corrective actions before our security would be degraded.

To stop the proliferation of nuclear weapons to other nations, we should be working on a global, verifiable ban on the production of all fissile material, the fuel of all atomic weapons. We should seek to control the spread of long-range ballistic missiles to other countries. Together, these arms control measures would significantly reduce the risks of nuclear war.

*The comprehensive test ban (CTB).* To stop the qualitative advances in technology that has fueled the arms race for 40 years, we would complete the work started by John F. Kennedy in 1963 with the signing of the limited test ban treaty (LTBT). The LTBT outlawed nuclear explosions in the atmosphere, under the sea, and in outer space, but permitted both nations to continue developing new weapons by exploding them underground. The CTB had been a goal of all Presidents from Eisenhower through Carter, but President Reagan refused to negotiate an end to underground nuclear testing, and President Bush has regrettably continued this short-sighted policy despite the ending of the Cold War. Ironically, while past U.S. Presidents wanted a CTB and their Soviet counterparts did not, the tables are reversed now, with Mikhail Gorbachev calling for a halt and unilaterally stopping all Soviet testing for 18 months in 1985–86, and Presidents Reagan and Bush refusing to negotiate.

*Missile flight test ban.* To bolster stability and the deterrence-only regime, we should seek a mutual ban on all ballistic missile flight tests to preclude further improvements in missile accuracy and novel flight trajectories that might put the minimal retaliatory force of the opponent at risk. While accuracies have already been improved to the point of making U.S. and Soviet ICBMs dangerously destabilizing, at least when the opponent has key assets at fixed sites, future progress could further undermine stability. U.S. programs include earth-penetrating warheads and precision guided maneuvering reentry vehicles, and the Soviets may have (or could have, should relations sour in the future) similar developments in progress.

Of course, if we and the Soviets removed all of our land-based missiles in fixed silos, the danger of Soviet improved accuracy diminishes. But further improvements in accurate nuclear delivery systems might still threaten command and communication facilities. Faced with the risk of lost communications, leaders might push the nuclear button early in some future crisis.

Continued missile developments including depressed trajectory flights would further undermine security. By flying low, submarine-launched ballistic missiles might evade detection and in any case would reduce warning time and increase the risk of catching bombers on the ground or the President in the White House. Such a low-flying ballistic missile would require development and testing. The extra buffeting of the atmosphere in a low level flight might require modifications to the structure of existing missiles or changes in their methods of operation. Today neither superpower has tested missiles on a depressed trajectory. A flight test ban would preclude this destabilizing development.

A flight test ban would also reduce Soviet leader's confidence in their ability to launch a coordinated first strike. Untested weapons would eventually become less reliable, undermining any plans to launch a massive attack.

*De-MIRVing.* We should seek to remove all multiple warhead (MIRV'd) warheads on both sides, starting with ICBM's in fixed silos. We should negotiate with the Soviets to remove their 10-warhead railroad-mobile SS-24 missiles, in exchange for our abandoning the MX rail garrison project.

*Sea-launched cruise missiles.* Both superpowers are developing and adding sea-launched cruise missiles to both submarines and surface ships. These cruise missiles are pilotless jet aircraft with current ranges up to 1,500 miles. Armed with nuclear weapons, they could attack deep inside any country. It is in the best interests of the United States to ban these weapons, since our two long sea coasts leave us vulnerable and exposed to these weapons. We have the most to lose if SLCMs become commonplace in future navies.

Some military planners hope to keep at least conventionally armed cruise missiles. This would significantly complicate verification, since a nuclear armed SLCM could be made to look like one armed with conventional explosives. Indeed, a nation could remove the bulky conventional chemical bomb from a SLCM, and replace it with a lighter nuclear weapon while significantly increasing range. Thus a long-range nuclear-armed SLCM could easily be camouflaged as a short-range conventional SLCM.

If a technique could be developed to distinguish between nuclear and conventional SLCMs, such as checking for nuclear materials at the exits of the SLCM factories on each side, and then marking each SLCM with a tamper-proof tag, then a ban on nuclear SLCMs while allowing conventionally armed SLCMs might work. In our judgment, however, we would be better served by banning all SLCMs, since even conventionally armed SLCMs would undermine our security in the future. Our long sea coasts have been a major strategic asset in the past, shielding us from the land armies that have plagued European superpowers for centuries. Proliferation of SLCMs would undermine this geo-strategic American advantage.

*Submarine sanctuary.* While submarines are quite secure, we could provide more insurance through innovative arms control measures. For example, we could negotiate submarine sanctuaries near the borders of both superpowers. All ASW activity and attack submarines of the opponent would be banned from these sanctuaries. Nuclear-armed submarines would patrol during peacetime in these sanctuaries, able to retaliate if necessary, but the opponent could not come close to test out ASW techniques against the real target. Without actual test data, neither side could gain confidence that their ASW sensors would work should war occur.

*Anti-satellite (ASAT) test ban.* We should seek a mutual, verifiable ban on the testing of all dedicated ASAT weapons. We could not ban all weapons with ASAT capability, because nuclear-tipped ballistic missiles could be used with little modification to destroy some satellites. Therefore, as long as we have some ballistic missiles on land or on submarines to satisfy our nuclear deterrence doctrine, then satellites in low earth orbit will be at risk.

In our judgment, the development and deployment of a dedicated ASAT system is the first step toward the weaponization of outer space. We have an opportunity to prevent an arms race in space by stopping ASAT weapons now, before the first fully capable systems are deployed. Because of our concern, we review the ASAT problem in some detail, beginning with an overview of past ASAT activities.

Reading newspaper accounts in the 1980s, one would get the impression that the Soviet Union has a monopoly on ASAT weapons. Their crude, coorbital ASAT system is referred to as "the world's only operational ASAT system." Actually the U.S. demonstrated an ASAT weapon first in 1959, when a Bold Orion rocket was fired from a B-47 bomber, entering outer space and passing within lethal range of the U.S. Explorer 6 satellite, many years before the Soviets began their ASAT development.

The U.S. was also the first to deploy an operational nuclear-armed ASAT in May of 1964. We placed nuclear armed missiles on Johnston Island in the Pacific; these missiles would have lifted nuclear warheads into the path of Soviet satellites in wartime. Accuracy was not critical, because the nuclear explosion could have killed most satellites tens of miles away. This ASAT system was operational for 11 years until dismantled in 1975.

The Soviets developed a coorbital ASAT system in the 1960s. This ASAT weapon is lifted into orbit from one of two launch pads at Tyuratam when the target satellite passes overhead. The Soviet ASAT weapon is then maneuvered during one or two orbits (one to three hours) into close proximity of the target, exploding like a land-mine when sufficiently close. The Soviet Union unilaterally stopped testing this ASAT system in 1982, asking the U.S. to join in a mutual ban. The Reagan and Bush administrations have refused to negotiate an ASAT weapons ban.

During the 1980s, the U.S. developed a much more versatile non-nuclear ASAT that could be fired from an F-15 fighter plane. This ASAT missile used infrared sensors to home in directly on satellites in space, eliminating the long maneuvering time of the Soviet coorbital system. Since it was fired from a fighter plane, the U.S. ASAT was not limited to attacking satellites passing over a fixed launch pad. The American F-15 ASAT was successfully tested on September 13, 1985, when it destroyed an aging U.S. scientific satellite in space. Congress denied funds for further testing, however, and the Air Force dropped this ASAT program in 1989.

The United States is pushing ahead on several fronts to develop much more effective ASAT weapons, derived primarily from research on the Star Wars ballistic missile defense weapons. Although Ronald Reagan vowed that Star Wars would be purely defensive, the first fruits from Star Wars research will be used for offensive ASAT missions. (See Appendix A for details on Star Wars.) Shooting down a few critical satellites flying in prescribed orbits is much easier than destroying thousands of Soviet missiles carrying tens of thousands of warheads and decoys.

The military wants ASAT weapons to destroy Soviet reconnaissance satellites during a conventional war. The Soviets have two classes of satellites that are used to monitor our ship movements around the world: the Radar Ocean Reconnaissance Satellite (RORSAT) and the Electronic Ocean Reconnaissance Satellite (EORSAT). The RORSAT radars search for U.S. ships, while the EORSAT satellites eavesdrop on U.S. fleet communications and radars on our ships. In a war, the U.S. Navy would like to shoot down these Soviet eyes and ears in space.

However, developing ASAT capability has serious drawbacks, when (not if) the Soviets copy our advances. The existing Soviet coorbital ASAT is slow (takes an hour or two to reach the target), has limited range (low-earth orbit only—a few hundred miles altitude), must wait to attack when the satellite is nearly overhead, and has limited capacity (a few shots per week, since the two pads must be refurbished and reloaded after firing the first two-shot volley). Both superpowers have the technical capability to build much more effective ASAT systems. Improvements of the existing kinetic energy, hit-to-kill weapons, such as those being developed in the Star Wars program, could be designed to kill satellites by direct ascent, with little warning. Multiple ASAT missiles could be installed at geographically separate sites, so that many satellites could be destroyed within a few minutes. New technologies such as powerful ground-based lasers could also be developed to damage at least unprotected satellites.

Our common security would be degraded if we allow these new ASAT weapons to be developed, tested and deployed. We and the Soviets rely on satellites for communications, for verification of arms control treaties, and for early warning of missile attack. Satellites permit us to peer into the Soviet Union, to monitor major military activities such as the building of missiles silos, large weapons plants, nuclear reactors and uranium enrichment plants that manufacture the fissionable material of all nuclear weapons. The loss of surveillance satellites in peacetime would exacerbate arms race stability. In a crisis situation, the loss of critical satellites might trigger a nuclear holocaust. In our opinion, a mutual ban on all ASAT tests would be in the best interests of both nations.

If both sides had very effective ASAT capability, then the side shooting first in a crisis could gain significant advantage. President Bush's National Security Advisor, Brent Scowcroft, co-authored a piece that graphically describes the destabilizing nature of ASAT weapons:

> Suppose that each side believed the other could blind or destroy its warning and communication satellites within minutes of a decision to strike. The instabilities of this situation in a crisis would be enormous. Fearing preemption, each side might be driven to nuclear alert levels that were inherently unstable. An accidental collision of spacecraft in GEO [geosynchronous orbit] or an unexpected maneuver could prompt a decision to attack the other side's ASATs. Worst of all, preemption against satellites might be viewed as the wiser course—if, in preempting, the attacker thought it could stave off a coherent missile strike by the other side. Like the prospect of a nuclear first strike that has so worried strategists, it would be a seemingly crazy act made logical by desperate circumstances.[7]

---

[7]William J. Perry, Brent Scowcroft, Joseph S. Nye, Jr., and James A. Schear, "Anti-Satellite Weapons and U.S. Military Space Policy: An Introduction," *Seeking Stability in Space: Anti-Satellite Weapons and the Evolving Space Regime*, the Aspen Strategy Group and University Press of America, p. 10.

Another seldom discussed hazard created by ASAT weapons testing is space debris. Unlike a battle on earth where the destroyed weapons fall to the ground or sea-bottom, debris from an ASAT attack would remain in orbit, circling the globe at speeds of some 17,000 miles per hour. This lethal debris could destroy virtually any satellite. One space battle, or one ASAT test, could create a hazardous orbital band that could not be used for peaceful purposes for decades or even centuries at higher altitudes.

Already, there is increasing danger of collision with orbital debris from the breakup of many early space craft, and the debris from a few ASAT test shots. The Soviet Union created hundreds of discrete objects by exploding their coorbital ASAT weapon in 20 tests before their 1982 test moratorium. There are 63 detectable pieces of debris still in orbit from the first Soviet coorbital ASAT test on October 20, 1968. The one U.S. test of the F-15 launched ASAT created 287 objects above about four inches in diameter (the smallest tracked by radar) on September 13, 1985. As of July 1988, 117 of these objects were still in orbit.

By continuing to develop and test ASAT weapons, we run the risk of creating an avalanche of debris in space. Eventually, debris from one test could crash into other debris, filling space with lethal fragments. One group of space experts speculated that:

> Conceivably, the fragments produced by many antisatellite explosions could start a chain reaction of events, ending in the fragmentation of so many satellites that much of near-Earth space would be unusable.[8]

Therefore the current ASAT arms race threatens not only increased risks of nuclear war, but also jeopardizes the peaceful as well as non-weapon military uses of outer space.

Brent Scowcroft's group concluded that:

> We find it hard to identify a set of circumstances in which the benefits of using the limited existing ASAT systems markedly outweigh the potential risks . . .
> All scenarios involving the use of ASATs, especially those

---

[8]Donald J. Kessler, Preston M. Landry, Burton G. Cour-Palais, Reuben E. Taylor, "Collision Avoidance in Space," *IEEE Spectrum*, June 1980, p. 39.

surrounding crises, increase the risks of accident, misperception, and inadvertent escalation.[9]

Apparently General Scowcroft has either changed his mind, or more likely has been overruled or at least delayed by the bureaucracy, since the Bush administration is pushing ahead with ASAT weapons developments and is refusing to negotiate with the Soviets to curtail these dangerous weapons. The administration has requested a 181 percent increase for kinetic energy ASAT weapons for 1991.

Our national security would be improved significantly if we could prevent the Soviets and other future adversaries from ever developing effective ASAT weapons systems. Given the Soviets' unilateral ASAT testing moratorium since 1982, we could easily negotiate a verifiable treaty, banning the testing of all dedicated ASAT weapons. But, again, President Bush has disdained this opportunity to protect our future security in exchange for seeking a short-term military advantage by developing dedicated U.S. ASAT weapons.

The administration claims that we could not verify Soviet compliance or violations of an ASAT test ban. We disagree. Existing early-warning satellites use infrared detector arrays to monitor all missile launches. Any attempt to launch a kinetic energy ASAT weapon can be detected from outer space. The American ASAT system fired from an F-15 fighter plane, now abandoned in favor of more effective Star Wars weapons, would have been more difficult to detect, since it could be fired from any point on the Earth, and because the infrared signal from this smaller rocket would be less visible in space. Improved sensitivity might be required to see plane-launched missiles, but this should be feasible with existing infrared technology, or technology developed in the Star Wars research program.

It would be more difficult to detect the placement of "space mines" in orbit. One nation might deploy what looked to be an innocent communications satellite. Parked in geosynchronous orbit, it might be maneuvered close to a critical satellite in war and detonated. On-site inspections of all missile launches might alleviate this concern, as proposed below to verify a more general space weapons ban.

Ground-based lasers could also be used to disable or destroy satellites passing overhead in low earth orbit. We could monitor any high power

---

[9]Ibid., p. 11.

laser test shots by observing the light scattered by the atmosphere above the laser beam director. Special sensors on satellites in geo-synchronous orbits above the Soviet Union could also stare at suspect Soviet laser sites continuously, looking for laser radiation. Alternately, laser light sensors could be placed in tamper-proof boxes at each suspect laser site. Since lasers powerful enough to destroy satellites must have very large power sources (either electrical or chemical), and must have very large beam-directing telescopes, the existence but not necessarily the operating characteristics of these facilities could be detected by spy satellite. An ASAT test ban treaty could provide for challenge inspec-tions and installation of sensor "black boxes" at suspect laser sites identified by satellite.

*Space weapons ban.* All nations should agree to ban weapons from outer space. There is no need to carry our past war-making habits into space. Whenever explorers of old sailed forth, they needed weapons to protect themselves from wild animals and native homo sapiens. But there are no dangerous animals in outer space. We can safely leave our weapons on earth, and fulfill our pledge made when NASA was formed to maintain outer space as a sanctuary for peaceful activities by all nations.

Some in the military will seek to "gain the high ground" by placing weapons in space. They see only the short-term military advantage of being able to attack the enemy's satellites or ballistic missiles. Others may hope to attack airplanes, ships or ground targets from the high ground of outer space. At least one defense contractor has already proposed such a space-based ground attack system. But these short-term military advantages would be swamped by the long-term dangers as other nations followed our lead, turning outer space into a vast battleground, reducing our security here on earth as discussed in the Appendix A regarding the dangers of deploying a space-based ballistic missile defense system.

A space weapons ban could be verified in part by existing and improved surveillance systems in orbit and on the earth. We observe all objects in space with both radar and electro-optic sensors. Any tests of space-based weapons would be detected. Infrared sensors detect all space launches.

Ideally, the space weapons ban should include pre-launch inspections of all missile payloads. Some may object, because we have traditionally treated reconnaissance and communications satellites as high military secrets. But the details of sensitive satellites could still be protected to some degree, while allowing inspectors to observe all satellite components above a certain size. Inspectors might be chosen from neutral nations, similar to the makeup of some United Nations peace-keeping forces. They would not be allowed to take any pictures or measurements; their sole responsibility would be to assure that no weapons were concealed in any missile payload.

*Halting nuclear weapons proliferation.* Once we and the Soviets moved to the deterrence-only policy, we should jointly work to stop other nations from acquiring nuclear weapons—"horizontal proliferation" in nukespeak. ("Vertical proliferation" refers to the development of new nuclear weapons by existing nuclear weapons states.) The two superpowers could reduce if not completely stop horizontal proliferation, but changes would be required in our current practices.

First, there is little we can do to stop information on nuclear weapon design from reaching any nation or terrorist group with access to a few nuclear engineers and a good library. There are very few secrets about the basics of nuclear bomb design. In 1979 free-lance reporter Howard Morland, using totally unclassified sources, put together a description of a hydrogen bomb design so convincing that the government blocked its publication in *Progressive* magazine for six months. They relented only after Charles Hansen, a computer programmer and amateur nuclear weapons buff, sent letters describing a hydrogen bomb design to several newspapers.[10]

Most bomb secrets relate to methods for making the weapons smaller and more easily transportable, particularly for hydrogen bombs that were initially quite bulky. However, terrorists or Third World countries might be satisfied with atomic bombs, which are still capable of destroying whole cities, as Hiroshima and Nagasaki demonstrated.

An atomic bomb is a surprisingly simple device. It contains some type of "fissile" or fissionable material, either highly enriched uranium or plutonium. Bring enough fissile material together, and it forms a "critical mass": neutrons emitted by the uranium or plutonium split neighboring atoms. Each fission or splitting of an atom releases two to three more neutrons which in turn split other nearby atoms, setting up an explosive "chain reaction." An atomic bomb therefore consists of more than a critical mass of fissile material that is divided into two or more sub-critical parts until the time of explosion.

---

[10]Stephen Hilgartner, Richard C. Bell and Rory O'Connor, *Nukespeak: Nuclear Language, Visions, and Mindset*, San Francisco: Sierra Club Books, 1982, p. 66.

The Hiroshima atomic bomb was a gun-type device: one sub-critical mass of uranium was fired into contact with another. The Nagasaki bomb and the very first atomic test bomb exploded at Alamagordo, New Mexico, in July of 1945 used less than a critical mass of plutonium formed into a sphere. Chemical explosives surrounding this sphere compressed the plutonium into a much higher density at the center, an implosion bomb. At higher density, less plutonium is needed to reach a critical mass. If the chemical explosives squeeze the plutonium until its density doubles, for example, then four times less plutonium is needed to reach a critical mass.

*The fissile material production ban.* While we cannot prevent any country from designing a crude nuclear weapon, we should keep it from acquiring the necessary fissile materials, and from testing any nuclear device. All atomic bombs require fissile material. And all hydrogen bombs, the more powerful nuclear weapons, require an atomic bomb to trigger the hydrogen or fusion reaction. Therefore, if we could restrict or prohibit the availability of fissile materials, we could prevent other nations from ever building nuclear weapons.

Fortunately, fissile materials are very difficult to manufacture, and require either very large, energy-intensive facilities or very complex technologies that are difficult if not impossible to hide. Our best chance to prevent other nations from building nuclear weapons is to initiate a global ban on the production of fissile materials such as highly enriched uranium and weapons-grade plutonium.

Consider the process of making fissile bomb fuel: natural uranium mined from the earth contains only 0.7 percent of fissionable U-235, the uranium isotope with 235 protons and neutrons. The rest of natural uranium ore is U-238, with three extra neutrons, making 99.3 percent of this natural ore almost useless in starting a nuclear chain reaction. Rare U-235 atoms must be separated from the slightly heavier and plentiful U-238 atoms. Since both of these uranium isotopes have the same chemical characteristics, they cannot be separated by any chemical process. Instead, very complicated and energy intensive physical methods had to be devised to separate out the fissile U-235 based on its slightly smaller atomic mass.

The first technique developed at the Oak Ridge, Tennessee laboratories during the World War II Manhattan project used gaseous diffusion: the uranium ore was changed into a gas, uranium hexafluoride. This gas was then forced through many membranes in sequence. These membranes tend to stop the heavier molecules of uranium hexafluoride containing the U-238 atoms, while letting the lighter gas molecules containing the U-235 atoms pass through. After many hundreds of such diffusion stages, the ratio of U-235 was eventually increased above 90 percent, adequate for making an atomic explosion.[11]

The gaseous diffusion plants at Oak Ridge and two others constructed near Piketon, Ohio, and Puducah, Kentucky, are huge facilities. Each requires massive sources of electrical power to drive the diffusion process. Any nation wishing to develop a clandestine gaseous diffusion plant would find it very difficult to hide from the spying eyes of modern reconnaissance satellites.

There are two other methods to enrich uranium: centrifuge separation and laser isotope separation. The gas centrifuge works on the same principle as gaseous diffusion: separation relies on the U-238 gas molecules being heavier, but in a series of high-speed spinning centrifuges instead of passing through many membranes. A gas centrifuge isotope separation plant would be smaller and require less electrical power than a gaseous diffusion plant. In addition, a similar technique using curved nozzles to separate out the uranium isotopes has been discussed that would also be more difficult to detect from spy satellites. Therefore it may be necessary to monitor the flow of uranium from cradle to grave: inspectors would have to monitor all uranium mined from the earth, and follow it throughout the processing steps to assure that no state or terrorist group could divert enough uranium to build a bomb.[12]

The more modern laser isotope separation could be even smaller: a laser beam tuned to the excitation frequency of U-235 tags these molecules while leaving the U-238 unaffected. Electric or magnetic fields then split the two gas molecules into separate streams. It would be much easier to hide a laser isotope separation facility, but no nation has built one, and few have the high technology to do so.

Plutonium is the other atomic bomb fissile fuel. Plutonium is not a natural element. It is an artificial element created in the fuel rods of nuclear power plants. During normal operation of a nuclear power

---

[11]Enriched uranium is also needed to fuel commercial nuclear power plants, but commercial reactors need only 3 percent U-235, compared to 90 percent U-235 preferred for atomic weapons. Therefore, enriched uranium plants can produce fuel for electrical generation without making bomb-grade material, as long as inspections are required at all uranium enrichment plants to verify that only low-grade U-235 is being produced for peaceful power generation purposes.

[12]Private communication with Theodore Taylor, April 18, 1990.

plant, some of the natural uranium (U-238) atoms in the fuel rods absorb a neutron to form a very unstable isotope, U-239, which decays in 20 minutes or so to form a new element, neptunium. This neptunium atom is unstable and radioactively decays within a few days to create plutonium (Pu-239), a relatively stable element with a half-life of 24,100 years (that is, after 24,100 years, half the plutonium would remain, the rest having decayed slowly over the years into uranium). Plutonium builds up inside the nuclear reactor fuel rods over many months or years as a result of normal operation.

To make an atomic bomb, the plutonium, which might constitute only 1 percent of the material inside a fuel rod, must be separated from a witches' brew of other highly radioactive elements created in the fuel rods when the uranium atoms are split. Unlike uranium, plutonium can be separated from other unwanted atoms by chemical methods; no isotope separation plant is required. But very special chemical separation facilities, called reprocessing plants, are still needed to protect workers from the toxic and highly radioactive materials in radiated fuel rods.

The plutonium route to generating fissile material therefore requires two major facilities: a nuclear reactor, and a plutonium chemical separation plant to "reprocess" the exhausted fuel rods after irradiation in the reactor. While the military prefer to use special nuclear reactors to produce plutonium, so that they can carefully control the degree of "burn-up" of the uranium fuel, any nuclear reactor, including civilian power reactors, produces plutonium that can be used to build a nuclear bomb. The plutonium from commercial reactors includes undesirable plutonium isotopes that may reduce the bomb's yield due to excessive neutron emission, but civilian reactor-grade plutonium would still produce a very potent atomic explosion.

One major roadblock to nuclear proliferation, then, is to cut off the supply of fissile material. The United States and the Soviet Union both have enough enriched uranium and plutonium to supply their own weapons needs for centuries. The United States has not enriched uranium for bombs since President Johnson halted production in 1964. We stopped producing plutonium in 1988, not out of concern about proliferation, but because the military plutonium production reactors at Savannah River were deemed unsafe for further operation. Since we are not producing any fissile fuel now, we should be actively pursuing a joint treaty with the Soviet Union to encourage them to stop too, to put both nations on an equal footing. But the United States still plans to resume production of plutonium and the Department of Energy, the agency that produces all of our nuclear weapons, has requested $6 billion to build two new plutonium production reactors.

This is another example of the Bush administration continuing the destabilizing policies of the Reagan administration. President Reagan, in his push to build thousands of additional nuclear weapons, planned to build two new production reactors. Even if we did not conclude the START arms control treaty reducing nuclear warheads by about 10 to 30 percent, we do not need any more plutonium. As John Herrington, the Secretary of Energy, testified to a House appropriations subcommittee in 1988, we are "awash in plutonium ... we have more plutonium than we need."[13] If we do cut back our excessive nuclear arsenal, then plutonium taken from old warheads could be used to build more modern weapons. Of course, we would prefer if the plutonium were used as fuel in commercial reactors to gradually reduce the world's supply of plutonium. But President Bush continues to press for more capacity to generate new plutonium.

Cutting back on military stockpiles of plutonium would reduce the risks of plutonium diversions to Third World countries from various nuclear weapon production plants scattered around our nation and those in the Soviet Union. With lower inventories of plutonium in various stages of production, there would be less chance of significant quantities being stolen without detection. But we must also control the spent fuel rods from civilian nuclear power reactors around the world.

Fortunately, we do have a mechanism in place to implement a global policing of clandestine plutonium reprocessing: the International Atomic Energy Agency (IAEA). The IAEA was set up to monitor provisions of the Non-proliferation Treaty (NPT) of 1968—an agreement between the nuclear weapons nations and the nuclear "have-nots." In exchange for sharing commercial nuclear power technology with the nuclear "have-nots," the "haves" promised to:

> pursue negotiations in good faith on effective measures relating to cessation of the nuclear arms race at an early date and to nuclear disarmament, and on a treaty on general and complete disarmament under strict and effective international control.

---

[13]Eric Pryne, "DOE Chief: 'We're Awash in Plutonium,'" *Seattle Times*, February 23, 1988.

The "have-nots" pledged in return not to build their own nuclear weapons.

To make sure that the non-weapons nations do not use their civilian reactors to produce plutonium for atomic bombs, the IAEA periodically inspects civilian reactors and installs various monitoring devices including TV cameras and special seals at these reactors.

The NPT regime has one serious flaw: not all nations have signed the treaty, including some probable or near nuclear-capable countries such as Argentina, Brazil, India, Israel, Pakistan and South Africa. Many refuse to sign as long as the nuclear weapons nations continue the nuclear arms race. They are not willing to give up their right to build nuclear weapons while the superpowers continue to expand both the quantity and the quality of their arsenals.

Here is another example of missed opportunity. By persisting in building more nuclear weapons than we need and in producing more plutonium, President Bush is sending the wrong signals to Third World nations. He is effectively saying that nuclear weapons are not good for them, but the United States, despite our huge arsenal of nuclear weapons, must continue to produce more.

In one case, President Bush degraded President Reagan's already weak record on non-proliferation: Pakistan has been actively pursuing nuclear weapons capability to match the earlier accomplishment of India. Pressured by Congress, President Reagan solicited a promise from Pakistan's General Mohammed Zia ul-Haq in 1984 not to enrich uranium above 5 percent, which is suitable for nuclear power plants but not for nuclear weapons. In the summer of 1989, however, President Bush dropped this demand for nuclear restraint from Pakistan's new prime minister, Benazir Bhutto.[14] Apparently President Bush was more interested in gaining Pakistan's help in aiding the Afghan rebels than in stopping nuclear weapons proliferation, even after the Soviets pulled out of Afghanistan. France has also contributed to Pakistan's quest for nuclear weapons by agreeing to sell nuclear reactor technology to Pakistan in February of 1990, despite the lack of international safeguards on Pakistan's reactors.

Some members of the Bush administration are also pushing to lift an export ban on supercomputers to Brazil, India, and Israel. These high-

---

[14]Michele A. Flournoy, "Bhutto Visit to U.S. Puts Pakistan's Nuclear Activities in Spotlight," *Arms Control Today*, August 1989, p. 30.

speed computers can be used to design improved nuclear weapons and also to speed the design of ballistic missiles to transport nuclear weapons over intercontinental ranges. The Department of Energy estimates that modern nuclear weapons designed with the help of these supercomputers need only five actual nuclear test explosions, compared to 180 physical explosions needed in the 1950s to develop modern nuclear bombs without high-speed computers. Commerce Department regulations currently ban the sale of these sensitive computers to any nations that have not signed the Nuclear Non-Proliferation Treaty and are not firmly committed to non-proliferation efforts. Brazil, India and Israel all fail to meet these non-proliferation criteria, and yet the Bush administration is considering lifting the export ban for these nations.[15]

To reduce weapons proliferation, the United States should be actively negotiating with the Soviet Union to stop the reprocessing of all plutonium. We should be working with the International Atomic Energy Agency (IAEA) to expand its monitoring capabilities to include a global ban on the separation of all plutonium and a ban on all highly enriched uranium production. Instead, we are pursuing business-as-usual, continuing the weapons development habits of the last 40 years.

*Ballistic missile proliferation.* In addition to stopping the proliferation of nuclear weapons, all nations should curb the proliferation of the preferred nuclear delivery vehicle: ballistic missiles. As many as 20 Third World nations have or are seeking missiles, and the CIA estimates that up to 15 might be manufacturing ballistic missiles by 2000.[16] Loaded with chemical, biological or nuclear weapons, nations such as Libya, Iraq, North Korea or other future terrorist nations could pose significant threats to much of the civilized world. While we cannot stop most nations from eventually acquiring missiles, we should be trying to stem the tide, blocking or slowing the proliferation of missile technology.

Fortunately, the United States has taken the lead in this area, forming the Missile Technology Control Regime (MTCR) to slow missile proliferation. The MTCR discourages exports of key technologies, and has contributed to the slowing of Argentina's Condor missile development project.

---

[15]Gary Milhollin, "Why Are We Helping the Third World Go Nuclear?" *The Washington Post*, April 1, 1990, p. C1.
[16]Seth Carus, "Stopping Missile Proliferation," *World & I*, November 1989, p. 182.

## IMPLEMENTING THE DETERRENCE-ONLY POLICY

To implement the deterrence-only policy, we would propose a series of joint initiatives with the Soviets to slow the arms race and to gradually but steadily reduce nuclear weapons on both sides, beginning with the most destabilizing. We would *not* recommend the traditional approach of lengthy negotiations with the Soviets while the qualitative arms race continues. All too often, negotiations lasted for years, while technology raced ahead, outstripping any modest gains at the negotiating table.

Senator Sam Nunn, chairman of the Armed Services Committee, has recommended that we establish a second track for arms control initiatives. The first track would be the existing detailed negotiations on specific proposals that tend to drag on for years. The second track would consider broader initiatives, exploring more creative options without worrying about details. Once there was general agreement about a subject, it would be turned over to the negotiators to work out the specifics. Senator Nunn suggested that contentious issues like sea-launched cruise missiles or the complete ban on multiple warhead land-based missiles be considered on this second track.

Senator Nunn's two-step approach has great merit, but we would go one step further. We recommend that the United States take the initiative to rapidly convert from nuclear war-fighting to a deterrence-only posture. For example, we could stop all nuclear weapons testing or all missile flight testing for a prescribed period, inviting the Soviets to join our initiative.

Conservatives would complain that our weapons reliability would decrease over time, so the test ban offer could be limited to something like one or two years. If the Soviets agreed to stop testing, which is likely, then we could sit down and work out verification details at a leisurely pace, without any fear that new weapons developments might overtake the negotiations. Additional remote seismic stations could be set up, and joint experiments run, similar to those conducted by the Natural Resources Defense Council and the Soviet Academy of Sciences. Working together to improve seismic monitoring capability, our confidence would grow that we could detect any militarily significant test program, and a mutual, verifiable ban could be implemented. The focus could then shift to an international ban on nuclear weapons testing.

We might also begin reducing land-based missiles in small steps, since they would not be needed for a deterrence-only policy. We could begin by removing a small number, say 100 of our existing 1,000 fixed-silo missiles, and invite the Soviets to remove a similar number or a number in ratio to their larger fleet of ICBMs. We have the opportunity to regain the peace initiative from Mr. Gorbachev, returning the United States to its historic position as the world's acknowledged leader and champion of peace and justice. For maximum impact, the U.S. President could personally observe the removal or destruction of the first missiles, live on national television. He could take this small step unilaterally, with no strings attached, inviting the Soviets to reciprocate.

Again, imagine the effect on world opinion of these bold actions. If the Soviets failed to respond to our initiatives, their international image would suffer. Our security would not be degraded in any case, since we do not need land-based missiles to deter the Soviets. We have nothing to lose, and much to gain by such dramatic initiatives.

Since the Soviet's submarine force is not considered as reliable as ours, they might want to replace fixed-silo ICBMs with mobile single-warhead ICBMs. We should accept this trade-off, since mobile missiles, and particularly single-warhead mobile missiles like the Soviets' SS-25, are stabilizing. If they accepted our offer to remove fixed silo ICBMs, then we would remove another 100, until all were eliminated on both sides, leaving our existing 5,300 nuclear warheads on submarines and 5,000 on bombers.

Some hard-liners would surely try to scare the American public by calling these actions "unilateral disarmament." But these shrill cries would fall on deaf ears if the public were well informed on nuclear matters, and realized that we could improve our security by removing destabilizing weapons like the MX and the Soviet SS-18.

There is historical precedent for such initiatives. On June 10, 1963, President John F. Kennedy made a memorable speech at American University: he congratulated the Soviet people for their heroism in stopping the Nazi invasion in World War II. He went on to announce a unilateral moratorium on atmospheric testing of nuclear weapons, inviting the Soviets to join the ban. Within weeks, Khrushchev agreed, and the Partial Test Ban Treaty was signed on August 6, 1963, less than two months after President Kennedy's original initiative. Negotiations on a test ban treaty had gone on for years before 1963, so we shouldn't expect such quick action in response to all unilateral initiatives. However, since Gorbachev did stop underground nuclear weapons testing unilaterally for 19 months starting in August of 1985, and has promised to stop again anytime the U.S. does, we could have a complete test ban within months if our President took the initiative.

President Nixon also successfully used the unilateral initiative to produce a major arms limitation treaty. On November 25, 1969, he unilaterally renounced the use and possession of biological weapons. There were no negotiations. There were no on-site inspections or data exchanges. There were no strings attached. President Nixon simply renounced biological warfare and ordered the Defense Department to dispose of all stocks of biological agents and weapons. On February 14, 1970, Nixon extended the ban to include toxins, which are poisonous chemicals produced by biological processes. This unilateral action stimulated action in the United Nations, eventually leading to the Biological Weapons Convention signed on April 10, 1972. This Convention bans the development, production and stockpiling of any toxins or biological agents. Remarkably, it contains no verification provisions, yet has been signed by 111 nations.[17]

Once all fixed-silo ICBMs were removed on both sides, we could begin a similar series of gradual reciprocal reductions in submarine and bomber-based nuclear weapons. Our preference would be to reduce nuclear-armed bombers first, both because the bomber force is the most costly to operate, and because the submarine force is most survivable.

To summarize our prescription for nuclear sanity, we would:

- Declare a policy of deterrence-only: henceforth, we keep nuclear weapons only to deter their use by others.
- Initiate the process leading to deterrence-only through a series of small initiatives, inviting reciprocal Soviet steps.
- Negotiate very deep, verifiable reductions in Soviet and American nuclear weapons, keeping only a few hundred nuclear warheads on submarines, bombers or possibly some mobile single warhead land-based missiles, eliminating all fixed-silo ICBMs.
- Negotiate a global, verifiable ban on all nuclear test explosions, all missile flight and all anti-satellite tests, and ban sea-launched cruise missiles and all weapons in space.
- Negotiate a global, verifiable ban on the production of fissile material, weapons-grade enriched uranium and plutonium.
- For the long term, seek a stable geopolitical environment that would permit complete nuclear disarmament.

---

[17]*Arms Control and Disarmament Agreements*, Washington, D.C.: United States Arms Control and Disarmament Agency, August 1980, p. 120.

Unfortunately, the Bush administration has shown little inclination for any significant initiatives in national security matters. Mr. Bush and his advisers have chosen incrementalism and day-to-day management over dynamic, visionary leadership. They are continuing the pre-Gorbachev Cold War mentality, protecting and expanding all nuclear weapons developments, even if it means sacrificing troop strengths and perpetuating our out-of-control federal deficits.

# CHAPTER 10

# Conventional Force Reductions and Restructuring

SUMMARY

During 40 years of Cold War, the United States has assembled a massive peacetime army, with 60 percent of those forces justified on the basis of stopping a surprise Warsaw Pact attack on Western Europe.[1] Now that the 1989 revolutions in Eastern Europe have virtually eliminated the Warsaw Pact as an effective fighting force, we can begin reducing up to half of our military forces over the next decade. For maximum stability at minimum cost, both sides should significantly reduce and restructure their conventional forces into a "non-offensive defense" posture: much smaller forces would be equipped and trained to defend but not conquer territory. Both sides would give up the ability to attack the other, recognizing that in the nuclear age there is no U.S. security without Soviet security, and there is no Soviet security without U.S. security. There is only common security.

---

[1]Alice C. Maroni and John J. Ulrich, "The U.S. Commitment to Europe's Defense: A Review of Cost Issues and Estimates," Congressional Research Service Report No. 85-211 F, November 7, 1985, p. 12.

The United States must have strong military forces. There will be threats to America, such as Saddam Hussein, even if the Soviets were to become trusted allies. But no other nation or group of nations could justify keeping 2.1 million men and women in uniform, and there is no compelling reason to continue a crash program to build a new generation of conventional weapons, weapons that are not needed to meet the expected threats in the years ahead.

## CONVENTIONAL FORCE REDUCTIONS: EUROPE

While we are most concerned about an unbridled competition in nuclear weapons—particularly the proliferation of nuclear weapons to other, less stable nations—no analysis of our nation's security can ignore the vast accumulation of sophisticated conventional weapons. Roughly 80 percent of our military budget, or $240 billion per year, pays for conventional weapons: tanks, planes, ships, missiles, guns, and all the people and infrastructure necessary to operate and bring these weapons to distant lands. Even if nuclear weapons were never invented, the modern conventional arsenals of both superpowers, if ever unleashed, would create unparalleled death and destruction.

If we are to solve or ameliorate our major social problems, we must cash in the "peace dividend," and reduce the costs of maintaining the two largest peacetime military forces in the history of the planet. We have built up our mammoth military machine to counter Soviet military strength, fearing that the Soviets might suddenly invade Europe or encourage client states to establish a global Communist empire. That possibility may have been valid during the turmoil and uncertainty in Eastern Europe following World War II. But the Warsaw Pact has virtually disintegrated as a fighting force, and the chances of the Soviets invading Western Europe are extremely small. As the Senate Armed Services Committee Chairman Sam Nunn stated:

> The threat of a large-scale Warsaw Pact attack against Western Europe has virtually been eliminated, and the chances of any Soviet go-it-alone attack across Eastern Europe against the West are very remote.[2]

---

[2]Sam Nunn, "The Changed Threat Environment of the 1990's," *Congressional Record*, March 29, 1990, p. S3444.

Yet Dick Cheney and the Defense Department continue to act as though the Soviets might strike any day. We keep 326,000 American troops stationed in or near Europe, four decades after the war ended. Most of these troops now bring their wives and families along, which is great for morale, but also a clear signal that we don't really expect a military conflict.

President Bush has called for reducing our troops in Europe by 80,000, leaving 225,000 in place. This is a welcome step, but if the Soviet threat continues to recede, we should be planning for much larger withdrawals. The President has unfortunately stated that he will not consider cuts below this 225,000-person level (195,000 in central Europe and 30,000 elsewhere in Europe), calling it a floor.

*Warning time.* This enormous standing army in Europe has been justified exclusively by the fear that the Soviet Union, through the Warsaw Pact, could launch a major attack on Western Europe with only 10 to 14 days warning. Due to this short warning time, NATO has maintained huge active duty forces, forward-deployed weapons and ammunition, and built the infrastructure to rapidly beef up our forces in Europe should war begin. With short warning, we would not have time to draft and train an army or build new weapons if the Soviets ever launched an attack. We would need massive airlift capability, since we could not even rely on ships to transport weapons and equipment on such short notice. The 10- to 14-day warning time has been the primary justification for the United States spending on the order of $180 billion per year for the rapid defense of NATO.

In the fall of 1988, however, the CIA, the DIA (Defense Intelligence Agency) and the JCS (Joint Chiefs of Staff) agreed in a secret report that the Pentagon would have a minimum of 33 to 44 days, and most likely up to six months warning of Soviet attack, primarily because of "hollow" Soviet forces. That is, the Soviets would have to call up reserves to fill in their ranks before attacking, activities that would be detected well in advance. Furthermore, this assessment was made *before* Gorbachev's unilateral withdrawal of 50,000 troops and 5,000 tanks from Europe took effect, *before* the crumbling of the Berlin Wall, *before* every Warsaw Pact nation dumped their hard-line Communist rulers, and *before* several of these new governments asked the Soviet army to leave. While no official assessment has been released to the public since the European revolutions of late 1989, it seems likely that we would now have several years warning of any possible Soviet attack, since they would most likely have to resubjugate Poland, Czechoslovakia and what was East Germany to reach Western Europe. This increased warning time *has virtually eliminated the primary justification for a huge peacetime military force in Europe, and with it, the justification for up to 60 percent of U.S. military expenditures.*

*Gorbachev: A time to act.* Our conservative friends have warned that we must not act rashly by reducing our military budget, that Gorbachev may not survive much longer. While his policy of glasnost has been a success by our standards, opening up the once secretive Soviet society to scrutiny unimagined just a few years ago, his policy of perestroika has yet to succeed at home. Economic conditions are not improving, despite efforts to restructure the centrally planned Soviet economy. Ethnic strife continues to simmer and even boil over, as those Soviet citizens in the outer provinces watch their counterparts in the Warsaw Pact nations achieve greater independence. If Poland can establish a non-Communist government independent of Moscow, why not Lithuania? Or even Georgia or Armenia?

If ethnic turmoil and economic distress continue, it is entirely possible that President Gorbachev will be replaced. We cannot base our national security policy on wishful thinking, on the hope that Gorbachev will succeed.

However, we contend that the possibility of Gorbachev's replacement is reason for action, not inaction. As long as he is in power, we apparently have little to fear from the huge Soviet military machine. If Gorbachev will not raise a finger to stop Communist governments from falling in Warsaw Pact nations, how much less likely is he to invade Western Europe? Particularly when he would have to march through those very nations that are now gaining their independence. But if he is driven from power (or dies from a heart attack) tomorrow, he could conceivably be replaced by a hard-liner. A future Soviet leader could once again resort to military force in Europe, possibly to rally popular support at home or to distract attention from internal chaos. As long as the Soviet military has the power in place to squash Eastern Europe, we cannot rule out some future rash act.

Hence we should be working now, while the Gorbachev window of opportunity is open, to reduce Soviet military forces, so that future Soviet leaders, even if predisposed to use force, would not have the military tools available to resubjugate Eastern Europe.

Instead of caution, we should be vigorously pursuing deeper conventional arms reductions in the CFE (Conventional Forces in Europe)[3] negotiations. Instead of worrying about losing the offensive edge in some class of weapon, we should be taking the initiative, reducing weapons levels and inviting Gorbachev to follow our lead. We should be reclaiming our historical heritage as champions of peace and freedom, not following the leader of the "evil empire." We should be leading the charge to significantly reduce and restructure Soviet military power in Europe, so that new-found freedoms in Poland, Czechoslovakia, East Germany, Hungary and Romania can flourish and grow without the fear of Soviet military interference, no matter who sits in the Kremlin.

## CONVENTIONAL FORCE REDUCTIONS: THE PACIFIC

Turning to the Pacific, our military posture isn't quite so out of tune with reality, but we still keep 40,000 troops in Japan and 45,000 troops in Korea, three decades after the "police action" ended on that troubled peninsula. Clearly, Japan is able to take care of itself. American taxpayers now cough up six times as much per person for military forces as each Japanese citizen. Relieved of most of their military burden, the Japanese can concentrate on consumer products and beat the socks off us in international trade.

South Korea is a different story, with a hostile neighbor to the North. But we should ask probing questions here as well. The South Korean economy is eight times stronger than the North Korean economy ($171 billion vs. $20 billion) and growing four times faster (12 percent vs. 3 percent growth rate). The South Koreans outnumber North Koreans by almost two to one (43 million vs. 22 million).[4] The U.S. does provide valuable reconnaissance information to South Korea, monitoring activities in the North. We could continue these activities until the South Koreans obtain their own capability, but there is no compelling reason to continue stationing 45,000 troops in South Korea. Indeed, their presence sometimes exacerbates anti-American feelings, and could be counterproductive in establishing a stable environment.

We could begin a gradual withdrawal of ground troops. This would not end our commitment to defend South Korea should they ever be

---

[3]These talks were originally called the Conventional Armed Forces in Europe negotiations, but apparently someone did not like the frivolous acronym "CAFE."
[4]CIA World Fact Book (1989), July 1988.

attacked, any more than the absence of U.S. troops in Israel indicates we would not support them if attacked, but it would reduce our economic burden, particularly if these troops were demobilized.

## THE MILITARY BUDGET

Our conventional military forces are based on old threats that have faded to the point of insignificance over the last three decades. The budgeting process that feeds the military machine is totally out of touch with this reality. Each year, the military budget is drawn up primarily by making incremental adjustments over the previous year's budget. Instead of asking the prudent question—what do we need for our defense against the actual threat?—planners in the Pentagon effectively ask how much of an increase or how little of a decrease in weapons and forces can they glean from Congress and the American taxpayer. Interservice rivalry drives the budget more than any assessment of the real threats to our security, as each service vies for a larger share of the budget pie.

In recent years, the military services have been forced to make mild reductions in their requests, and the Pentagon's budget authority (the amount of new money they can allocate for current and future years) has not kept pace with inflation since 1986. But even these reductions have been modest, with real cuts after inflation of 11.5 percent, far less than the 54 percent increase in military spending between 1980 and 1985. Indeed, the budget authority for the military **exceeded funding authority at the peak of the Vietnam war from 1983 through 1990** (see Figure 10-1), even after accounting for inflation. We are still **spending about 50 percent more in constant dollars than in previous peacetime periods** following the Korean and Vietnam wars, despite vastly improved international relations and the reduced threats facing our nation.

Furthermore, the actual defense outlays (the dollars actually spent each year) kept increasing until 1988, and fell by only 0.8 percent after correcting for inflation in 1989 and by 3.3 percent in 1990. Since 1986, military planners have been asked to make small, incremental reductions in their plans, leaving in place the massive weapons procurement machine assembled by the Reagan-Bush administration to fight the Warsaw Pact with only 10 to 14 days warning time. We continue to spend at wartime levels in a period of unprecedented peacetime opportunity.

FIGURE 10-1. MILITARY SPENDING IN CONSTANT, 1990 DOLLARS

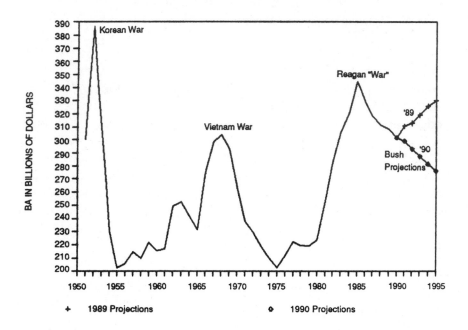

Secretary of Defense Cheney recognized that we cannot continue spending at warlike rates, given the federal budget deficit, the reduced Soviet threat, and pressing domestic needs. In the fall of 1989, he announced, with great fanfare, the possibility of "cutting" $180 billion from future defense budgets. This sounded substantial, compared to the $300 billion annual military budget, and was reported as "very deep cuts" by some newspapers. In reality, this proposed "cut" was a paper cut only. The Pentagon had been planning on *increases* of about $200 billion over the five-year period from 1991 to 1995. Mr. Cheney's proposed $180 billion cut would have merely reduced the planned increases. Actual spending levels would have remained at the nominal $300 billion per year wartime levels, with inflation slightly eroding Pentagon purchasing power each year.

The administration and other champions of more military hardware often disguise the true size of the military budget by quoting it as a percentage of the gross national product (GNP). As our economy grows (and it is still growing faster than inflation), the percentage of GNP spent on the Pentagon would naturally decrease, even though the actual spending was constant. For example, military spending is about equal to the peak of the Vietnam War level in constant (inflation-adjusted) dollars. As a percentage of GNP, however, military big spenders can claim that the Pentagon budget has "fallen" from 9.6 percent of GNP in 1968 to "only" 5.5 percent of GNP in 1990. They don't mention that this entire drop is caused by our rising GNP, not by reduced military budget authority.

Measuring military spending as a percent of GNP may be useful as an indicator of the nation's ability to pay for Pentagon operations, or to compare the burden on our economy with that of our allies (for example, Japan spends only 1 percent and our NATO allies about 3 percent of their GNP on the military versus our 5.5 percent), but it should not be used to judge the appropriate level of spending. Just because our nation produces more refrigerators or washing machines, we do not need more tanks or airplanes. The country does not become more difficult to defend every time we sell more hamburgers or milkshakes. Our military budget should be determined on actual need, the numbers of weapons and troops required to meet the real threats to our security. It should not be based on some arbitrary rubber yardstick such as GNP.

## WHAT FORCE LEVELS DO WE NEED?

Rather than continuing current military spending levels, nudging the budget a few percent one way or the other, we should be asking what military forces we need to meet the real external threats of the 1990s and beyond. Suppose we had to start over. Suppose we had no military forces and no weapons. How many troops and what kinds of weapons would we need to defend the United States and meet our other obligations around the world?

We should ask under what circumstances military forces might be needed in the future, and then design our forces and hence our military budget to counter the expected threats. Here are some possibilities for using military force in the 1990s:

1. To stop a Soviet invasion of Europe.
2. To intervene in other countries (eg., Vietnam, Nicaragua, El Salvador, Panama, Lebanon, or elsewhere in the Middle East).
3. To protect U.S. mainland from attack.

4. To protect sea-lanes for commerce (e.g., Persian Gulf oil tanker operation).

5. To support allies and meet treaty obligations (e.g., Israel, South Korea).

6. To protect American citizens abroad (e.g., the failed Iran hostage rescue or Grenada).

7. To stem anti-terrorist activities.

8. To conduct drug interdiction missions.

Let's look at each of these possible uses of military force in today's world. How likely is each threat? How many troops and how much military hardware do we need to accomplish each mission?

*Soviet invasion of Europe.* The Soviet Union clearly maintains an enormous military machine. Hard-liners claim this Soviet might far exceeds their legitimate defensive needs. Apparently Gorbachev agrees, and is cutting back Soviet forces while offering to make further asymmetrical reductions in the CFE negotiations. Others point to the historical record of repeated invasions of the Russian homeland from the west and the loss of tens of millions of Russians, to explain their paranoia and commitment to keep western armies far from Moscow. Whether justified or not, this Soviet capability has been the primary motivation for maintaining our own vast peacetime military forces. And, of course, our continued buildup of military capability has been used by Soviet hard-liners to justify their own excesses, forming a positive feedback circuit that has driven the arms race on both sides before the arrival of Mr. Gorbachev in 1985.

A detailed analysis of the conventional military balance in Europe is beyond the scope of this book, but we can highlight some of the issues. As shown in Table 10-1, the Soviets have more troops and more weapons than the United States, but the more appropriate measure prior to 1989 was the Warsaw Pact nations compared to the NATO alliance. Clearly, the United States would not have to stop a Soviet invasion by itself. We have reliable allies who would have far more to lose by any invasion from the east.

As shown in the Table, the NATO/Warsaw Pact military balance was more nearly equal. In fact, NATO held a slight edge in active-duty ground forces in Europe by some estimates. The two sides do not agree on exact numbers, however, due in part to differing definitions of what constitutes a "tank" or a "fighter aircraft," or, for that matter, whether a railroad construction worker paid by the army should be included in troop counts. The estimates of weapons and manpower differ even on the western side, with most analysts accepting the more objective European estimates such as those of the London-based International Institute for Strategic Studies. In any case, small differences in these numbers are not significant.

TABLE 10-1.   1989 MILITARY FORCE BALANCE[5]

|  | U.S. | USSR | NATO | WP* |
|---|---|---|---|---|
| Active Military (M) | | | | |
| Worldwide: | 2.1 | 4.2 | 5.5 | 6.4 |
| Europe: | 2.2 | 3.1 | | |
| Reserve Military (M) | 1.6 | 5.5 | 8.2 | 8.2 |
| Active ground forces | | | | |
| Worldwide: | 0.766 | 1.6 | 2.9 | 2.8 |
| Europe: | 0.209 | 2.38 | 2.29 | |
| Central Europe: | 0.202 | 0.55 | 1.02 | 0.99 |
| Main Battle Tanks | | | | |
| Worldwide: | 15,992 | 53,350 | 31,300 | 68,300 |
| Europe: | 6,000 | 37,000 | 22,200 | 52,200 |
| Europe, post 1965: | | | 18,000 | 18,000 |
| Central Europe: | | | 13,600 | 18,000 |
| Central, post-1965: | | | 12,000 | 9,500 |
| Bombers and ground-attack aircraft | | | | |
| Worldwide: | | | 5,675 | 4,301 |
| Europe: | | | 2,393 | 2,594 |
| Central Europe: | | | 1,238 | 1,024 |
| Helicopter gun-ships | | | | |
| Worldwide: | | | 2,020 | 2,130 |
| Europe: | | | 780 | 1,630 |

| Economic Measures | | | | |
|---|---|---|---|---|
|  | U.S. | USSR | NATO | WP |
| Population (M) | 249 | 289 | 647 | 396 |
| GNP (billion $): | 4,900 | 2,400 | 7,975 | 3,068 |
| Military spending: | 300 | | 410 | 315 |

*Warsaw Pact

The events of late 1989 have further eroded the Soviet threat. For all practical purposes, the Warsaw Pact has ceased to exist as a viable fighting force. The three major Warsaw Pact nations separating the Soviet Union from West Germany (Poland, Czechoslovakia and East

---

[5]The International Institute for Strategic Studies, *The Military Balance, 1989-1990*, London: Brassey's, 1989 and *Soviet Military Power, 1988*.

Germany) have rejected former Communist leadership and have become much more independent of the Soviets. Poland, Hungary and Czechoslovakia have asked that most or all Soviet troops be removed from their soil within a year or two, although Poland is having second thoughts about ejecting all Soviet troops with a unified Germany on their western border.

Gorbachev has demonstrated that he will not use force to stop this trend toward multi-party, independent governments in Eastern Europe (although he apparently will use force within the Soviet Union and the Baltic states of Lithuania, Estonia and Latvia). It was always questionable whether Polish or East German troops would have remained loyal or enthusiastically supported a Soviet invasion of West Germany, but now it seems clear that no Soviet leader could count on the support of any Warsaw Pact nation for an attack on the West.

Suppose, however, that Gorbachev is replaced by an aggressive Soviet leader 10 or 20 years from now. Could another Stalin have any chance of conquering any NATO nation? If we assume that the Eastern bloc nations remained neutral, and neither supported nor hindered a Soviet attack on NATO, then future Soviet leaders would have seen a balanced force of 2.2 million troops on each side before Gorbachev's unilateral troop withdrawals. However, after Gorbachev unilaterally pulled out 50,000 soldiers from Europe and reduced 500,000 overall, NATO troops outnumber Soviet troops. The Soviets would have more tanks, artillery and other hardware, but even these numerical advantages will be eliminated by the Conventional Forces in Europe (CFE) agreements.

Given these nearly equal "bean counts" of weapons and troops on both sides, there is little probability that any Soviet leader would attack the West. But we should also look beyond these bare numbers. Military capability also depends on the quality of the weapons, the readiness of the troops, the level of training, the ability to sustain military operations, and, most importantly, the industrial and human resources available to the two sides should an armed conflict ensue.

Consider the quality of the tanks on both sides. Many of the Soviet tanks contributing to their lead in this category were over 25 years old. Israeli sources describe their experience with captured Soviet tanks:

> Shifting gears in a Soviet tank sometimes requires a "sharp blow from a heavy hammer." And poor ventilation means that exhaust fumes from the turret gun cause the tank's fighting compartment to fill with carbon monoxide. To compound these problems, an

ejection device designed to expel spent shell casings is often knocked out of alignment when the tank travels over a rough road, causing empty shell casings to ricochet "at high speed around the cramped fighting compartment."[6]

Soviet tanks have no laser range finders and no gyro-stabilized turrets, making it very difficult to fire while moving. Even the Soviets' much publicized numerical advantage in tanks was somewhat misleading. They had a 3.8 to 1 advantage over the U.S. in all tanks. But Warsaw Pact advantage over NATO in Europe (from the Atlantic to the Ural mountains) was 2.3 to 1. If we exclude tanks made before 1965, then the old Warsaw Pact lost its advantage: both sides had about 18,000 modern tanks in Europe. On the main central front, the Warsaw Pact had a 1.4 to 1 advantage in all tanks, but NATO had a 1.26 to 1 advantage over the Warsaw Pact in modern (post-1965) tanks. And Gorbachev's promise to destroy 10,000 tanks, including 5,000 in Central Europe, will further improve NATO's lead.

Most observers grant NATO a substantial lead in other qualitative factors such as training and readiness. American soldiers fire more ammunition and American pilots fly more hours than their Soviet counterparts.

Finally, we should always ask whether it was necessary to match the Soviets weapon for weapon in order to have prevented any attack in Europe. Rather than spending our limited resources on building 2,000 more M1 tanks at a cost of $3 million each to catch up to the Soviets, why not develop and build 50,000 effective anti-tank weapons for $20,000 each or one sixth the total cost? Or install (unobtrusive) tank barriers in Germany? We had no desire to invade the Soviet Union. We should have concentrated on defensive weapons, if stopping a Soviet invasion was our only objective.

In short, no Soviet leader would have any confidence of winning a war with the West, should Mr. Gorbachev be replaced by an aggressive leader. However, this does not eliminate the chances of war started by a desperate, suicidal Soviet boss. And so we should strive to further erode their ability to attack by jointly reducing troop levels and weapons, while an accommodating Gorbachev remains in power.

*Intervention in Third World countries.* Will there be any more

---

[6]Jack Mendelsohn and Thomas Halverson, "The Conventional Balance: a TKO for NATO?" *Bulletin of the Atomic Scientists*, March 1989, p. 30.

Vietnams? Would the American public ever let this nation become immersed in another Third World civil war, in a no-win situation? Many books have been written about the lessons of Vietnam. Certainly one lesson is that all of our expensive, high-tech hardware and excessive firepower are no match for an indigenous, dedicated insurgent force.

Another lesson is that the domino theory is suspect, if not invalid. Remember the claims that all of Southeast Asia would fall to Communism if we "lost" Vietnam, as if it was ours to lose! Well, guess what? We "lost" Vietnam and not a single domino fell! If anything, the dominoes are falling the other way, as one by one the nations that came under Soviet rule after World War II have thrown off the yoke of Communism.

The United States has intervened since Vietnam, but not with any major American troop involvement. We have poured hundreds of millions of dollars of military support to prop up a right-wing government in El Salvador, but used only 55 military "advisers." We covertly mined the harbor in Nicaragua, but hired the Contras to do most of the dirty work, undermining our own democratic process as a few misguided zealots tried to run an illegal war out of the White House basement. We put hundreds of Marines into a hotel in Lebanon as a symbol of our military strength, and brought 241 of them home in body bags. We sent 25,000 troops to dispose of Panamanian dictator Manuel Noriega, after training and supporting him, after looking the other way as he profited from drug sales, and after sending Noriega fat CIA paychecks because we wanted him to help the Contras in Nicaragua.

One key question is whether we will ever be able to justify intervention again in the internal affairs of other nations. Intervention is always cloaked in the mantle of national security, as if a totally belligerent Nicaragua could ever succeed in crossing through Mexico and invading or even damaging the United States.

Officially our security is based on "forward defense." Forward defense means that our wars are fought on other people's land. It means that innocent Nicaraguan men, women and children are murdered in the name of peace, freedom and democracy; that is, peace, freedom and democracy for us, sitting safely in our suburban homes back in the U.S.A., assured that any spill-over from the nasty war in Nicaragua would fall mainly on Honduras, still far from our borders.

Despite the lessons from these ill-advised escapades, the U.S. could be involved in future wars. The world is full of nasty dictators like Saddam Hussein with fanatical aspirations and total disregard for human life. We must be prepared to deal with future despots, should they threaten American interests or those of our allies, and should all efforts to resolve conflicts through diplomatic channels fail.

Yet the list of possible future "enemies" (Table 10-2) could at best justify a small fraction of our current forces. Our 2.1 million military establishment is needed only to stop the Soviet Union. As Secretary of Defense Frank Carlucci wrote in 1989, "No other nation poses a military threat to the United States and its allies *even remotely comparable* to that posed by the Soviet forces."[7]

While China has a large army, they have little capability to project power much beyond their vast territory; China spends at least 15 times less on its larger army than we do, indicating the condition and number of Chinese weapons.

Iraq has one million men in uniform, but spends 20 times less on their military forces than the U.S. Based on our superior weapons and overwhelming air superiority, we do not have to match Iraq's army soldier-for-soldier. So far, less than 10 percent of U.S. forces have deterred Saddam Hussein from attacking Saudi Arabia.

But the United States does not have to police the Middle East alone. A United Nations peacekeeping force would not only spread the financial costs of stopping Iraq's naked aggression, but it would eliminate a major cause of anti-American sentiment that could undermine anti-Iraq efforts of moderate Arab nations. If we shared the costs of defending Saudi Arabia based on relative GNP of the free world nations (basically the European community, Canada and Japan), then the U.S. would shoulder about 40 percent of the burden. More appropriately, if we shared the burden based on percentage of Persian Gulf oil imported to each nation, then the U.S. would pay only 20 percent of the costs. Our average "fair share" would then be 30 percent. If 100,000 UN peacekeeping troops were needed, the U.S. should supply 30,000, which is less than 2 percent of our current forces.

We conclude that the United States does not need a large standing army for interventions in other nations. The large heavily mechanized forces of today were justified solely by the Soviet threat. No other nation requires such extraordinary peacetime military forces. If future conditions deteriorate, we would have time to call up the reserves, as we did to block Iraq, or even to draft and train more troops, as we did for Korea and Vietnam. A fraction of today's U.S. military forces could handle any

---

[7]Frank C. Carlucci, *Annual Report to the Congress*, Fiscal Year 1990, p. 12.

TABLE 10-2.  CHARACTERISTICS OF POTENTIAL "ENEMIES"[8]

| | Military Spending ($ Billion) (ACDA/IISS)[9] | Armed Forces (Million) | Main Battle Tanks | Fighter Aircraft | Major Combat Ships |
|---|---|---|---|---|---|
| U.S. | 300 | 2.1 | 15,992 | 3,205 | 387 |
| USSR | 303/120 | 4.2 | 53,350 | 4,500 | 654 |
| China | 21/ 6.6 | 3.0 | 8,000 | 4,000 | 56 |
| Iraq | /12.9 | 1.0 | 5,500 | 143 | 5 |
| Iran | 22/ 9.9 | 0.6 | 500 | 15 | 8 |
| N. Korea | 5.8/4.2 | 1.04 | 3,200 | 290 | 2 |
| Syria | 3.3/1.6 | 0.40 | 4,050 | 306 | 2 |
| Libya | 3.0/1.4 | 0.07 | 1,980 | 282 | 3 |
| Cuba | 1.7/2.2 | 0.18 | 1,100 | 112 | 3 |
| Nicaragua | 5.5/1.4 | 0.08 | 130 | 0 | 0 |
| Angola | /0.8 | 0.10 | 500 | 75 | 0 |
| Panama | /0.1 | 0.004 | 0 | 0 | 0 |

conceivable conflict in the Third World. As we discuss at the end of this chapter, many military analysts are now suggesting that we reduce our force levels by up to 50 percent by the 1995–2000 time period. Given the likely threats to our security, these reductions seem prudent. Given our fiscal and societal deterioration, they are mandatory.

*Protect the U.S. from invasion.* You rarely read anything about protecting the United States from external invasion. And for good reason. Our posture of "forward defense" has pushed the possible battle lines far from our shores. No nation, including the Soviet Union, has the sea lift and necessary air cover to support an invasion of our homeland. We are protected by two friendly neighbors and two vast oceans.

The only real external threat we face is from nuclear annihilation. We can be destroyed but not invaded. Given our favorable geographic position, we could defend our country from external invasion with 10 percent of our current forces. We certainly do not need two million troops and 500 warships to protect our country from invasion.

---

[8]Unless otherwise noted, data are from the International Institute for Strategic Studies, *The Military Balance 1989-1990* (London: Brassey, 1989).
[9]ACDA-Arms Control and Disarmament Agency; IISS-International Institute for Strategic Studies.

*Protect sea lanes.* One primary mission for the Navy is to protect commercial and military ships on the high seas. This requirement assumes a replay of World War II, where it was essential to protect our troop and supply ships from German U-boats. Again, the only nation with naval forces large enough to seriously challenge our free access to the world's oceans is the Soviet Union. If we accept that they are becoming less belligerent and less likely to ever attack our forces, then the need for a large standing navy diminishes.

The Soviet Union has indicated a willingness to jointly reduce naval forces. They have already reduced their naval activities in the Far East, including withdrawal of some forces from the former U.S. base at Cam Ranh Bay in Vietnam. Former Reagan administration officials including Paul Nitze, the dean of arms control advisers, and Admiral William Crowe, former chairman of the Joint Chiefs of Staff, have recommended that the two superpowers consider eliminating all tactical nuclear weapons from naval vessels. They reason that the United States has a superior Navy, including 14 aircraft carrier battle groups. The Soviet Union has no large deck carriers of this type. The only weapon that could destroy a carrier and eliminate this U.S. advantage is a nuclear bomb. Thus, Nitze and Crowe reason, it would be to our advantage to jointly eliminate what amounts to a Soviet equalizer weapon. Unfortunately, the Bush administration has refused to discuss possible reductions in naval power, either nuclear or conventional.

The primary cost of the Navy is due to our aircraft carrier battle groups. Each of our 14 carriers requires an armada of defensive ships and supply ships. These carriers are the backbone of the naval component of "forward defense," carrying the battle to distant lands. The Reagan administration insisted in building up to 15 aircraft carriers, with an official JCS goal of 21 carriers, so that we could simultaneously fight several wars around the world, including the use of carriers to attack the Soviet homeland. Nonsense! As if a huge aircraft carrier could get close enough to the USSR with thousands of nuclear weapons available to blast this sitting duck target. And we certainly do not need 15 aircraft carrier battle-groups to fight Moammar Gadhafi or Manuel Noriega.

We did use our Navy to protect tankers in the Persian Gulf during the Iran-Iraq war. Ironically, our expensive, sophisticated ships, designed to fight World War III with the Soviet Union, were not appropriate for protecting ships in the crowded Persian Gulf. First, we did not have minesweepers to cope with the major threat to shipping: World War

I-vintage mines. We had to beg our allies to send minesweeping ships. Then we sent in the Vincennes, equipped with the latest technology Aegis weapons system, and accidentally shot down a civilian airliner, killing more innocent people (290) than we lost in the entire operation.

The Persian Gulf may be typical of the types of conflicts we will be involved with in the future: small, regional battles between Third World countries with far smaller forces and resources. At the peak of the Persian gulf operation, the U.S. Navy had about 48 ships on duty; we used about eight percent of our total fleet of 570 vessels. We could cut back the Navy substantially, and still conduct operations much larger than protecting the oil lanes in the Persian Gulf.

*Support our allies.* The United States may need military forces in the future to support our friends and allies anywhere in the world. The last major attack that required U.S. forces occurred over 30 years ago, when the North Koreans invaded the South. The Korean "police action" showed both superpowers that modern conventional war is futile, with both sides losing in the stalemate. There have been no significant confrontations between client states of the superpowers since, and little likelihood that either side would permit such a confrontation.

Still, it is possible that we might be called on to protect an ally with belligerent neighbors, such as Israel. Some military power projection forces should be maintained to support our friends around the world. Here again, though, we see a reduction in the required levels, as more nations join the ranks of those seeking peaceful solutions to conflicts, recognizing the futility of military solutions to political problems. As discussed above under possible interventions in Third World countries, a small fraction of our current military forces could handle any possible adversary, particularly if we acted in concert with the growing number of free and independent nations around the world.

It is conceivable, if the current trends in superpower relations continue, that the United States and the Soviet Union may once again join together, possibly under U.N. auspices, to block future tyrants from aggressive acts. During the Persian Gulf war, the Soviet Union did cooperate with the U.S. Navy by sharing information regarding the location of mines and minelaying ships. The Soviets also agreed to the UN resolutions condemning Iraq's invasion of Kuwait, and they agreed to the embargo on Iraq. After all, it is the superpowers who would suffer the most in a global nuclear war. We have the most to gain by keeping the lid on Third World hot spots.

Secretary of State James Baker reportedly agreed to endorse the use of Soviet military force to intervene, if necessary, to help the new government of Romania when the Ceausescu regime was toppled in December of 1989. If superpower cooperation becomes more commonplace, then each side would need even less military force to keep the peace.

*Protect U.S. citizens abroad.* We may need military forces to rescue Americans overseas at any time. As the fiasco during the Iran hostage rescue mission showed, however, our large standing army is ill-equipped to handle small, long-range missions. Even the Grenada "invasion," justified in part to "rescue" American students—even though they didn't know they needed rescuing!—was plagued by poor coordination and lack of communication between participating services. U.S. soldiers reportedly had to use pay telephones to call back to Washington for instructions, with each military service controlling its own troops with insufficient coordination. Apparently these command and control deficiencies were corrected in time for the Panama invasion, where a single commander was in charge of all services participating in the battle.

Partially as a result of these experiences, the Pentagon has expanded what is becoming a new branch of the military: the Special Operations Forces (SOF). Drawn from all branches of the military, the SOF has been given a full command status, with its own commander in chief. It includes Navy Seals for quiet infiltration, Army Green Berets, Rangers, Civil Affairs, Psychological Operations, Delta Force, and some Air Force SOF with a total troop strength of about 30,000. The Seals were the first covert forces that preceded the invasion of Panama in December of 1989, while the Delta Force rescued an American CIA agent and several former Panamanian soldiers from two jails just as the attack began. These small, highly trained forces are best suited for future hostage rescue and other covert operations as an adjunct to regular military forces.

We do have some reservations about these covert forces. They have formed a psychological and civilian affairs division, which smacks of failed covert CIA operations. The risk of abuse seems high with psychological operations assigned permanent status in peacetime to a military organization. Unlike the CIA covert operations, the SOF has no reporting requirements to Congress. Senator Jim Sasser has warned of the danger that these special forces could be used by the CIA and thus "skirt congressional review." Lt. General John T. Chain, then Air Force deputy chief of staff for operations, warned Congress that having Special Forces is "like carrying a loaded gun." He recommended that the SOF only be used to support traditional overt military operations, and not as a covert force to circumvent democratic oversight and control.[10]

In any case, the number of troops required for SOF operations is far less than our current 2.1 million. We used about one (1!) percent of our forces in the invasion of Panama, 25,000 out of 2.1 million. It is difficult to imagine many more Panamas in our future, given the special circumstances that converged to justify the Panama invasion (large American civilian population, defense of the canal, belligerent Panamanian president, shooting death of American officer and threats against another officer and his wife, etc.). Even if the U.S. forces deployed in Saudi Arabia reach the 200,000 level, this is less than 10 percent of our active forces and about 5 percent of our total forces (active, guard and reserves).

*Anti-terrorist operations.* While military actions between industrialized nations are on the decline, terrorist attacks seem to be on the rise. Military action might be required on rare occasion, but individual terrorists usually cannot be traced reliably to known terrorist groups for retaliation. Military actions would usually be limited to rescue operations, and the small SOF type groups, currently less than 2 percent of our active duty forces, would suffice.

*Drug intervention.* Similarly, the recent calls to use more military forces for drug intervention would not require heavily mechanized divisions. Even here, the use of military forces instead of DEA agents raises the risk of escalation without much benefit. Using sophisticated SOF squads to burn a few cocaine crops may not be worth the effort or risks of escalation. The military has contributed with reconnaissance and surveillance of drug transportation activities, and naval forces may play a larger role in stopping the flow of drugs to our shores. The Air Force might conceivably help in chasing errant planes, forcing them to land at airports for appropriate inspections by custom officials, but large-scale military forces would not be productive in the "war" on drugs. The drug wars will be won primarily through education, treatment and rehabilitation programs within our borders.

To summarize, our military forces have really evolved into two distinct forces: a large standing army that will probably never be used in conflict, and a set of small special operation forces and light infantry divisions that will be used as quasi-police forces to protect Americans

---

[10]"America's Secret Soldiers: the Buildup of U.S. Special Operation Forces," *The Defense Monitor*, Vol. XIV, No. 2, Center for Defense Information, 1985.

and fight terrorists or possibly help stop drug operations. The large standing army is needed only to counter the Soviet Union, since no other potential adversary would require such massive force. As the Soviet "threat" recedes, we should be reducing our large, heavily mechanized and armored military divisions.

## CONVENTIONAL FORCE ALTERNATIVES FOR THE 1990S

Based on this evaluation, we conclude that there is no conceivable threat approaching that of the Soviet Union. Since the Pentagon formerly justified over 60 percent of our military budget on the basis of a surprise Soviet attack, and since that threat is no longer credible, then we can consider reductions approaching 50 percent.

William Kaufmann, a Pentagon adviser to Secretaries of Defense in the Kennedy through Carter administrations, has recommended major reductions in military forces over the next decade. Assuming that the U.S. and the Soviet Union conclude both CFE negotiations reducing conventional forces and the START negotiations cutting nuclear weapons, then Kaufmann, in a Brookings Institution report, estimates that defense spending could be cut nearly in half by the end of the century, from $300 billion down to $160 billion.

The media, usually supportive of large military budgets throughout the Cold War, have joined the chorus calling for at least a reevaluation of our military forces, if not outright cuts. *Fortune* magazine, after interviewing 20 defense experts, suggested in July of 1989, before the European revolution gathered full steam, that the United States should cut back military spending from $300 billion to $185 billion by the year 2000.[11] The *Fortune* prescription called for cutting the Army from 18 to 8 divisions, the Air Force from 24 to 16 tactical air wings, the Navy from 563 to 500 ships, and strategic nuclear weapons from 13,000 down to 4,000. By December of 1989, with the dismantling of the Berlin Wall and disintegration of the Warsaw Pact, even the conservative *Business Week* chimed in with a cover story entitled "The Peace Economy: How Defense Cuts Will Pay Off for America" and *U.S. News & World Report* ran the even more provocative cover question: "Do we need an Army?" (Answer: "Of course. But its size and mission are about to change.") And the *New York Times* editorialized on March 8, 1990, that the United

---

[11]Lee Smith, "How Big a Military Does the U.S. Need?," *Fortune*, July 31, 1989, p. 140.

States should aim for defense spending of $150 billion by the year 2000, a 50 percent cut from current levels. The *Times* editorial included suggestions for weapons cancellations to meet this goal.

Major changes in our military posture are even being suggested by members of the hard-line Reagan administration, at least those now out of office! Admiral Crowe, former chairman of the Joint Chiefs of Staff (JCS), has suggested that we negotiate with the Soviets to remove tactical nuclear weapons from our naval vessels, and that we consider eliminating one leg of the nuclear triad. Crowe stated that the need for nuclear weapons to stop a Soviet invasion of Europe is no longer credible. Larry Korb, a Reagan Pentagon appointee now with the Brookings Institution, has endorsed a plan to cut military spending in half by the year 2000.

And even Richard Perle, former Assistant Secretary of Defense, nicknamed the "Prince of Darkness" for his persistent advocacy of weapons of war, has now admitted that the changes in Eastern Europe could permit the United States to postpone building the next generation of weapons. Perle, testifying before the Senate Armed Services Committee in January of 1990, stated that "I believe we can safely reduce the investment we make in protecting against a massive surprise Soviet nuclear attack." He suggested that we could give up both the MX rail garrison and Midgetman missiles (as did four former chairmen of the JCS), and the new advanced tactical fighter. With regard to conventional and nuclear arms control negotiations, Perle testified that "I would urge that we consider and propose cuts far deeper than anything we have tabled so far."[12] This from a man long considered Washington's most successful derailer of effective arms control treaties.

Despite these calls for major change from across the political spectrum, the Bush administration's 1991 budget supports all of the nuclear weapons systems, with an average funding hike of 30 percent, and most of the conventional weapons proposed in the Cold War era by the Reagan administration. The Bush administration did call for small, 2 percent per year reductions in military spending over the next five years, but military programs were not cut sufficiently even to reach this modest goal. Reductions in troop levels and unspecified Defense Management Report savings were included, along with some proposed base closings. However, this base closing proposal was clearly a political

---

[12]R. Jeffrey Smith, "Perle Rules Out Warsaw Pact Attack," *Washington Post*, January 25, 1990, p. A11.

ploy, since 91 percent of the proposed base closings and 99 percent of the lost jobs would have been in Democratic districts, while 87 percent of proposed base expansion jobs would have been created in Republican districts.

This status quo military budgeting is not acceptable. We must restructure our forces substantially. Possible characteristics of U.S. military forces in the year 2000 are summarized in Table 10-3 under three proposals for major military cuts:

TABLE 10-3:   KAUFMANN/BROOKING, PROPOSAL FOR 2000 A.D.

|  | Current Levels: | Kaufmann:[13] |
|---|---|---|
| NUCLEAR FORCES: | | |
| ICBM Warheads | 2,450 | 300 |
| SLBM Warheads | 5,312 | 3,264 |
| Bomber Warheads | 5,238 | 492 |
| CONVENTIONAL FORCES: | | |
| Army Divisions | 18 | 7-9 |
| Marine Divisions | 3 | 3 |
| Marine Air Wings | 3 | 3 |
| Air Force Wings | 25 | 12 |
| Total Military (Millions) | 2.17 | 1.2 |
| Aircraft Carriers | 14 | 6-9 |
| Military Budget ($1990 billions) | $300 | $160-200 |

Other former military leaders who have called for large reductions in military forces include General Andrew J. Goodpaster, former aide to President Eisenhower and NATO Supreme Allied Commander from 1969 to 1974; Jonathan Dean, former Ambassador to the Mutual and Balanced Force Reductions (MBFR) talks; and Robert McNamara, former Secretary of Defense for Presidents Kennedy and Johnson. Both Ambassador Dean and General Goodpaster called for 50 percent cuts in NATO and Warsaw Pact forces, which does not necessarily translate into 50 percent cuts for American forces worldwide. But Robert McNamara

---

[13]William W. Kaufmann, *Glasnost, Perestroika, and U.S. Defense Spending*, The Brookings Institution, November 1989, and "A Plan to Cut Military Spending in Half," *Bulletin of the Atomic Scientists*, March 1990, p. 35.

has suggested that U.S. military expenditures could be cut by 50 percent by 1995–1997, freeing up $150 billion per year (in 1990 dollars) for domestic needs.[14]

The Kaufmann study recommends that we reduce military force levels by 43 percent by the year 2000, from 2.1 million men and women down to 1.2 million. Mr. Cheney has suggested that we must avoid rapid reductions, since our forces are all volunteers. They have chosen the military as their long-term career, and should not be dismissed arbitrarily. However, a 43 percent reduction over ten years requires reductions of 5.5 percent per year, or about 115,000 troops in 1991. This is less than half the normal annual military attrition rate of 300,000 per year. While there may not be balance in all services and in all types of personnel, most of the suggested reductions could come from normal attrition, without disrupting careers.

Everyone agrees that the military budget will decrease. The remaining questions are by how much, how fast and how best to structure and equip a smaller military force to meet the challenges of the 1990s. In the process of cutting back, we must take care that budget pressures do not force us to make the wrong choices. For example, the Gramm-Rudman deficit reduction law calls for very steep reductions in the federal budget deficit each year, the so-called outlays or the money actually spent during the year by the federal government.

This is a laudable goal, but the Gramm-Rudman law has a detrimental effect on military personnel. Not all money authorized each year by Congress is spent during that year. For fiscal year 1991, the Bush administration is requesting $1,396.5 billion in budget authority for all functions of government. But only $753.3 billion or 54 percent would be spent during FY 1991.

If Congress authorizes $1 billion for a new aircraft carrier, for example, only 4 percent or $40 million would actually be spent during the first year. The remaining $960 million would be spent slowly over four or five years or longer until the carrier was completed. In Congressional language, aircraft carrier funds are in a "slow-spending" account. If Congress cut $1 billion in budget authority (BA) for a new aircraft carrier, it would reduce outlays and therefore this year's budget deficit by only $40 million.

Other military accounts spend funds much more quickly, as shown in Table 10-4. In particular, over 90 percent of personnel costs and over 70

---

[14]Robert S. McNamara, *Out of the Cold*, New York: Simon and Schuster, 1989.

percent of operation and maintenance funds are paid in the year Congress authorizes the money. These are the "fast-spending" accounts. Research and development funds for projects like Star Wars fall in the middle, spending about 50 percent during the first year money is authorized.

TABLE 10-4.  SAMPLE MILITARY ACCOUNT OUTLAY RATES

(Percent of budget authority spent each year)

|  | First Year | Second Year | Third Year | Fourth Year | Fifth Year |
|---|---|---|---|---|---|
| PROCUREMENT |  |  |  |  |  |
| Aircraft | 5.4% | 28.2 | 37.6 | 15.7 | 6.7 |
| Army Missiles | 5 | 30 | 49 | 13 | 1 |
| Air Force Missiles | 20.6 | 22 | 30.3 | 15.1 | 3 |
| Ammunition | 34 | 14 | 37 | −2 | 11 |
| Shipbuilding | 4 | 17 | 23.3 | 14.7 | 15 |
| RESEARCH and DEVELOPMENT |  |  |  |  |  |
| Army | 51 | 36.5 | 8.3 | 2.2 | 1.4 |
| Navy | 56 | 34.2 | 8.8 | 0.5 | 1.6 |
| Air Force | 51.2 | 35.3 | 8.5 | 2.3 | 1.2 |
| PERSONNEL |  |  |  |  |  |
| Army | 94.9 | 4.9 |  |  |  |
| Navy | 95.5 | 4.3 |  |  |  |
| Air Force | 95.8 | 4 |  |  |  |
| OPERATION-MAINTENANCE |  |  |  |  |  |
| Army | 78.6 | 16 | 3.1 | 1.7 |  |
| Navy | 77 | 19 | 2.8 | 0.8 |  |
| Air Force | 76.7 | 18.8 | 2.1 | 2 |  |
| DOE ATOMIC ENERGY |  |  |  |  |  |
| DEFENSE ACTIVITIES | 65 | 30 | 5 |  |  |

To cut this year's deficit, then, the administration and Congress tend to focus on fast-spending money in personnel, operation and maintenance. Troops and civilian workers are eliminated and maintenance budgets cut, while expensive new weapons procurements are often ignored, since they do not contribute much to immediate deficit reduction.

This is another example of short-sighted planning. While cutting budget authority for new weapons procurements may not reduce this year's deficit, it would significantly reduce outlays and therefore budget deficits in the years ahead. Conversely, by continuing to grant new budget authority for expensive weapons systems, Congress and the administration fill up the pipeline for future military outlays, making it ever more difficult to cut the deficit in future years. In fact, the Pentagon now has about $280 billion dollars in prior-year money available for continuing weapons production. The Congress could cut the Pentagon's budget authority to zero for 1991, and defense contractors would still have a backlog of $280 billion to spend. This is all the more reason to make significant cuts in budget authority this year, to regain control of Pentagon spending and bring our fiscal priorities back into balance with our real security needs.

Some new weapon procurements should be cancelled because of the reduced Soviet threat. The production of other weapons should at least be postponed until they are properly tested. During the Reagan years, many weapons systems were rushed into production before they were tested, the so-called concurrency problem. The B-1 bomber is the most famous example: 100 bombers were produced at a cost of $20 billion before testing was finished on the first bomber. When it was learned that the B-1 could not penetrate advanced Soviet radars as advertised due to problems with its electronic countermeasures system, it was too late. Now all 97 surviving B-1s will have to be retrofitted at great expense.

The Soviet threat was used to justify excessive concurrency in the 1980s. There is no rush today. Yet the administration is proposing to build several new weapons systems before testing is complete. For example, had Congress approved the administration's original request to quickly build 132 stealth B-2 bombers, about 36 bombers would be purchased at a cost of $48 billion before testing was finished on one bomber.

Other examples of excessive concurrency include the C-17 transport aircraft, the AMRAAM missile, the Seawolf SSN-21 attack submarine and the Arleigh Burke DDG-51 destroyer. The Navy plans to buy 29 Seawolf submarines at a total cost of $37 billion; over half of these submarines will be in production and $20 billion spent before the first sub enters sea trials. Similarly, 33 Arleigh Burke destroyers are planned at a cost of $27 billion. Again, over half of the destroyers will be purchased at a cost of $15 billion before the first goes to sea.[15]

With no imminent threat, we should postpone production of weapons until the need is established and they are fully tested. These weapon procurement postponements or cancellations would not be irreversible.

---

[15]John D. Dingell, letter of February 9, 1990 to President George Bush.

We would still maintain an adequate stock of weapons to meet our real defense needs. We could continue research and development of promising new weapons technologies, if necessary, but there is absolutely no rationale to rush into another round of weapons procurements now to stop a surprise Soviet attack on West Germany, as proposed by the Bush administration.

We could build more weapons in the future, if conditions deteriorate. But we would have many years' warning of any future Soviet threat, since their society would have to go through the convulsions of replacing Mikhail Gorbachev with a hard-line leadership, followed by the conquest and resubjugation of Eastern Europe.

We could also reduce active duty troop strength without withdrawing any troops from Europe. Any troop withdrawals from Europe should be accompanied by Soviet reductions, either through the CFE talks, or through reciprocal initiatives. However, we maintain six active-duty divisions here in the United States which are to back up the four divisions deployed in Europe within 10 days. Some of these home-based active divisions could be demobilized or shifted to the reserves while waiting for consummation of the CFE negotiations to reduce forces in Europe.

In general it costs far less to maintain troops in the Reserves or National Guard. The Army National Guard costs only 25 to 30 percent of an active-duty army division. Training an Air National Guard force costs approximately 55 percent of an active duty air wing, and Air National Guard pilots consistently score better than their active duty counterparts in mock battles, presumably because the Guard pilots are more experienced even though they now fly fewer hours per year. It takes longer to mobilize Guard and Reserve forces, but, again, we have time now that the Soviet and Warsaw Pact forces are receding. The military budget could be trimmed substantially by transferring most of our heavy active divisions to Reserve or Guard status.

We should be saving money by consolidating Air Force bases. Many air bases have been operating well below capacity for many years. Very few bases have been closed, even though the total number of aircraft have decreased from 25,000 to 9,200 over the last 35 years, and the number of flying hours is down 63 percent. One Pentagon analysis suggests that 36 of the 64 major Air Force bases operate below 50 percent of their capacity.[16] At one extreme, Whitman Air Force Base has

---

[16]Stephen G. Tompkins, "Livid Top Brass Squelch Report of Under-Use of Air Force Bases," *Washington Times*, April 26, 1989, p. 1.

no fixed wing airplanes, but maintains a 12,400 foot runway for B-52 bombers.

While the Pentagon should decide the right mix of weapons, troops and bases to meet our future (reduced) security needs, we believe that cutting budget authority for weapons procurements alone could save $30 billion in 1991. We could cut about $14 billion in budget authority for nuclear weapon systems such as the MX rail garrison, the Midgetman mobile missile, the B-2 Stealth bomber, the Trident II (D-5) missile, a new Trident submarine, anti-satellite weapons, and we should certainly cut Star Wars research. But we can also safely postpone or terminate production of many conventional weapons, such as the M1 tank, the Bradley fighting vehicle, two new advanced fighters, among others. Budget authority for these conventional weapons could be cut by $16 billion for FY 1991. At the very least, production should be postponed until all weapons systems have been thoroughly tested.

Finally, we should begin cutting back the number of aircraft carrier battle-groups by retiring older carriers, with a goal of reducing to six to nine carriers by 2000. We should retire, once and for all, the four World War II battleships (President Bush has recommended retiring two of the four). And we must bring congressional control back to the so-called black budget, the supersecret weapons programs that spend up to $30 billion per year without adequate congressional oversight.

Congress and the American people must insist that all new nuclear weapons production be stopped, except for legitimate one-for-one replacement of aging parts or systems to maintain a credible deterrent. In the conventional arena, there is much room for debate about which weapons are appropriate.

Let the debate begin. But let us not fall into the trap of making incremental changes from last year's budget, when that budget is far more than we need for our defense.

Several possible paths for military spending over the next decade are plotted in Figure 10-2. We are recommending that the fiscal year 1991 budget authority be cut by 10 percent,[17] with reductions to $200 billion

_____

[17]The recommended budget authority for the 050 account, which includes both the Department of Defense and the Department of Energy's nuclear weapons activities, would be about $282 billion in 1991 dollars, assuming four percent inflation. This is equivalent to about $271 billion in 1990 dollars, or a 10 percent cut from the 1990 level of $301.5 billion for this function. Note again that the media often follow the Pentagon in reporting only the Department of Defense figures, the 051 function, which excludes about $9 billion for nuclear weapons and other defense-related activities.

by 1995 and to $150 billion by the end of the century, assuming no major new threats arise, all in constant, 1990 dollars. The Bush administration projection assumes continued gradual reductions of 2 percent per year for ten years (the Pentagon has projected spending to decrease at 2 percent per year over the next five years in constant dollars. Since inflation is increasing at 4 percent per year, however, the actual dollar figure going to the Pentagon would increase by 2 percent each year in their scenario).

The rising military projection curve of Figure 10-2 illustrates the fallacy of presenting military spending as a percentage of GNP. At least one member of Congress has proposed that the defense budget be "reduced" to 4.5 percent of the GNP by the year 2000. He claimed that this would represent a 25 percent cut in spending, failing to take into account that GNP generally rises over time.[18] If the GNP follows historic trends, it would grow at about 3.1 percent per year above inflation. Over the decade, the GNP would then increase from its projected level of $5.48 trillion for 1990 to about $7.44 trillion by 2000; then 4.5 percent of the GNP would equal $335 billion (in 1990 dollars) for the Pentagon in 2000, or an *increase of 11 percent in actual defense budget* in 10 years, as shown by the upper curve in Figure 10-2.

When this Congressman was asked whether he had really intended to recommend a major increase in military spending, he tried to salvage his faulty framework by suggesting that the GNP might grow by only 1.5 percent per year over the entire decade. For a Republican, this would be an extraordinary projection, equivalent to assuming that economic growth during the 1990s would be the worst since the Great Depression. Even then, GNP would still grow to $6.34 trillion. In this case of extreme pessimism, 4.5 percent of GNP would still equal $286 billion in the year 2000, only a 4.6 percent decrease from today's warlike military levels. Even the Bush administration, with its minimal cuts of 2 percent per year, would dip below $286 billion by 1993 in constant 1990 dollars. Such are the perils of basing military spending on GNP. A 25 percent "cut" turns into a mushy, ill-defined proposal that could result in anything from an 11 percent increase to a 4.6 percent decrease by 2000, if we had another depression.

---

[18]He also assumed incorrectly that the 1990 military budget is six percent of the current GNP; in fact it is only 5.5 percent—$300 billion out of $5.48 trillion. Starting from this faulty base line, he apparently made a simple calculation, reducing the six percent figure by 25 percent, arriving at the number of 4.5 percent of GNP to represent his 25 percent "cut" in the year 2000.

FIGURE 10-2.    DEFENSE BUDGET AUTHORITY PROJECTIONS

(Billions of constant, 1990 dollars)

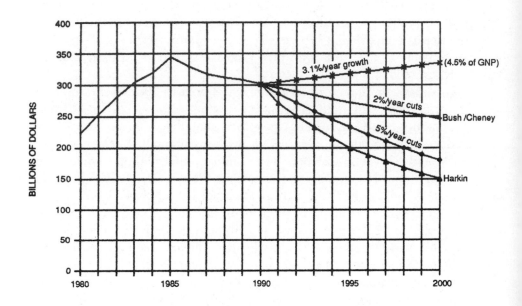

Figure 10-2 can also be used to compare the costs of the Korean, Vietnam and "Reagan" wars. If we make the assumption that $200 billion has been the historic peacetime spending level since World War II, then the money in excess of $200 billion could be attributed to the costs of each war. For those who appreciate graphs, this cost is proportional to the area between the $200 billion line and the actual spending curve for each war. Of course, the "Reagan war" is not over yet. The total costs of the Reagan-Bush war will depend on how fast we cut back, now that the Cold War is ending (see Table 10-5).

TABLE 10-5.    ESTIMATED COST OF THREE WARS

(Constant 1990 $billions)

| | |
|---|---|
| Korean War: | 430 |
| Vietnam War: | 700 |
| Reagan War, ended by: | |
| Harkin proposal: | 1,220 |
| −5 percent/year: | 1,430 |
| Bush proposal: −2 percent/year: | 2,000 |

If we allow the Bush administration to prolong the Reagan war, decreasing spending only 2 percent per year, then we will have spent $2 trillion over and above the "normal" peacetime levels of $200 billion per year. This would mean that the unprecedented Reagan-Bush peacetime buildup would cost the American taxpayers almost five times more than the real Korean War, and almost three times more than the real Vietnam War.

Note also the rapid rate of decline in defense spending in Figure 10-2 after the Korean and Vietnam wars. The U.S. cut back dramatically in the first three years following the Korean War, with real cuts of 17.7, 26.7 and 12.6 percent in 1953, 1954 and 1955. These cuts were far more draconian than the 10 percent cut we are proposing for 1991 or the average 6.7 percent per year cut needed to halve military spending by 2000. The post-Korean War cuts represented much larger shares of the GNP, and would therefore been expected to have a larger effect on the economy. In 1953, military spending represented 15 percent of the GNP, compared to about 5.5 percent in 1990. However, the GNP still grew by a healthy 4.4 percent per year averaged over these three post-Korean War years despite large military cuts.

The military reductions following the peak of the Vietnam War were less drastic, but we still cut the military by 9.9 percent and 9.7 percent in 1970 and 1971, even though the war did not end until 1973, and the last Americans did not leave Vietnam until 1975. Economic growth was a sluggish 2.8 percent per year averaged over 1970 and 1971, but economists attribute this to other economic problems unrelated to ending the war in Vietnam.

From the historic perspective, our economy can accommodate military cuts on the order of 6 to 10 percent per year. Whether Congress and the American people have the will to force the Bush administration to make these reductions is another matter.

### JOBS AND DEFENSE SPENDING

Some worry that cuts in military spending will reduce employment and drag down the economy. Throughout the Cold War, we have been told that defense spending creates jobs and stimulates the economy through "spin-offs" to the commercial sector. Now that military budgets are shrinking, one would expect a negative economic impact, according to this reasoning.

Certainly some geographic areas and some professions and trades will suffer initially from reductions in military spending. However, most experience and most studies conclude that both employment and the economy, averaged over time and over all geographic areas, will actually improve as a result of reduced military budgets.

For example, the Pentagon has an Office of Economic Adjustment to help communities that lose large contracts or suffer from base closings. Over the last 25 years, 100 bases have been closed. The Pentagon reports that employment *increased* by 47 percent in the communities involved as a result of these cuts. That is, 138,138 new jobs were created by turning military bases into industrial parks, schools and even a jail, more than making up for the 93,424 jobs lost initially as a result of base closings.

A study conducted for the United States Conference of Mayors concluded that transferring $30 billion per year from military spending to urban projects such as education, housing, mass transit, public health and other human services would create 197,500 additional jobs.[19] Indeed, military spending is one of the least efficient ways to create jobs. Military projects require highly skilled and high-paid workers, in addition to very expensive hardware and raw materials. Each military dollar therefore hires fewer workers than each civilian dollar. This study for the conference of mayors did show that some geographic areas would lose net jobs as defense contracts were cancelled or not renewed, but other areas of the country would add even more to the payrolls.

Given our huge federal budget deficits, some of the so-called peace dividend from reduced military budgets should go to reducing the deficit. Even in this case, however, the net effect over time could very likely increase employment. *Business Week* magazine hired an economic consulting firm to analyze the effects of cutting the defense budget by five percent per year for just four years, holding steady thereafter at about $244 billion per year to the end of the century. Assuming that these modest cuts were used to reduce the deficit, then this computer modeling predicted that the gross national product (GNP) would grow 20 percent faster by the year 2000 than if we continued on the Bush-Cheney plan of steady military spending. This increased GNP would create more jobs in the commercial sector.

---

[19]Employment Research Associates, "A Shift in Military Spending to American Cities," 1988.

## NON-OFFENSIVE DEFENSE

In addition to cutting back conventional forces to match the real threats of the 1990s and beyond, we should consider restructuring the remaining forces into a "non-offensive defense" posture. The basic concept of non-offensive defense (also called "non-provocative defense" or "defensive defense") is to equip and train troops to be able to defend but not to conquer new territory. This example of "new thinking" originated among West Germans, who had great incentive to find alternatives to NATO's policy of using tactical nuclear weapons to "save" Germany from a Soviet invasion. In 1976, a West German defense analyst, Horst Afheldt, proposed replacing heavily armed NATO divisions with small groups of "technocommandos," equipped with anti-tank weapons.[20] In a non-offensive defense system, weapons would generally have shorter range and less mobility, and fighting units would be dispersed about the defended territory, rather than centralized where they would provide an easy target.

For example, large, heavily armored tank divisions would be replaced with small, lightly armed troops with anti-tank weapons. Bridging equipment needed for offensive attacks would be replaced by tank traps and land mines. Long range ground-attack aircraft would be replaced by anti-aircraft guns and surface-to-air missiles.

While all weapons have both offensive and defensive capability, some are inherently better suited to offense than defense. Mobile bridging equipment is essential for offensive forces to cross rivers, but useless for defenders—unless they want to take the offensive to punish retreating armies.

One major design change to the Advanced Tactical Fighter (ATF) to make it more defensive was reportedly considered by the Pentagon. The ATF was designed for offensive penetrations far behind Soviet lines, part of the follow-on forces attack (FOFA) plan. During the reviews of military hardware in early 1990, Secretary of Defense Cheney was offered the option of a "mini-ATF," a scaled-down single engine fighter for defensive air operations near the battlefront.[21] This mini-ATF would have been one third cheaper and would have required less development

---

[20]Horst Afheldt, "New Policies, Old Fears," *Bulletin of the Atomic Scientists*, September 1988, p. 24.
[21]Barbara Amouyal, "Pentagon Proposes Dramatic Change in ATF Design, Mission," *Defense News*, February 26, 1990, p. 1.

cost than the full-scale deep-strike ATF, and would have contributed to a non-offensive defense posture. Unfortunately, Mr. Cheney chose the deep-strike offensive version of the ATF.

If both sides began removing their offensive forces, such as main battle tanks and deep-strike aircraft, then the other side would gain confidence that they could defend their territory against the smaller remaining tank force. The positive feedback of the Cold War era, where an increase of offensive forces on one side would stimulate the other to add more weapons, would be replaced by the negative feedback of non-offensive defense: each decrease in offensive firepower would creative incentive for the opponent to reduce force levels and to continue the restructuring to non-offensive defense. This mutually reinforcing peace race would provide much greater stability than the offensive arms race.

As with major nuclear arms control proposals, the United States would not have difficulty "selling" the concept of non-offensive defense to Mr. Gorbachev. Indeed, he was briefed on these Western ideas early in his tenure, and endorsed the concept in principle. Gorbachev has renounced the use of offensive military power, and claims to be restructuring Soviet forces into a more purely defensive role which he calls "reasonable sufficiency." Admiral Frank Kelso, Commander of the U.S. and NATO forces in the Atlantic, testified that Soviet naval forces were apparently pulling back to reflect this new Soviet non-offensive defense. Admiral Kelso concluded "the Soviets have espoused a defensive doctrine," and "they've pulled back to support that defensive doctrine."[22]

The Kremlin had effectively told Syria to scale down its drive to add offensive weapons including ballistic missiles to match Israel. Instead, the Soviets are encouraging Syria to adopt the concept of defensive deterrence.[23]

Before the fall of the Berlin Wall in 1989, Gorbachev told the President of Finland:

The events that are now taking place in the countries of Eastern Europe concern the countries and peoples of that region. We have

---

[22]Molly Moore, "Anti-Submarine Effort May Be Cut by Navy," *Washington Post*, February 8, 1990, p. 30.
[23]James Bruce, "Soviets Urge Defensive Deterrence on Syria," *Jane's Defense Weekly*, December 9, 1989, p. 1264.

no right, moral or political right, to interfere in events happening there.[24]

Gorbachev backed up these virtuous words with actions (or inactions) as the Eastern European nations raced toward independence and multi-party systems in late 1989. If our intelligence confirms that the Soviets are continuing to move toward a non-offensive defense posture by removing offensive weapons, then our own security and that of Europe would be improved if we too moved toward some form of non-offensive defense.

Non-offensive defense should become more beneficial as Soviet troops withdraw from Eastern Europe. Former Warsaw Pact nations such as Poland and Czechoslovakia are becoming concerned about their neighbors, now that Soviet influence is waning. The non-offensive defensive posture of Sweden and Switzerland could become a model for these former Pact nations. By acquiring forces to repel potential invaders but not the capability for major offensive thrusts, these nations could maintain stability in central Europe. The non-offensive defense structure could be particularly beneficial for a united Germany, both to protect its borders at minimum cost and, more importantly, to reassure its neighbors that a unified Germany poses no offensive threat.

If the major nations vigorously adopted the non-offensive defense posture, then we could remove most of our troops from Europe before the turn of the century, and we could reduce our military budget by up to 50 percent. This would not mean the abandonment of the alliance concept. We would still be available in time of crisis to aid our European allies, as we did in the last two world wars, should conditions deteriorate or deterrence ever fail. However, deterrence would be much less likely to fail if both sides adopted a non-offensive defense posture.

In our judgment, the days of major world conflict between the great industrial powers are gone forever, like dueling to resolve personal spats, or slavery to support agriculture. There will still be civil wars or wars between less developed or more fanatical countries, but world wars are simply too destructive to be contemplated by any rational indus-trialized nation. Still, there is much we can do to further reduce the chances of another major war, and to minimize the probability of local war between developing countries from mushrooming out of control.

---

[24]Bill Keller, "Gorbachev, in Finland, Disavows Any Right of Regional Intervention," *New York Times*, October 26, 1989, p. 1.

To summarize our recommendations for reducing and restructuring conventional military forces, we should:

- immediately cut the fiscal year 1991 military budget authority by 10 percent or $30 billion, by reducing some troop levels and postponing or cancelling the production of the next generation of nuclear and some conventional weapon systems;
- reduce military spending from $300 billion per year to previous peacetime levels of $200 billion per year (in constant, inflation-adjusted 1990 dollars) by 1995;
- assuming conclusion of conventional and nuclear arms reductions treaties with the Soviet Union and no new military threats, we should further reduce forces and expenditures to the $150 billion level by the year 2000, corresponding to a 50 percent reduction from today's levels;
- move toward a posture of non-offensive defense;
- and rely on joint United Nations forces to keep the peace in trouble spots requiring military force or the threat of force.

The savings from these reductions and restructuring could be enormous. We estimate that the United States could reap a $1 trillion "peace dividend" during the 1990s. That is, we could spend about $1 trillion less on the military compared to the Bush administration projections.

These savings would be used to fight the internal enemies that we identified in Chapter 3. While there are many options for dividing up the "peace dividend," we would recommend that the bulk (say 50 percent) of these savings be used to reduce the federal deficit, our number one economic enemy. This action alone should help to restore jobs lost by the cancellation of military procurement contracts. The other half of the peace dividend should be used to help retrain defense workers for the civilian economy, for the war on drugs and to reinvigorate essential programs cut during the Reagan years, including education, health care, repair of our infrastructure and renewable energy research. Ultimately, these human services and infrastructure investments will pay off for the commercial economy, as healthy workers contribute to greater business success.

With this dramatic reorientation of American priorities from deficit military spending to civilian and human services programs with fiscal responsibility, the United States will be much stronger as we enter the 21st century.

# CHAPTER 11

# What You Can Do

### SUMMARY

ONLY CITIZEN ACTION CAN STOP THE ARMS RACE! You are the key to diverting tens of billions of dollars from wasteful and dangerous military spending to the much more important task of averting impending environmental, energy and economic disasters.

People do make a difference. Citizen action ended slavery and brought women into the voting booth. Concerned citizens stopped atmospheric testing of nuclear weapons. Concerned citizens aroused Congress to limit the MX to 50 missiles, and to temporarily ban the testing of anti-satellite weapons. Concerned and courageous citizens toppled governments in Eastern Europe with striking speed. Now Americans must create the political climate so that progressive officials can be elected, officials who will implement the deterrence-only nuclear weapons policy and a large reduction and restructuring of conventional military forces.

### PEOPLE DO MAKE A DIFFERENCE

It is easy to become cynical, to feel that one person cannot make a difference. Yet, throughout our history, ordinary Americans, working together, have changed the course of our nation. When most citizens

271

were content with or at least condoned slavery, a concerned few worked for decades to rid our country of the blight of human bondage. They were not a majority, but they were dedicated to their cause, and persevered. Later, a minority of women banded together and struggled to earn the right to vote. Without the power of the ballot box, they used the force of the written and spoken word, sprinkled with demonstrations, to coerce their opposite sex to grant them equal status. Those working for sane defense policies have one powerful advantage over suffragettes: the right to elect responsible and visionary representatives.

Citizen action has also made a difference in nuclear issues. Fear of radioactive Strontium-90 in milk led many Americans to protest the explosions of nuclear weapons in the atmosphere in the 1950s. This public pressure contributed to the Limited Test Ban Treaty of 1963 that at least kept radioactive contamination mostly underground. Many credit citizen protests over the war in Vietnam for bringing that unhappy chapter in our history to a quicker end. And the popular Nuclear Weapons Freeze Campaign, while failing in its primary goal of capping the nuclear arms race, did have a major effect on the course of nuclear weapons and arms control policy in this country.

George Bush, while he was campaigning for the presidency, asserted that the Intermediate Range Nuclear Forces (INF) Treaty proved once and for all that the nuclear weapons Freeze was a bad idea. He and like-minded conservatives believe that NATO resolve in deploying the Pershing-II and ground-launched cruise missiles (GLCMs) in the early 1980s, against the popular will in Europe, coerced the Soviets to negotiate the INF Treaty, forcing them to remove all of their three-warhead SS-20 mobile missiles. Had we agreed to a nuclear weapons Freeze in 1980, according to the standard conservative litany, then the United States could not have deployed Pershing-II and ground-launched cruise missiles, and the Soviets would have over 1,600 nuclear warheads on INF missiles in Europe. By resisting the popular urge to freeze nuclear weapons at their 1980 levels, and by adding new weapons, they claim, the United States forced the Soviets to remove all intermediate-range nuclear weapons, a clear victory for "peace through strength."

This representation ignores the bigger picture. The INF Treaty covers less than 4 percent of all nuclear warheads, only those on missiles with a range between 300 and 3,400 miles. Between 1980 and 1988 when the INF Treaty was signed, the Soviet Union added about 3,300 long-range strategic nuclear warheads that are not included in the

INF discussion. In 1980, they had about 880 intermediate-range warheads that were later removed under the INF Treaty.[1]

Thus a Freeze in 1980 would have stopped the deployment of 3,300 additional strategic warheads that can reach the United States in exchange for the Soviets keeping 880 INF warheads then deployed. A 1980 Freeze would have left the Soviets with 2,400 *fewer* warheads today than as a result of waiting for the 1988 INF Treaty. And a Freeze in 1980 would have saved the United States about $110 billion in new nuclear weapons added after 1980, plus annual reductions in research and development costs. We would have avoided the absurd spectacle of paying defense contractors over $6 billion to build the Pershing II missiles and ground-launched cruise missiles, and then to pay them to destroy those same missiles a few years later.

Furthermore, it is possible that Gorbachev would have cut back on SS-20 missiles even if we had agreed to a bilateral nuclear weapons Freeze in 1980. After all, Gorbachev agreed to remove all shorter-range (between 300 and 600 miles) Soviet missiles in the INF agreement, even though the United States had no weapons in this category. We did *not* have to add shorter-range missiles to force the Soviets to eliminate theirs. A Freeze in 1980 would also have prevented the qualitative advances like the MX missile that have decreased crisis stability.

Although citizens did not succeed in the Freeze itself, the Freeze Campaign did increase public awareness of the dangers of the new generation of nuclear weapons. This increased awareness translated into public pressure on Congress to block weapons like the MX. The Pentagon originally asked for 200 MX missiles. As the public and the Congress began to appreciate the destabilizing nature of the MX, the request was reduced to 100 missiles, and Congress eventually established a limit of 50 missiles. Although the Pentagon did try to add another 50 MX missiles on railroad cars in 1988, congressional resistance spurred by public pressure has kept the 50-missile limit in place. Instead of having 2,000 accurate, first-strike capable warheads on line, the original Pentagon plan, we have only 500. Those extra 1,500 accurate MX warheads would have given the United States the ability to destroy most Soviet land-based missiles, if we struck first. Thus citizen action

---

[1]In 1980, the Soviets had deployed about 350 SS-4s, 50 SS-5s, each single-warhead INF missiles, and 160 of the triple-warhead SS-20s, or a total nuclear warhead count of 880. See John M. Collins and Dianne E. Rennack, *U.S./Soviet Military Balance: Statistical Trends, 1980-1988*, August 8, 1989, p. 39.

has prevented the U.S. from acquiring a destabilizing posture, at least until more of the D-5 submarine missiles are deployed, as planned by the Bush administration.

Citizen pressure also stopped the testing of the F-15 launched anti-satellite (ASAT) weapon in the mid-1980s. In this case, the test ban was approved in the House but not in the Senate. However, the ASAT test ban was accepted in the conference between House and Senate, in exchange for dropping a ban on nuclear underground testing that was also passed by the House but not the Senate. After several years with only one test against an actual satellite, the Air Force cancelled the program in 1989. Like many victories of the peace movement, however, this one needs to be won again. The Pentagon has initiated several new ASAT programs, including a 181 percent increase for the kinetic energy ASAT program in their fiscal year 1991 budget request, using technology developed for the supposedly defensive Star Wars program.

Public support for the Freeze also encouraged several organizations to adopt nuclear weapons arms control as part of their agenda. Prior to 1982, for example, the Union of Concerned Scientists lobbied against nuclear power, but not against nuclear weapons. They have since joined the fight against destabilizing nuclear weapons. Common Cause and the League of Women Voters also jumped on the anti-nuclear weapons bandwagon in the early 1980s. Some of these organizations continue to lobby on behalf of sensible nuclear weapons policies on Capitol Hill, a positive remnant of the Freeze campaign. And in 1987 the Freeze campaign itself merged with SANE, an older peace organization, forming SANE/Freeze, with a combined membership of 173,000.

Finally, public support for the Freeze movement had a pronounced effect on President Reagan. Entering office condemning all arms control treaties, he left office with the INF Treaty signed and ratified, and with nominal 50 percent cuts within reach in the START negotiations. Robert McFarlane, then his National Security Adviser, has stated that the March 23, 1983, Star Wars speech was due in part to the Freeze movement. President Reagan wanted to capture the moral "high ground" from the Freeze, doing the movement one better by promising to eliminate the threat of nuclear weapons, not just freezing them at their current obscene levels. One might even trace the brief discussion of eliminating all nuclear weapons at the Reykjavik summit to the Freeze movement.

Part of President Reagan's conversion from an evil empire hater to friend of Mikhail Gorbachev may be attributed to one person with unique skills and knowledge of the Soviet Union. Suzanne Massie is fluent in Russian, and has visited the Soviet Union more than 20 times, becoming an expert on Soviet history and culture. She lectures frequently on Soviet issues and has written *Land of the Firebird: The Beauty of Old Russia*.

In early 1983, Massie became concerned by deteriorating U.S.-Soviet relations. The Soviets had shot down the Korean airliner. During one of her frequent journeys to the Soviet Union, officials there told Massie they were frightened by sagging U.S.-Soviet relations. Massie managed to gain access to President Reagan through Senator William Cohen and Robert McFarlane. She accomplished something none of the State Department officials could: the humanization of the Soviet enemy. By anecdotes of ordinary Russians, over a series of dozens of briefings, some lasting over an hour and a half, she convinced the arch Communist hater, Ronald Reagan, that these were real people, with feelings, families, hopes and fears, like all of us. One person, equipped with knowledge and conviction, opened the President's mind to Gorbachev's new thinking. One person can make a difference.

Now American citizens can improve international stability, by working to elect responsible officials who will solidify and advance the gains in superpower relations begun in the Gorbachev era. Americans must challenge the assumptions that have supported the Cold War for 40 years.

## CHALLENGE THE ASSUMPTIONS—NUCLEAR WEAPONS

Citizen activists should set two very challenging goals: to create the political climate that will permit progressive presidential and congressional candidates to run for office on platforms dedicated to reforms (or encourage incumbents to work for reform or risk defeat), and to press specifically for the deterrence-only nuclear weapons policies, major military cuts and a reorientation of our national priorities to pressing domestic problems.

Neither task will be easy. Given the almost total lack of substantial debate in the 1988 presidential campaign, you may wonder how we could ever elect a President sympathetic to the deterrence-only policy or to major cuts in military spending. We'll discuss process (education, letter writing and organizing) in the next section, but for now let's concentrate on substance: assuming you have a public forum, what issues should you raise to generate support for ending the arms race and reorienting national priorities?

In our judgment, you should challenge the assumptions that have propped up the arms race for decades. These assumptions, generated by a nuclear elite, have been repeated so often that they are accepted as gospel by the establishment in Washington. They form the basis for justifying new nuclear and conventional weapons and for delaying reasonable arms control proposals. Rather than reacting to each new weapons system, we need to challenge these underlying assumptions, to remove the justification for any new weapons that would undermine stability. Rather than debating the merits of the B-1 versus the B-2 bomber, we should be discussing the need for any new manned bombers. Rather than debating whether we should add the MX on rail cars or a new Midgetman on trucks, we should be challenging the assumption that we need any new land-based missiles, or any land-based missiles at all given our other massive retaliatory capability by air and by sea.

We believe that there are nine major assumptions that drive the nuclear arms race. In our judgment, all nine would wilt in the light of *informed* public debate. If we could reach a majority (or at least a vocal minority to start) of Americans with the message of this book, they would rapidly conclude that these basic assumptions are fatally flawed. Without these roots, there would be no source to feed the arms race. These are the critical issues that you should be debating and raising with your elected officials:

*Assumption #1: **The United States must have the capability to destroy those targets that the Soviets value most: their strategic rocket forces and themselves***. This cuts to the heart of the nuclear debate: what deters the Soviets? The nuclear "experts" have concluded that the Soviets are *not* deterred by the threat of 13,000 hydrogen bombs raining down on their homeland. They are not deterred by the fear of losing most of their industrial infrastructure, of seeing the fruits of seven decades of struggle to enter the industrial age wiped out in a few hours. They are not deterred by the fear of losing most of their conventional military infrastructure, their airbases, their navy ports, their fuel depots, their ability to generate electricity. And they are not deterred by the possibility of tens or hundreds of millions of their citizens killed, and millions more subjected to lingering pain and misery of unimaginable dimensions.

No, say the nuclear "experts," Soviet leaders are only concerned about losing two treasures: their beloved ICBMs and their own skins. As long as they believe that they could escape with their own lives and their missiles, then they might consider unleashing the nuclear holocaust. Therefore we must have the ability to destroy underground command bunkers and buried missile silos, the things they hold dear.

Of course, the same people who say we must be able to attack ICBMs and command bunkers will tell you that deterrence has worked for 40 years. Deterrence worked, even though we did not have the ability to attack hardened targets such as ICBMs and command bunkers. Are we to believe that it will become harder to deter in the future? Or is this a smoke screen to hide other goals, like being able to regain nuclear superiority or to fight and "win" or at least "prevail" in a nuclear war?

*Assumption #2: We must have prompt, hard-target kill capability.* In plain English, this oft-repeated phrase means that we need to build new, more accurate nuclear weapons to quickly destroy Soviet ICBMs and command and control bunkers that are hardened against nuclear attack in underground concrete silos. This second assumption flows directly from the first. If you swallow the rationale that we must be able to destroy the targets that the Soviets value most, then you must accept the need for accurate weapons to implement the first goal. This assumption is used to justify the MX missile with 10 accurate warheads, the new D-5 submarine missiles with 8 accurate warheads each, as well as the Pershing-II missiles before they were destroyed as part of the INF agreement.

We must challenge this pernicious assumption at every opportunity. We only need prompt, hard-target kill capability to fight a nuclear war, not to deter one. As we discussed in detail in Chapter 5, this capability undermines stability, giving both sides strong incentive to push the button early in a crisis situation.

As we've said before, you don't have to be a military expert to judge the effects of hard-target kill capability. Just put yourself in the shoes of a Soviet military leader when a crisis develops. Compare two scenarios: a crisis with today's U.S. weapons versus a crisis when we add thousands of extra hard-target kill capable weapons like the D-5. Today, the Soviet leadership could afford to wait out an attack, or the (possibly false) warning of attack. They know that they would survive in their command and control bunkers, and they know that most of their ICBMs would survive to retaliate even if the warning signals were real and the bombs began exploding.

But, if the U.S. adds thousands of new hard-target kill capable weapons, putting the Soviet leadership bunkers and ICBMs at risk, the situation changes. Soviet leaders would be concerned that they might lose control. They might not be able to retaliate if communications were destroyed, or if ICBMs or the leaders themselves were wiped out. They would be under pressure to "use them or lose them," or to fire them before the lights go out.

Why would we ever want to place the Soviets into a position where they must fire their missiles early? Why in heaven's name would we ever want to force the Soviets to rely on their early warning sensors and computers to launch a nuclear attack? Would you feel more comfortable knowing the fate of the earth depends on the reliability of Soviet computers? Yet our weapons procurements are generating this dangerous situation. We have it in our power, unilaterally, to avoid this predicament.

*Assumption #3: **We must have over 20,000 nuclear weapons with various capabilities to support the "flexible response" doctrine.*** This should be at the center of debate about nuclear weapons: exactly how many and what type of nuclear weapons are needed to deter the Soviets from attacking? The U.S.-NATO position since 1967 has been called "flexible response." We need a wide range of nuclear weapons to be able to respond to any form of Soviet aggression. With numerous nuclear weapons spread around the European landscape, the Soviets would more likely believe that some might be used, and deterrence would be enhanced. Short-range tactical weapons are needed in case of a conventional attack. Longer range battlefield nuclear weapons are needed to attack behind the Soviet lines if they try to bring up reinforcements, and, of course, we need intercontinental range missiles and bombers in case the Soviets attack the United States homeland. The latest SIOP (Single Integrated Operational Plan), the super-secret plan that designates Soviet nuclear targets, reportedly includes 15,000 separate sites. As long as the military is told that it must attack 15,000 targets with nuclear weapons, the arms race will continue. The SIOP target list must be shortened dramatically to remove the justification for more nuclear weapons.

If you feel that you do not have the experience to judge what number or type of nuclear weapons are needed for deterrence, relax. There are no experts when it comes to deterring nuclear war, and certainly there are no experts in fighting a nuclear war. Your judgments are just as good as those of the nuclear high command. Here's what former presidential science adviser Jerome Wiesner had to say on this crucial topic:

Each citizen should realize that on such critical issues as what constitutes a deterrent and how many nuclear weapons are enough his or her judgments are as good as those of a president or secretary of defense, perhaps even better since the layperson is not subject to all of the confusing pressures that influence people in official positions. It is important for citizens to realize that their government has no monopoly on wisdom or special knowledge that changes the common-sense conclusion that nuclear weapons have only one purpose—to prevent their use—and that can be accomplished with a small number of secure weapons on each side.[2]

With such sound advice, is it any wonder that presidents after JFK have downgraded the position of Scientific Adviser?

*Assumption #4: **Nuclear weapons are needed to deter conventional war***. How many times have you heard someone say that nuclear weapons have kept the peace in central Europe for 40 years, the longest period of peace in modern history? Say it often enough, and it becomes the gospel truth. However, no one can ever prove what facet of our defense, if any, prevented superpower war all these years.

Times are changing. The industrialized nations have resorted less and less to direct warfare to settle disputes among themselves (unfortunately the same cannot be said with regard to our treatment of less fortunate Third World countries or for wars between Third World countries). The destruction of a modern conventional war may be sufficient to deter any industrialized nation from attacking another. The added threat of nuclear weapons may augment deterrence, as accepted by many observers, but it cannot be proved.

John Mueller, a political scientist at the University of Rochester, has suggested that major wars are now obsolete, even without nuclear weapons.[3] Like slavery and dueling, war is becoming unthinkable, and the propensity to consider military actions will decrease in the future. The Soviets, being cautious, would never have considered invading Europe, even before Gorbachev and the collapse of the Berlin Wall. While this may not give everyone sufficient reason to accept nuclear disarmament, it certainly lends credence to the thesis that a few

---

[2]Jerome B. Wiesner, "A Militarized Society," *Bulletin of the Atomic Scientists*, August 1985, p. 102.
[3]John Mueller, *Retreat from Doomsday: The Obsolescence of Major War*, New York: Basic Books, 1989.

hundred nuclear weapons are enough, particularly when our European allies, Britain and France, have over 1,000 nuclear weapons between them. In other words, it seems perfectly sensible to remove all tactical nuclear weapons from Europe, relying on the threat of conventional war and, if some insist, the threat of British, French or U.S. nuclear weapons from submarines or aircraft to deter Soviet conventional aggression.

*Assumption #5: We could terminate a nuclear war on terms favorable to the United States*. We doubt that very many U.S. war planners or government officials really believe this in their hearts, but it does appear in written propaganda from time to time. It supports the need for accurate war-fighting weapons. If deterrence fails, we want accurate weapons to destroy any remaining Soviet ICBMs, to limit damage on the U.S., and to come out in a better relative position. In truth this type of discussion is obscene, unbefitting for our great nation that was founded on the principle that all men and women are created equal. To even think that 100,000,000 American deaths would be acceptable, if only 120,000,000 Soviet citizens were murdered in a nuclear holocaust. To even suggest that it would matter who was ahead after a nuclear armageddon.

*Assumption #6: We must "modernize" our nuclear weapons to maintain deterrence*. If nuclear warheads or their delivery vehicles were rusting away, unable to reach their targets, then they should be *replaced* on a one-for-one basis, not modernized, as long as we rely on nuclear deterrence to keep the Soviets from attacking. However, the modernization excuse has been used to cover up our futile quest for a nuclear war-fighting capability for many years. The most glaring example is the replacement of the C-4 (Trident-I) submarine-launched ballistic missiles with the first-strike capable D-5 missiles. The C-4 is perfectly capable of hitting all military and industrial targets in the Soviet Union, except underground silos. The C-4 is our best deterrent, and has several decades of service life left. There is no reason to "modernize" the C-4 with the D-5, except to enhance our nuclear war-fighting capability.

Modernization has also been used as the excuse to dramatically beef up our bomber forces. The old B-52 bombers equipped with cruise missiles are perfectly capable of retaliating against the Soviet Union, along with our 97 brand-new B-1 bombers. There is absolutely no justification for adding any B-2 Stealth bombers, and we certainly cannot afford the $82 billion plus price tag for 132 B-2 bombers.

*Assumption #7: Nuclear testing is required to keep our deterrent reliable*. This is one of the few assumptions that does require some technical judgment. However, citizens can rely on experts outside the government (and many inside who have the courage to speak out) to evaluate claims that we need to continue nuclear explosive testing. In fact, most bomb components that could degrade over time can be checked by disassembling the weapon and running non-explosive component checks. And past history is a guide: on the average, only one weapon has been taken out of our stockpile every two years to check for reliability by explosive testing, compared to an average of 30 to 40 nuclear explosions over the same period. All the other nuclear explosions at the Nevada test site are to develop new weapons or to test the radiation hardness of other components.

In any case, the Soviet Union has signaled its desire to stop testing with its 18-month unilateral moratorium started in 1985. If they are willing to live with the purported loss of reliability as a result of stopping all nuclear testing, then we should be willing too. Since reduced confidence affects the side contemplating a first strike more than the retaliator, stability would be increased by a general decline in confidence of nuclear weapons performance.

*Assumption #8:* **We must have an anti-satellite (ASAT) weapon system.** The Pentagon has listed two reasons for building an ASAT weapon: to deter the Soviets from using their crude ASAT system, and to shoot down Soviet ocean reconnaissance satellites in a war. Of course, we can't do both: if we use an ASAT to shoot down Soviet satellites in a war, then we would encourage the Soviets to reciprocate instead of deterring them from using their ASAT. By building an ASAT capability, we would place all of our critical satellites at risk as the Soviets added effective ASAT capability, undermining stability, and jeopardizing the peaceful uses of outer space.

As Brent Scowcroft, the National Security Adviser to President Bush, wrote: "all scenarios involving the use of ASATs, especially those surrounding crises, increase the risks of accident, misperception and inadvertent escalation."[4] If we all agree that the use of ASATs increases the risks of war, why should we try to build effective ASAT systems, knowing full well that the Soviets will copy our lead? The Soviets

---

[4]William J. Perry, Brent Scowcroft, Joseph S. Nye, Jr., and James A. Schear, "Introduction: Anti-satellite weapons and U.S. Military Space Policy," Chapter 1 of *Seeking Stability in Space: Anti-Satellite Weapons and the Evolving Space Regime,* Edited by Joseph A. Nye and James A. Schear, University of America Press, Inc., 1987, p. 12.

offered to ban all ASAT weapons in 1981 and 1983. Why not take them up on their offer? Why not improve our common security?

*Assumption #9: **A partial ballistic missile defense is better than no defense at all**.* This assumption has great surface appeal: how can we leave our citizens defenseless? Isn't it better to stop a few nuclear weapons, even if you can't stop them all?

Any thinking citizen can refute these simplistic arguments, assuming you have a chance to reach the audience subjected to the Star Wars propaganda. There are twin dangers to pursuing a partial, leaky defense, the only defense possible as admitted by the Joint Chiefs of Staff who set a goal of stopping only 15 percent of Soviet strategic warheads: arms race instability and crisis instability. Possibly the best way to illustrate arms race instability is to quote Caspar Weinberger, no dove on defense. He wrote to President Reagan that we would have to increase our offensive nuclear forces to overcome any possible Soviet ballistic missile defense, exacerbating the arms race.

You could also refer to the probable number of warheads targeted on Moscow: we have probably aimed 100 more nuclear warheads at Moscow to compensate for the 100 defensive interceptor rockets they have installed. Since not all of their interceptors will succeed in stopping one warhead, more nuclear bombs will explode over Moscow than before they installed their "defensive system." In other words, any unilateral effort to install partial defenses would result in more nuclear explosions, not fewer.

Crisis instability as a result of a partial defense is more difficult to describe to an uninitiated audience. You could discuss how a partial Star Wars defense would be more effective mopping up a ragged Soviet retaliatory strike than a coordinated Soviet first strike, assuming that some Soviet ICBMs would be destroyed in the U.S. first strike. For a more advanced audience, you might try describing how a U.S. first strike would disrupt Soviet command, control and communications, causing their retaliatory response to straggle on for hours or even days. A partial space-based defense would be much more effective against this stretched-out retaliatory response than against a coordinated first-strike, since battle stations on the other side of the earth at the start of the battle could come into the field of view over the Soviet missile fields to mop up late Soviet retaliatory missile launches. Thus a partial Star Wars defense would be much more effective in support of an offensive U.S. first strike than as a defensive system responding to a Soviet first strike. Therefore both sides have much to gain by striking first in a crisis, creating crisis instability.

### CHALLENGE THE ASSUMPTIONS—CONVENTIONAL WEAPONS

Just as certain underlying assumptions gird the nuclear arms race, other assumptions have justified the building of conventional weapons over the last 40 years. The liberalization of Eastern Europe in 1989 has virtually eliminated the basis for most of our conventional forces, but old ideas die hard. Citizens need to keep elected officials honest. If the buildup of conventional military forces is predicated on a surprise Soviet attack on NATO, then, in light of the breakdown of the Warsaw Pact, other justifications must be provided or else the military must be trimmed substantially. Here are five Cold War assumptions that should be challenged in the military debates of the 1990s:

*Assumption #1—**Warning time of 10 to 14 days.*** We have been told for many years that we must respond to a massive Soviet attack in Europe with only 10 to 14 days of warning. Now that even the official Pentagon bureaucracy has admitted that warning time of Soviet attack would be 33 to 44 days minimum, and more likely six months, we need to reevaluate our entire force structure and readiness posture.

Even though this fundamental assumption has been overturned by events, citizens must demand that our military forces be reduced and restructured to meet the new reality. During a hearing of the Senate Armed Services Committee in December 1989, Senator Sam Nunn was told that the FY 1991 military budget would NOT take into account the vastly increased warning time. This must be corrected.

*Assumption #2—**Military measured as fraction of GNP.*** Those favoring excessive military spending have for years quoted the military burden in terms of the gross national product (GNP). With this frame of reference, they are able to say that military spending has been decreasing steadily over the years, when in fact it has been holding relatively steady in constant (inflation-adjusted) dollars until the rapid rise in military spending during the Reagan/Bush administration. (See Figure 10-1.)

This bookkeeping ruse is based on a rising GNP. Since the Second World War, the GNP has been increasing at an average of about 3.1 percent per year above inflation. By measuring the military spending as a fraction of a steadily increasing number, the military burden appears to be decreasing. But there is no reason that military spending should increase just because our economy is growing. We do not need more tanks or planes just because the country produces more washing machines or hamburgers. Military spending should be based on real defense needs, not an arbitrary economic measure. We should be allocating funds that are needed, not all that we can afford.

Reference to GNP might be appropriate if we had another war and if there were any question about how much we could afford. Indeed, during World War II, defense consumed something like 35 percent of our GNP. During the Korean and Vietnam wars, military spending was 14 percent and 9.6 percent of GNP respectively. In 1990, the military budget is about 5.5 percent of the GNP, implying that we are not spending as much as we did at the peak of the Vietnam War. Not true! The 1990 defense budget authority requested by President Bush was higher than in 1968; the fact that GNP has grown by 88 percent since 1968 masks the true military burden.

The GNP comparison is also used erroneously to compare Soviet and American military spending. We spend only 5.5 percent of our GNP on armed forces while the Soviets are estimated to spend something like 15 to 18 percent. Therefore they are winning the military spending race, right? Wrong! Our GNP is about two times larger than the Soviets', and given all the other difficulties of estimating Soviet economic conditions, including ruble-to-dollar exchange rate, our two nations seem to be feeding our military machines at about the same rate.

*Assumption #3—Bargaining Chip.* We are often told that we must increase both nuclear and conventional forces to coerce the Soviets into reducing their force levels. This may have been valid in pre-Gorbachev days, but now he seems quite anxious to decrease the Soviet military burden, even if it means bargaining away Soviet advantages. In the Conventional Armed Forces in Europe (CFE) talks, for example, the Soviet Union would have to remove 420,000 troops from central Europe versus only 110,000 for the U.S., if they accept a ceiling of 195,000 for each side. Furthermore, the U.S. would be allowed to keep 30,000 of these troops in Europe, outside the central zone, so we would actually remove only 80,000 to 420,000 for the Soviets. We did not need to add 340,000 active-duty troops to force the reluctant Soviets to negotiate deep reductions.

Similarly, we did not have to build up to match Soviet tank levels. They have agreed to reduce to equal levels without our adding thousands of expensive new M-1 tanks. So too with artillery, armored personnel carriers, aircraft and helicopters. The Soviets have agreed to cut substantially more in each of these categories.

*Assumption #4—**Threats other than the Soviets are growing so that we cannot make substantial reductions.*** Throughout the 1970s and 1980s, the Pentagon justified about 60 percent of our force structure on the basis of stopping a surprise Warsaw Pact attack. Now that that threat has evaporated, we are suddenly hearing that other threats are really much more substantial than we have been told in the past. We do not accept this assessment. As we discussed in Chapter 10, there is no plausible combination of potential enemies that could justify even 50 percent of our current force structure, absent a credible Soviet short-warning threat.

After the invasion of Panama in December of 1989 and after American troops were deployed to Saudi Arabia in August of 1990, President Bush implied that there could be no "peace dividend." In reality, the entire Panama operation used just over 1 percent of our forces, and we have sent less than 10 percent to Saudi Arabia. We could cut our conventional forces by 50 percent as proposed here, without affecting our ability to conduct Panama or Saudi Arabia style operations, particularly if we rely more on UN peacekeeping forces around the world. In fact, by restructuring our forces away from heavy armored divisions bogged down in Europe, Korea and Japan to lighter, more mobile forces to meet Third World type threats, U.S. military forces could more effectively stop aggression at much lower cost.

*Assumption #5—**Peace through strength.*** The cry of "Peace through Strength" echoes through the halls of Congress each time anyone tries to question the need for a new weapons system. If you want peace, prepare for war. A new weapon might not have much military justification, but we must show our manhood, sending messages to the Russians just how tough we are.

We need to redefine the term "Peace through Strength" to include economic strength and social strength, in addition to military strength. Our nation must be strong socially, economically, and morally if we are to continue our post World War II role as leader of the free world. Our new motto should be "Strength through Peace," recognizing that in a peaceful world, our broadly-based social system coupled with our competitive economic system and a free and open political system, will make us the strongest nation on earth.

## How Can I Be Effective?

All right, you have the information to challenge the establishment assumptions, but how can you help? Who will listen to an ordinary citizen? What can you do?

First, you do not have to give up your current job to work full-time on peace issues (although some peace activists have chosen this route, and many dedicated, full-time people will be required to organize and staff any movement to reverse the arms race). You do not have to spend hundreds of hours each month to come up to speed on military issues. Again quoting Jerome Wiesner:

> I am often told that this subject is too complicated for average people to understand, and so even though they are frightened by what they see and hear, they have no choice but to accept what the "experts" say. These people are wrong. These issues can indeed be understood by anyone who is willing to make a sustained effort to do so. Just a few hours of study and discussion a week can make a person knowledgeable, if not expert, and a truly knowledgeable citizenry will lead to sounder national policies.[5]

You can make an impact right where you are; you do not have to come to Washington, D.C. In fact, you're better off outside the beltway so that you're not infected by nuclear numbing. By working through existing organizations and contacts in your everyday life, you can influence and raise the awareness of people who would never be affected by pronouncements emanating from Washington or military think tanks.

We suggest six activities to contribute toward a sane military policy:

1. Join together with an existing peace group.
2. Educate yourself and others.
3. Destroy enemy images.
4. Reach out to others in your community.
5. Lobby your elected officials.
6. Support a local political party.

*Join a group.* While some can be effective working alone, most of us work better in a supportive group setting. There are many peace

---

[5]Wiesner, op. cit., p. 105.

groups, some very old, some new, and most reinvigorated during the early 1980s when nuclear weapons issues dominated the news. Many professions have formed an organization that deals with the arms race:

Physicians for Social Responsibility
Psychologists for Social Responsibility
Union of Concerned Scientists
Federation of American Scientists
Educators for Social Responsibility
Computer Professionals for Social Responsibility

Women may want to consider joining:

WAND (Women's Action for Nuclear Disarmament)
Peace Links
Women's International League for Peace and Freedom

And all citizens may want to join a local chapter of SANE/Freeze. Since these are generally grassroots oriented, they may have different local names, such as Interfaith Council for Peace. If your community doesn't have a local chapter, write to the national office and ask if there are members in your area who might want to get together.

Many churches and synagogues have peace and justice programs. The American Catholic bishops issued an analysis of the nuclear arms race in 1983 called *The Challenge of Peace: God's Promise and Our Response*. This bishops' letter supported the Nuclear Weapons Freeze, a comprehensive test ban, renounced NATO's policy of first use of nuclear weapons, renounced the quest for superiority and first-strike capable weapons, and accepted nuclear deterrence only as a temporary measure while we negotiate nuclear disarmament.

In 1986 the Methodist Bishops went one step further in their document, *In Defense of Creation: The Nuclear Crisis and a Just Peace*, condemning the possession and *any* use of nuclear weapons, even in a deterrence role. Unfortunately, these sensible documents and visions have not been adopted by most local churches. Like many of us, churches are caught up in their own problems of budgets, maintaining the church property, and the rituals of religious life. Many do not have the time for contemplating grave moral problems like reliance on weapons of mass destruction to deter war.

*Education.* We all need to educate ourselves on national issues to hone our positions, to counter criticisms, and to adapt to changing conditions. While the paramount nuclear issue—what deters the Soviets—and the need to reduce conventional forces require only good judgment and a modest knowledge base, other information is often necessary to fend off the complex scenarios and contorted reasoning used to justify new weapons. Hopefully this book will provide some of the information you will need to make a contribution to ending the arms race.

Sometimes we can educate others just by asking the right question. For example, polls regarding the Star Wars program show that roughly 50 percent favor SDI research. However, when pollsters asked how many would favor a defense that was only 20 percent effective, only 8 percent were supportive. By pointing out that the initial phase of Star Wars would stop at best 15 to 20 percent of Soviet nuclear warheads, we could eliminate most support for this futile and costly system.

We cannot all become experts on all issues. This is one of the virtues of joining a group. Members can specialize, providing the depth necessary to respond to criticism and to changing conditions over time, and to generate new ideas for reducing risks and costs of our military. We suggest that at least one member of your local group subscribe to each of these periodical publications to keep current on military affairs:

*The Bulletin of the Atomic Scientists*
6042 South Kimbark, Chicago, Illinois 60637
   (A monthly magazine with 7–10 articles on the arms race, both conventional and nuclear, including analysis of arms control efforts—or lack thereof.)
*Arms Control Today*
11 Dupont Circle, Washington, D.C. 20036
   (Monthly publication of the Arms Control Association, the organization of past arms control negotiators and specialists.)
*The Defense Monitor*
Center for Defense Information
1500 Massachusetts Avenue NW, Washington, D.C. 20005
   (The Center for Defense Information is run by retired military officers—primarily from the Navy. The *Defense Monitors* are published 5–7 times per year; each *Monitor* is devoted to a single topic such as Star Wars, conventional weapons balance, the defense budget, etc.)

One Iowa organization exemplifies citizen education in the nuclear age: "Business for Peace," a group of 115 presidents and executive officers from various businesses in Des Moines. These men and women have been drawn together for one purpose: to study the arms race, and to consider reasonable, consensus approaches to various defense issues such as SDI, the INF Treaty, conventional weapons, and defense procurement practices. The members of Business for Peace are nearly equally divided by political party: Republicans, Democrats and independents. They do share one unusual trait: none have any major vested interest in the arms race. They each subscribe to the following declaration, which is remarkable considering their political diversity:

Business men and women, like others, have concerns which transcend their daily activities. Many of us share a common belief that the overriding concerns in today's world are:
• the increasing reliance on military force, and
• the threat of nuclear war.
In particular, we believe that:
1. **War doesn't work anymore.** In the face of nuclear extinction, alternatives to war and terrorism must be found. For humanity to survive, nations and their foreign policies, like businesses, must adapt to change.
2. **"National Security" means global security.** Business has learned that its own well-being depends on a global economy. Similarly, one nation's security can no longer be purchased at the price of another's insecurity.
3. **The arms race *must* be halted.** Today's nuclear arsenals can wage 1,000,000 Hiroshimas. More nations seek nuclear weapons. Conventional weapons are in mass production. Chemical weapons ("nerve gas") are widely held. Biological weapon research continues. Allowing nuclear and conventional weapons to proliferate further—in both stable and unstable nations—destroys any sense of security we may think we have.
4. **An arms race is not an intelligent allocation of human and capital resources.** The application of resources to disease reduction, food distribution, population growth, reduction in human rights abuses, and improved living standards reduces the chance of war and enhances national security.
5. **National economies are hurt, not helped, by arms spending.** In the long run, a disproportionate use of a nation's best talent and

resources to prepare for war impairs its relative economic progress. Both the U.S. and the U.S.S.R. are examples.

6. **We do not favor unilateral disarmament.** Disarmament must flow from verifiable agreements and we must move forward with such agreements. However, until such agreements are implemented, a U.S. military force—sufficient to deter a nuclear first strike and a conventional attack—is a necessity.

7. **The number one item on today's foreign policy agenda must be multilateral disarmament**. Trust among nations is not a prerequisite; however, a long-term view and the identification of mutual interests are necessities for progress.

**Peace is a respectable word.** As business men and women, we support the work of others who are committed to a process of peace making—a process that must show results if the nation is to be secure.

We pledge to educate ourselves and speak out on policy options.
We urge businesspeople, and others, to join us.
Together we can—and must—build a world without war. It's a matter of our survival.

Business for Peace did not stop with this eloquent plea for a new way of thinking about war and peace. They went on to form several study groups to analyze various defense issues. They invited speakers on both sides of an issue like SDI, read relevant literature, and composed a three- to four-page position paper. The draft paper was then submitted to all members for comment, followed by revisions and, eventually, endorsement by the group.

Business for Peace is an excellent example of responsible citizenship. These men and women have taken time from their busy professional lives to look beyond their immediate business and private worlds. They cared enough to educate themselves on important defense issues, and to express their views to their elected officials. Einstein would be proud of their new way of thinking and acting.

If you would like tips on starting a "Business for Peace" group in your community, contact:

Robert E. Larson
711 High Street
Des Moines, Iowa 50309
(515) 247-5173

*Destroying enemy images.* Every major war has been accompanied by propaganda campaigns to dehumanize the enemy. Killing other human beings is rejected by most religions, so the enemy soldiers must be portrayed as less than human, to ease the pain and overcome normal civilized inhibitions regarding the taking of any human life. By working diligently to learn about the Soviet Union, its customs, its history, its people, we can all work to tear down the enemy images and create an environment for better cooperation.

Admiral William J. Crowe, then the Chairman of the Joint Chiefs of Staff, the highest military officer, destroyed his enemy image through personal contact with his counterpart, Marshal Sergei Akhromeyev. The power of people-to-people contact is potent indeed. Crowe called his one-week visit with Akhromeyev the most fascinating in his life. They have since corresponded frequently. Later, when asked if the Soviets were still the enemy, Crowe responded:

> They are a potential adversary. When you say enemy, I don't know quite what that means. Maybe they're your enemy. They're not my enemy ... incidentally, the last major war we were in, they were our allies.[6]

This breaking of enemy images worked both ways. Marshal Akhromeyev later told Senator Bumpers that he had truly believed throughout his adult life as a Soviet military officer that the United States was preparing to attack the Soviet Union, and would do so at the right moment. The meeting with Admiral Crowe changed his mind. Marshal Akhromeyev, relieved of his enemy images, is now an adviser to President Gorbachev.

Whenever possible, we should seek out person-to-person contact with our designated enemies, to break down stereotype enemy images. We should encourage exchange programs and increased business activities with the Soviets. We must actively work to solidify the gains made in superpower relations during the Gorbachev era.

*Outreach.* Once you or your group have reached a comfortable level of knowledge regarding the arms race, it's time to reach out to others in your community. Outreach is much more difficult than education. Anyone can go to the library and study the arms race to any degree on

---

[6]Bob Woodward and R. Jeffrey Smith, "U.S.-Soviet Pact to Curb Incidents," *Washington Post*, June 7, 1989, p. A1.

his or her own. Reaching others requires creativity, sensitivity and imagination. As we've discussed earlier, most citizens have very limited horizons in time and space. Most are concerned about yesterday, today and maybe tomorrow. Most limit their concerns to their immediate family, school or workplace. Their horizon may extend to their neighborhood or city, especially if something goes wrong: high taxes, poor schools, crowded freeways, potholes in the road, and so on. But few are motivated to look beyond their immediate surroundings, to consider the long-term implications of new weapons. One of the greatest challenges we face is how to break this barrier, how to motivate more of our fellow citizens to become involved with global issues.

To be effective, you have to start where people are. Your best chance of success is to reach them within existing groups such as local service clubs (Lions Club, Kiwanis, Rotary), church social concerns groups, PTAs, unions, community colleges, etc.

We suggest that you try to make *connections* between the arms race and local issues. If your community is concerned with homelessness or hunger, you might suggest that our country would have more resources to solve these problems if we reduced the military burden. If employment rates are high in your area, you could collect and report data on how military spending is the least efficient method to create jobs. Similarly, if an existing group is worried about the environment or energy production, or the greenhouse effect, you could point out at every opportunity that reducing military research budgets would release thousands of scientists and engineers to attack these other problems.

Once you have reached a person or group with the economic impact of military spending, you can move on to describe the other destabilizing aspects of the next generation of nuclear weapons. Without the connections to other societal issues closer to home, however, we are unlikely to move many people from apathy to action. Writing letters-to-the-editor of your local newspapers is very effective. You can reach a wider audience, including many who would never attend public or organizational meetings. And elected officials pay special attention to any material appearing in newspapers within their district.

*Lobbying.* The end goal of education and outreach is to generate a grass roots movement to lobby for changes in our military policy. All the education and motivation in the world will be useless if it is not translated into action to stop the arms race. Our society is replete with examples of popular issues that are not translated into legislative action.

For decades, a large majority of the American public has favored sensible gun control laws such as requiring a waiting period to purchase a handgun or outlawing non-sporting guns such as "Saturday nite specials" and more recently semi-automatic "assault" rifles. And yet these gun control efforts have been thwarted by a vocal and well-financed minority, headed by the National Rifle Association.

So too with the Nuclear Weapons Freeze. Poll after poll showed that 80 percent or so of Americans favored the Freeze, but it was never implemented. A majority is not sufficient unless they are motivated enough to work for change.

How? By lobbying your elected officials. Citizen pressure does work. You can write, visit or call. One of the first questions elected officials ask on a controversial issue is "How are the letters from constituents running?" We do not always vote blindly according to the latest letter tally, but it is one important ingredient. If we suspect that most letters are written by a highly motivated minority of our constituents, such as those citizens impacted by a new highway passing through their community, we may opt to vote against their concerns if the benefits to the silent majority outweigh the inconveniences to the vocal minority. But often, contacts from our constituents make a major difference.

Both quantity and quality of letters are important. All letters are read and counted, and all letters from constituents are answered. Often, Senators and Representatives make note only of the number of pro and con letters. But a well-written, thoughtful letter, particularly one raising new issues or challenging a previously stated position, will penetrate the letter-counting regime and receive a more thoughtful response. Challenging letters with well-documented facts can often change an official's position. Letter writing is effective.

We suggest that you organize letter writing for both quantity and quality. That is, generate as many short letters as possible calling for a comprehensive test ban (CTB). If your Senator or Representative writes back that he or she opposes the CTB because it is unverifiable, then begin to generate more technical letters addressing the verification issue. Appoint one or two people in your group to gather the (now plentiful) information on seismic verification capabilities for monitoring a CTB, and supply pertinent information to your elected officials. Be persistent. Be polite, but tenacious. Continue to write until the argument is answered, or until the official shifts to the next excuse for postponing the CTB, probably the reliability question. Then generate new technical letters addressing the reliability issue in depth.

Your group should visit its elected officials periodically, either in Washington or at home during recess periods. Large numbers are not necessary (and can even be counter-productive), but 8 to 10 people can make an effective presentation, particularly if each is prepared to discuss one aspect of arms control in depth. Time is usually limited to half an hour or less, so you can't expect to discuss many topics. The most effective approach is to press just one issue per visit, but be prepared to discuss other issues if they come up. In most cases, you will know the official's position from previous visits, voting records or correspondence, so you should move quickly to the key area of disagreement, providing your arguments rebutting the Senator or Representative.

Occasionally, visits have to be cancelled at the last minute. Don't be discouraged. The fact that you cared enough to set up an appointment makes an impression, and the staff has to prepare material to brief the Senator or Representative for the meeting. Just preparing for your meeting brings the issue of arms control to the forefront for the staff, if not the member of Congress.

And don't be discouraged if you don't see any change in your representative's voting record. Just forcing him or her to face the detailed rebuttals and preparing responses to your letters is part of the process. Even if you can't convince them to change their vote, you will at least weaken their confidence in some of these old arguments against sensible arms control proposals. You may plant the seeds that will germinate and grow years later, when the political climate is better. You will at least let them know that there are citizens out there who care, citizens who share a new way of thinking. And citizens who may vote for the next challenger who supports rational arms control proposals.

Don't be discouraged if you can't meet frequently with your Representatives or Senators. They lead very busy lives, with every hour of every day scheduled weeks in advance. However, you should insist on meeting with the staff person responsible for arms control or defense issues. She or he usually has direct access to the elected official, and knows that official's position in depth. The staff person is one of the key routes of communication to the Senator or Representative, and wields that greatest Washington power: access. Converting her or him to your point of view may not be sufficient to change a vote, but it is a very positive step, and may succeed with time. Your goal should be to get on a first-name basis with the staff person, so that he or she will immediately take or return your call. Next to developing a rapport with your elected official, getting to know and communicate frequently with the defense LA (legislative assistant) is your most likely road to success.

As with education, lobbying need not take considerable time. And the lobbying effort can also be educational. One of the more innovative and effective organizations lobbying for arms control is a group called "20/20 Vision." This organization, started by Lois Barber of Amherst, Massachusetts, is based on the principle that most advocates of sensible arms control are too busy in their everyday lives to be able to lobby effectively. The 20/20 Vision therefore supplies a service to interested citizens: for $20 per year and 20 minutes of time per month, each subscriber becomes a very effective lobbyist.

Here's how it works: a core group of five or more people within each Congressional district meets at least monthly, and studies various arms control issues. Once a month, members of this core group call the Washington lobbyists from peace groups like PSR, SANE/Freeze, etc., asking about the latest arms control issues in Congress. Each month they select one topic for a letter-writing campaign to their Representative and two Senators. The information for each letter campaign is condensed down to a single post card. This post card is then mailed to each subscriber, asking them to write their elected officials. No four-page fund-raising letter. No 10-page newsletter. No need to read long books like this one. Just 20 minutes a month to read one post card and write one or more letters.

And it works! Started in 1986, 20/20 Vision already has core groups operating in 35 Congressional districts. The 20/20 Vision technique has helped convince Senators to sponsor our bill to ban weapons in space. Like Business for Peace, the 20/20 Vision project is another example of creative new ways of thinking that will stop and reverse the arms race.

If you would like to start a 20/20 Vision core group, write to Lois Barber at 69 South Pleasant Street, Amherst, Massachusetts 01002. If you decide to start your own 20/20 Vision local chapter, they will provide you with an excellent "do-it-yourself" packet in a three-ring binder. This notebook was professionally designed to provide everything you need to get started: names and addresses of peace group lobbyists in Washington, camera-ready logos and materials for letters and post cards.

If you are too busy to sit down and write a letter, then at least call or write a post card, particularly before key votes in Congress. Elected officials also get reports on the number of phone calls and post cards on each subject. They can also make a difference.

*Support a political party.* Finally, if you are so inclined, become involved with local political campaigns. All elected officials depend on volunteers in their home states to provide most of the people-power necessary for election campaigns. Even if you can't find a candidate who supports all of your positions, you should at least become involved with the candidates or party most nearly in line with your desire to end the arms race. Over time, if enough men and women sympathetic to rational arms control policies become integrated into the local political process, you can begin to influence who gets elected and who decides to run in the first place.

Above all remember: one person *can* make a difference in our democratic society.

CHAPTER 12

# Conclusion:
# Peace Through Economic and
# Social Strength

## THE OPPORTUNITY

The world faces its best opportunity in 40 years to end the nuclear arms race, curtail excessive military spending, and shift priorities toward solving our common problems of a polluted environment, decaying cities and infrastructure, overreliance on fossil fuels, and lack of food, housing and medical care for much of the world's population. Mikhail Gorbachev has overturned decades of fear and mistrust of the Soviet Union, to the point where only 6 percent of the British public now considers the Soviets a serious threat to their security, and, even before the collapse of the Berlin Wall, 80 percent of West Germans felt that there was no longer a threat from the east.[1] By allowing the Eastern bloc nations freedom to pursue their own destiny, he has released decades of pent up yearnings for freedom and democracy. These are indeed times of great promise, but also great peril.

---

[1] Jack Beatty, "The Exorbitant Anachronism," *Atlantic Monthly*, June 1989, p. 44.

The changes wrought by Gorbachev in five short years (1985–1990) are startling. For most of the Cold War period, hard-liners accepted these truths about the Soviet Union:

- The Soviets would never agree to asymmetric reductions of weapons in arms control talks.
- They would never agree to on-site inspections.
- They would never voluntarily withdraw from conquered territory such as Afghanistan.
- They would never allow Soviet Jews to freely emigrate or release those in exile such as Andrei Sakarov.
- No Communist government would ever be removed from power except by overwhelming military force.
- They would never allow free, multi-party elections in Eastern bloc nations.

In five short years, Gorbachev shattered each one of these conservative elements of faith, leaving American hard-liners with little basis to justify a continuation of the nuclear arms race or a massive peacetime standing army. The Communist governments of Eastern Europe not only fell in 1989, but most changes required little or no violence. Lech Walesa proudly boasts that Solidarity brought down the Polish Communist government without so much as breaking a pane of glass. And even in Romania, the death toll from massive civil disobedience against armed secret police was minor compared to the likely carnage from an attempted military overthrow of the Ceausescu regime.

For the future, Gorbachev's promises for reductions and drastic restructuring of the massive Soviet conventional army offer even greater hope. If he follows through on his pledge to reduce offensive forces and to restructure the remaining forces in a defensive mode, he will have eliminated any remaining basis for our large standing peacetime army and huge military budget. All indications are that he intends to fulfill these promises. But even if Gorbachev were removed from power tomorrow, a less accommodating Soviet leader could not likely reverse the epoch-making happenings of 1989 in Eastern Europe. As former Secretary of Defense James Schlesinger testified:

> The lines of force that have governed international relations in the postwar period have now been *permanently* altered. To proceed as

if transformation had not occurred would ultimately be self-defeating.[2]

CIA Director William Webster also concluded that the changes in Europe are probably irreversible:

> Even if a hardline regime were able to retain power in Moscow, it would have little incentive to engage in major confrontations with the United States. New leaders would be largely preoccupied with the country's urgent domestic problems, and would unlikely to indulge in a major military buildup.[3]

The United States has the potential to benefit from this unprecedented opportunity. We are still the leader of the free world, with the world's most productive economy and its most progressive political system. Not that we do not have problems. As Winston Churchill said, democracy is the worst form of government in the world—except for all the rest! But our economic and political difficulties pale in comparison to those of many other nations.

For those who are concerned about our relative economic decline (and we share this concern), consider this: the United States still has the world's most powerful economy, although the European Community will come close or surpass our economic production in 1992. Our gross national product is still largest in the world and at least twice that of the Soviet Union, and the U.S. per capita GNP ranks near the top.

Americans constitute about 5 percent of the world's population, and yet we produce 25 percent of the world's goods and services, five times more than the average worker. This is a decline from our previous position, to be sure, when we produced 50 percent of the world's total after the Second World War, but this decline is a measure of the *success* of our foreign policy. After World War II, we set out to help our former allies and enemies to recover from the devastation of war. We succeeded beyond our expectations. It was inevitable that as other nations became economically self-sufficient, our relative position would decline. This is a victory for our progressive policies following the war.

This leveling of the world economic activity is desirable. A world split into the rich and the poor is a breeding ground for friction and strife. As

---

[2]Quoted by Sam Nunn, *Congressional Record*, March 29, 1990, p. S3447.
[3]Ibid., p. S3446.

long as some nations and some people within nations do not have access to basic human needs, as long as grating poverty and illiteracy are the fate of so many, as long as those in power exploit their less fortunate brothers and sisters, we will have the underlying causes of conflict and war.

While our policies and foreign aid have helped to turn our former enemies, Japan and West Germany, into economic giants, those nations forced into Communism by the Soviets after the war have become economic basket cases. Communism has stifled initiative and creativity. Communism's central planning has failed as an economic system. Gorbachev has had the courage to say so, and has begun some free enterprise experiments within the Soviet economy. Unfortunately, some of these experiments have failed, since generations of Soviet citizens have been taught that profits are evil, and workers who benefit from their enterprise and hard work are enemies of the people. The Eastern bloc nations have thrown off the yoke of monolithic Communist control, and are moving inexorably toward more open economic and political systems. The message is clear: free enterprise has its problems, and abuses occur, but it is the best approach for unleashing human creativity and initiative, and for rewarding workers by giving them the opportunity to share in the fruits of their labor.

The stark contrast between free enterprise and Communism's central planning is best seen in Germany. Normally it is difficult to conduct a controlled experiment in the social sciences. There are too many variables in geography, natural resources, climate and population to draw conclusions by comparing the economic experiences of two nations. But after World War II, the artificial separation of Germany into sectors created a direct comparison of the two economic systems, operating side by side with similar people, geography and resources. West Germany has flourished under tutelage of the western nations with a free enterprise economy. East Germany, while performing better than any other Warsaw Pact country (including the Soviet Union), has done poorly compared to West Germany, with a claimed per capita GNP of $12,500 compared to $18,000 for West Germany (right behind the U.S. at nearly $20,000 per capita). However, the intelligence community estimates of Communist nation's economies have probably been exaggerated. The actual differences were much greater, which was graphically displayed on November 9, 1989, as thousands of East Germans poured through the opening in the Berlin Wall to sample the fruits of the West German free enterprise economy.

Politically, the United States is still the envy of the world, and rightly so. The forces of peace and democracy are sweeping the globe. Free and contested elections were held in the Soviet Union for the Congress of People's Deputies. Although this Congress has limited power, it shows that even progressive Communist leaders feel obliged to cater to the will of the people to some degree. Offered free elections on June 4, 1989, voters in Poland overwhelmingly rejected Communist candidates; Lech Walesa's Solidarity won 99 of 100 seats in the Senate, and the subsequent coalition government includes 20 non-Communists and four Communists.

The Communist Party was renamed the Socialist Party in Hungary, but they won only 8.3 percent of the seats in the new Parliament on April 8, 1990. The Hungarians are asking that all Soviet troops leave their country. Czechoslovakia has a non-Communist president and a cabinet with 11 non-Communists and 10 Communists, and non-Communist minorities share power in Bulgaria. In less than a year, Communists lost exclusive power in all six Warsaw Pact nations. At this writing, former Warsaw Pact member Albania remains the only authoritarian Communist nation in Europe.

The rise of democracy in Communist nations was not limited to Eastern Europe. Who can forget those brave Chinese students, quoting Jefferson and Madison while erecting a replica of the Statue of Liberty in Tiananmen Square? Their aging leaders may have temporarily squashed democracy and freedom with military power, but the message is clear: left to their own devices, people the world over will choose democracy, not Communism and authoritative rule. We have not heard the last from the younger generation in China.

In 1795, Immanuel Kant wrote of three "conditions for peace":

First, governments should be "republics," meaning that their power would flow from the consent of the people. Since the people suffer the most from war, they would be less inclined to permit governments to use military force to resolve conflicts.

Second, the republics should have market economies, with the goal of improving the well-being of its citizens. Since war would disrupt beneficial international trade, citizens would avoid military action.

Third, such liberal republics would respect international law.

The number of liberal republics has been growing steadily since Kant wrote his prescription for international peace. While we would not yet classify the Eastern European nations as liberal republics, they have made giant steps in that direction during the last two years. If we can help to encourage this movement, we will improve the chances for the rule of law prevailing over the use of force as we enter the 21st century.

The United States has the economy, the political structure, and the world leadership potential to help bring unprecedented peace, prosperity and justice to the world. But will we take advantage of this unique opportunity? Can we adapt to changing times? Can we restructure our foreign policies, our national priorities to fully exploit this (possibly fleeting) chance for a more secure and humane future?

## The Problems

Unfortunately, our nation is not prepared to take advantage of perestroika. For over four decades, our foreign policy and our military establishment have been focused on one threat: world Communist domination. We have accumulated our vast arsenal of conventional and nuclear weapons to contain the perceived Soviet threat. President Bush recognized the need for change, and called on his new administration to conduct a major review of national security strategy in 1989. After months of inter-agency review, the bureaucracy cranked out the inevitable result: there is no need for change, conduct business as usual. Not too surprising, since the bureaucrats who offered up this advice were the bureaucrats who have been a driving force in the Cold War. One Pentagon official called this strategic review a "complete sham."[4] Without any guidance for change from the bureaucracy, President Bush coined the phrase "beyond containment" to symbolize the need for new direction, but we need more than symbols.

We need our own glasnost and perestroika. We need to shed the chains of secrecy and subterfuge that characterizes much of our national security decision-making. We need to admit to past errors and excesses, and openly debate remedies for our national shortcomings and deficiencies. We need our own restructuring of nuclear policies and weapons, a restructuring to gear our national resources to the problems of the 1990s and not those of the 1950s.

---

⁴David Wood, "Soviet Withdrawal Befuddles U.S.," *Newark Star-Ledger*, August 6, 1989, p. III-3.

Communism is dying. Communism was not defeated on the battlefield, but in the hearts and minds of millions of people who have experienced it and found it wanting. Military force did not destroy Communism in China. It was books and words, not bombs and bullets, that convinced Chinese students and workers that democracy is the wave of the future. Communism is not our major national security threat.

The primary external threat to our security in the 1990s is still the risk of nuclear war. Despite the collapse of the Warsaw Pact, we believe that the threat of nuclear war is growing as less stable nations attempt to build nuclear weapons capability, and as the superpowers add a new generation of destabilizing nuclear weapons, weapons that would more likely be used in some future international crisis. Ironically, continued reduction in superpower tensions might inadvertently contribute to this growing threat of nuclear war, as citizens become complacent and do not insist that the nuclear nations put an end to nuclear proliferation and the production of destabilizing new nuclear weapons.

Other internal enemies will also threaten our real national security in the 1990s. Over the last few decades, other, more potent enemies have quietly supplanted Communism as a major threat to the health and security of our nation. While we have been devoting most of our discretionary national resources to the military, we have allowed major deficits to build up within our society. Each could degrade our standard of living. Taken together, these deficits could destroy from within what military forces are supposed to protect from external destruction. These societal deficits include:

*The federal budget deficit.* It took the federal government 200 years to accumulate its first trillion (1,000,000,000,000) dollars of debt, and only four years to accumulate the next trillion during the presidency of Ronald Reagan, the candidate who promised a balanced budget. The debt reached three trillion in 1990. Gross interest alone on this growing mountain of debt consumes 52 percent of our personal income tax dollars, robbing funds that could be used to reduce the other deficits on this list. The administration disguises the true magnitude of the annual budget deficits by including the surpluses from the trust funds in their calculations, effectively using the regressive social security payroll tax to hide much of the yearly deficit. In the process, the administration is breaking its vow to the American public to maintain adequate Social Security surpluses or to make appropriate investments that will create the economic growth needed to provide for the baby boomers as they retire in the 21st century.

*The drug war deficit.* We have allowed the scourge of illegal drugs to run rampant in our cities and towns. Americans are dying and suffering daily from a very real drug war, while the federal government devotes most of its discretionary resources to preparing for a most unlikely war, a surprise Soviet invasion of Europe. We have not invested enough resources in drug education, drug rehabilitation, law enforcement, or drug surveillance and interdiction efforts.

*The education deficit.* We are falling behind much of the industrialized world in our number one resource for tomorrow: our children. Our youngsters are not receiving adequate education, particularly in science and math, to carry them into the 21st century as leaders of a highly technological society.

*The environmental deficit.* We have been adding pollutants to our air, water and soil faster than they can be assimilated by nature, building up a large deficit that will have to be reversed by future generations to avoid major repercussions. The primary threats include acid rain; too much ozone in cities which damages our lungs, and too little ozone in the upper atmosphere to effectively shield out harmful ultraviolet rays; toxic chemicals that have accumulated in our air, water and soil; the potential for gradual warming from the burning of fossil fuels as extra "greenhouse gases" accumulate in the atmosphere; lack of adequate methods to store radioactive waste from reactors, and the mismanagement and disregard for public safety in our nation's nuclear weapons production facilities; and lack of landfill to handle our society's burgeoning solid waste.

*The commercial competitiveness deficit.* Our nation's businesses have been losing competitive position in many industries, but particularly in consumer electronics. Only one U.S. company now makes color televisions. Even when we invent new technology, we fail to capitalize on those inventions by bringing new products to market.

*The trade deficit.* As a result of our continuous consumption binge and disdain for saving for the future, we have become a net debtor nation, importing more goods and services than we sell outside our country. The United States is a net exporter in only three major categories: agriculture with an $18.2 billion positive trade balance in 1989, commercial aircraft and chemicals. We finance our global overindulgence by selling off large chunks of American real estate and business assets to foreigners.

*The infrastructure deficit.* We have not maintained our nation's infrastructure of roads, sewers, bridges, airports and railroads. We have been particularly delinquent in building or even repairing the existing stock of low-cost housing in America, to the point where homelessness is a major problem in most cities. Again, future generations will have to make up this deficit.

*The energy deficit.* We are borrowing from the past in the form of fossil fuel consumption. We could never repay this deficit, since it took nature millions of years to accumulate the fossil fuel we burn in one year. We will eventually run out of economically recoverable fossil fuel. The question is when, not if. And the time depends on population growth and rising standards of living around the globe. The only solution is to develop alternative renewable sources of energy, so that our grandchildren can continue to enjoy the benefits of plentiful energy without reliance on foreign sources of oil, without exacerbating the greenhouse effect, and without polluting the environment.

*The social deficit.* The United States is number 1 in military strength and gross national product, but ranks 20th in number of physicians per capita, 34th in number of hospital beds per person, and 13th in infant mortality rate. Twelve million children in America have no health insurance. The degree of hunger, poverty and homelessness in America is a national shame, given our status as the world's richest nation. As the wealthiest nation the earth has ever known, we should at least be able to provide adequate health care for all of our citizens. On a global scale, less than 1 percent of the U.S. military budget, or $2.8 billion would be adequate to save the lives of more than 2.8 million children in developing countries, by vaccinating them against preventable diseases such as polio, tetanus, diphtheria and tuberculosis.[5]

Any one of these deficits alone could lead to a substantial decline of our health or standard of living. But taken together, these deficits, if not reduced, could act synergistically to degrade our future position in the world community: the total damage would be larger than the sum of the parts. Without trained scientists and engineers, we won't be able to reduce our dependence on foreign oil. Without non-polluting, renewable sources of energy, it will be much more difficult to clean up the environment. Without trained workers or cheap sources of energy, it will be difficult to regain our competitive advantage in the world's

---

[5]Susan Okie, "Health Crisis Confronts 1.3 Billion," *Washington Post*, September 25, 1989, p. A1.

marketplace. And if we fail to reduce the federal deficit, we will not have the funds to invest in education, energy research, environmental clean-up or low-cost housing.

Instead of addressing these deficits before they occurred, our nation chose to invest most of our discretionary federal funds in more nuclear weapons and more robust military forces. We chose to borrow from our children and grandchildren, leaving the burden of these nine deficits to them, all in the name of "national security."

Conventional Washington wisdom holds that "only" 26 percent of the federal budget goes to the military. However, the military consumes about 60 percent of the federal discretionary funds, the money that Congress appropriates each year. The rest of the federal budget is set by law, including interest on the debt, entitlement and other mandated programs.

Another important function of the federal government is to provide research money to help solve societal ills that cannot be addressed by the private sector. In 1989, the military consumed 67 percent of all federal research money, up from 50 percent at the beginning of the Reagan administration in 1980. In 1988, the federal government spent 6.5 times more on military research than on energy research, 24 times more on the military than on the National Science Foundation, 103 times more than on environmental research, and 263 times more than on education research. During the Reagan years, military research grew by 84 percent after adjusting for inflation, while energy research fell by 26 percent, transportation research by 48 percent, environmental research by 27 percent, and education research by 27 percent. Over just the last 27 months, the U.S. spent more on military R&D than on all biomedical research since World War II, including all research on cancer, AIDS, arthritis, diabetes, Alzheimer's disease, and so on. Are these the proper priorities to lead our nation into the 21st century?

But it isn't just the money, as we've emphasized throughout this book. The next generation of nuclear weapons would be much more dangerous than our current arsenal. Not because they would be more powerful—we've long passed the levels of explosive power that would devastate any civilization—but because these new nuclear weapons would be more likely to be used in some future conflict. Weapons such as the MX missile, the Trident-II (D-5) submarine-launched missile, and even a partial, space-based defense would create incentives for both sides to strike first in a crisis, to "use them or lose them."

While stopping the nuclear arms race would save some money,

conventional military forces account for about 80 percent of the military budget, or about $240 billion dollars per year. Most of this vast sum, about $160 to $170 billion goes for defending our allies in NATO, providing active-duty troops to respond within two weeks to a surprise Soviet attack. This was prudent when our allies were prostrate after World War II. But is this prudent today, when they are catching up to us and, in the case of Japan, passing us by in many economic indicators? Do we really need to keep 305,000 troops (or 225,000 if the CFE Treaty goes into force) in Europe 40 years after the end of the war? Or 45,000 troops in Korea 35 years after that "police action" ended? Or 40,000 troops to defend what has become one of the world's most powerful economic nations, Japan?

This is not to imply that we do not need military force. We live in a dangerous world. Force is sometimes necessary when nations or terrorist groups resort to violence. But consider the types of military force needed over the last few decades. We did not need 2.2 million active duty soldiers to rescue a few students in Grenada, to dispose of an unruly Panamanian dictator, or to stop Iraq from invading Saudi Arabia. If 5 percent of our troops were adequate to block Saddam Hussein, could we not safely cut troop strength in half?

And even if our nation did decide that some future Vietnam-style war was justified, should we continue to support a 2.2-million member standing army indefinitely in peacetime, or should we wait for future events to dictate our military needs? After all, we did mobilize from 1.4 million troops in 1950 to 3.2 million in 1951 to fight the Korean War. If our primary potential adversaries are Third World countries like Iraq or Libya, do we really need B-2 bombers and MX missiles, or, for that matter, thousands of M-1 tanks or 15 aircraft carrier battlegroups or World War II battleships?

International terrorism will be with us as long as there are fanatical groups willing to die for a cause. Drug trafficking is a real and growing menace to the world community. And simmering conflicts between Israel and the Palestinians who have become refugees in their own land, between Iraq and its neighbors, and between Pakistan and India could explode in violence at any time. We should gear our forces to respond to these realistic threats, and we should rely more on UN peacekeeping forces.

In short, we cannot properly address the threats and the societal deficits accumulated over the last several decades, if our policies are frozen in the 1950s. Our military forces are tied down in fixed locations far from the probable sources of conflict, with heavy-duty equipment suited to refighting World War II instead of countering today's threats of terrorism, drug dealers, and so-called low intensity wars between lesser developed countries.

## POSSIBLE SOLUTIONS

There are many options that would better position the United States to address our national problems, and to take advantage of Mikhail Gorbachev's reforms within the Soviet Union and Eastern Europe. We prescribe three major changes in our federal policy: a nuclear policy of deterrence-only, major reductions and restructuring of our conventional forces with an emphasis on non-offensive defense, and reorientation of our federal budget from military to societal concerns.

*Deterrence only.* As discussed in detail in Chapter 9, we would propose a drastic change in our attitudes toward and accumulation of nuclear weapons. We subscribe to the views of Robert McNamara, who served longer as Secretary of Defense than any other since World War II, when he wrote that "nuclear weapons serve no military purpose, save to deter their own use."

We should renounce any other use of nuclear weapons, including the futile quest for nuclear superiority, or their use in intimidating other nations. We should stop building weapons to attack Soviet hardened assets such as buried ICBM silos and command and control bunkers.

Our intermediate goal should be to eliminate all but a few hundred nuclear weapons on each side, beginning with the most destabilizing weapons: MIRV'd ICBMs in fixed silos. The remaining nuclear weapons would be on survivable platforms such as submarines or mobile land-based missiles. We could make some initial reductions first, say by destroying 100 of our 1,000 ICBMs under international supervision, inviting the Soviets to join our disarmament race. If they followed our lead, new steps would be taken to gradually move from our current level of 13,000 strategic warheads down to a few hundred on each side. Each new step would depend on reciprocal Soviet reductions. Detailed treaties could be ratified during the process to codify verification and challenge procedures. We must not let the arms control negotiators bog down discussions in endless details until the Gorbachev window of opportunity is closed.

Simultaneously, we would stop the qualitative arms race, the development of new weapons technologies that would make nuclear war more likely in some future crisis. As Glenn Seaborg, former chairman of the Atomic Energy Commission that oversaw the initial development of our nuclear arsenal, wrote:

> The litmus test of true dedication to meaningful arms control is the continued pursuit of a comprehensive test ban treaty. We must stop the qualitative improvement of nuclear weapons. Even now, significant new weapons are being developed or considered that could make the current "balance of terror" much more unstable.[6]

Again, initiatives should be taken to speed progress toward halting new nuclear weapons developments. Specifically, we and the Soviets should negotiate permanent, verifiable bans on:

- underground nuclear explosions—the comprehensive test ban,
- missile flight tests,
- all tests of dedicated anti-satellite (ASAT) weapons,
- all weapons in outer space,
- and the production of fissile material, the fuel of all nuclear weapons.

Once these mutual bans were negotiated with the Soviet Union, we and Soviets should join together with the Soviets to convince all nations of the world to accept these restraints. Together, we and the Soviets would develop advanced verification sensors to police a global ban on nuclear, ASAT, and missile flight tests, and the production of all fissile material. Together, we would prevent an arms race in outer space, before it begins.

For the longer term, we would not abandon the hope of eventually eliminating all nuclear weapons. Our verification efforts, especially with respect to the fissile material production ban, should be directed toward the goal of complete nuclear disarmament. This prospect may seem remote in today's international environment, but the world is changing. Who would have dreamed in 1945, for example, that we would be encouraging the Japanese to rearm, or giving nuclear weapons to the Germans? And who would have imagined just 15 years ago that President Nixon's opening to China would result in a mass demonstration for democracy in the heart of Communist China? Change is possible. We should be prepared to propose and enforce nuclear

---

[6]Glenn T. Seaborg, "Weapons Labs Need New Thinking," *Bulletin of the Atomic Scientists*, July/August 1989, p. 11.

disarmament whenever political conditions and verification technologies permit.

*Conventional weapons reductions and restructuring.* As we proceed with reducing the quantitative and qualitative nuclear arms races, we should reduce and restructure our conventional forces.

Our fixation with a replay of World War II or the Korean War has skewed our military forces toward heavy armored force that is ill-suited to the expected threats to our national security in the 21st century. We should seriously consider removing our troops in foreign lands, not precipitously, but slowly, with prior consultation with our allies.

We should set a goal of reducing military spending from current levels of $300 billion per year for both the Department of Defense and the Department of Energy, down to $200 billion by 1995 after adjusting for inflation. This level corresponds roughly to previous post-World War II peacetime spending levels in constant, 1990 dollars.

Given current world conditions, with no large-scale threat to our security, we should also aim toward 50 percent reductions in our total force structure by the year 2000. That is, if the Soviet Union continues its "hands-off" posture relative to Eastern Europe, and if CFE talks progress as expected, reducing both sides to parity by the 1992-1994 period, then we should set a goal of reducing U.S. military spending to $150 billion by 2000, in constant 1990 dollars, with about 1.2 million men and women in uniform, compared to 2.2 million today.

We should vigorously pursue the West European concept of non-offensive defense, now accepted by Gorbachev. Whatever forces remain from NATO and the Warsaw Pact should be reoriented for purely defensive roles. The distinction between offensive and defensive weapons is not always clear, but weapons should have short-range and limited mobility to permit the defense of territory but not the conquest of new territory. Anti-tank weapons and tank barriers would be preferred over tanks. Short-range fighter aircraft over long-range bombers. Short-range fixed artillery over long-range mobile artillery.

Unfortunately, NATO strategy over the last decade has moved in the opposite direction, with the follow-on forces attack (FOFA) and AirLand Battle doctrines that call for deep strikes behind Warsaw Pact lines to prevent reinforcements from reaching the front. These deep strike forces would have to be restricted because of their offensive potential. However, if the Soviets are willing to significantly reduce their offensive forces, then NATO's need for deep strike forces is drastically diminished.

Ironically, Gorbachev's decision to allow the independence movements to flourish unimpeded by Soviet tanks in Eastern Europe could lead to civil unrest and violent disturbances at any moment. The democracy movements have not solved deep economic problems. Without dictatorial, iron-fisted governments, Eastern Europe is ripe for strife, more unstable now than at any time since 1914. It is imperative that we work to reduce conventional forces on both sides now, so that these reforms have a better chance of working without Soviet military intervention in some future Prague spring.

The Bush administration has preached caution. They warn that Gorbachev's reforms may not be permanent. They fear, apparently, that if we withdraw our forces, then the Soviets might rearm suddenly and attack or intimidate the West. In the case of suppressing internal dissent in the Eastern bloc, the only likely use of Soviet forces should Gorbachev be disposed, it doesn't matter how many NATO troops are in place, but it does matter how many Soviet troops can be brought in to suppress revolt.

In 1956, it didn't matter how many troops we had opposite Hungary. We would not risk a world war to save the Hungarian freedom fighters, even though we had overwhelming nuclear superiority. Again in 1968, the Soviet military power was used to crush the Prague spring without regard to NATO force levels. Thus we should be working now, while the opportunity exists, to encourage the offensive force reductions Gorbachev desires. Sustaining the reforms in Hungary, Czechoslovakia, East Germany, Poland, Romania or Bulgaria could depend on our ability to negotiate substantial reductions in the Soviet military machine now, while Gorbachev is still in power.

Based on possible threats to our nation requiring the use of military force, it appears that a much smaller, lightly armed military, similar to the Special Operations Forces would be adequate for many missions. These forces, numbering some 30,000, could perform international policing operations, drug interdictions, hostage rescue operations and counter-terrorist raids if they are deemed necessary—provided that adequate congressional checks and balances were developed to prevent another Iran-Contra illegal war. Larger active duty forces with up to one million troops would be available for larger military actions, with the rest of our capability in the Reserves and National Guard.

We should also reevaluate our role as international policeman. The Persian Gulf operation illustrates the deficiencies of an all-U.S. peacekeeping operation. First, our high technology equipment was not well-suited to the operation. We did not have the minesweepers essential to clearing crude World War II-vintage mines. Our advanced Aegis radar system on the Vincennes led our Navy to shoot down an innocent airliner. Second, the mere presence of American ships stirred anti-American feelings in Iran that could have exacerbated the war. A joint peacekeeping operation among several nations under the auspices of the United Nations would have been much more effective. A U.N. force would have also spread the financial burden of the operation.

*Shifting the federal budget priorities.* We believe that the changes in military posture, moving toward deterrence-only and toward a smaller, defensive-oriented conventional force, would free between $100 to $150 billion annually for other needs within 10 years. As Charles Schultz, former chairman of the Council of Economic Advisors, said:

> We could have more housing and more investment. Think what lower interest rates would mean to the financial markets, to the [Third World] debt problem. A defense cut of $100 billion would do incredible things.[7]

Over the next decade, this spending level would save about $1 trillion compared to a continuation of current military spending levels. This money, and the national resources it would command, should be shifted to relieving the nine deficits outlined earlier, with half going to reduce the federal budget deficits and the rest to urgent domestic needs.

### IMPLEMENTATION

Achieving these three objectives (deterrence-only, non-offensive defense at half current force levels, and reorientation of budget priorities from military to societal needs) will be a major challenge in today's political climate. We have a classical chicken-and-egg dilemma: to elect progressive officials to implement these policies, we need an informed and motivated citizenry. But to effectively inform and motivate our citizens, we need a strong, progressive President, or else an exceptional, charismatic leader who can use some other national platform to reach millions of Americans, to honestly discuss our problems and the dangers that lie ahead if we do not change course.

---

[7]James McCartney, "Is America Prepared for Peace?" *Philadelphia Inquirer*, November 26, 1989, p. 7C.

The only other obvious event that would cut through the apathy and indifference of most Americans would be a major crisis related to one of the nine societal deficits. A major economic depression that touched the pocketbooks of most Americans, another oil embargo that once again created long lines at the gas pumps, or another Bhopal or Chernobyl type environmental disaster might trigger massive citizen reaction. Certainly the use of even one nuclear weapon anywhere in the world would raise awareness and presumably lead to a reassessment of our antiquated nuclear policies.

But, needless to say, we would hope that changes can be made before these crises arise. We would hope that our nation's leaders would have the foresight to predict the possibility of these impending disasters, and the courage and honesty to openly warn the public of what the future holds if we do not take remedial action soon.

These changes will probably require a bold, visionary President. The President alone has the forum to effectively reach the American public on national security issues, particularly when old myths and habits must be erased. The President would have to orchestrate the diverse departments of the executive branch to make this landmark shift in our weapons policies. And, of course, the President alone has the responsibility for negotiating treaties to seal the stability of deterrence-only. We need a bold, courageous and visionary new leader, someone with sufficient stature, knowledge and self-confidence to survive and defend his or her position against the sure cries of "soft on Communism" and "weak on defense."

Congress might be able to adopt the deterrence-only position without presidential cooperation, but the likelihood that Congress could move beyond its customary role of making marginal changes to the defense budget seems remote. Congress has the constitutional obligation to provide funding for the military services, and the Senate is charged with providing its "advice and consent" in the making of treaties. If a majority of both houses of Congress were convinced that deterrence-only would strengthen and stabilize our nation's future, then we could cut off all funds for underground nuclear testing, missile flights, ASAT weapons and weapons in space.

Congress has had limited success initiating arms control policies in the past. During the Reagan years, Congress did cut off funds for testing of an American anti-satellite (ASAT) weapon against objects in space, as long as the Soviets continued to abide by their unilateral ASAT testing moratorium. This action created a temporary ban on space weapons, but the Bush administration has started a whole new series of ASAT weapons programs that threaten to extend the arms race into outer space.

Congress also initiated a ban on depressed trajectory missiles that could sneak under radar coverage from submarines off shore as part of a surprise attack. In this case, the Bush administration accepted the logic of this congressional initiative, and has offered to make the depressed trajectory ban permanent through the START treaty. But without executive branch agreement, congressional action has been limited in the arms control area.

To implement a deterrence-only policy, Congress could in principle cut off funds for operating some existing land-based ICBMs, and even cut off operating funds for all but a minimum deterrence arsenal of nuclear weapons, with "escape clauses" dependent on Soviet restraint in each area. But without concurrence of the executive branch, such a drastic change in our nuclear posture would be extremely difficult. If the President vetoed these measures, then two-thirds of both houses of Congress would have to support the deterrence-only strategy. If enough Americans accepted our position to elect two-thirds majorities in both houses, then it seems likely that they would also elect a President sympathetic to this approach.

At best the Congress might drag a reluctant President down the road toward deterrence-only. The legislative route would surely take longer, increasing the risk that the Gorbachev window of opportunity might close before we reached our goal.

We can envision the process for change, once progressive leaders are elected or once incumbent lawmakers come to see and deal with the dangers we face. We recommend that four agencies be substantially strengthened or reoriented within the federal government: a new President's Advisory Council, the Arms Control and Disarmament Agency, a new Verification Bureau, and a U.S. Peace Academy.

*The President's Advisory Council.* We would suggest that the President revamp the executive planning process, beginning with the National Security Council. The intent is to expand our definition of "national security" to include all the threats to our nation, economic, environmental, societal and infrastructure decline, as well as direct military threats. The NSC should be replaced as our premier planning vehicle with a Presidential Advisory Panel that includes the military component via the NSC, but also includes on an equal basis the President's Council of Economic Advisors, the Council on Environmental Quality, and spokesman for the real energy concerns, and for the poor (housing, etc.). This planning body might sound like the President's cabinet, but our intent is to focus on long-term planning, not day-to-day operations of the government, and to include a panel of experts in each deficit area.

This Advisory Council would be charged with zero-based budgeting. They would start by defining the threats to our nation's health and security. They would consider the nine deficits and other needs of our society, with emphasis on long-term planning, projecting the effects of neglecting our accumulating deficits several decades into the future. Priorities would be assigned to each deficit based on the costs of neglecting or postponing remedial action. Resources would then be allocated to meet each threat, not on the basis of last year's funding, but on the basis of projected need and the predicted consequences of not acting. If we did not have the resources to meet some critical needs, then the President would go to the American people, explain the circumstances, outline a long-term plan to address the myriad of problems, and, if necessary, request the resources from Congress.

*The Arms Control and Disarmament Agency (ACDA).* ACDA was established by Congress in 1961 to provide an independent advocate for arms control and disarmament within the executive branch. This agency was envisioned as a counterbalance to the enormous political and economic clout of the military-industrial complex. While it has had some successes over the years, ACDA has effectively been assimilated into the establishment, losing any independent voice it once had. During the Reagan administration, ACDA's leaders were generally opponents of arms control who saw negotiations as a necessary evil to placate the public. Arms control proposals were designed to appear reasonable, while being so one-sided that they would be totally unacceptable to the Soviets. Only the rise to power of Mikhail Gorbachev foiled these plans, since he began to accept these asymmetrical proposals, such as the so-called zero-option that became the INF Treaty.

ACDA should be reinvigorated with true advocates of arms control, such as President Carter's ACDA director, Paul Warnke. Warnke was successful as negotiator of the SALT II accords, but was replaced by Carter in a futile attempt to buy votes for Senate ratification of the Treaty. ACDA should be enlarged, to provide a true counterbalance to the Pentagon. Today, the Pentagon's budget is about 10,000 times larger than the ACDA budget. While we do not suggest anything close to parity, a healthy increase in ACDA's budget, say from $30 million up to the $50 to $60 million range would provide a more stable base of technical support for concluding verifiable arms control and real disarmament treaties. This modest increase in funding (by federal government standards) would give ACDA needed clout in the bureaucratic inter-agency process.

*The Verification Bureau.* Along with augmenting ACDA, we recommend that a permanent agency be established to develop, procure, and operate hardware to verify compliance with past and future arms control treaties. Today the U.S. spends only a few hundred million dollars on verification technology research, compared to $40 billion dollars on military research. We spend about $900 million developing laser weapons for Star Wars and ASAT programs, but researchers were reluctant to take a congressionally mandated $2 million contract to verify our ability to detect laser weapons, for fear that an arms control treaty would kill the laser weapons research program. Verification research is conducted at the national weapons laboratories at Los Alamos, Sandia and Livermore, raising an obvious conflict of interest question. Do we really want those who profit by a continuation of the arms race to be in charge of developing technology to verify an end to the arms race?

The results from this study in conflict of interest have been mixed to date. The weapons laboratories have set up small but separate verification technology research groups. The Los Alamos group did develop a portal monitoring system to check the material exiting the Soviet manufacturing plant that formerly made SS-20 missiles. But when it came to the bread and butter business of Los Alamos and Livermore nuclear weapons testing, the two weapons laboratories not only dragged their collective feet on verification procedures, but actively lobbied Congress (at taxpayer expense) not to legislate a comprehensive test ban. It was a private group, the Natural Resources Defense Council, that actively pursued seismic verification technology, initiating a joint test program with the Soviet Union, much to the embarrassment of the Reagan administration. While NRDC provided a valuable service, breaking ground for a CTB, private groups do not have the financial or scientific resources needed to fully develop verification technology.

We would recommend that this verification bureau be administered by a reinvigorated ACDA. The ACDA research budget would have to be expanded, since they only have a few million dollars available each year. ACDA could then contract with companies and the national weapons laboratories to develop new verification technology and techniques. There are undoubtedly many individual scientists and engineers at Los Alamos, Livermore, Sandia and other government labs who would gladly work on verification technology if funds were available, and if the national leadership promoted verifiable arms control and disarmament as being in our nation's best interest.

These verification projects could form part of the economic conversion process, moving scientists and engineers from designing and building nuclear weapons to designing and developing technology to detect potential test ban cheaters. Much of the scientific work would be similar. Those intimately familiar with the radioactive emissions such as gamma rays and neutrons from nuclear weapons, would be well qualified to design devices such as gamma ray spectrometers to detect clandestine fissile material, or to measure the isotopic content of material withdrawn from nuclear power plants as part of plutonium and enriched uranium inventory control.

*The United States Peace Academy.* For many decades, prominent Americans have called for the establishment of a Peace Academy to train our young people in the skills of diplomacy and peaceful resolution of conflicts. Each year we spend about $300 million directly on the three service academies, teaching young people how to fight wars. In addition, there are several war colleges to educate our officers, and much of the $300 billion military budget trains soldiers directly how to fight wars. Why not spend a minute fraction to train the next generation on how to settle disputes without violence?

Conflict resolution techniques should become an integral part of our education system beginning in elementary schools. We need to teach our youngest children that every conflict does not need to produce winners and losers. They must learn to seek out "win-win" compromises in every situation, from squabbling over toys to community and business conflicts to international disputes. We must train more of our young people to become mediators at all levels of our life, until mediation becomes the norm for resolving disputes.

Congress did act at the end of the Carter administration, spurred by the tireless efforts of the late Senator Spark Matsunaga from Hawaii, and the U.S. Institute of Peace was established during the Reagan administration. Reagan was not thrilled with this idea, and stalled for several years in making the required appointments to the USIP board. Reagan appointments, not surprisingly, were conservative, so the first projects were tilted toward conservative causes.

But the U.S. Institute of Peace has survived, and the new president, Samuel Lewis, is a career diplomat who participated in President Carter's Camp David Peace Accords, culminating in the agreement between Israel and Egypt. The Peace Institute awards grants to various institutions and individuals to conduct research on peace and conflict resolution topics, and they fund scholars directly for various competitively selected projects.

While the USIP is a good start, this activity is too little compared with the need for diplomats and negotiators skilled in non-violent conflict resolution. The entire USIP budget in 1989 was about $7 million dollars, just 2.3 percent of the operating budgets of the military academies, and 42,000 times smaller than the total military budget! We would like to see the USIP develop into a major institution on the American scene, so that in the 21st century, graduates of the U.S. Academy of Peace will be employed around the world as mediators, and other nations will call on our diplomats to help resolve international disputes and young people from across the globe will come to the United States Peace Academy to learn the art of conflict resolution.

We could not accomplish any of these changes without the support of the American people. As we discussed in Chapter 11, it is up to you, our readers, to go from here. We have no delusions that this book alone could move enough people to act, but if we convince even a few voters of the merits of our case, and if you become involved in reaching others, we will have made a difference. And maybe, just maybe, one of you will use these humble thoughts as a springboard to bringing about the nuclear perestroika that we envision.

We enter the last decade of the 20th century with unprecedented opportunity to advance the cause of peace, freedom and democracy around the globe. Our fear is that we will not take advantage of this historic opportunity. Our nation could struggle on without cutting back military spending. We could make sacrifices and build more new nuclear weapons. We could continue business as usual, developing new weapons and making small, incremental changes in the military budget. Our economy is strong enough to afford the MX missile, the B-2 bomber, and we can afford to keep 2.2 million troops on the active-duty rosters; this might not bankrupt our nation. And even if we did continue down this "business as usual" path, international relations might continue to improve and we might avoid wars between Third World nations.

Even if we did not cash in the "peace dividend" and divert many billions from military spending to other societal needs, we might not suffer. Global warming may not occur, or might be less onerous than we fear. Deficits may not ruin our economy, or we may struggle along as a strong, but second-rate economic power. And we may learn, somehow, to cope with the drug war without new resources.

But the larger issue is whether we can do better, whether we can take the initiative before it is too late to improve our future, before the crisis happens. This is the responsibility of true leaders: to look into the future, to analyze and predict the likely outcome of various actions, and to minimize the risks and maximize the positive outcomes. Our leaders should once again *lead*, by energizing us to follow the best course, not the easiest, status quo course.

William Kaufmann, the ex-Pentagon adviser who has recommended that we cut military spending in half by the year 2000, tells of his experience during the 1963-64 time period when Nikita Khrushchev made unilateral cuts in the Soviet military. Khrushchev pulled tanks and troops out of East Germany, and invited the U.S. to do the same. President Kennedy did consider making reciprocal cuts, but increased military spending instead to fight the Vietnam War.

In retrospect, Kaufmann believes that we missed a unique opportunity to wind down the arms race and improve superpower relations: "The one regret I have is that we did not respond nearly enough to Khrushchev." Kaufmann called our failure to react "the big missed opportunity" of the Cold War, and went on to say that "we can't afford to miss again."[8]

Let's hope that future U.S. leaders do not have to regret our lack of response to the far greater Gorbachev window of opportunity.

As we approach the 21st century, it is our dream that our grandchildren will look back on the 1990s as the time when Einstein's new way of thinking about nuclear weapons took hold. A time when the earth's inhabitants rejected the possession and use of nuclear weapons. A time when a majority rejected the use of war to settle international disputes, just as our grandparents rejected dueling to settle personal disputes. A time when nations turned from building expensive homes for missiles to building low-cost housing for their people. A time when

---

[8]Fred Kaplan, "Seize Moment, Says Pentagon Veteran," *Boston Globe*, November 29, 1989, p. 16.

people began removing pollutants from the environment faster than they were added. A time when all the nations recognized that there is no security for one until there is security for all—there is only common security. A time when peace was not just the absence of war, but the presence of justice for all.

We hope you share this dream, and will help us to make it a reality. No one can do it alone.

# Glossary

ABM (Anti-Ballistic Missile)—
A defensive missile to shoot down an opponent's offensive missile which may be armed with nuclear weapons.

ABM TREATY—
Treaty banning development of nationwide defenses against ballistic missiles. (See Appendix B)

ADVANCED CRUISE MISSILE—
Advanced air-launched cruise missile which will use stealth technology to reduce radar detection, and may fly at supersonic speeds. (See Cruise Missile)

ALCM (Air-Launched Cruise Missile)—
A cruise missile launched from an aircraft. (See Cruise Missile)

ASAT (Anti-Satellite) Weapons—
Weapons to shoot down the opponent's satellites in space.

ASW (Anti-Submarine Warfare)—
Weapons systems to attempt to find and destroy the opponent's submarines. Despite decades of spending billions of dollars per year, there is little likelihood that ASW systems will be able to succeed in destroying submerged submarines.

ATOMIC BOMB—
The initial nuclear weapon used on Hiroshima and Nagasaki, with power derived by splitting very heavy atoms of uranium or plutonium. (See also Hydrogen bomb)

B-1 BOMBER—
Modern strategic nuclear bomber; 100 were deployed in 1986–87 to penetrate Soviet radar, although electronics problems persist in the 97 surviving bombers.

B-2 STEALTH BOMBER—
Initially a supersecret strategic bomber using advanced composite materials to reduce radar and infrared detectability. Thirteen of these costly (over $500 million each) and controversial planes have been ordered, with

321

132 originally planned at a cost exceeding $80 billion. Latest plans call for building 75 B-2 bombers at a cost of $815 million each.

B-52 BOMBER—

The oldest U.S. strategic bomber; about 243 of the newer G and H models remain in the strategic force, with 61 older models reserved for conventional bombing missions. Each B-52 can carry four nuclear gravity bombs, six short-range attack (SRAM) missiles, and 16 air-launched Cruise Missiles (ALCM).

BALLISTIC MISSILES—

Missiles that are powered on takeoff by one to three rocket engines, but coast through outer space at very high speeds on a free-fall "ballistic" trajectory after the engines burn out, much like a bullet after it leaves the barrel of a gun.

BMD (Ballistic Missile Defense)—

The name for research into stopping ballistic missiles before President Reagan introduced the Star Wars concept in 1983.

CEP (Circular Error Probability, or Circle of Equal Probability)—

A statistical measure of weapon accuracy. The CEP is the radius of a circle surrounding the intended target, into which half the bombs aimed at that target would fall. A small CEP corresponds to an accurate weapon system.

COUNTERFORCE ATTACK—

Attack against military targets.

COUNTERSILO ATTACK—

Attack against underground missile silos.

COUNTERVALUE ATTACK—

Attack against cities or economic/industrial targets.

CRUISE MISSILE—

Small (20 foot long), slow, pilotless, inexpensive, low-flying jet aircraft that can carry either nuclear or conventional explosives. Cruise missiles can be fired from planes (Air-Launched Cruise Missiles—ALCM), ships (Sea-Launched Cruise Missiles—SLCM), or from the ground (Ground-Launched Cruise Missiles—GLCM). Cruise missiles are considered destabilizing because their improved accuracy can destroy hardened missile silos and their small size makes verification difficult, but they are considered stabilizing because of their long flight time and hence long warning time compared to ballistic missiles.

D-5 MISSILE—

See Trident-II submarine launched ballistic missile.

DEPLOYMENT—

The act of installing and making a weapon system ready for operation.

DESTABILIZING—

Tending to reduce the inhibitions of one or both superpowers to use nuclear weapons in a warlike situation (crisis instability), or tending to force one or both superpowers to build more nuclear weapons during peacetime to overcome advances in nuclear weaponry by the adversary (arms race instability).

DETERRENCE—

The threat of retaliation with nuclear weapons that keeps any rational government from starting a nuclear war.

DEUTERIUM—

The hydrogen isotope with a neutron in its nucleus, useful for fusion reactions (ordinary hydrogen has one proton, one electron, and no neutrons).

DEW (Directed Energy Weapons)—

Weapons such as high-power lasers that kill with high-speed energy instead of physical projectiles like bullets or missiles.

FIRST STRIKE—

The act of setting off the first nuclear explosive in a war, generally taken to mean an attempt to gain advantage by attacking the nuclear arsenal of the opponent before the adversary can launch its weapons.

FISSION—

The nuclear reaction from splitting large atoms such as uranium and plutonium, the process that drives the atomic bomb and also commercial nuclear power plants.

FUSION—

The nuclear reaction of fusing or combining two small atoms such as hydrogen to form helium, the process that drives the hydrogen bomb and the sun. To date, scientists have not harnessed the fusion reaction for peaceful purposes, but two major research programs, magnetic confinement fusion and laser or inertial confinement fusion, have that goal.

GLCM (Ground-Launched Cruise Missile)—(See Cruise Missile)

HARD TARGET—

A target such as a missile silo or an underground command and control bunker that has been "hardened" or protected against nearby nuclear explosions, usually by burying in deep, underground concrete and steel silos.

HARD TARGET KILL CAPABILITY—

The capability to destroy hardened military targets such as buried missile silos, usually by achieving great missile accuracy combined with large nuclear explosive power.

HYDROGEN BOMB—

The more powerful bomb using an atomic bomb trigger to drive a fusion or thermonuclear reaction.

ICBM (Intercontinental Ballistic Missile)—

A ballistic missile, usually carrying one or more nuclear weapons, that can propel those weapons from one continent to another in less than half an hour by traveling through outer space.

INF TREATY—
   Intermediate Range Nuclear Forces Treaty eliminating all nuclear
   weapons with a range between 300 and 3,400 miles. (See Appendix B)
IRON TRIANGLE—
   The three elements of society that tend to drive the nuclear arms race: the
   military, defense industries and Congress.
ISOTOPE—
   A form of an element characterized by a different number of neutrons than
   normally occurs for that element. For example, over 99 percent of natural
   uranium has 238 neutrons and protons...the U-238 isotope of uranium.
   U-238 cannot be used to start a nuclear reaction but the isotope U-235,
   with three fewer neutrons, is a primary fuel for atomic bombs. U-235 and
   U-238 are chemically identical, but have vastly different nuclear proper-
   ties. Most elements with extra neutrons are radioactive.
ISOTOPE SEPARATION—
   The process of separating one isotope from another, such as extracting the
   rare U-235 isotope from the plentiful U-238 isotope in a gaseous diffusion
   plant.
KILOTON (KT)—
   A measure of nuclear explosive power, equivalent to one thousand tons of
   TNT chemical explosive. The bomb dropped on Hiroshima had an
   explosive power of about 13 kilotons—13,000 tons of TNT—although the
   bomb weighed only 4.5 tons; the bomb produced 2,800 times more power
   than a TNT bomb of the same weight.
KEW (Kinetic Energy Weapons)—
   Weapons such as bullets or interceptor rockets that kill by direct impact.
   Kinetic energy weapons have no chemical or nuclear explosive.
LASER—
   A device that produces a narrow beam of coherent light at one wavelength
   or color. Because of the purity of this radiation, it can in theory be focused
   to a small spot to damage objects at a great distance.
LANCE MISSILE—
   A short-range tactical nuclear weapon with 64–88 launchers deployed in
   Europe; the current Lance missile has a range of 70 miles with a 1–100
   kiloton nuclear bomb. The Pentagon originally planned to develop a
   "Follow-on to Lance" missile with much longer range, up to the 300-mile
   limit of the INF Treaty.
LAUNCH-ON-WARNING—
   The strategy of launching ICBMs automatically after receiving signals
   from surveillance satellites that the opponent has launched its missiles.
   Some fear that accurate new nuclear weapons could force one or both
   superpowers to adopt this launch-on-warning posture in some future
   crisis, to avoid losing control during the fog of battle.

MEGATON (MT)—
Explosive power equivalent to one million tons of TNT chemical explosive.

MINUTEMAN MISSILES—
Nuclear armed missiles in the U.S. arsenal, consisting of 450 Minuteman-II single-warhead missiles carrying 1–2 megaton nuclear bombs, and 500 Minuteman-III missiles each armed with three warheads with 170 to 335 kiloton yield.

MIRV (Multiple, Independently Targetable Reentry Vehicles)—
The vehicles placed inside the nose cone of modern ballistic missiles that carry more than one nuclear bomb which can be independently aimed at more than one target. MIRV'd missiles are considered extremely destabilizing, since one missile can in theory destroy many missiles of the opponent...but only by striking first.

MAD (Mutual Assured Destruction)—
The "balance of terror" whereby each superpower threatens to destroy much of the industry and infrastructure of the opponent should it ever attack. MAD implies a massive, all-out spasm attack; in reality, the U.S. has had options and plans for much more limited attacks since 1963...the strategy of "flexible response."

MIDGETMAN MISSILE—
Also called the Small ICBM or SICBM, the Midgetman is a proposed single-warhead U.S. ICBM that would be mounted on a truck to provide mobility; not knowing where the Midgetman trucks would be at any time, the Soviets could not reliably target these missiles.

MOBILE MISSILE—
A nuclear-tipped ballistic missile place on a moving platform such as a truck or train to prevent an opponent from targeting missiles in fixed underground silos. Technically, submarine-launched ballistic missiles (SLBM) are mobile missiles, but the term mobile missile is usually applied to land-based missiles.

MX MISSILE—
The most modern U.S. ICBM (first deployed in 1986), carrying 10 very accurate 300-kiloton hydrogen bombs. Fifty MX missiles with 500 nuclear weapons have been deployed in old Minuteman-III underground silos. The MX is considered highly destabilizing, since its ten warheads are a lucrative target, and they could in theory destroy 5 to 10 Soviet ICBMs— if we struck first! The Pentagon wants to put these 50 MX missiles on railroad cars to hide them on commercial rail lines in event of an international crisis.

NEUTRON—
The uncharged or neutral atomic building block; all atoms are composed of electrons (negative charge), protons (positive charge) and neutrons.

Neutrons have no effect on ordinary chemical reactions, but play the dominant role in nuclear reactions.

PERSHING MISSILE—
The Pershing-II missile was a short-range (450 miles) nuclear-armed (60–400 kiloton) ballistic missile deployed in West Germany...a "tactical" nuclear weapon. The Pershing-II was an intermediate range (1,000- to 2,400-mile), highly accurate missile that could have destroyed Soviet ICBMs...if we struck first. The Pershing-II was eliminated as part of the INF Treaty of 1987.

PLUTONIUM—
The 94th chemical element, highly toxic and radioactive, a primary nuclear bomb fuel produced in all nuclear reactors in the course of bombarding uranium with neutrons. All plutonium must be created in nuclear reactors, since it does not exist in any natural deposit.

POSEIDON SUBMARINE—
A nuclear-powered submarine originally carrying 16 Poseidon missiles, each armed with 10 to 14 40-kiloton nuclear warheads. Thus one Poseidon submarine could explode 160 nuclear weapons, with each explosion over three times the power of the bomb that destroyed Hiroshima in 1945. The U.S. had deployed 31 Poseidon submarines, but the older subs are being retired as Trident submarines enter the fleet. In addition, 12 of the Poseidon submarines have been retrofitted with 16 of the new Trident-I or C-4 missiles, each carrying eight 100-KT hydrogen bombs.

PROLIFERATION—
The continued expansion of nuclear weapons. "Horizontal proliferation" refers to the spread of nuclear weapons to other nations. "Vertical proliferation" is the expansion of new nuclear weapons technologies within the arsenals of the six acknowledged members of the nuclear weapons club (the U.S., USSR, U.K., France, China and India).

REENTRY VEHICLE—
The canister within the ballistic missile that contains the nuclear explosive and the heat-resistant shield that protects the nuclear bomb as the vehicle reenters the earth's atmosphere at high speed, prior to exploding over the target.

SS-18 ICBM—
U.S. name for the heavy Soviet land-based, MIRV'd missile. Each of 308 SS-18's can carry 10 500-kiloton hydrogen bombs. The START treaty eliminates half of these missiles.

SS-24 ICBM—
New Soviet 10-warhead mobile ICBM which can be deployed on trains, similar to the proposed U.S. MX rail garrison system.

SS-25 ICBM—
Soviet single-warhead ICBM mounted on trucks, similar to the proposed U.S. Midgetman system.

SALT I (Strategic Arms Limitation Talks)—
Negotiations that resulted in two agreements between the Soviet Union and the United States in 1972: the ABM Treaty and the interim agreement on nuclear weapons delivery vehicles. Both sides agreed not to build more missiles than were in existence or planned at that time. (See also Appendix B)

SALT II—
Negotiations that further restrained nuclear delivery vehicles and placed caps on those carrying more than one nuclear warhead. The SALT II treaty was signed in June of 1979, but was never ratified by the Senate; both sides agreed nonetheless to abide by the numerical limits until President Reagan intentionally exceeded those limits in 1986.

SDI (The Strategic Defense Initiative)—
The formal name for "Star Wars," President Reagan's dream of an impregnable defensive shield to physically stop ballistic missiles from hurling nuclear weapons toward our nation. (See Appendix A)

SDIO (The Strategic Defense Initiative Organization)—
The Pentagon organization that runs the Star Wars research program.

SILO—
The underground vertical concrete cylinder containing one ICBM.

SLBM (Submarine-Launched Ballistic Missile)—
Long-range (intercontinental) strategic missiles loaded with nuclear weapons that are fired from submarines. Considered to be the most stabilizing element of our nuclear forces, since a submerged submarine is virtually invulnerable to enemy attack, and therefore does not invite attack in a crisis situation.

SLCM (Sea-Launched Cruise Missile; see Cruise Missile)

STABILITY—
The condition where no nation perceives any advantage in using nuclear weapons, even if a conventional war should start (crisis stability), and no nation has any incentive to build more nuclear weapons (arms race stability).

START (Strategic Arms Reduction Talks)—
Talks leading to a treaty between the United States and the Soviet Union which was advertised as cutting nuclear weapons by 50 percent. In reality only certain classes of ballistic missiles will be cut drastically, with U.S. strategic nuclear warheads falling from about 13,000 to 11,000 warheads, although Congress may not appropriate funds to buy enough bombers to reach these levels. (See Chapter 6 and Appendix B)

STRATEGIC NUCLEAR WEAPONS—
Nuclear weapons with the range to reach deep inside the opponent's country, capable of destroying targets of strategic importance.

TACTICAL NUCLEAR WEAPONS—
Short-range weapons that can only be used in the local battlefield or theatre.

TRIAD—
Refers to the three methods of delivering strategic nuclear weapons: bombers, land-based and submarine-based missiles.

TRIDENT-I (C-4) SLBM—
A modern submarine-launched ballistic missile first deployed in 1979 and retrofitted into 12 of the Poseidon submarines, replacing the older Poseidon missiles. The first eight Trident submarines carry Trident-I missiles, although DOD plans to replace these missiles with the more accurate (and therefore more destabilizing) Trident-II missiles. Each Trident-I missile carries eight 100-kiloton nuclear bombs.

TRIDENT-II (D-5) SLBM—
Latest Trident submarine-launched ballistic missile, first deployed in 1990, with improved accuracy capable of destroying Soviet ICBMs in their underground silos—if the U.S. strikes first with nuclear weapons! Each Trident-II missile carries eight nuclear bombs with an explosive power of 100 to 450-KT. Although the D-5 is our most modern missile, it may be vulnerable to an accidental explosion, since its designers used older, more accident-prone chemical detonators to achieve greater yield for killing underground silos, and because they packed the eight warheads around the third stage rocket fuel. A handling accident could possibly set off the rocket fuel which in turn might trigger the older chemical explosive to set off one or more of the eight nearby nuclear warheads.

TRIDENT SUBMARINE—
The most modern nuclear-powered submarine carrying 24 Trident missiles, also called the "Ohio Class" submarine after the name of the first ship. The U.S. has ordered 17 Trident subs (18th requested in the FY 1991 budget, with plans for several more).

URANIUM—
The main source of fissionable material for atomic bombs. About 0.7 percent of natural uranium contains the fissionable U-235 isotope, and the rest, U-238, can be converted into plutonium, another fissionable material, by neutron bombardment in nuclear reactors.

VERIFICATION—
The process of confirming compliance with arms control treaties. The first step in verification is to monitor the opponent's activities, usually with external devices or "national technical means" such as spy satellites, but more recently by on-site inspections in the INF Treaty.

VULNERABILITY—

Being susceptible to destruction from nuclear or conventional attack.

WARHEAD—

The device in missiles containing the nuclear bomb—the term "bomb" is usually reserved for gravity bombs dropped from airplanes.

WINDOW OF VULNERABILITY—

The theoretical vulnerability of land-based missiles to preemptive attack by accurate Soviet missiles. This "window of vulnerability" is not strategically significant, given our ability to retaliate with submarine ballistic missiles and bombers on alert. In fact, only 19 percent of our nuclear weapons are on land-based missiles, with 5,300 safely at sea on invulnerable submarines.

YIELD—

The explosive power of nuclear weapons, measured in tons of TNT equivalent power.

# Appendix A
# The Strategic Defense
# Alternative

SUMMARY

President Reagan dearly wanted to find a substitute for mutual assured destruction; he challenged scientists and engineers to erect a defensive shield—Star Wars—to destroy nuclear missiles. Although virtually everyone outside the White House rejected Reagan's dream as unrealistic, costly and even dangerous, President Bush continues to spend several billion dollars each year chasing the Star Wars fantasy, requesting over $4.6 billion for 1991 alone.

Unfortunately, Star Wars is a cruel hoax on the American public. Even Vice President Dan Quayle, an enthusiastic Star Wars supporter, admitted that President Reagan's claims were inflated for political effect:

The Reagan administration ... talked about this impenetrable shield that was going to be completely leak proof ... I believe that in the semantics of let's say political jargon, that that was acceptable. But it clearly was stretching the capability of a strategic defense system.[1]

---

[1]Dan Quayle, "SDI's Straw Man," *The Wall Street Journal*, September 18, 1989, p. 16.

Conceived as a technical fix to end the scourge of nuclear weapons for all time, building Star Wars would, in fact, exacerbate the arms race, bankrupt our nation, and make nuclear war more likely in some future crisis. Exotic Star Wars weapons like particle beams or lasers, if they ever proved feasible in the next century, could be used by the Soviets or other future adversaries to shoot down our Star Wars sensors and weapons in space . . . Star Wars contains the seeds of its own destruction. To protect our people and cities from nuclear attack would require the cooperation of the Soviet Union: we would have to reduce our nuclear forces dramatically, approaching nuclear disarmament . . . Star Wars would only work if it was not needed!

For those of you who share our disdain for Star Wars, please skip this appendix. Our nation has already wasted far too many resources chasing the mirage of missile defenses. The real alternatives to the offensive arms race are discussed in Chapters 9 through 11.

For those readers who are uncertain about SDI, read on. And a special apology to any who still hope that technology might someday provide the answer to our nuclear dilemma. We do not like to shatter dreams, but it's better to face reality honestly, and to place our trust and resources in alternatives that are feasible, realistic and affordable. Nuclear weapons will become "impotent and obsolete" only when we humans become wise enough to devise alternative methods to assure the security of all nations. In the meantime, there is much we can do to reduce the risks of nuclear war, but pursuing an active defense to unilaterally disarm the opponent is not one of them.

## INTRODUCTION

In 1983, President Reagan sensed the need for dramatic change, and proposed a major revision of our nuclear posture: Star Wars or the Strategic Defense Initiative (SDI). Even before he reached the White House, President Reagan yearned for an alternative to replace deterrence or mutual assured destruction (MAD), correctly calling it immoral to murder innocent citizens of another land, no matter what their leaders might have done. On March 23, 1983, he called on scientists and engineers to build a defensive weapon system that would replace deterrence and render nuclear weapons "impotent and obsolete." In the great American tradition, he sought a technological solution to a vexing political and moral problem.

President Reagan's motives were exemplary. Instead of deterring by threat of massive reprisals, how much better to deter by denial, by building a shield to physically protect us from nuclear weapons. We would shoot down Soviet missiles or the "warheads" carrying the nuclear bombs before they could reach our soil. Our security would then be in our own hands; we would no longer have to rely on the good will and rational behavior of Soviet leaders for our continued existence as a viable civilization.

Some opponents of the Star Wars program may have assumed that it would die once its chief cheerleader (and virtually sole true believer) left the White House. But President Bush, while avoiding hyperinflated claims for a Star Wars defensive shield, nonetheless continued asking for billion dollar per year increases in SDI funding. He has rejected the advice of the Joint Chiefs of Staff that, in exchange for a permanent START treaty with the Soviet Union, cutting some categories of offensive nuclear weapons by up to 50 percent, we agree *not* to deploy Star Wars. Congress rejected President Bush's request for further increases in Star Wars funding, but the program continues at three to four times its pre-Reagan funding levels, making it the largest research program in the world. The impact of the Reagan dream lives on, unfettered by reason or fiscal responsibility.

### SOME CONSEQUENCES OF NUCLEAR DEFENSES

President Reagan's 1983 Star Wars speech stood four decades of nuclear logic on its head. Instead of threatening an immoral act (nuclear retaliation) to achieve a moral end (preventing war), he wanted to substitute a totally moral act (self-defense). However, as we shall see in a moment, by pursuing this moral end we would in fact stimulate an open-ended arms race, further bankrupting our two nations, while increasing the chances for nuclear war in a crisis. In this case seeking a moral end could produce the ultimate immoral action ... nuclear omnicide, or, at best, if we managed to avoid the actual use of nuclear weapons, it would accelerate our nation's economic decline.

Yes, building defenses against nuclear weapons could actually *increase* the chances for nuclear war. The supporters of SDI frequently ask, however, how can we leave the American public defenseless?

What's wrong with trying to protect the people? Even if the defense is only partially effective, isn't it better to at least stop *some* of the ballistic missiles in the event of war?

Not necessarily. In the upside-down nuclear world, apparently beneficial intentions like physical defense can have unintended consequences. We must always consider the *actual* effects of our actions, not the *intended* effects. Let's look at two examples of supposedly beneficial "defensive" actions: civil defense and the limited Soviet ballistic missile defense system around Moscow.

Civil defense measures would seem prudent on the surface. In the event of nuclear war, it seems wise to try to save as many civilians as possible. But what if the very action of preparing for civil defense would increase the chances for nuclear war in the first place? What if our adversary interpreted our efforts to save our leaders and civilians as preparations for fighting and surviving a nuclear war? What if Soviet leaders thought we would be more likely to push the button if U.S. officials believed that most of our population would survive? Or at least that more Americans than Russians would survive? In other words, what if preparing for nuclear war were a self-fulfilling prophecy, making it more likely?

If this thinking sounds bizarre, consider the space devoted to the Soviet civil defense measures in past issues of *Soviet Military Power*, the Pentagon's annual assessment of Soviet military strength. For many years, U.S. military planners counted Soviet underground bunkers for Soviet leaders and for industrial machinery as part of their military capability, part of their ability to continue governing during and after a nuclear war. In the Reagan years, the mere existence of Soviet civil defense efforts was offered as proof of Soviet preparation to fight and win a nuclear war.

Paul Nitze, one of President Reagan's senior arms control advisers, was clearly concerned about the Soviet civil defense effort: "As the Soviet civil defense program becomes more effective it tends to destabilize the deterrent relationship."[2]

He apparently did not consider our own efforts in civil defense as equally destabilizing. As an American, that is understandable, but we cannot expect the Soviets to be as sanguine.

---

[2]Paul H. Nitze, "Assuring Strategic Stability in an Era of Detente," *Foreign Affairs*, Vol. 54, No. 2, p. 223.

Suppose that we did build shelters for our citizens, or suppose we did initiate "crisis relocation," the current plan to move citizens into the countryside when our leaders thought nuclear war was imminent. What would be the effects of the President ordering people into the corn fields? Would the Soviets take this as a signal that we were about to attack?

And suppose that the President did move people out of the cities, and nothing happened. Presumably the action to evacuate cities would not have been taken lightly. Some grave international crisis would have precipitated the action, convincing our leaders that there was a good chance that the bombs might start flying. Once millions of Americans were in the field, there would be strong pressure on the President to escalate the war, before hungry and cold Americans began drifting back into the cities in search of food and shelter. How many would leave their homes a second time, if the crisis deepened? The President would be faced with a daunting dilemma: if he or she waited, then more citizens would be back in the cities, sure to be killed initially if an all-out war ensued. If the American President was convinced that a nuclear exchange was going to occur sooner or later, then there would be a perceived advantage in striking while more Americans were away from the cities.

In short, civil defense evacuation could be the trigger for a nuclear war, with little chance of saving many lives over the long term. Even if many survived the initial blast, fire and radiation, how many Americans could live off the land? How long could the typical urban American cope without food and water? How long would it take to replenish food supplies without any sources of energy to grow, harvest, process and transport the food? Once a war began, civil defense might do little more than change how, when and where we die. If the mere act of preparing for civil defense increases the chances of using nuclear weapons by any small degree, then it should not be attempted, given the minimal impact of such preparation on the outcome of a nuclear holocaust.

Note that civil defense by itself is not destabilizing. Countries without nuclear weapons or significant offensive forces, such as Sweden and Switzerland, have extensive civil defense programs. These civilian protection efforts are very stabilizing, in the sense that they reduce the chances of a potential aggressor achieving his objectives, without threatening the opponent. It is the combination of aggressive forces such as nuclear weapons with civil defense that becomes destabilizing. This is somewhat analogous to a sword and a shield: a shield by itself is not threatening. But add a sword to a warrior with a shield, and he becomes much more of a potential menace than a soldier with a sword alone.

The limited Soviet ballistic missile defense system surrounding Moscow illustrates another deficiency of a partial physical defense. The Soviets have installed up to 100 nuclear-tipped interceptor rockets around the city, as permitted by the ABM Treaty of 1972. If the U.S. ever attacked Moscow with nuclear weapons, the Soviets could explode nuclear weapons in the path of up to 100 incoming U.S. warheads, destroying them high in the atmosphere before they could damage objects on the ground. Before this "defensive" system was installed, the U.S. aimed a certain number of bombs on missiles at Moscow . . . say 30 hydrogen bombs. When the Soviets added their 100 defensive interceptors, the U.S. war-planners probably made the usual worst-case (for us) assumption: all 100 Soviet interceptor rockets would work perfectly.

Therefore U.S. planners would have aimed 100 **extra** warheads at Moscow to overcome the ballistic missile defenses. (No great stress, since we have 13,000 available strategic warheads.) However, in an actual battle, not all Soviet interceptor rockets would work flawlessly. Some would probably misfire, never leaving their silos. Guidance systems might fail on others, sending the interceptors in the wrong direction. Battle-management computers might err, aiming two or more interceptors at the same U.S. warhead. Some Soviet interceptor bombs might not explode.

Assume that 70 percent of the Soviet defensive interceptors did work (very optimistic by usual military standards), taking out 70 of the 130 incoming warheads. Then 60 hydrogen bombs would explode on Moscow, compared to only 30 before they installed their defensive system. *Adding "defenses" would actually double the number of hydrogen bombs exploding on Moscow* in this example. Was this a wise use of Soviet resources? Should we spend our hard-earned tax dollars to build a partial defense against Soviet missiles?

Some of you may be thinking that we're being too pessimistic. After all, prominent scientists once said that we could never build an atomic bomb. Others predicted that we could never land a man on the moon. But given enough time and money, American scientists and engineers rose to the challenge. Why can't we repeat history? With enough time and money, why can't we build a defensive shield against nuclear missiles?

Unfortunately, building a defense against nuclear weapons faces one obstacle totally absent from both the Manhattan and Apollo projects: a dedicated and determined adversary. There was no one at Los Alamos trying to stop Robert Oppenheimer and friends from developing the first atomic bomb in the 1940s. There was no one on the moon shooting at Neil Armstrong when he took those first, historic steps. Scientists and engineers were fighting only the laws of nature.

However, any attempt to build a nationwide defense would be opposed by the Soviet Union. Their national security, their very existence as a nation-state, like ours, depends on the ability to retaliate with nuclear weapons should we or our French or British allies (or the Chinese) ever attack them. Or so they believe. They would do everything in their power and commit all the resources necessary to defeat, circumvent or destroy any Star Wars defensive system. And so would we if the Soviets ever attempted to build a nationwide defense against our retaliatory missiles, giving them the ability to attack us with impunity.

Paul Nitze, the senior arms control adviser to President Reagan, established three criteria to judge the success of the Star Wars program—the "Nitze Criteria." First, the defensive shield should be militarily effective. Second, it should be survivable (to a Soviet attack). And, third, it should be "cost effective at the margin," meaning that it should cost less for us to add defenses than it would cost the Soviets to defeat the system (by adding more offensive missiles, for example). These Nitze criteria cannot be met with existing technology: scientists and engineers have been attempting to meet these objectives of a ballistic defense system for over 30 years without success, and they are not much closer today after spending over $20 billion in the 1980s, more than the entire Manhattan project that successfully created the first atomic bombs.

## HISTORY OF BALLISTIC MISSILE DEFENSE

The quest for a defense against ballistic missiles did not begin with President Reagan's Star Wars speech in March of 1983. In fact, ballistic missile defense (BMD) was studied by think-tanks like the RAND Corporation prior to 1957, when the Soviets first launched Sputnik into orbit ... before there were practical ballistic missiles to defend against. The United States has had a vigorous BMD research program for over three decades. We were spending just under $1 billion per year on missile defenses at the time of the 1983 Star Wars speech.

The debate over strategic defenses also predated 1983. Ballistic missile defense was vigorously discussed in the late 1960s, one of the few times in the nuclear age that we did openly debate the merits and risks of building a particular weapons system ... before it was built. In that case, our nation eventually agreed that building a defense would be destabilizing. That is, if one side built a defense, the other would be forced to add more offensive weapons to penetrate the opponent's defenses, thereby escalating the arms race, like spilling gasoline on a fire.

There is one interesting bureaucratic difference between the current SDI program and the ballistic missile defense program of the 1960s. At that time the Army was developing ballistic missile defense systems. The Army made the convenient assumption that the Soviets would *not* add more offensive missiles if we began to deploy defenses. However, Secretary of Defense Robert McNamara organized a Systems Analysis Office within the Pentagon to independently assess ballistic missile defenses. This independent office looked at scenarios where the Soviets did react to our defenses by adding offensive forces and other counter-measures, and concluded that the ballistic missile defense effort would be futile.[3]

Unfortunately, Secretary of Defense Weinberger never established an independent group to evaluate SDI within the Pentagon; the SDI organization that is conducting the research is also providing the "red teams" that conjure up Soviet responses to SDI.

Ironically, in the late 1960s the Soviet Union did not agree with our assessment that defenses would be destabilizing. President Johnson had to convince Premier Kosygin in the 1967–68 time period that defenses spur the adversary to add more weapons. Eventually the Soviets agreed, and we signed the Anti-Ballistic Missile (ABM) Treaty in 1972, part of the SALT I Treaty. The ABM Treaty limits each side to building two (later amended to one) defensive weapon installation, located near either the capital city or near a missile field. Each side could have no more than 100 interceptor rockets. The Soviets chose to defend Moscow, and we chose to build a defensive system near Grand Forks, North Dakota, to protect the nearby missile field. We did build a limited defensive system at Grand Forks in 1974–75, including nuclear-tipped interceptor rockets and a giant phased array radar to track incoming

---

[3]Alain C. Enthoven and K. Wayne Smith, *How Much is Enough? Shaping the Defense Program, 1961-1969*, Harper & Row, 1971, p.112.

nuclear warheads. However, we dismantled the system in 1976 since it was too costly and ineffective. The Soviets have continued to improve their defensive system around Moscow, despite its limited effectiveness, and despite its political liability in this country, as hard-liners point to the Moscow system as the world's only operational ballistic missile defense system, with predictions of doom if we don't copy their lead.

For those of us who believe in rational constraints on nuclear weapons deployments, the ABM Treaty is the stellar example of how the democratic process should work. A free and open debate was held *before* the proposed weapon system was developed and deployed. We looked ahead, and predicted the consequences of actually deploying defensive weapons. We considered the reaction of the adversary. As a nation, we concluded that any attempt to build a nationwide defense would be destabilizing, causing the opponent to build more offenses, and so we negotiated and signed a permanent treaty banning all but a token deployment of these destabilizing weapons.

In retrospect, we and the Soviets made one major mistake by not banning all missile defenses. Allowing one active ABM site plus two test sites left the door open for developing more advanced ballistic missile defenses, raising doubts on both sides about the intentions of the other. We worry that the Soviets might use their Moscow ABM system to start a nationwide defense, and the Soviets fear that we will develop a partial Star Wars defense based on tests conducted at the White Sands Missile Range in New Mexico and at our Kwajalein facility in the Pacific. While we should not and could not ban laboratory research on defensive systems and particularly countermeasures to defeat potential defenses, we could have banned all tests outside the laboratory, the tests that can be verified by spy satellites or listening posts around the world.

The testing loophole in the ABM Treaty will also permit the development of anti-satellite (ASAT) capability, a destabilizing development, in our opinion. Had we and the Soviets agreed to ban all ABM systems in 1972, then we would not be faced with the threatened development of more effective ABM and ASAT systems today.

### THE STAR WARS DEFENSIVE SYSTEM

As you can see, President Reagan's Star Wars speech did not break new ground. He was actually reopening old wounds, revisiting territory covered 11 years earlier. To be sure, technology had improved as a result of 11 years of BMD research near the $1 billion per year level. But had the technology changed enough to justify quadrupling BMD research (SDI funding reached $4 billion per year in 1989) and scrapping the ABM Treaty, as any SDI deployment would require? Indeed, could any improvement in technology justify building defenses?

Any defensive system would require three components: sensors (the eyes of the system), weapons and computers. There has been much discussion in the literature regarding the technical feasibility of building these three major elements of SDI. Some have said that building adequate sensors would be extremely difficult; millions or even tens of millions of individual infrared detector elements might be needed in each of dozens of sensor satellites to accurately determine the location of each Soviet missile and warhead. Some have said that we could never design the computer software to run the Star Wars battle in outer space, because of the complexity and speed required to coordinate the global space-age battle. This computer system would have to work perfectly the first and only time it was used in a full battle. Others say that we could not afford a full Star Wars system, which might cost one trillion dollars.

But we take a different approach here: suppose that all this technology could be developed and built. Assume that it all worked perfectly the first time it was ever tested . . . when World War III began. Assume that the nation decided to make sacrifices and provide up to a trillion dollars for strategic defenses. Under these grossly optimistic circumstances, would we want to proceed with Star Wars? As you may have gathered, we think not. We discuss the reasons below, after a brief review of Star Wars weapons technology.

## STAR WARS WEAPONS

Consider the weapons that would be needed by any Star Wars system, assuming perfect sensors and perfect battle-management computers and software. The SDI research program is investigating two general classes of weapons: kinetic energy weapons (KEW) and directed energy weapons (DEW). Kinetic energy is the energy of motion. A kinetic energy weapon is one that kills by impact. A gun is a kinetic energy weapon, since it kills by accelerating a bullet. (Leave it to the wordsmiths to camouflage a simple concept!)

Directed energy weapons are the exotic laser beams and particle beams that gave SDI its Star Wars reputation. DEWs kill by transmitting energy, rather than a physical projectile such as a bullet or interceptor rocket. Actually, DEWs are ancient, too, if Archimedes really used many mirrors to burn wooden ships with focused sunlight. But the modern reincarnation would revolutionize warfare, if it could be perfected, since the DEW energy travels at or near the speed of light. Targets like ballistic missiles could be zapped in fractions of a second, whereas interceptor rockets might take several minutes to reach a missile from a space-based battle station. Given enough power and very precise and high-speed beam-directing optics, a space-based laser could fire at literally hundreds of targets thousands of miles away, look to see if they were destroyed, and fire again in a small fraction of the time an old-fashioned interceptor rocket took to fly out and collide with one target.

However, most knowledgeable scientists agree that directed energy weapons would not be available for several decades, if ever. The American Physical Society, after receiving fully classified briefings on Star Wars, concluded:

> Even in the best of circumstances, a decade or more of intensive research would be required to provide the technical knowledge needed for an informed decision about the potential effectiveness and survivability of directed energy weapon systems.[4]

This "decade or more" of research would be required just to make an intelligent decision. The Congressional Office of Technology Assessment predicted that the additional time needed for developing, producing and deploying DEWs would take at least another 10 to 15 years. They concluded that:

> It is unlikely that any DEW system could be highly effective before 2010 to 2015 at the earliest.[5]

As a result, the early phases of SDI, as currently proposed, would use older kinetic energy weapon technology, the only weapons available with any chance of even partial success. In particular, the SDI organization planned in 1988 to place something like 1,500 space-based interceptor (SBI) rockets on 150 orbiting battle stations in outer space.

---

[4]The American Physical Society Study Group, *Science and Technology of Directed Energy Weapons*, April 1987, p. 2.
[5]Office of Technology Assessment, *SDI Technology, Survivability, and Software*, Washington, D.C.: U.S. Government Printing Office, May 1988, p. 154.

These SBI bullets would be fired at Soviet missiles in their critical boost phase of flight, as they lifted off from silos in the Soviet Union.

The SBIs would not be ordinary bullets or projectiles. They would be "smart bullets" or "smart rocks." They would have infrared "eyes" to track the hot exhaust gas from the missile booster engine, inertial guidance units for orientation, maneuvering jets to orient and steer the bullet, communication gear to receive instructions from external sensors, power supplies, and a computer to calculate the necessary maneuvers, guiding the SBI into a collision course with the ICBM.

In 1989, the SDI organization shifted rhetorical gears, replacing the SBI "smart rocks" with the latest SDI fad: "brilliant pebbles," as their primary candidate for space-based defenses. These brilliant pebbles have all the same features as space-based interceptors, including sensors and divert propulsion motors to steer a collision course with Soviet ICBMs. But the brilliant pebbles would have very capable computers, and each pebble would be autonomous. Instead of placing 10 SBI "smart rocks" on every battlestation, each brilliant pebble would be deployed by itself in outer space. This autonomous arrangement was previously rejected by all five defense contractors paid to design a Star Wars "system architecture." The major objection was that some autonomous interceptors would choose the same ICBM target, wasting limited bullets in space. A better coordinated system would be more efficient, and each interceptor rocket could have less sophisticated and less expensive computers and sensors.

The SDI organization (SDIO) claimed that these brilliant pebbles would be faster, lighter, and cheaper than the previous year's SBI rockets, even though the brilliant pebbles would have to perform more functions than the SBI. The main architect of the brilliant pebbles concept was none other than Lowell Wood of the Lawrence Livermore nuclear weapons lab, who, along with Edward Teller, energized President Reagan with inflated statements about the abilities of the X-ray laser. When the X-ray laser claims were exposed as grossly exaggerated and it was dethroned as the Star Wars miraculous weapon-of-the-year, Lowell Wood came up with the brilliant pebbles scheme based on conventional rocket technology to keep Star Wars hopes alive. It now appears that brilliant pebbles will have no better success than the X-ray laser.

Claims that brilliant pebbles could be as cheap as only $100,000 to $1,000,000 each are suspect because each pebble would have to be stored in its own "life jacket"—a container that would include a solar panel for energy, batteries, communication gear—the functions that the previous SBI battle-station satellites provided to 10 SBI rockets. The brilliant pebbles system would have ten times as many solar panels, batteries and communication links.

If the brilliant pebbles could indeed be made faster, lighter and cheaper than SBIs, then the defense contractors designing SBIs have not used the best technology. Or, more likely, the defense contractors have been more realistic in their estimates, knowing that they may have to actually design and build the space-based interceptors, while SDI enthusiasts are grasping for gimmicks to resuscitate the dying Star Wars program.

To have any chance of success, any SDI system would have to destroy most Soviet ICBMs in the boost phase of their flight. During the boost phase, the ICBM would produce a hot plume of gas that could be seen easily from outer space, would be relatively fragile (as the Space Shuttle Challenger accident tragically demonstrated), and most ICBMs would carry more than one warhead . . . the SBI bullet could kill more than one bird with one stone.

If the Star Wars defense waited until after the ICBM booster engines have burned out, all of these advantages would disappear: the reentry vehicles released into space are relative small, have no significant heat source to give away their location, travel at speeds of 15,000 miles per hour, and are "hardened" to withstand the tremendous heat due to the friction of reentry into the earth's atmosphere, and therefore are very difficult to destroy.

For all these reasons, the SBI bullets or brilliant pebbles would have to be fired and reach their targets during the few minutes that the Soviet ICBM booster engines were burning; this means that we would have to pre-position Star Wars weapons in space over the Soviet Union in peacetime.

The SDIO also hopes to destroy some warheads while they are still on the post-boost vehicle or "bus" that aims and releases each warhead in space after the last booster engine burns out; current Soviet buses have hot gas steering engines that offer some heat signal to the SBI infrared sensors, but this signal is often 1,000 times weaker than from the booster rocket. Detecting and tracking post-boost vehicles would be much more difficult than killing the missile booster rocket. Furthermore, the Soviets could reduce the time for the bus to disperse warheads, and they could change to cold gas thrusters to aim the warheads, eliminating the hot gas signal that gives away the location of current post-boost vehicles.

The booster rockets on most existing liquid-fueled Soviet ICBMs burn for about five minutes. Newer solid-fueled ICBMs that the Soviets introduced in the 1987-88 time period, such as the SS-24 10-warhead, train-mobile missile and the single warhead SS-25 truck-mobile missile, burn for about three minutes. Thus the SBI bullets must be fired and must intercept their targets within three to five minutes after the Soviets launch their attack, to maximize the defense effectiveness.

If the Star Wars battle station were 600 miles away from the planned impact point, and if the SBI bullet could be accelerated to speeds of 12,000 miles per hour, then it would take at least three minutes for the SBI bullet to reach the ICBM. For the case of the solid-fueled ICBM that burns out in three minutes, the SBI would have to be fired the instant the ICBM was launched to reach it before engine burnout ... the Star Wars battle management would have to anticipate when the ICBM would be launched and what its probable trajectory would be. Obviously this is not possible, so the SBI must be closer than 600 miles from the ICBM at impact with these assumptions. This means that many Star Wars battle stations or brilliant pebbles would be needed to be able to intercept most Soviet ICBMs, and faster-burning ICBMs would require more battle stations. In this manner, the Soviets, by reducing the burn-time of their ICBMs, can force SDI to add extra space battle stations or brilliant pebbles just to maintain limited defense effectiveness.

Since these SBI "smart rocks" must be on orbiting battle stations a few hundred miles above the earth, they must travel very fast to generate enough centrifugal force to counter the earth's gravity and stay in orbit. Only at very high altitudes, far from the earth, is the earth's gravity reduced enough so that satellites can slow down and still stay in orbit. At the low SBI orbits, each SBI battle station or brilliant pebble would circle the earth every 90 minutes or so. As a result, most would be on the other side of the earth or out of range of the Soviet missile fields when a Soviet nuclear attack began. This is the "absentee ratio" problem ... only 5 to 10 percent of the 1,500 SBIs could reach the Soviet ICBMs during the crucial boost phase. Therefore the originally proposed SDI system of 1,500 SBIs would have only 75 to 150 bullets within range to shoot down 700 to 1,400 ICBMs, assuming that the Soviets strike first with a coordinated attack. Thus this SDI system could at best destroy 5 to 20 percent of the Soviet ICBMs.

Some SDI proponents argue that the Soviets would never fire all 1,400 ICBMs in a massive first strike ... they would undoubtedly keep some in reserve. But the Pentagon predicted in 1989 that, even without Star Wars to pressure the Soviets to increase their offensive forces, the Soviets could have from 16,000 to 21,000 nuclear warheads and 2,000 missiles by the 1996 time period, when the SDI organization originally estimated we might have a partial phase 1 system in place. But Secretary of Defense Carlucci admitted before leaving office in 1988 that even this token defense could not be placed in orbit until 1999 or 2000. Thus the Soviets could have 2,000 ICBMs in place four years before the first phase of SDI could be deployed; the Soviets could fire 1,400 ICBMs in a first strike and still have 600 or more missiles in reserve.

Returning to the absentee ratio question, we would have only 75 to 150 SBI bullets or brilliant pebbles available if the Soviets struck first. But suppose that the United States struck first.

You may be thinking that we are the "good guys" with the white hats ... we would never strike first. But do the Soviets believe that? In a crisis situation? Let's look at it from the Soviet perspective:

If the United States ever struck first with nuclear weapons in some future crisis, we would probably knock out some Soviet ICBMs on the ground, particularly if we continue to add accurate, first-strike capable weapons like the MX and the D-5 submarine-launched missiles. However, even if we didn't destroy any Soviet ICBMs with our first strike, we would certainly disrupt their command and control and communications network. The Soviets could not plan and execute a coordinated second-strike retaliation. Instead of firing 700 to 1,400 ICBMs within a few minutes, their retaliation would probably straggle out over several hours or even days.

But in 90 minutes, SBI battle stations travel around the earth. Battlestations that were on the other side of the earth when the first Soviet retaliatory ICBM took off, would come into range of the missile fields with a full load of smart bullets to shoot down subsequent Soviet launches. Instead of using only 75 to 150 SBI bullets in support of SDI as a defensive shield, we could use 750 to 1,500 SBI bullets or brilliant pebbles to support a U.S. first strike.

Therefore a partial space-based defense could be **10 times more effective** in mopping up a ragged retaliatory response than in stopping a coordinated Soviet first strike. This gives strong incentive in a crisis for both sides to strike first: the Soviets, knowing that their retaliation could be degraded significantly by SDI if they waited until the U.S.

opened fire, would be under pressure to launch a coordinated preemptive strike. The U.S., although we could never have any confidence in stopping all Soviet warheads, would see a major advantage in going first in a severe crisis ... we could reduce Soviet warheads exploding on American soil from 10,000 down to a few thousand, or maybe even a few hundred. If we thought that nuclear war was inevitable in a deteriorating situation, then there would be strong pressures on our civilian and military leaders to strike first, to reduce the anticipated damage. **Thus a partial space-based defense such as that proposed by SDI creates significant crisis instability, giving both sides strong incentive to strike first.**

While the United States would never go first, let's turn the tables. Suppose that we go ahead with SDI space-base defenses, as planned. What happens when the Soviets (or other future adversaries) copy our lead and deploy their own space-based "defense." Then they would have one component of a first-strike capability. Do we really want to embark on a course that would ultimately permit a future enemy to acquire first-strike capability or weapons that would give them a major advantage in striking first? Or at least a capability to reduce damage to their homeland from 10,000 to "only" a few hundred nuclear detonations? If you were a Pentagon war planner, accustomed to assuming that most of our 12,000 strategic warheads would be available to hit Soviet targets, would you want the Soviets to have the capability to stop all but a few hundred warheads?

Just imagine the political fireworks in a future election if a challenger claimed that the incumbent President had allowed the Soviets to build a partial defense that might stop 12,000 of our 13,000 warheads, if they struck first. Recall that the "window of vulnerability" scare tactic used so effectively by Ronald Reagan in the 1980 presidential election would have affected only 2,100 of the 10,000 strategic warheads in our nuclear arsenal at the time, had the Soviets ever launched a first strike. Abandoning the ABM Treaty and allowing the Soviets to build a space-based defense would be far more destabilizing. And to think the seeds of this destabilizing enterprise were sown by Ronald Reagan, the author of the "window of vulnerability" scare.

Before leaving our description of SDI hardware, let's return for a moment to directed energy weapons (DEWs). Suppose that two or three decades from now, SDI research does prove the feasibility of a DEW. Would this change the previous conclusions that space-based defenses are destabilizing?

Not really. In fact, if DEWs, like Edward Teller's favorite, the X-ray laser, or particle beam weapons, ever were proved feasible, they would spell the death knell of Star Wars. These weapons could be used at lower power levels (earlier stages of development) by the Soviets to shoot down our space-based Star Wars assets. Star Wars must have space-based sensor satellites and space-based battle stations (or possibly huge battle mirrors in space to reflect laser beams from ground-based lasers in the United States to the Soviet ICBMs on the other side of the earth). If we went ahead with this technology, we must assume that the Soviets would follow suit. (Proponents of increased defense spending usually claim that the Soviets are ahead, although history usually shows these claims to be highly exaggerated.) The Soviets could then shoot down our critical space platforms as a prelude to attack. In this sense, Star Wars contains the seeds of its own destruction: the better it works, the less it would succeed!

By now it should be apparent that SDI has serious flaws, even with the optimistic assumptions that all technical challenges are met. The Soviets have several options to confuse, overwhelm, underfly, or defeat any conceivable Star War system. They could:

- add more offensive nuclear weapons ... more ballistic missiles and warheads on land and at sea to overwhelm SDI; this would be far cheaper for the Soviets, using existing missile technology developed over several decades to defeat exotic new U.S. Star Wars technology.
- add decoys—light objects such as aluminum foil-covered balloons— to their missile nose cones along with the real warheads to fool SDI. Or place warheads inside foil-covered and insulated balloons—anti-simulation: making warheads look like decoys.
- use electronic transmitters to jam the SDI communication channels.
- shoot down critical SDI assets such as space-based sensors essential to any defensive system, using nuclear or non-nuclear interceptor rockets or space mines.
- develop "depressed trajectory" submarine-launched ballistic missiles—those fired on low paths to fly under the SDI system that is designed to attack objects in outer space.
- build more cruise missiles or bombers to fly under SDI. (The SDI system would attack ballistic missiles and warheads in space; another defensive system, called the Air Defense Initiative or ADI, has been started to develop the technology necessary to intercept bombers and cruise missiles.)
- use high power lasers or particle beam weapons, the same technology

we're developing for Star Wars, to shoot down our Star Wars battle stations and sensor satellites in space.

## THE DANGERS OF STAR WARS

As you may have gathered, we are rather skeptical about the merits of SDI, even if the technology could be developed. But our opposition goes much deeper. It's not just that SDI could never protect our people and cities as advertised, but rather that SDI would degrade our security. We count five major flaws:

*Arms race instability.* If the United States ever attempted to build a defensive shield against ballistic missiles, the cheapest and least technologically challenging response by the Soviet Union would be to add more offensive nuclear weapons. They wouldn't need to develop any new technology. They could simply add more ballistic missiles, something they've been doing for decades. New technology would help to thwart SDI, but it wouldn't be necessary. They would probably add more of the faster-burning solid-fueled ICBMs like the SS-24 and SS-25, to minimize the booster engine exposure time to the SBIs or brilliant pebbles. They might add more cruise missiles, either on bombers, submarines or surface ships, or depressed trajectory submarine launched missiles. They have many options to add offensive weapons, additions that would probably spur the U.S. to add more to keep up with the Soviets, arms race instability.

The Reagan administration frequently claimed that SDI would cause the Soviets to *reduce* their offensive forces. Their logic went something like this: if we continue SDI research, and if we could convince the Soviets that SDI would be very effective, then they would realize that their ICBMs were becoming less valuable, and they would dismantle them or bargain them away!

This is absurd! Just consider U.S. reactions to possible Soviet defenses. In the late 1960s, we feared (overreacting, as usual) that the Soviets were about to deploy a nationwide defense. Did we roll over and play dead, dismantling our offensive forces? Hardly: we invented new ways to increase our offensive forces. The end product was MIRV . . . multiple independently targetable reentry vehicles . . . we added many warheads on each missile to be able to penetrate Soviet defenses. As a result, the total number of U.S. strategic nuclear warheads grew from about 5,000 in 1970 (before MIRV) to about 13,000 today, all started by the threat of a *potential* Soviet defensive system, a defense that still hasn't materialized 20 years later.

We can even quote one of President Reagan's true Star Wars believers, then Secretary of Defense Caspar Weinberger, on our likely reaction should the Soviets build a defensive system. Just before the first Reagan/Gorbachev summit, Weinberger wrote:

> Even a probable territorial defense would require us to increase the number of our offensive forces and their ability to penetrate Soviet defenses to assure that our operational plans could be executed.[6]

We would *increase* our offensive forces, but we expect that the Soviets would *decrease* their forces in response to SDI. Consistency and logic was not one of the hallmarks of the Reagan administration.

*Crisis Instability.* As discussed earlier, the orbital mechanics for a space-based defensive system are much more suitable for mopping up a ragged retaliatory response in support of a first strike, than for attempting to stop a coordinated attack by the opponent. This gives a major advantage to the side striking first in a crisis. The hardware, once in place, could drive decisions of future leaders in the wrong direction: they would have strong incentives to strike first, to use the SDI system to gain an advantage in a crisis, to come out of a nuclear war in a better relative position. Conversely, the Soviets would have strong incentive to strike first themselves, to avoid the large U.S. advantage from going first.

*Diversion of Resources.* SDI research programs are already undermining our nation's economic strength by diverting thousands of engineers, scientists, and other national resources away from more productive activities. In the past, many military programs have contributed in some degree to the civilian economy. Computers and aircraft come to mind. But the bulk of Star Wars research has little application in civilian life. What could you do with a neutral particle beam weapon? Roast hot dogs? Or heat-seeking interceptor rockets? Chase down speeders on the freeway? The SDI organization has been bending over backwards trying to find "spin-offs" to justify their research program, now that most knowledgeable observers realize SDI cannot protect

---

[6]Caspar Weinberger, quoted in the *Washington Post*, November 18, 1985.

people. Congress even got into the act and designated that part of the free electron laser (FEL) research money should be used for medical research. Actually, the medical FEL research was started long before SDI began free electron laser experiments, using university FEL systems. In fact, the power levels proposed by SDIO would blow away a patient. We don't need SDI research to conduct medical research.

Not only are the scientists and engineers diverted from solving other societal problems as discussed in Chapter 5, but they are learning skills and technologies that, in many cases, will not contribute to our society after Star Wars research ends. The longer they work on dead-end, gold-plated military projects with unlimited research budgets, the more difficult it will be to rejoin the competitive commercial world.

*Weaponization of Space.* One of the gravest long-term consequences of Star Wars, if we went ahead with deployment, would be the weaponization of space. We have military satellites in outer space today, but they are used for non-threatening applications like communication, navigation and weather forecasting, or for stabilizing missions like verification of arms control treaties and early warning of missile attack. But Star Wars would place weapons in space, crossing a new threshold in the arms race. President Reagan insisted that Star Wars would be purely defensive. Despite his pious intentions, however, every Star Wars weapon could more easily be used in an offensive mode to shoot down the opponent's satellites than in a defensive mode to shoot down ballistic missiles or particularly small, hardened warheads.

Satellites are literally sitting ducks. They travel in prescribed orbits. Attacks can be planned days or weeks in advance, while Star Wars would have to react in seconds to a sudden Soviet missile launch. Unlike missiles or warheads, satellites have vulnerable components including communication antennas, sensors and huge solar panels to collect energy. These solar panels could be destroyed much more easily than finding and shooting down a nuclear warhead in space. For all these reasons, Star Wars weapons, whether American or Soviet (or Libyan or Iranian) would make potent offensive anti-satellite (ASAT) weapons.

As one Defense Intelligence Agency (DIA) analyst noted:

> The Soviet Union could deploy a prototype particle beam weapon with a capability of disrupting satellite electronics in the 1990s. Sometime thereafter, a particle beam weapon that could destroy satellites will be possible. A weapon capable of destroying missile boosters in flight would undoubtedly take longer ... kinetic

energy weapons in space as antisatellite or satellite defense weapons could take place even earlier that deployment of a true antimissile weapon.[7]

Placing weapons in space would, in our judgment, threaten all of the peaceful and non-weapons military uses of outer space. Unlike a fighter airplane dogfight or a war at sea, a space battle would create debris that could poison vast orbital bands of space for years, decades or even centuries depending on altitude. The junk from an airplane duel or a damaged ship falls to the ground or the sea bottom. Not so in space. Junk from a battle or even a Star Wars test collision would continue to orbit the earth at speeds of 17,000 miles per hour. Even a paint chip becomes a lethal weapon at these speeds. Only the slight friction from residual air molecules in low orbits would cause this debris to "de-orbit" ... to fall back into the atmosphere and burn up. Above a few hundred miles, debris would continue to circle the earth for many years, jeopardizing all peaceful activities long after the battle ended.

Once the Soviets or other future enemies followed our lead, placing weapons in space, both sides would be tempted to knock out the communications and early-warning satellites of the other in a crisis. Speed-of-light weapons would be particularly destabilizing, if they could ever be developed, because the side striking first could blind the enemy in a fraction of a second. There would be no warning in a space-age shoot out, leading to a dangerous, hair-trigger environment. If we continue down this road to the weaponization of space, we may someday look back and envy today's conditions, where we at least have 25 minutes warning of missile attack. We will also wonder why we didn't do more to prevent such dangerous developments when we had the chance.

*Cost.* The research costs of SDI are large ($4 billion per year,) but the costs to engineer, build, deploy and maintain an actual space-based weapons system would be staggering. The first phase of SDI was originally estimated at $40 billion, but rapidly grew to the $75 to $150 billion range, by SDIO estimation. This first phase was supposed to stop 50 percent of the Soviet SS-18 heavy ICBMs, and about 30 percent of a Soviet attack using about half of their warheads. The original design

---

[7]Rear Admiral Thomas A. Brooks, "Soviet Strategic Defense Initiatives," *Signal, Journal of the Armed Forces Communications and Electronics Associations,* 41, No. 4, December 1986, p. 29.

called for 3,000 space based interceptors (SBI) orbiting the earth, and about 1,000 ground-based interceptor rockets. To reduce costs, the SDIO cut the proposed number of expensive SBIs in half in the fall of 1988, to about 1,500, and increased the less expensive ground-based interceptors to 1,700. The new cost estimate: "only" $69 billion.

This estimate is highly suspect, however, since the new redesigned system shifts the burden from space-based interceptors to ground-based interceptors. But the ground-based interceptors can be fooled by decoys released in the vacuum of space, and the $69 billion price tag could not pay for the necessary sensors to discriminate between cheap decoys and the real warheads. The ground-based SDI interceptors could be overwhelmed by several hundred thousand decoys, according to some estimates.

But keep in mind that this $69 billion is just the beginning. This is only the cost of producing the defensive weapons. It does not include the additional research and development needed to reach the production phase. The SDIO estimated that another $45 billion or so would be required for R&D. And the $69 billion does not include operating costs including space-based maintenance or replacement of defective SBI interceptors. Thus the total costs for a 15 percent effective system against today's Soviet threat would exceed $100 billion.

When it became apparent that our nation could not afford this $100 billion price tag for a partial defense, SDI came up with the "brilliant pebbles" clearance sale. These interceptor rockets were touted to be several times less expensive, so that several thousand could be orbited for "only" $25 billion. One has to be very skeptical of these cost estimates, made in desperation as previous cost estimates have been rejected as unaffordable. Indeed the latest official SDIO estimate for the first phase of brilliant pebbles is now up to $55 billion, just $14 billion less than the previous year's estimate for space-based interceptor (SBI) rockets. The government's General Accounting Office (GAO) reported that even $55 billion would not be enough for a brilliant pebbles defensive system. The total cost to complete the Phase I development and deployment, in addition to the $15.7 billion spent to date, would be $87 billion, not $55 billion. Furthermore, taxpayers would have to dish out another $10.1 billion for operation and maintenance of the Phase I system during deployment, and another $26 billion for non-Phase I research between 1990 and 1994 on the later phases necessary to overcome the inevitable Soviet countermeasures. The total cost for a Phase I brilliant pebbles system, capable of stopping about 15 percent of

Soviet warheads, would be $139.2 billion through 1994, not $25 billion claimed by some outside SDI enthusiasts.[8]

Furthermore, these costs are based on SDIO estimates. GAO did not independently audit the actual cost estimates for the various components of a defensive system. Given that the brilliant pebbles design is not complete, cost will undoubtedly grow.

An outside group of experts, called the JASONs, evaluated this brilliant pebbles scheme in the summer of 1989. Their spokesman, in a briefing to Congressional staff, stated that he didn't have any idea how to cost brilliant pebbles, since it hasn't been designed. While the main cheerleaders of brilliant pebbles claim that it could use inexpensive "off-the-shelf" components, the JASONs group said that new components would have to be developed, if the system is to work effectively. In effect, you can have cheap brilliant pebbles, or ones that work, but not both!

The Defense Science Board (DSB), a group of experts used by the Pentagon to evaluate military projects, cast further doubt on the cost estimates of a brilliant pebbles system, since the system design in not complete:

> The BP design is neither complete nor stable, nor is there yet a well-defined program acquisition strategy for transistioning BP into system acquisition . . . .several critical issues do exist and have yet to be resolved. In order to keep down the weight and cost, some components are marginal in performance and may need upgrading.[9]

Subsequently, brilliant pebbles advocates conceded that these orbiting bullets would be vulnerable to attack in time of war. The brilliant pebbles would therefore have to be redesigned to include decoys, to maneuver to avoid attacks, and to have "shoot back" capability... additional "bullets" for self protection. All of these countermeasures will add weight and cost to the brilliant pebble scheme.

This initial SDI system of interceptor rockets, whether SBIs or brilliant pebbles, would have to grow to keep pace with Soviet offensive

[8]"Strategic Defense Initiative: Funding Needs Through Completion of Phase I System," Washington, D.C.: United States General Accounting Office, GAO/NSIAD-90-79FS, January 1990.
[9]Charles E. Bennett and Tom Ridge, "Science Board Doubts 'Pebbles'," Washington, D.C.: U.S. House of Representatives, April 5, 1990.

improvements, just to keep the defense effectiveness at 30 percent assuming that the Soviets fire only half their missiles. (That is, 70 percent of the Soviet warheads would get through.) The SDIO system architecture contractors had designed two more phases of defense. The second phase would add more effective discrimination capability and more SBIs. One of the national laboratories estimated the life cycle costs of this phase at $541 billion.[10]

The third phase of SDI would add the exotic laser beam or particle beam weapons, if they ever proved feasible. Estimating the cost of complex laser weapons systems still in the research phase is highly speculative, but certainly $500 billion would be the right ball park. Thus $1 trillion has been bandied about as a possible cost for the total SDI system.

By virtue of the measure-countermeasure game, however, the SDI system would never be finished. We would continually be reacting to Soviet improvements in their offensive forces if we chose to continue the nuclear arms race into outer space. This is the mark of arms race instability ... the costs go on and on.

President Reagan sensed this inevitability, and suggested that we would avoid this arms race by sharing our SDI technology with the Soviets. Then we could both be secure, having the capability to reliably shoot down the opponent's missiles. This scheme has several flaws which stem from the offensive and defensive capability of most weapons. Reagan liked to classify weapons as offensive or defensive. In this black and white world, we could comfortably share defensive weapons, because they would hurt no one. In the real world, every Star Wars weapon can be used as an offensive weapon to shoot down the opponent's satellites. We would be giving away our most modern weapons technology. The Soviets would also learn how to defeat our latest weapons if we shared our technology with them. The concept would never be seriously considered in the Pentagon, but this didn't stop the Reagan White House from suggesting the sharing concept to paper over fundamental flaws in the Star Wars concept.

The economic burden and instabilities of pursuing a defense against nuclear missiles seemed to be recognized even by Robert "Bud" McFarlane, who, as National Security Adviser, had coaxed President

---

[10]James T. Bruce, Bruce W. MacDonald, and Ronald L. Tammen, *Star Wars at the Crossroads: The Strategic Defense Initiative after Five Years*, Staff report to Senators Bennett Johnston, Dale Bumpers, and William Proxmire, June 12, 1988.

Reagan to propose the Star Wars program in 1983. Writing in *Foreign Affairs* in 1988, McFarlane stated:

> Because there is no current basis for confidence that a survivable defensive shield is within reach, and in view of the very substantial problems of political, economic, and military stability attendant to making a commitment to such a shield, the adoption of a defensive doctrine, even as a goal, would be imprudent.[11]

But McFarlane went on to say that we should continue a healthy Star Wars research program, that SDI, properly structured, is "essential to our national security." He apparently subscribes to one or more of the rationales for continuing SDI research described in the next section.

## WHY CONTINUE WITH SDI RESEARCH?

We have shown that SDI is futile, dangerous and exorbitantly expensive. Then why continue Star Wars research? The leaders of the SDIO and our military are rational people. They want to provide the best possible defense for this country, and most recognize the need to cut defense expenditures in this age of obscene federal deficits and falling threat. If deployment of SDI would really be so expensive and destabilizing, why do they continue the program?

As with most military programs, there is no simple answer. There are many players, each with different motivations to keep working on SDI research. Many work on the program because it is technologically challenging and rewarding. Most feel they have no choice, being forced to go where the money is. Some may still cling to the belief that we could some day protect our people from attack, but virtually every knowledgeable observer admits that complete protection is not feasible without substantial arms reductions. To their credit, even the leaders of the SDI program have admitted from the start that a perfect defense is not within reason.

Lt. Gen. James Abrahamson, the cheerleading Director of the SDI in the Reagan administration, stated:

---

[11]Robert C. McFarlane, "Effective Strategic Policy," *Foreign Affairs*, 1988, p. 40.

A perfect astrodome defense is not a realistic thing[12] ... there is no perfect weapons system, there is no panacea.[13]

And Gerold Yonas, the first chief scientist for the SDI program, wrote in *Physics Today*:

I know we agreed at the start that there was no perfect defense against a determined adversary, and it is *not likely there ever will be*.[14]

They clearly acknowledge that we could not stop all nuclear weapons. SDI would always remain a leaky defense, if the Soviets tried to defeat it, as they surely would. True SDI proponents do not abandon the hope that we could someday eliminate the threat of nuclear weapons, but that could only be achieved through negotiating very deep reductions in nuclear weapons, bordering on nuclear disarmament. But if the Soviet-American relations improve to the point of trusting one another to disarm, then SDI would not be needed.

On the other hand, if we ever did agree to eliminate all nuclear weapons, then a modest, *ground-based* defense might be justified as an insurance policy, to guard against other countries ever developing nuclear-tipped ICBMs or SLBMs. If we had no nuclear weapons, defenses would be stabilizing!

## THE TRANSITION PROBLEM

But wait, you say: if defenses are stabilizing in the case when we have no nuclear weapons, why don't we begin to add defenses now? Why don't we rely on a mixture of offenses and defenses while we work cooperatively with the Soviets to reduce offensive nuclear forces?

The SDI organization has suggested just such a mixture of offense and defense. However, as long as we and the Soviets rely on offensive nuclear retaliation, any addition of defenses effectively nullifies the corresponding offenses on the other side. The opponent then is compelled to increase offenses to compensate and maintain retaliatory capability, instead of reducing offensive forces, the desired reaction.

---

[12]*Public Interest Report*, 38, Federation of American Scientist, March 1985, p. 3.
[13]*Science*, 226, November 9, 1984, p. 673.
[14]Gerold Yonas, "Strategic Defense Initiative: The Politics and Science of Weapons in Space," *Physics Today*, 38, June 1985.

This is the transition problem: how do we make the transition from security based on offensive nuclear retaliation to security based on defenses? As far as we know, no one has ever proposed a feasible scenario to make this transition from offense to defense, even assuming full Soviet cooperation through the arms control process. The Congressional Office of Technology Assessment concluded that "OTA was unable to find anyone who could propose a plausible agreement for offensive arms reductions and a cooperative transition" to a defensive posture.[15]

What then are the reasons to continue SDI research? We list ten possible goals for SDI in order of increasing difficulty. Some of these goals are supported by the SDIO, some are rarely discussed, and some are vehemently rejected. Some are approved by members of Congress, but with varying degrees of enthusiasm. The first five goals could be accomplished just by spending money on research; no SDI hardware need ever be built or deployed.

Goal #1—*Preempt the Freeze Movement.* Prior to President Reagan's Star Wars speech in March of 1983, the Nuclear Weapons Freeze Campaign had reinvigorated public concern over the escalating nuclear arms race. A bilateral U.S.-USSR freeze on nuclear weapons production, testing and deployment would have stopped the nuclear "modernization" projects that were at the heart of the Reagan military buildup, which President Bush has continued with vigor. Many of President Reagan's advisers felt that accurate weapons like the MX, the submarine-launched D-5, and the various types of cruise missiles were essential to "fight and win" or to "prevail" in a nuclear war. President Bush and his conservative Secretary of Defense, Dick Cheney, have continued to press for all of these new weapons including a 30 percent increase in funding for the top 11 programs for 1991. The Freeze movement was a clear and present danger to the Reagan-Bush nuclear war-fighting plans.

Robert McFarlane, the President Reagan's National Security Advisor in 1983, has been credited with the idea of announcing the SDI program to derail the popular Freeze movement.[16]

---

[15]The United States Congress, Office of Technology Assessment, *Ballistic Missile Defense Technologies*, OTA-ISC-254 Washington, D.C.: U.S. Government Printing Office, September 1985, p. 33.
[16]Kent D. Lee, "The role of scientific advisers in the strategic defense initiative," *Technology in Society, 8*, 1986, p. 293.

The President could claim the "moral high ground," eliminating the scourge of nuclear weapons, instead of the very modest step of freezing in the horror of nuclear weapons at their current levels. Star Wars would substitute the promise of a nuclear-free world sometime in the distant future, in place of an immediate freeze of the nuclear arms race at existing high levels. Some would say that this Star Wars goal of derailing the Nuclear Weapons Freeze Campaign was achieved.

Goal #2—*Research spin-offs*. The spin-off argument is used for most military programs, particularly those that have weak military justifications. Proponents claim that military advances "spin-off" improved technology that helps the civilian economy. While this may have been true to some degree in the past, the high technology aspects of much SDI research would seem to be ill suited to commercial applications. We should always ask the obvious question: how much more could be accomplished if we spent our research dollars directly to solve civilian problems like the environment, energy, transportation, health, etc. Simon Ramo, the founder of TRW, one of the largest SDI contractors, claims that the United States has lost more than a decade in commercial technology advancement by emphasizing military over civilian research.[17]

Goal #3—*Hedge against Soviet breakout of the ABM Treaty*. This is, in our judgment, the only legitimate reason to continue some SDI research. Our security, for better or worse, depends on being able to attack the Soviet Union with nuclear weapons should they ever attack us. While none of us can imagine Gorbachev ever contemplating, let alone carrying out, a nuclear attack on the United States, we must always consider what would happen if some future Soviet leadership should regress to the Brezhnev or Stalin period. If they ever attempted to build a Star Wars system, then we should have the technology to thwart that system. Just as our Star Wars weapons could be confused, overwhelmed, or destroyed by Soviet countermeasures, we must be aware of possible Soviet ballistic missile defense (BMD) technologies so that we could penetrate any potential Soviet defenses. Some believe that just by having such a research program, we deter the Soviets from ever trying to build a nationwide defense.

The United States had a vigorous BMD program in place for 25 years before President Reagan suggested SDI, with nearly one billion dollars

---

[17]Peter H. Stone, "Star Wars Draws New Fire," *Boston Globe*, January 6, 1987, p. 17.

allocated for BMD research in 1983. Adjusting for inflation, we might justify a $1.5 billion research program, but not $3.8 billion (1990 level) or $4.7 billion (President Bush's request for fiscal year 1991).

Approximately one seventh of the $4 billion SDI program is allocated to projects that could even remotely be interpreted as needed to thwart a Soviet system. The fiscal year 1988 budget included $510 million for countermeasures, lethality evaluation, hardening, data collection and survivability... activities needed to penetrate future Soviet defenses. If we include high-power laser research (excluding high-power demonstration projects), on the grounds that we should determine what power levels the Soviets could achieve, another $220 million might be justified. This accounts for 13 percent of the $5.7 billion request for 1988.

The Senate Armed Services Committee concluded that the ERIS (exoatmospheric reentry vehicle interceptor system) ground-based missile program would be "an adequate hedge" to prevent Soviet "breakout" of the ABM Treaty, along with the penetration aids mentioned above.[18] The ERIS program accounts for about 4 percent of the FY 1988 request.

Thus we might be able to justify 17 percent of the SDI budget as a "hedge" against Soviet breakout, or about $700 million.

The Congressional Budget Office (CBO) was more generous in their evaluation of Star Wars. They analyzed several options for SDI, and concluded that $2.6 billion per year would be adequate to provide a hedge against Soviet breakout of the ABM Treaty. While this funding level would be a major improvement over the $3.8 billion appropriated for 1990, we feel that Star Wars research program should be reduced to the $1 to $1.5 billion per year level, in the next few years, bringing it back into line with the pre-Reagan levels. If $1 billion was adequate in 1983 in the pre-Gorbachev era, why should we be spending three times that amount with a substantially reduced threat?

Even this justification for SDI research will diminish as more intrusive arms control inspection regimes are introduced in the years ahead. That is, as we obtain better means to assure that the Soviets could not rapidly deploy a nationwide defense, then we could cut back our research efforts.

Goal #4—*Bargaining chip.* Throughout the nuclear age, controvers-

---

[18]*National Defense Authorization Act for Fiscal Years 1988 and 1989*, Report 100-57, May 8, 1987, p. 119.

ial weapons systems have been declared "bargaining chips." We supposedly build them to force the Soviets to negotiate reductions in nuclear weapons. MIRVs (multiple warheads on missiles) and cruise missiles were bargaining chips . . . until they were ready for deployment. Then the military found them too valuable to bargain away. A bargaining chip must be cashed in to gain value. As President Reagan showed at the Reykjavik summit, however, he was not willing to give up Star Wars research, even in exchange for the elimination of all ballistic missiles. (This is truly ironic, because only by eliminating all missiles could President Reagan's dream of an effective defense ever be realized.)

The bargaining chip argument might have carried some weight with previous Soviet leaders. President Gorbachev, however, seems independently motivated to seek meaningful arms control agreements, based on improving the Soviet economy as well as reducing the risks of nuclear war.

Despite President Bush's reduced enthusiasm for Star Wars, his national security team has refused to heed the advice of the Joint Chiefs of Staff (JCS), the nation's highest military officers, when they recommended that the United States agree to abide by the ABM Treaty and agree not to deploy Star Wars in exchange for concluding a permanent START treaty cutting offensive nuclear weapons. Thus President Bush continues our past practices of refusing to cash in "bargaining chips," even if it would lead to major reductions in Soviet nuclear weapons. In fact, a START treaty would accomplish the stated JCS goals for Star Wars (cutting 50 percent of Soviet SS-18 warheads and at least 30 percent of all others) much faster, with far more certainty, and with far less cost. Why spend $100 billion or more for a Star Wars system that might stop 10 to 20 percent of Soviet ICBM warheads sometime in the next century, when an arms control treaty could eliminate 50 percent of their warheads next year with absolute certainty and negligible cost? This is one bargaining chip we should enthusiastically bargain away.

Goal #5—*Block arms control agreements*. It is no secret that President Reagan and many of his national security advisers came into power distrusting all arms control treaties. They firmly believed that any treaty would always favor the Soviets, because, they claim, Soviets always cheat while the U.S. public and Congress force the United States to honor our international commitments.

To the hard-liners in the Reagan administration, Star Wars was a perfect shield . . . against arms control treaties. The Soviet Union would never agree to any significant cut in offensive nuclear weapons while we planned to build a defense against their remaining forces. At the very best, they would merely state that they would no longer be bound by the treaty if the U.S. went ahead with Star Wars deployments. Thus Star Wars allowed President Reagan to suggest even total elimination of all nuclear weapons at Reykjavik, knowing full well that Gorbachev would never agree as long as the President clung to his Star Wars dream. (One could also argue that Gorbachev played the same game . . . knowing that Reagan would never give up Star Wars allowed Gorbachev to propose the elimination of all missiles.)

Goal #6—*Stop accidental or terrorist attacks.* Senator Sam Nunn suggested to the Arms Control Association that the United States should explore using Star Wars technology for an accidental launch protection system (ALPS), to shoot down a few errant warheads fired by accident or by a deranged submarine commander. He had in mind a very limited ground-based system, probably using the ERIS interceptor rockets based in the U.S.

The proposed SDI space-based system such as brilliant pebbles would not be suitable for an ALPS system. Space-based defenses require almost immediate release of weapons, within at best one minute after launch to hit the missiles in their vulnerable boost phase. There would not be time to authorize weapons release if just one or two missiles were accidentally fired with no warning in peacetime. Automatic destruction of missiles could not be permitted without jeopardizing peaceful and manned Soviet missile launches. Indeed, since the SDI weapons travel around the earth, all space launches, including our own, would be vulnerable to an errant SBI or brilliant pebble space mine. Undoubtedly any Star Wars space-based system would require prior warning of impending crisis and the confirmed launch of many missiles simultaneously before weapons could be released, making them unsuitable for an accidental launch protection system.

Ground-based interceptors such as ERIS could in principle be used to attack the warheads released by accidentally launched ICBMs. There would be time (up to 15 minutes) to make a decision, and possibly time to communicate with the Soviet military command. However, any effective ALPS system would jeopardize the ABM Treaty and provide potent anti-satellite capability, both destabilizing actions in our judgment. The ABM Treaty provides stability by assuring each side that they do not need to add more offensive weapons to maintain their deterrent capability. But, to be effective, ALPS would violate the ABM Treaty in two areas. First, the ABM Treaty limits each side to 100 interceptor rockets. But an accidental or unauthorized launch of just two missiles with 10 warheads each and 100 light decoys each would produce 220 targets. We would need at least 220 and preferably 440 interceptors to aim two at each target.

Second, ALPS would have to violate the ABM Treaty restriction of one defensive site. ERIS rockets based near Grand Forks, North Dakota, our one allowed site, could intercept warheads fired from ICBMs in the Soviet Union, but not SLBMs fired at coastal targets from submarines off our coasts. We would need several sites to stop the SLBM threat.

Once multiple missile sites were allowed with a nationwide radar system, it would be very difficult to assure each side that the other was not moving toward a full national defense. Building ALPS would undermine if not trash the ABM Treaty.

As for stopping terrorist attacks, it is unlikely that a terrorist organization would bother to build ICBMs. It would be much easier to use an airplane, ship or truck.

We should also explore alternatives to ALPS to eliminate the threat of accidental launches. Each side could put radio-controlled explosives on their own missiles, to be detonated if one were accidentally fired. All of our unmanned missiles have such self-destruct mechanisms so that the range safety officer can blow up an errant missile headed for a populated area. Many American missiles have been intentionally blown up in the past after they strayed off course. The military has been reticent to equip our nuclear missiles with explosives, fearing that the enemy might discover the radio signal used to trigger the explosive. However, with modern high-speed computers and sophisticated codes, we should be able to develop a foolproof self-destruct mechanism for our missiles. Again, this would be far less expensive and more effective than building a Star Wars defensive system.

Goal #7—*To complicate Soviet attack plans.* This is the first official goal of the SDI program. They claim that we would benefit from an initial leaky Star War space-based defense (say one that could stop 10 to 30 percent of Soviet nuclear warheads) by making Soviet nuclear attack planning uncertain. The Soviets would not know which of their warheads would get through. If they wanted to knock out all 1,000 of our ICBM silos, for example, and they fired 2,000 of their 6,450 ICBM-based warheads at our silos, and if SDI did stop 30 percent or 600 of the 2,000 Soviet warheads, then the Soviets couldn't be sure of destroying all of our ICBMs with a preemptive first strike attack. They couldn't be sure that they could achieve their military objective, so they would not attack. According to this reasoning, by complicating their attack plans, a partial defense would therefore enhance deterrence and make nuclear war less likely.

We hope most of you found the previous paragraph rather unconvincing. This convoluted thinking represents the primary justification for a partial defense in SDI circles. This reasoning is faulty on three levels. First, to swallow this justification, you must assume that the Soviets are **NOT** deterred now by the threat of massive U.S. retaliation with at least 3,000 and probably closer to 5,000 submarine-launched nuclear warheads. These warheads could be fired even if the Soviets could destroy all of our ICBMs, even if they did achieve their military objectives. These surviving SLBM warheads could destroy Soviet military bases, airfields, radar stations, anti-aircraft facilities, barracks, fuel depots, ammunition dumps, ports, space-launch facilities, weapons factories, electrical generation plants, industrial plants, and, yes, cities. In short, they could destroy everything except Soviet ICBMs and buried command and control bunkers. Those would be safe for eight to twelve hours until our bombers arrived with better accuracy to finish them off. (It's hard to imagine why any Soviet silos would contain live missiles eight hours after a nuclear holocaust, or why their elimination would make much difference, but that hypothesis is needed to justify manned bombers.)

Second, even if creating more uncertainty were necessary (and we find it totally unnecessary), there are other less costly and less dangerous methods to increase uncertainty. Great uncertainty already exists in their ability to destroy all our land-based missiles, since neither superpower has ever fired missiles over the North Pole, the required wartime route, and neither nation has ever attempted a coordinated launch of tens of missiles, let alone thousands. But if more uncertainty was needed, we could greatly complicate their attack planning by deploying mobile missiles, such as the planned Midgetman small ICBM that would move around on special trucks. We could negotiate a treaty banning missile flight testing, thereby creating uncertainty over time as each side lost confidence in their ability to launch a coordinated first strike. Better yet, if we and the Soviets agreed to eliminate all fixed-silo ICBMs, then the Soviets wouldn't have any target to shoot at; we would have created *total uncertainty* in their ability to destroy any of our nuclear weapons. We could create this total uncertainty in Soviet attack plans with arms control within months instead of decades to develop and build SDI, with no research program, and with negligible cost.

To protect our command and control network, another Soviet target, we would have to continue our program of hardening communication satellites like MILSTAR, proliferating communication channels, adding mobile communication vans and airborne command posts, etc. A small fraction of the resources devoted to SDI could increase command and control survivability significantly.

The third flaw in the "complicate Soviet attack plans" justification is its narrow focus. It considers just one possible effect of a partial defense on Soviet actions. It totally ignores the destabilizing aspects of a partial space-based defense, including the significant advantage to the side striking first, as discussed earlier in this appendix. This is one of the most blatant examples of presenting the purported advantages of a weapons system without even mentioning let alone discussing the disadvantages or alternatives. The American public and the Congress deserve much better.

Commenting on this concept that SDI would complicate Soviet attack plans and therefore enhance deterrence, Brent Scowcroft, President Bush's current National Security Advisor, stated that the first phase of SDI "would enhance deterrence only in the sense that it would force a very heavy attack" by the Soviets. He went on to say that "I think there is a real problem with enhancing deterrence at the cost of increasing crisis instability or at least arms-race instability."[19]

Despite his personal reservations, however, he did not succeed in reducing the first Star Wars budget proposed by the new Bush administration to reasonable levels.

Goal #8—*To enhance deterrence by protecting missiles.* Some have suggested that we deploy a limited ground-based defensive system to protect our ICBMs. Missile silos are much easier to defend than cities. Silo defense does not have to be perfect to permit the survival of some missiles for retaliation, thereby enhancing deterrence ... assuming it needs to be enhanced. A silo defense need only work for a few minutes, long enough for the authorities to confirm an attack and launch the retaliatory strike. Furthermore, Soviet warheads could be destroyed within a few hundred feet above the silos, using ground-based, nuclear-

---

[19]Charles E. Bennett and Tom Ridge, "A Star Wars Proposal," *Christian Science Monitor*, March 20, 1989, p. 19.

tipped interceptor rockets close to the missile fields. These low-altitude nuclear blasts would decimate a city (both Hiroshima and Nagasaki were destroyed by atomic bombs exploded in the air), but would not destroy buried missile silos. By waiting until the enemy warheads had reentered the atmosphere above the target, the silo defense could take advantage of the atmosphere to slow down lightweight decoys, avoiding wasted shots at decoys.

Point defense of silos is not an official SDI goal. President Reagan called for the elimination of deterrence, not for its enhancement. SDI supporters fear that any plan for silo defense would siphon off funds for their more ambitious space-based weapons and thereby diminish the chances of ever building the more comprehensive Star Wars weapons system.

Like the goal to "complicate Soviet attack plans," the goal of silo defense has very weak justification, and, even if it were needed, could be obtained at lower cost and risk by other means. Just as Soviet attack plans don't need more complication, deterrence doesn't need enhancing. Again, in our judgment, the threat of retaliation by 3,000 to 5,000 submarine-launched nuclear warheads is more than enough to deter any rational Soviet leader. We don't need to protect ICBMs to assure a retaliatory capability.

And, even if ICBM survivability was essential for deterrence, we should consider less expensive alternatives to defensive systems. Placing our ICBMs on mobile trucks (the "Midgetman") would assure their survivability with much less cost than a Star Wars weapons system and without the risk of an accelerated arms race.

Goal #9—*To strive for a first-strike capability.* This is an unspoken motivation for Star Wars. Administration officials deny any intent to create a shield that would allow us to attack with nuclear weapons and fend off the sure retaliation. However, most ardent pro Star Wars advocates must realize that a partial defense combined with very accurate missiles like the MX and particularly the large number of D-5 submarine-launched warheads that were first deployed in 1990, would make a potent and destabilizing mix. President Reagan alluded to this possibility in his 1983 Star Wars speech when he said that "I clearly recognize that defensive systems have limitations and raise certain problems and ambiguities. If paired with offensive systems, they can be viewed as fostering an aggressive policy."

For some hard-liners, Star Wars fits into their continual quest for nuclear superiority. They would like to turn back the clock to the 1950s when we had absolute superiority in deliverable nuclear weapons. They deny any desire for a first-strike capability. But they push for first-strike capable weapons, and they want Star Wars as part of a nuclear war-fighting capability to limit damage or to "prevail" should deterrence fail.

Goal #10—*Anti-satellite (ASAT) capability.* Anti-satellite weapons are not an explicit goal, but rather an inevitable outcome of BMD research and development. As discussed above, every Star Wars weapon could be used to shoot down satellites long before ballistic missiles or warheads. President Reagan consistently denied any offensive intent for Star Wars weapons, but, before he even left office, his Secretary of Defense, Frank Carlucci, requested funds to utilize Star Wars kinetic kill interceptor rockets as an ASAT system for the Navy. They want these weapons to be prepared to shoot down Soviet ocean surveillance satellites during a war. These satellites help the Soviets to track Navy ships at sea, although then Secretary of the Navy, John Lehman, testified that the Navy could cope with these satellites by a combination of electronic jamming and maneuvering to avoid detection.[20]

In our opinion, this ASAT capability may be the most dangerous legacy of Star Wars. If we proceed with a dedicated ASAT system, or if we deploy a limited ALPS defensive system with 100 interceptor rockets that could easily shoot down satellites, we would be extending the arms race into outer space. Once we crossed this threshold, we might foreclose any opportunity to preserve the peaceful uses of outer space.

To summarize, we have examined 10 potential goals for continuing the Star Wars program. We find two of the goals to be unfortunate (slowing the Nuclear Weapons Freeze movement and blocking meaningful offensive arms control), five of the goals have no significant merit (research spin-offs, the bargaining chip, complication of Soviet attack plans, enhancing deterrence by protecting missiles, and stopping accidental launches), and two are very dangerous (anti-satellite capability and first-strike capability). This leaves but one legitimate goal for continued SDI research: to provide the United States with options should the Soviet Union ever attempt to build a nationwide defense. However, this function would require only $700 million to $1 billion per year, compared to the $4 billion wasted annually on SDI research now.

Star Wars was a cruel hoax. Offered by President Reagan as a panacea to eliminate the threat of nuclear weapons once and for all, it would

---

[20]Paul B. Stares, *Space and National Security*, Washington, D.C.: The Brookings Institution, 1987, p. 132.

instead exacerbate the arms race, make nuclear war more likely in a crisis, and bankrupt our nation. While President Bush may be less enthusiastic about Star Wars, he has permitted SDI research to continue at three to four times its historic levels, robbing our national treasury of much needed research funds for other, more worthwhile activities, and he has allowed Star Wars to interfere with a timely conclusion of a permanent START treaty to limit offensive nuclear weapons.

Brent Scowcroft, before he became the National Security Adviser to President Bush, co-authored an article that clearly stated the limitations of Star Wars:

> While the president's vision is both clear and desirable, it is not realistic within any operative time frame. We see virtually no prospect of building a significant and effective population shield against a responsive enemy inside of this century, and there is great uncertainty about the long term.

Scowcroft also warned that deployment of a partial Star Wars defense could significantly reduce our national security:

> Correspondingly, while limited forms of SDI may be more plausible, it is unlikely that they will meet the administration's own criteria of cost-effectiveness and survivability. If they do not meet these technical criteria, premature efforts to deploy a system could stimulate a costly offensive and defensive arms race and reduce stability at a time of crisis. Both effects would reduce rather than enhance our security.[21]

We can only hope that General Scowcroft is able to translate these sane and rational judgments into action in his current capacity. So far, the entrenched bureaucracy within the Bush administration has managed to push Star Wars down the costly and dangerous path toward the premature early deployment feared by Scowcroft and many others.

The *intent* of Star Wars was the type of bold new direction that we need to break out of the Cold War mentality that has been driving our

---

[21]William J. Perry, Brent Scowcroft, Joseph S. Nye, Jr., and James A Shear, "How to Proceed with SDI—Realistic Priorities," *National Interest*, Spring 1987, p. 68.

military policies for four decades. But Star Wars is not the answer. As we discussed in Chapter 9, there are other alternatives to the nuclear arms race, alternatives that are safer, much less expensive, and require no technological breakthroughs.

# Appendix B
# Arms Control Treaties

The United States and the Soviet Union are party to 19 major arms control treaties, most of them related to nuclear weapons, but including two treaties on chemical and biological weapons and one on weather modification. While there have been repeated charges that the Soviets have cheated or violated many of these treaties, almost all so-called violations have involved secondary, peripheral issues. For the most part, the Soviets have a good record in meeting the main limitations of these treaties. Even the one "major" violation, the building of the large, phased array radar at Abalakova near Krasnoyarsk, a technical violation of the ABM Treaty of 1972, as the Soviets have now admitted, did not result in an operational ballistic missile defense system, which means that the main objective of the ABM Treaty—banning nationwide ballistic missile defenses—was sustained.

These are the treaties in chronological order, followed by a summary of the two major ongoing arms control negotiations:

## GENEVA PROTOCOL OF 1925

This treaty, initiated by the United States after World War I, bans the use (but not the production and storage) of chemical and bacteriological weapons. Most major nations including the Soviet Union signed the Geneva Protocol before World War II, except for Japan and the United States, and chemical weapons were not used in the Second World War.

In 1966, several Communist countries objected to the U.S. use of tear gas and chemical herbicides in the Vietnam War. A U.N. resolution condemning the use of all chemicals was approved by a vote of 80 to 3, with only the U.S., Australia and Portugal voting no. The United States did not ratify the Geneva Protocol for 50 years—until 1975.

## THE ANTARCTIC TREATY OF 1960

This treaty sets aside the Antarctic region for peaceful scientific exploration, prohibiting "any measures of a military nature, such as the establishment of military bases and fortifications, the carrying out of military maneuvers, as well as the testing of any type of weapons." The Antarctic Treaty sets several interesting precedents with regard to verification: each signatory agreed to complete access to all facilities. Challenge inspections of other nations' facilities can occur at any time without advance notice. Overflights are also permitted at any time without warning. Since 1964, the United States has inspected stations occupied by six nations, including those of the Soviet Union. Twenty-two nations have signed the treaty.

In our judgment, the Antarctic Treaty has several interesting parallels to our proposal to ban all weapons in outer space. Access to both outer space and the Antarctic is limited, making it difficult to smuggle weapons in. In both cases, there are no wild animals or local inhabitants that would require weapons for self-defense. In both cases, all nations have declared that the region should be used only for peaceful exploration and for scientific experiments.

## THE "HOT LINE" AGREEMENT OF 1963

Following the scare of the Cuban missile crisis in October of 1962, both superpowers agreed to set up a telegraph communication link between the two countries, to be used in an emergency. This link was used during the Israeli-Arab wars of 1967 and 1973 to avoid misunderstanding regarding American ship movements in the region.

## LIMITED TEST BAN TREATY OF 1963

The LTBT prohibits nuclear weapons explosions in the atmosphere, under water and in outer space. Unfortunately, it does not stop nuclear explosions in underground tunnels, since the negotiators stumbled over adequate measures to detect underground explosions, and because the military establishments of both sides wanted to continue developing nuclear weapons. The LTBT is effectively an environmental treaty, removing the airborne radioactive fallout from above-ground testing. The nuclear arms race simply moved underground, where both superpowers have continued to develop new nuclear explosives. The LTBT has been signed by 108 nations, including all nuclear powers except France and China. The last atmospheric nuclear explosion was set off by China on October 16, 1980.

### OUTER SPACE TREATY OF 1967

This treaty prohibits the placement of nuclear weapons or "any other kinds of weapons of mass destruction" in outer space or on celestial bodies, and declares that outer space is not subject to national sovereignty, but is open to all nations for peaceful purposes. The treaty does not, however, prohibit conventional (non-nuclear) weapons such as those being developed by the Star Wars program.

### LATIN AMERICAN NUCLEAR-FREE ZONE TREATY OF 1968

The Latin American countries pledge to use nuclear power only for peaceful purposes, and not to develop, acquire or test nuclear weapons on their soil. The nuclear weapons states agree in a separate protocol to respect the nuclear-free zone by not introducing nuclear weapons or threatening the use of nuclear weapons against the Latin American countries.

### NON-PROLIFERATION TREATY (NPT) OF 1968

The NPT is essentially a compact between the nuclear weapons states and the "have-nots." The "haves" agree to share nuclear power technology with the "have-nots," and to seek nuclear disarmament, in exchange for the "have-nots" pledging not to acquire nuclear weapons capability. The goal is stop the proliferation of nuclear weapons to other nations.

The pledge of the nuclear weapons states is particularly challenging; Article VI reads:

Each of the parties undertakes to pursue negotiations in good faith on effective measures relating to cessation of the nuclear arms race at an early date and to nuclear disarmament, and on a treaty on general and complete disarmament under strict and effective international control.

The nuclear "have-nots" frequently claim that the nuclear weapons states have not seriously followed the dictates of Article VI, particularly since the superpowers have still not agreed to a comprehensive test ban (CTB), banning all nuclear weapons explosions.

## SEABED ARMS CONTROL TREATY OF 1971

Signatories agreed not to place nuclear weapons on the sea bed beyond a 12-mile limit.

## "ACCIDENTS MEASURES" AGREEMENT OF 1971

The superpowers agreed to reduce risks of accidental nuclear detonations, to notify the other immediately if such an accident occurred, and to give advance notice of any missile launches that would travel outside national boundaries.

## HOT LINE MODERNIZATION AGREEMENT OF 1971

Replaced wire telegraph circuit with satellite hookup, keeping a radio link as backup.

## BIOLOGICAL WEAPONS CONVENTION OF 1972

Signatories agreed not to develop, produce or acquire biological agents or toxins.

## SALT I: STRATEGIC ARMS LIMITATION TALKS OF 1972

The SALT I agreements covered both offensive and defensive weapons:

### ABM (ANTI-BALLISTIC MISSILE) TREATY

The ABM Treaty, part of the SALT I accords, prohibits the development of a nationwide defense against ballistic missiles, on the theory that if either nation begins to erect such a shield, then the opponent would add offensive nuclear weapons to overwhelm the defenses and maintain the "balance of terror." Each nation was allowed two defensive sites (later amended to one), and each country was also allowed to develop and test (but not deploy) new ABM systems at two test sites. Both sides agreed not to develop, test or deploy sea-based, air-based or space-based ABM systems or their components, which precludes effective testing of most Star Wars components.

### INTERIM AGREEMENT

The Interim Agreement on offensive nuclear weapons, also part of SALT I, set an upper ceiling on the number of ICBM and SLBM missile launchers allowed on each side, equal to the number of launchers then in place or under construction.... essentially a freeze at existing or planned levels. This agreement was to last for five years, when a more stringent SALT II treaty would take over.

## PREVENTION OF NUCLEAR WAR AGREEMENT OF 1973

Although the two superpowers could not agree on reductions in offensive nuclear weapons in SALT I, the process of negotiation did lead to an agreement to avoid confrontations anywhere in the world, and to consult with each other should conflicts occur.

## THRESHOLD TEST BAN TREATY (TTBT) OF 1974

This treaty banned all nuclear explosive tests with a yield above 150 kilotons, roughly 10 times the power of the Hiroshima bomb. The two sides agreed to exchange information on the geology of their test sites to aid the other side in measuring the yield of the opponent's underground explosions. This treaty has still not been ratified by the U.S. Senate.

## PEACEFUL NUCLEAR EXPLOSION (PNE) TREATY OF 1976

The PNE Treaty extended the 150-kiloton limit to peaceful nuclear explosions used for constructing canals or underground caverns away from the military test sites. It included elaborate agreements for on-site inspections. The Senate has not yet ratified this treaty, as the Bush administration continues the practice of the Reagan administration, stalling on ratification of the TTBT and PNE treaties to postpone negotiations on a comprehensive test ban, outlawing all nuclear explosions.

## ENVIRONMENTAL MODIFICATION CONVENTION OF 1977

Both sides agreed not to modify the climate in any way in an attempt to gain military advantage.

## SALT II TREATY OF 1979

The SALT II Treaty established a set of indirect limits on the number of nuclear warheads in the arsenals of the two superpowers. The numbers would have required the Soviets to slightly reduce the number of warheads on land-based missiles; otherwise this treaty, like SALT I, merely put a cap on the arms race at very high levels. With the Soviet invasion of Afghanistan in December of 1979, President Carter withdrew the treaty from the Senate, and it was never ratified. Both sides agreed to abide by the numerical limits of the treaty until President

Reagan breached the number of allowed warheads in December of 1986 by deploying additional air-launched cruise missiles on B-52 bombers. With the lapse of the SALT II Treaty, there are currently no limits on offensive nuclear weapons, although the Soviet Union is informally abiding by the SALT II numerical limits.

## INF TREATY OF 1988

The INF (Intermediate Range Nuclear Forces) Treaty eliminated all tactical nuclear weapons with a range between 300 and 3,400 miles. This treaty set several important milestones. It was the first treaty to abolish an entire class of weapons. It established the precedent of asymmetrical reductions: Mr. Gorbachev agreed to eliminate about twice the number of INF missiles with four times the number of nuclear warheads and nine times the explosive power. And the treaty established intrusive, on-site inspection, including challenge inspections and on-site resident inspectors who are stationed outside the gates of former missile manufacturing plants in both countries.

Unfortunately, the INF Treaty covers less than 4 percent of the world's arsenal of nuclear weapons. It does nothing to curb the longer-range strategic nuclear weapons.

The United States and the Soviet Union have negotiated two major treaties to reduce conventional and nuclear forces:

## CONVENTIONAL ARMED FORCES IN EUROPE (CFE)

The CFE talks include the 23 members of the two alliances: the North Atlantic Treaty Organization (NATO) and the Warsaw Treaty Organization. The two alliances were attempting to make significant reductions in conventional forces in the "Atlantic to the Urals" region— from the Atlantic Ocean to the Ural mountains in the Soviet Union— when the revolutions of 1989 essentially shattered the Warsaw Pact. Before late 1989, the NATO goal was to reduce the Soviet and Warsaw Pact advantages in tanks, troops and artillery by establishing equal ceilings in these and other categories of weapons. After the revolutions, the Soviets will most likely be forced to remove all of their forces from Warsaw Pact nations, and so the CFE process could ironically act as a brake on the removal of Soviet troops from Eastern Europe by legitimizing higher Soviet troop levels than would have resulted from negotiations between the Warsaw Pact nations and the Soviets.

Nonetheless, the CFE Treaty is valuable, because it requires the destruction of tens of thousands of conventional weapons, rather than their withdrawal to the Soviet Union, and it sets up intrusive on-site inspection procedures so that we can monitor troop and military equipment movements, assuring that no future Soviet leader could reimpose hegemony over Eastern Europe.

## START (THE STRATEGIC ARMS REDUCTION TALKS)

The START Treaty aims to reduce the levels of strategic (long-range) nuclear warheads by up to 50 percent. Due to "counting rules" that favor bombers, however, the actual reductions may be closer to 10 percent for the U.S. and 40 percent for the Soviet Union. That is, each bomber is counted as having only one hydrogen bomb, even though it might carry up to 24 in the case of the B-1 bomber, and each bomber may be counted as carrying 10 air-launched cruise missiles (ALCM) even though it actually has 20.

If concluded, the START treaty would represent the first strategic arms control treaty to make significant cuts in the nuclear arsenals. However, in their rush to get an agreement, both superpowers are leaving several large loopholes in the treaty that will permit the nuclear arms race to continue. The treaty at this time (spring 1990) does not cover sea-launched cruise missiles, except in a non-binding "gentlemen's agreement" not to exceed 880 missiles. Second, both sides have agreed to ignore the Star Wars program for the moment; the Soviets have made it perfectly clear, however, that they would abrogate any START treaty if the U.S. started to test a Star Wars system (and so would we if the Soviets ever attempted to test and build a nationwide defense). And, as we emphasized throughout the book, the START treaty would do nothing to stop the destabilizing qualitative arms race, the technological advances that would increase the chances of nuclear weapons being used in some future conflict.

# Index

377